TECHNOLOGY FOR PHYSICAL EDUCATORS, HEALTH EDUCATORS, AND COACHES

Enhancing Instruction, Assessment, Management, Professional Development, and Advocacy

Seth E. Jenny, PhD
Slippery Rock University of Pennsylvania

Jennifer M. Krause, PhD
University of Northern Colorado

Tess Armstrong, PhD
Grand Valley State University

HUMAN KINETICS

Library of Congress Cataloging-in-Publication Data

Names: Jenny, Seth, author. | Krause, Jennifer M., 1981- author. | Armstrong, Tess, 1983- author.

Title: Technology for physical educators, health educators, and coaches : enhancing instruction, assessment, management, professional development, and advocacy / Seth E. Jenny, Jennifer M. Krause, Tess Armstrong, Authors.

Description: Champaign, IL : Human Kinetics, [2021] | Includes index.

Identifiers: LCCN 2019057448 (print) | LCCN 2019057449 (ebook) | ISBN 9781492589341 (paperback) | ISBN 9781492589365 (epub) | ISBN 9781492589358 (pdf)

Subjects: LCSH: Physical education--Study and teaching. | Educational technology. | Health education--Study and teaching.

Classification: LCC GV361 .J46 2021 (print) | LCC GV361 (ebook) | DDC 372.86--dc23

LC record available at https://lccn.loc.gov/2019057448
LC ebook record available at https://lccn.loc.gov/2019057449

ISBN: 978-1-4925-8934-1 (print)

The web addresses cited in this text were current as of December 2019, unless otherwise noted.

Acquisitions Editor: Scott Wikgren; **Senior Developmental Editor:** Melissa Feld; **Managing Editor:** Miranda K. Baur; **Copyeditors:** Tom Tiller and Heather Gauen Hutches; **Indexer:** Kevin Campbell; **Permissions Manager:** Dalene Reeder; **Graphic Designer:** Whitney Milburn; **Cover Designer:** Keri Evans; **Cover Design Associate:** Susan Rothermel Allen; **Photograph (cover):** Monkey Business/Adobe Stock, troyek/Getty Images, and Dannon G. Cox, M.Ed.; **Photo Asset Manager:** Laura Fitch; **Photo Production Coordinator:** Amy M. Rose; **Photo Production Manager:** Jason Allen; **Senior Art Manager:** Kelly Hendren; **Printer:** Walsworth

Printed in the United States of America   10 9 8 7 6 5 4 3 2 1

The paper in this book was manufactured using responsible forestry methods.

Human Kinetics
1607 N. Market St.
Champaign, IL 61820
Website: www.HumanKinetics.com

In the United States, email info@hkusa.com or call 800-747-4457.
In Canada, email info@hkcanada.com.
In the United Kingdom/Europe, email hk@hkeurope.com.

For information about Human Kinetics' coverage in other areas of the world, please visit our website: **www.HumanKinetics.com**

E7766

Tell us what you think!
Human Kinetics would love to hear what we can do to improve the customer experience. Use this QR code to take our brief survey.

For Angie, Miles, and Calvin. Thanks for reminding me who the "real doctor" is in the family! – SEJ

For Aaron for your continued encouragement; for Charlotte, who inspires me to want to inspire her; for Alex, who arrived midway through writing this and should probably be listed as a co-author; and for my mom for your support since day one. – JMK

For Montana and Maddy, who always keep my priorities in check and encourage me to get outside and keep moving. – TA

Praise for *Technology for Physical Educators, Health Educators, and Coaches*

"If you can learn about and implement one third of the resources mentioned in this text you will be way ahead of the average teacher. You will set yourself apart and stand out as a knowledgeable educator that knows how to motivate and engage students and you will increase your productivity and effectiveness at your job."

Ben "The PE Specialist" Landers
NBCT Elementary PE Teacher, ThePEspecialist.com

"At last a book has been written that guides educators towards the best, most effective way to incorporate technology in all aspects of their professional life. While a teacher's tech tool of choice will change over time, best practice will remain a constant, and this is the book to empower all teachers."

Andrew Milne
2017 SHAPE America Health Education TOY, www.slowchathealth.com

"Some coaches may be hesitant or intimidated to initially use or add new technology to their coaching practice, but this book eases that fear...I would highly recommend this textbook to coaches and coach educators"

Dr. Scott Douglas
Board of Directors, United States Center for Coaching Excellence; Sport Coaching Program Coordinator, University of Northern Colorado

"This is a text that embraces the current professional expectations of health educators, physical educators, and coaches within a twenty-first-century classroom."

Collin Brooks
PhD Candidate, former Elementary PE Teacher, Co-creator Physedagogy.com

"The chapter 'Meeting Special Needs and Abilities Through Technology' provides an excellent overview of a wide range of assistive technologies and guides the reader on how to incorporate specific equipment, devices, and apps in order to support students with disabilities in engaging with the health and physical education curriculum in a meaningful way."

Dr. Scott McNamara
CAPE, Adapted PE Professor, University of Northern Iowa

"More than a how-to manual, the text...presents a student-centered model for engaging the current generation of digital natives in exciting ways...It is an excellent resource for today's educators and coaches committed to healthy lifestyles."

Dr. Joanne Leight
Chair, Department of Health and Physical Education, Slippery Rock University of Pennsylvania; Author of Technology for Fitness and Wellness Professionals

CONTENTS

Foreword   viii | Preface   ix

Acknowledgments   xiii

Part I   Introduction to Technology in Physical Education, Health Education, and Coaching   1

1   Introduction 3

Technology in Physical Education   6 | Technology in Health Education   8 | Technology in Coaching   10 | Conclusion   12 | Review Questions   12 | Discussion Questions   12

Part II   Technology for Class and Team Management and Communication   13

2   Management Technology 15

Course and Sport Management   16 | Teaching and Coaching Time and Task Management   19 | Student and Athlete Management   21 | Budget and Equipment Management   25 | Document Management   25 | Data and Assessment Management   27 | Conclusion   28 | Review Questions   28 | Discussion Questions   28

3   Communication Technology 29

Overview of Communication Technology   30 | Electronic Mail   33 | Text Messaging   36 | Social Media   37 | Cloud-Based File Sharing   38 | Scheduling Tools   40 | Reminder Tools   42 | Video Calls and Videoconferences   44 | Conclusion   49 | Review Questions   50 | Discussion Questions   50

Part III   Technology for Instruction   51

4   Technology for Health Education Classroom Instruction 53

Displays   55 | Microsoft Applications   56 | Google Applications   63 | Student Feedback and Involvement   69 | Apps   73 | Video Integration   74 | Learning Management Systems   78 | Websites and Technology Management   79 | Conclusion   80 | Review Questions   81 | Discussion Questions   81

5 Technology for Motivation 83

Motivating with Technology 85 | Motivating with Music 87 | Motivating with Video Games 88 | Motivating with Augmented Reality and Virtual Reality 98 | Motivating with Interactive Video Projection 99 | Motivating with Gamification and Technology 99 | Technology-Integrated Activities that Motivate Movement in the Classroom 100 | Motivating with Technology-Related Extrinsic Rewards 104 | Conclusion 104 | Review Questions 106 | Discussion Questions 106

6 Technology for Lifelong Health and Fitness 107

Lifetime Health Technologies 108 | Physical Health 108 | Mental Health 126 | Social Health 130 | Conclusion 133 | Review Questions 134 | Discussion Questions 134

7 Meeting Special Needs and Abilities Through Technology 135

Disability and Legal Mandates 137 | Brief Recommendations for AT Implementation and Pedagogy 139 | Mid-Tech and High-Tech Assistive Technology 140 | Apps for Individuals with Disabilities (Blindness/Visual Impairment, Deafness/Hearing Impairments, Cognitive Impairments, Physical Disabilities) 150 | Video Gaming for Individuals with Disabilities 152 | Conclusion 155 | Review Questions 157 | Discussion Questions 157

8 Online Instruction and Remote Supervision 159

Online Instruction 161 | Flipped Instruction 179 | Online Physical Education 181 | Online Coaching 185 | Remote Supervision Using Digital Video Technology 187 | Conclusion 195 | Review Questions 197 | Discussion Questions 198

Part IV Technology for Assessment   199

9 Wearable Technology for Assessment 201

Heart Rate Monitors 202 | Pedometers 214 | Accelerometers 224 | GPS Units and Other Wearable Coaching Technologies 228 | Wearable Technology for Health Education 233 | Conclusion 234 | Review Questions 235 | Discussion Questions 236

10 Other Forms of Technology for Assessment 237

Health-Related Fitness Assessment Technology 239 | Quiz and Survey Technology 240 | Video for Assessment 245 | Creating and Utilizing Rubrics with Technology 252 | Data Collection, Mining, and Reporting Considerations 252 | Conclusion 253 | Review Questions 254 | Discussion Questions 254

11 Basic Digital Video Recording and Editing 255

Digital Video Recording Equipment 257 | Digital Video Recording 265 | Digital Video Editing 266 | Conclusion 274 | Review Questions 275 | Discussion Questions 276

Part V Technology for Professional Development and Advocacy   277

12 Technology for Professional Development 279

Informal Professional Development 280 | Formal Professional Development 282 | Identifying Appropriate and High-Quality Online Professional Development 285 | Building and Maintaining Your Professional Presence with Technology 286 | Conclusion 289 | Review Questions 290 | Discussion Questions 290

13 Technology for Advocacy 291

Advocacy Issues in Physical Education, Health Education, and Coaching 292 | Technology Tools for Advocacy 293 | Advantages and Limitations of Using Technology for Advocacy 301 | Conclusion 302 | Review Questions 302 | Discussion Questions 302

14 Technology Resources (available online only) 303

Part VI Legal and Financial Aspects of Technology   305

15 Legal Aspects of Technology Use 307

Student Use of the Internet 308 | Understanding Copyright Laws 310 | Capturing and Sharing Student Photos, Videos, and Work 318 | Digital Communication 320 | Conclusion 323 | Review Questions 324 | Discussion Questions 324

16 Opportunities and Ideas for Acquiring Technology 325

School and Community-Based Lending Programs 326 | School-Based Funding 328 | Fundraising 331 | Crowdfunding 331 | Grants 334 | Smart Technology Purchases for Your Budget 338 | Conclusion 339 | Review Questions 340 | Discussion Questions 340

References 341 | Index 359

About the Authors 368

FOREWORD

The difficulty with writing a textbook on integrating technology in teaching and coaching is that technology is always changing. New apps, updates, and categories of tools are emerging at such a breakneck pace that it can feel impossible to keep up. Attempting to capture a snapshot of the current state of educational technology is like trying to hold a river in your hands.

This book, however, undoubtedly will assist with that endeavor. The fundamental principles that support best practices in teaching and learning do not share the same kinetic nature of today's technology landscape and this text supports these principles. By using best practices as our lens, we can filter out the flashy, the unnecessary, the "FOMO" (fear of missing out), or gadgets, applications, and platforms that so desperately want our attention. Instead, we should mindfully choose the best tools for the job; the most effective solutions to our problems.

This text is not a collection of trendy apps and tools. It is an extensive resource that has been developed with a clear understanding of best practices in health education, physical education, and coaching. This book has been put together by educators who understand the problems teachers and coaches face on a daily basis and it presents technology-related solutions to those problems.

While specific technology tools may change over time, the reasoning behind the selection of these tools, the understanding of how they link to best practices, the sense of why they can be so powerful when it comes to student learning—these things will not change. This stellar book will help give you the confidence and competence you will need to effectively integrate technology into your teaching or coaching in a purposeful and intentional way for years to come.

Happy Teaching!
Joey Feith
Physical Education Teacher
Founder, ThePhysicalEducator.com

PREFACE

Health and physical educators strive to ensure that all individuals gain the knowledge, skills, and dispositions they need in order to lead a healthy lifestyle and be physically active for life. Similarly, sport coaches use both teaching and training programs to help athletes prepare for athletic competition. Taken together, these professionals serve as teachers who promote movement and encourage healthy behaviors, and they do so in environments that call for effective instruction, assessment, management, communication, professional development, and advocacy. And all of these dimensions of practice can be enhanced by technology—if it is used appropriately!

Even so, you might feel, understandably, that technology presents a barrier to achieving some of your objectives. Indeed, technology can draw both children and adults away from physical activity and healthy lifestyle choices—and toward a life spent in front of a screen. However, despite this potential pitfall, effective use of technology can enhance your ability to teach and coach, as well as motivate your students and athletes to be active and healthy, both for sport competition and for life. The key to success lies in how you approach technology; therefore, helping you make full use of what technology offers is the purpose of *Technology for Physical Educators, Health Educators, and Coaches.*

Put simply, we love technology! Indeed, if we did not, we would not write a book about it. At the same time, we are cognizant of the fact that technology should not be used simply to "add technology" into your teaching or coaching. To the contrary, it should be used *only* if it enhances the teaching or coaching process, and the subsequent learning or performance of the students or athletes. More specifically, integrating technology into your practice should accomplish goals such as the following:

- Solving a problem
- Increasing teaching effectiveness
- Improving classroom or training session management
- Engaging and motivating learners
- Meeting lesson or training objectives
- Enhancing communication
- Promoting lifetime health and fitness
- Increasing student and athlete safety
- Improving assessment possibilities and accuracy
- Expediting data mining and reporting
- Providing online instruction and remote supervision opportunities
- Meeting special needs and abilities
- Advocating for your program
- Providing opportunities for professional development and networking

To ensure that technology use serves such goals, practitioners must ask questions such as, "What is the utility of this technology?" and "Does using this technology help me accomplish this task more effectively than not using it?" In this book, we provide many technology-related ideas and suggestions to help you develop into a more effective teacher or coach. Successful practitioners continuously evolve as they self-reflect and discover ways to improve their teaching or coaching. This text will aid you in this quest as we share with you how to use technology to meet your objectives—whether in the gym, on the playing field, or in the classroom.

TEXT ORGANIZATION

Part I consists solely of chapter 1, which introduces the topic of technology in physical education, health education, and coaching. More specifically, it defines technology and addresses how using it can help you meet specific goals and objectives in each of these three domains. In particular, it addresses how technology can help practitioners fulfill the national standards for physical education and sport coaching established by the Society of Health and Physical Educators (SHAPE America), as well as the health education standards created by the Joint Committee on National Health Education Standards. Chapter 1 also includes brief examples of the types of technology that are discussed in more detail later in the text.

The remainder of the book is organized according to certain key functions or uses of technology, and the utility of each category is highlighted by the relevant chapter title. **Part II** covers technology for class and team management and for communication. Chapter 2 (Management Technology) discusses specific organization and management technology that practitioners can use in the gym, in the classroom, or on the playing field. Much of this technology is designed to help you organize lessons and practice sessions in order to maximize time on task and increase the likelihood of meeting each session's objectives. Next, chapter 3 (Communication Technology) provides ideas for using specific technology for various modes of communication and for digital file sharing with key stakeholders, such as students, athletes, parents, administrators, colleagues, and members of the community.

Part III centers on technology for instruction. That is, whereas part II focuses on the planning phase, this part highlights ideas for using technology to facilitate teaching and learning *during* instruction. Chapter 4 (Technology for Health Education Classroom Instruction) reviews technology geared toward health pedagogy, and chapter 5 (Technology for Motivation) covers ideas for motivating classes and teams through technology-based approaches such as motion-based video games, interactive video, gamification, and virtual and augmented reality. Next, chapter 6 (Technology for Lifelong Health and Fitness) focuses on a multitude of technologies used to optimize physical, mental, and social health over a lifetime. Examples include nutrition and physical activity trackers and technology-related lifetime activities, such as geocaching. Chapter 7 (Meeting Special Needs and Abilities through Technology) provides an overview of assistive digital technologies for supporting differentiated instruction techniques to meet the accessibility needs of learners in a variety of settings. Finally, chapter 8 (Online Instruction and Remote Supervision) presents ideas and best practices for online, hybrid, and flipped instruction, as well as remote supervision via videoconferencing.

Part IV covers technology for assessment. Chapter 9 (Wearable Technology for Assessment) highlights devices such as heart rate monitors, pedometers, accelerometers, and GPS units. Chapter 10 (Other Forms of Technology for Assessment) addresses additional tools, such as fitness, quiz, survey, and digital video options. Moreover, chapter 11 (Basic Digital Video Recording and Editing) reviews best practices for recording video, as well as rudimentary digital video editing. These skills are compulsory for many preservice and practicing teachers. Digital video samples are required for National Board certification and by the Education Teacher Performance Assessment (edTPA), which is being adopted by more and more teacher preparation programs and state education departments. In addition, sport coaches will benefit from knowing how to record and edit digital video for use in motion analysis and provision of feedback to their athletes.

Part V addresses technology for professional development and advocacy. Chapter 12 (Technology for Professional Development) covers ideas for growing and learning as a professional through technology that aids in networking, staying up to date on research and trends, and participating in distance learning. Next, chapter 13 (Technology for Advocacy) discusses technology that can help professionals promote and advocate for their programs through utilizing websites, social media, and other digital avenues. Finally, chapter 14 (Technology Resources; available only in the book's online component) presents excellent resources related to technology in physical education, health, and coaching (e.g., websites, blogs, Twitter handles, organizations) that you can explore for more information about all technology-related topics presented in this book.

The text concludes with **part VI**, which covers the all-important legal and financial aspects of technology. Chapter 15 (Legal Aspects of Technology Use) considers the laws applicable to certain types of technology that are common in health and physical education and in sport coaching—in particular, recording and sharing digital pictures and videos, as well as interacting with students or athletes through technology outside of class or practice. The book closes with chapter 16 (Opportunities and Ideas for Acquiring Technology), which provides specific suggestions for using school and community technology resources, acquiring money to purchase technology through fundraising or grants, and making wise technology purchases.

TEXT GOALS

Whether you are a teacher or a coach, this book gives you practical information that will help you become both more effective and more efficient by using technology to do the following:

- Improve your management efficiency so that you can devote more time to instruction.
- Improve your communication with stakeholders.
- Improve your instruction, both inside and outside of the traditional classroom, so that all learners can better understand concepts, apply skills, and increase motivation.
- Improve the inclusion opportunities you provide for all learners.
- Improve your online instructional effectiveness and create more opportunities to use this approach.
- Improve your assessment so that it supports learning and is fair, accurate, and insightful.
- Improve your skill at recording and editing digital videos.
- Improve your ability to advocate for your program.
- Improve your access to opportunities for high-quality professional development.
- Improve your understanding of the legal implications of using technology.
- Improve your knowledge of opportunities for acquiring technology equipment and technology-related funding and grants.

SPECIAL ELEMENTS IN EACH CHAPTER

- *Research overviews.* These elements address the effectiveness of certain technological options and provide practical suggestions for using them. These overviews are often included in a section titled What Does the Research Say?

- *Differentiating technology.* Where appropriate, the text provides examples of how the type or use of the technology might vary depending on level (primary, secondary, collegiate, elite) or domain (physical education, health education, sport coaching). Much of the technology, however, can be applied to multiple settings.

- *Practitioner tips and examples.* These elements provide specific examples and suggestions from practicing professionals who use certain types of technology; they appear both in the print text and in the online resources.

- *Chapter features.* Each chapter includes a set of objectives, key terms with definitions, review questions, and open-ended discussion questions (which could be used for online discussion boards).

- *Instructor materials.* Instructors who adopt the text are provided with an extremely detailed chapter-by-chapter instructor guide with sample content-specific assignments, online chapter quizzes that are compatible with learning management systems (LMSs), as well as PowerPoint presentations covering each chapter, along with corresponding figures and images.

WEB RESOURCE

This book includes the key code for a robust variety of online resources, such as additional practitioner interviews focused on technology, ancillary examples, website and video links, podcasts, sample handouts, and other activities and resources from practicing professionals that augment each chapter. Moreover, chapter 14 (Technology Resources) is available only online. All of these materials provide specific examples of technology used by physical educators, health educators, and sport coaches today. Finally, because we know that technology changes virtually every day, we will work with our many contributors to keep these online resources updated so that the most current tools are always at your disposal.

SOCIAL MEDIA

In addition, the authors have created social media accounts on Twitter: @Tech4HPE-Coach and Facebook: @Tech4HPECoach for the book that are meant to be user-driven online discussion boards (i.e., forums) where you can share ideas, pose questions to fellow readers/practitioners, and post content you have created that relates to Technology for Physical Educators, Health Educators, and Coaches. Also, use the hashtag #Tech4HPE-Coach across these and other varying social media platforms (e.g., Instagram, Pinterest, etc.) to further connect and share ideas!

NO CONFLICTS OF INTEREST DISCLOSURE

Neither the authors nor Human Kinetics received compensation from any company that produces any product mentioned in this text. The views expressed in the interviews in this book and web resource are solely the opinion of the interviewees and do not necessarily represent the views of the authors or Human Kinetics. While we highlight specific equipment, brands, applications, and resources, we encourage consumers to research products prior to purchase, as all programs are unique and technology resources are always changing.

ACKNOWLEDGMENTS

Thank you to the many health and physical education teachers, coaches, students, and athletes who inspired us to write this book. Moreover, thank you to those teachers, coaches, students, athletes, and interviewees who shared your time, ideas, pictures, and artifacts with us for this book and corresponding web resources. Specifically, we would like to thank Veronica Adams, Jeff Bartlett, Andrew Becker, Laura Loretz Benson, Nicolas Besombes, Nicole Bosley, Collin Brooks, Jamie Cain, George Claypoole, Michael Cleary, Jon Coles, Colby Coulter, Dannon Cox, Matthew Cummiskey, Brian Danielson, Evan Dauenhauer, Jacob Dauenhauer, Victoria Demerest, Ashley Dugas, Becky Eidson, Craig Ellingson, John Ferry, Joey Feith, Zan Gao, Karen Lux Gaudreault, Ben Gordon, James Gunther, Matthew Hammersmith, Kimberly Hohman, Kendra Holtcamp, Alan Hough, Glenn Hushman, Frederick Jenny, Geraldine Jenny, Neve Johnson, Ingrid Johnson, Sarah Keaton, Joanne Leight, Brandy Lynch, Jeffrey Lynn, Tara McCarthy, Jaimie McMullen, Scott McNamara, Adam Mullis, Gloria Napper-Owen, Dan Ogden, David Pinero, Colleen Quinn-Maxwell, Tawn Reidel, Aaron Scheidies, Bre Snyder, Scott Sorensen, Rebekah Sweat, Andrea Taliaferro, Kevin Tiller, Kim Trgina, Lisa Warner, Robert Waugh, Kimarie Whetstone, Bradley Williams, Bradley Witzel, and Carly Wright. Finally, thank you *Human Kinetics* staff Scott Wikgren, Melissa Feld, Miranda Baur, Bill Sunderland, Bill Dobrik, Dalene Reeder, Lynn Kincaid, Tom Tiller, Heather Gauen Hutches, and others who worked "behind the scenes" in developing this book.

PART I

Introduction to Technology in Physical Education, Health Education, and Coaching

1

Introduction

Chapter Objectives

When you have completed this chapter, you will be able to do the following:

1. Define technology and its potential for application in physical education, health education, and coaching contexts.
2. Identify standards related to technology in physical education, health education, and coaching.
3. Identify basic functions of technology for management, communication, instruction, assessment, professional development, and advocacy.

Wavebreakmedia/iStock/Getty Images

Technology is everywhere. Now that it has become an integral part of day-to-day life, it helps people with **communication**, productivity, entertainment, and more. Think about all of the ways in which you use technology in your daily life. Did you wake up to an alarm clock this morning? Did you use any form of motorized transportation to get to school or work? Have you communicated with friends, family, or colleagues by way of text message, phone call, email, or social media? Will you engage in media-based entertainment, such as television, video streaming, or video gaming this evening? Have you tracked your physical activity levels today with a digital wearable device? Although some may argue that technology is not a necessity for life, it certainly has made its way into society and into our everyday operations. This is especially true for **digital natives**, who have spent most if not all of their lives in a technology-driven world.

When we think of technology in our modern society, we think most readily of digital gadgets. More generally, however, technology is defined as a manner of accomplishing a task using technical processes, methods, or knowledge. Thus it serves a problem-solving purpose and has been around for centuries, ranging from the invention of basic tools such as the wheel and the pencil to more advanced products such as the telephone and the Internet. In fact, technology has arguably evolved society, one invention at a time, and continues to do so at a rapid pace.

Even as technology has profoundly affected society in general, it has also been recognized as an integral part of the educational system. Its capacity to enhance teaching and learning, along with increasing affordability and availability, has led to greater integration of technology in both PK-12 schools and higher education settings. The days of questioning whether or not technology might aid in learning are long gone; now, experts are working to determine just how it can best be used to improve learning for all students (U.S. Department of Education, 2017). For example, educational settings now commonly use various kinds of technology, such as calculators, computers, tablets, software or applications (apps), and the Internet. In addition, more specific tools are used in particular subject areas. For instance, robotics and 3-D printers are used in science classrooms, whereas math classrooms use advanced calculators and statistical software. Ultimately, all subject areas are expected to infuse technology into the curriculum in order to enhance teaching and learning, as described in the **International Society for Technology in Education (ISTE)** standards. Specifically, ISTE has established seven Standards for Educators that include indicators for effective integration of technology in order to help students become empowered learners. The standards are shown in table 1.1.

Table 1.1 ISTE Standards for Educators

Learner	Learn from and with others and explore promising practices that leverage technology.
Leader	Seek opportunities to support student empowerment, help shape and shared vision and advocate for student equity.
Citizen	Inspire students to contribute responsibly in the digital world and guide them to be curious, wise, empathetic, safe, and ethical.
Collaborator	Collaborate with others to improve practice, discover and share resources, and solve problems with others around the globe.
Designer	Design authentic, learner-driven activities and environments that recognize and accommodate learner variability.
Facilitator	Model creative expression, empower students to take ownership of their learning and create opportunities for students to innovate and solve problems.
Analyst	Use data to drive instruction and provide alternate ways for students to demonstrate competency and use assessment data to guide progress.

Based on ISTE Standards for Students, ©2016, ISTE® (International Society for Technology in Education), iste.org.

ISTE also established seven Standards for Students, which include indicators that students are prepared to succeed in a world marked by continuously evolving technology. Table 1.2 shows what a digital-age learner looks like with achievement of the ISTE Standards for Students.

Abiding by the ISTE Standards for Educators is the responsibility of all educators in all subject areas, including physical education and health education. Doing so enables us to integrate technology effectively, thereby helping learners achieve the ISTE Standards for Students and preparing them for success in a digital world.

Although the ISTE standards can help us determine what to focus on when using technology, we must understand that simply knowing about technology is not enough. Granted, digital natives are generally more tech savvy than preceding generations due to their lifelong exposure to technology. However, being aware of and skilled with technology—also known as *possessing technology knowledge (TK)*—does not necessarily mean that educators will be able to teach well with technology. Shulman (1987) shared a recipe for success as a teacher, which included mastery of content knowledge (CK; e.g., health education), pedagogical knowledge (PK; i.e., teaching skills), and pedagogical content knowledge (PCK; e.g., how to teach health content). Once technology was found to be a major player in the world of education, Koehler & Mishra (2008) added TK, technological content knowledge (TCK), and technological pedagogical knowledge (TPK), which, when combined, create **technological, pedagogical, and content knowledge (TPACK)**. As illustrated in figure 1.1, TPACK constitutes the ability to successfully teach a particular content area with appropriate use of technology; as such, it serves as the gold standard for successful integration of technology. The various types of knowledge are summarized in table 1.3.

This chapter provides a basic overview of the integration of technology in physical education, health education, and coaching. The remainder of the book, in turn, expands in detail on technology integration for these three areas. Physical education and health education can benefit from the same technology used in general education classes, such as computers and apps. Along with coaching, they also offer more expansive possibilities

Table 1.2   ISTE Standards for Students

Empowered Learner	I use technology to set goals, work toward achieving them and demonstrate my learning.
Global Collaborator	I strive to broaden my perspective, understand others and work effectively in teams using digital tools.
Digital Citizen	I understand the rights, responsibilities, and opportunities of living, learning, and working in an interconnected digital world.
Creative Communicator	I communicate effectively and express myself creatively using different tools, styles, formats, and digital media.
Knowledge Constructor	I critically select, evaluate, and synthesize digital resources into a collection that reflects my learning and builds my knowledge.
Computational Thinker	I identify authentic problems, work with data, and use a step-by-step process to automate solutions.
Innovative Designer	I solve problems by creative new and imaginative solutions using a variety of digital tools.

Based on ISTE Standards for Students, ©2016, ISTE® (International Society for Technology in Education), iste. org.

for technology integration due to their unique context and content, especially when taught outside of the traditional classroom setting. Specifically, technology can be used to enhance the following functions necessary for successful teaching and coaching:

- Management
- Communication
- Instruction
- Assessment
- Professional development
- Advocacy

The following sections provide a brief overview of how technology aids achievement of standards related to physical education, health education, and coaching.

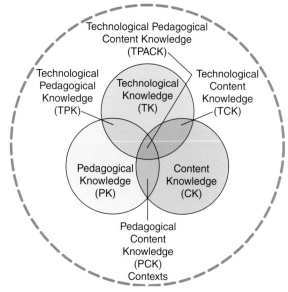

Figure 1.1 TPACK model.

Reproduced by permission of the publisher, © 2012 by tpack.org.

TECHNOLOGY IN PHYSICAL EDUCATION

The goal of physical education is to "develop physically literate individuals who have the knowledge, skills, and confidence to enjoy a lifetime of healthful physical activity" (Society of Health and Physical Educators, 2014, p. 11). This goal is accomplished through high-quality physical education programs that address the National Standards for K-12 Physical Education (figure 1.2).

High-quality physical education programs adhere to these standards through well-defined policies and environments that promote physical education for all students. They also use an established curriculum, provide rigorous **instruction**, and collect evidence of

Table 1.3 TPACK Knowledge Types

Knowledge type	Definition
Content knowledge (CK)	Knowledge of the subject matter to be learned or taught
Pedagogical knowledge (PK)	Knowledge of processes, practices, or methods of teaching and learning
Technological knowledge (TK)	Knowledge of working with technological tools and resources
Pedagogical content knowledge (PCK)	Knowledge of pedagogy related to teaching specific content
Technological content knowledge (TCK)	Knowledge of how technology and content affect and limit one another
Technological pedagogical knowledge (TPK)	Knowledge of how teaching and learning can be transformed when technology is integrated in a specific way
Technological, pedagogical, and content knowledge (TPACK)	Knowledge of pedagogy employed for subject matter content and carried out with appropriate technology

Figure 1.2   National Standards for K-12 Physical Education.

Standard 1: The physically literate individual demonstrates competency in a variety of motor skills and movement patterns.

Standard 2: The physically literate individual applies knowledge of concepts, principles, strategies and tactics related to movement and performance.

Standard 3: The physically literate individual demonstrates the knowledge and skills to achieve and maintain a health-enhancing level of physical activity and fitness.

Standard 4: The physically literate individual exhibits responsible personal and social behavior that respects self and others.

Standard 5: The physically literate individual recognizes the value of physical activity for health, enjoyment, challenge, self-expression, and/or social interaction.

Reprinted by permission from SHAPE America, *National Standards & Grade-Level Outcomes for K-12 Physical Education* (Champaign, IL: Human Kinetics, 2014).

student learning through appropriate assessments (Society of Health and Physical Educators, 2015). In addition, the benefits of integrating technology into teaching and learning can be brought to bear by applying technology in physical education programs. In fact, specific expectations call for physical education teacher candidates to be able to integrate technology as follows into their instruction, **assessment**, and **advocacy** for physical education, according to the National Standards for Initial Physical Education Teacher Education (Society of Health and Physical Educators, 2017):

3.e Plan and implement learning experiences that require students to use technology appropriately in meeting one or more short- and long-term plan objective(s).

4.e Analyze motor skills and performance concepts through multiple means (e.g., visual observation, technology) in order to provide specific, congruent feedback to enhance student learning.

6.c Describe strategies, including the use of technology, for the promotion and advocacy of physical education and expanded physical activity opportunities.

Physical education teachers who acquire the necessary knowledge and skills for integrating technology in these areas can use enhanced approaches to address both the National Standards for K-12 Physical Education and the ISTE Standards for Students. For example, an elementary physical education teacher might teach overhand throwing in order to address National Standard 1 ("competency in a variety of motor skills and movement patterns") and, more specifically, grade-level outcome S1.E14.3 (e.g., "throws overhand, demonstrating 3 of the 5 critical elements of a mature pattern" in a closed environment). The teacher could facilitate achievement of this standard by using technology to fulfill the ISTE Standard for Students 1C (i.e., "students use technology to seek feedback that informs and improves their practice and to demonstrate their learning in a variety of ways"). For instance, the teacher could use a motor skill analysis application on a tablet to provide feedback to students about their performance of the critical elements of the overhand throw (figure 1.3).

Table 1.4 provides additional examples of how physical education teachers can use technology for **management**, communication, instruction, assessment, **professional development**, and advocacy. More examples are provided in detail throughout the book.

TECHNOLOGY IN HEALTH EDUCATION

Health education provides students with the knowledge and skills to adopt and maintain healthy lifestyles through the development of health literacy. Health-enhancing behaviors are facilitated among students when we achieve the National Health Education Standards PreK-12 (Joint Committee on National Health Education Standards, 2007); see figure 1.4.

Health education teacher candidates are expected to be able to incorporate technology into their planning and implementation of instruction, as indicated in the following two components of the National Standards for Initial Health Education Teacher Education (Society of Health and Physical Educators, 2018):

Jennifer Krause

Figure 1.3   Evaluating motor performance using a skills analysis application.

Component 2.f: Candidates plan instruction that incorporates technology, media and other appropriate resources in order to enhance students' digital literacy and to engage all learners.

Component 3.b: Candidates implement instructional strategies that incorporate technology, media and other appropriate resources to enhance student learning and engage all learners.

Health education teachers who acquire the necessary knowledge and skills for integrating technology in these areas can use enhanced approaches to address both the National Health Education Standards and the ISTE Standards for Students. For example, a health teacher who delivers a lesson on the effects of drug use might want to address National Health Education Standard 3 ("ability to access valid information and products and services to enhance health").

Table 1.4   Sample Applications of Technology in Physical Education

Function	Technology applications
Management and communication	Use a classroom management app to track student behaviors (e.g., fair play) during physical education.
Instruction	Use heart rate monitors to teach students about heart rate zones, goal setting, and monitoring their own performance.
Assessment	Use a classroom response system (e.g., Plickers) to gather assessment data on students' content knowledge and beliefs.
Professional development and advocacy	Use social media to network with colleagues and advocate for your physical education program by sharing information about the benefits of PE and your program's achievements.

Figure 1.4 Focus areas of the National Health Education Standards PreK-12.

Standard 1: Health promotion and disease prevention

Standard 2: Influences on health behaviors

Standard 3: Valid information and products

Standard 4: Interpersonal communication skills

Standard 5: Decision-making skills

Standard 6: Goal-setting skills

Standard 7: Health-enhancing behaviors

Standard 8: Advocacy for health

Adapted from the Joint Committee on National Health Education Standards (2007).

The teacher could facilitate achievement of this standard by combining it with ISTE Standard for Students 3b ("students evaluate the accuracy, perspective, credibility, and relevance of information, media, data, or other sources"). For instance, students could use the Internet to research the effects of drug use while following guidelines for selecting appropriate and valid websites in order to ensure that the information they gather is accurate and credible (figure 1.5).

Technology can also be integrated into health education in a multitude of ways that go beyond planning and implementation, such as managing your classes, communicating with students and parents, and staying up to date professionally. Table 1.5 presents a selection of technology tools, and various examples are discussed throughout the book.

Christian Science Monitor/Getty Images

Figure 1.5 Students selecting valid health information online.

Table 1.5 Sample Applications of Technology in Health Education

Function	Technology applications
Management and communication	Use cloud-based file sharing (e.g., Google Drive) to organize, store, and share assignments and other documents with students, parents, and colleagues.
Instruction	Use collaborative tools (e.g., wikis) that enable students to collaborate and curate health information.
Assessment	Use online quiz tools (e.g., Kahoot!) to gather assessment data on students' content knowledge in a fun and competitive way.
Professional development and advocacy	Participate in webinars on health education pedagogy to stay up to date and refine your teaching methods.

TECHNOLOGY IN COACHING

Beyond traditional school settings, technology has become an important part of the coaching world. The National Standards for Sport Coaches (NSSC; Society of Health and Physical Educators, 2019), include 42 standards covering areas such as setting goals and standards; engaging in ethical practices; building relationships; creating a safe, positive, and inclusive environment; conducting practices; preparing for competition; teaching, assessing, and adapting; and striving for improvement. Of the 42 standards, only one specifically mentions technology, and it is for the purpose of assessment:

> Standard 34: Implement appropriate strategies for evaluating athlete training, development, and performance: Sport coaches evaluate athlete progress and performance to assist in making decisions about athlete training, development, and performance. Sport coaches will use evidence-based strategies and tools as well as athlete input to make decisions regarding: athlete selection, assignment of team roles, goal-setting and training plan development, daily evaluation of progress, and incorporation of technology in training.

For instance, integrating technology into athlete training might involve using heart rate monitors to track cardiorespiratory workload or using skill analysis software to evaluate motor performance of the critical elements of a particular skill. Moreover, although this standard includes the only mention of the word *technology* in the NSSC, technology can enhance coaching in many ways and aid in addressing many of the other standards, some of are discussed throughout this book. Some examples of technology use in coaching are presented in table 1.6.

WHAT DOES THE RESEARCH SAY?

Technology Use in Physical Education and Health Education

Technology can enhance instruction in both health education and physical education (Eberline & Richards, 2013), and each passing year brings greater awareness and availability of technology, as well as new and evolving options for using it. In addition, both in-service and preservice teachers are becoming more confident in their abilities to use technology for teaching and learning than ever before (Krause, 2017; Scrabis-Fletcher, Juniu, & Zullo, 2016). Health and physical education professionals participating in an online SHAPE America forum on technology held more discussions on the following types of technology than any other: activity monitors (e.g., pedometers, heart rate monitors), mobile devices (e.g., tablets), social media, active gaming, computers, and office tools (Krause, Franks, & Lynch, 2017). As practitioners continue to grow their technology knowledge and skills, and as a greater variety of options continues to become available, opportunities are increasing rapidly to integrate technology into health education and physical education; indeed, such opportunities are becoming a staple in our classrooms.

Table 1.6   Sample Applications of Technology in Coaching

Function	Technology applications
Management and communication	Use communication apps (e.g., Remind) to share up-to-date information with athletes and parents.
Instruction	Use whiteboard apps (e.g., Coach Note) to plan, record, and share strategies and tactics with athletes.
Assessment	Use video-delay apps to enable athletes to view and self-assess their performances within moments after the event.
Professional development and advocacy	Enroll in an online coaching-enhancement program (e.g., certificate or degree program) to enhance your credentials.

TECHNOLOGY TIPS FROM THE FIELD

Administrator Perspective: Technology Integration in Physical Education and Health Education

Lisa Warner
Principal and former health and physical education teacher
Marsteller Middle School, Bristow, Virginia

What are the technology integration expectations for health and physical education teachers in your school?
All teachers, including health and physical education, are required to plan and implement a technology-focused lesson quarterly, according to the Prince William County Public Schools Educational Technology Plan.

What types of technology do health and physical education teachers in your school have access to, and how do they use them?
They use projectors, pedometers, computers, and iPads. I've witnessed the use of projectors in the gym to reinforce demonstrations and lead fitness activities, where the teacher prerecords a video and then displays it for all students to view. They've also used iPads and laptops in the gym for students to track their own data. For example, students input their own data for FitnessGram on the iPads. Health classes often show PowerPoints or other interactive [material] . . . on the projectors and computers.

For you as the principal of the school, why is technology implementation important in health education and physical education, and what are your goals for its use in these settings?
I come from a unique perspective—not only as an administrator, but as a former health and physical education teacher. I probably care a little more about what's going on in these classes. I want our students to find something active that they love to do and can do for their whole lives. At this level, we want them to incorporate technology to use it to increase their physical activity levels. They are so tech savvy, and we need to keep up with them. We want to teach them to embrace the technology they are already using to enhance their lifestyles.

What suggestions do you have for health education and physical education teachers in using technology to teach?
Make it engaging, align to the standards, and be practical!

Conclusion

This chapter introduces technology integration in physical education, health education, and coaching. The opportunities are vast for professionals to use technology for management, communication, instruction, assessment, professional development, and advocacy. The remainder of this book, as well as the web resource, provide you with a wealth of ideas and applications for your own teaching and coaching practice.

Key Terms

advocacy—Practice of supporting, defending, or recommending an idea or cause.

assessment—Process and tools used by educators to document and gather data about students' behaviors, progress, and achievement.

communication—Process of exchanging information and meaning between people in a variety of settings.

digital native—Person who has spent most of life in a technology-driven world.

instruction—Practice of teaching someone how to do something.

International Society for Technology in Education (ISTE)—Epicenter of educational technology, which helps practitioners use technology to solve challenging problems in education.

management—Process and techniques used to keep teaching tasks organized and orderly and to keep students on task and productive.

professional development—Specialized training to help teachers improve their knowledge, skills, and effectiveness.

technological, pedagogical, and content knowledge (TPACK)—Ability to teach a particular content area with appropriate use of technology.

technology—Manner of accomplishing a task using technical processes, methods, or knowledge.

Review Questions

1. Define technology in your own words.
2. List three examples of historical technology and three examples of modern or digital technology.
3. What are the respective purposes of the ISTE Standards for Educators and the ISTE Standards for Students?
4. What are the expectations for an initial physical education teacher with regard to technology integration, according to the National Standards for Initial Physical Education Teacher Education?
5. Define TPACK.

Discussion Questions

1. Describe why successful teaching with technology requires more than basic technology skills.
2. How do you think technology will evolve in the next 5 to 10 years? How will this evolution affect physical education, health education, and coaching?
3. How can technology influence the achievement of standards?

PART II

Technology for Class and Team Management and Communication

2

Management Technology

Chapter Objectives

When you have completed this chapter, you will be able to do the following:

1. Identify a variety of high-quality management resources and tools.
2. Describe a variety of ways to use technology to enhance management for physical education, health education, and coaching.
3. Determine which types of technology are appropriate for various management needs.
4. Identify benefits of using technology for management.

Lorado/E+/Getty Images

Teachers and coaches must perform a multitude of tasks in order to enable a successful experience for learners. They must develop and deliver lesson or practice plans, assess student or athlete progress, and maintain an orderly and organized environment. Along the way, they must establish effective structure and organization, which includes setting up an orderly teaching or coaching space, managing students or athletes and their behavior, and handling documents and data. Table 2.1 presents several **management** standards for physical educators, health educators, and coaches developed by the Society of Health and Physical Educators (SHAPE America).

Features of effective classroom management include establishing and upholding order, managing students both as a group and as individuals, and preventing and handling discipline issues (Jones, 1996). Professionals who have a good handle on management can better focus their time and efforts on instruction and assessment, which enhances learning outcomes for students and athletes. Historically, tools for effective management have included the use of start and stop (or "freeze") signals, clipboards and roster sheets, think chairs, and class folders. In recent years, these practices have been simplified and facilitated by various forms of modern technology. This chapter presents technologies that can enhance the management experience for physical educators, health educators, and coaches.

COURSE AND SPORT MANAGEMENT

The challenge of organizing a course or team can seem overwhelming. Teachers must handle lesson plans, assignments, assessments, presentation materials, gradebooks, attendance rosters, crucial student information (e.g., medical notes), and more. Coaches must take care of team schedules, rosters, statistics, player availability, and many other items. Before the development of modern technology, teachers and coaches typically organized and managed their work through filing cabinets and three-ring binders, which were often unwieldy to handle in the limited space available. Now, however, digital technology offers practitioners

Table 2.1   Management Standards from SHAPE America

Profession	Standard(s)
Physical education	Implement *transitions, routines and positive behavior management* to create and maintain a safe, supportive and engaging learning environment. (Society of Health and Physical Educators, 2017, standard 4.d, emphasis added)
Health education	Candidates apply communication skills, feedback and *classroom management strategies* equitably to promote a safe, inclusive and supportive learning environment that meets the diverse needs of all learners. (Society of Health and Physical Educators, 2018, component 3.d, emphasis added)
Coaching	*Manage program resources* in a responsible manner. Sport coaches manage program documents. They have a basic understanding of fiscal and facility management specific to their program. (Society of Health and Physical Educators, 2019, standard 5, emphasis added)
	Understand components of *effective contest management*. Sport coaches understand the importance of preparing facilities for competition, securing licensed officials, and promoting and demonstrating positive behavior to all officials, coaches and spectators. (Society of Health and Physical Educators, 2019, standard 29, emphasis added)
	Craft daily practice plans based on sound teaching and learning principles to promote athlete development and optimize competitive performance. Sport coaches create daily practice plans . . . [while] *instituting behavioral management practices*. (Society of Health and Physical Educators, 2019, standard 32, emphasis added)

Reprinted from SHAPE America (2017); SHAPE America (2018): SHAPE America (2019).

Can Technology Improve Classroom Management?

Classroom and practice management are among the most challenging aspects of teaching and coaching; more specifically, classroom discipline and the organization of class work have long been perceived by beginning teachers as two of their most daunting tasks (Veenman, 1984; Melnick & Meister, 2008). In response, some experts have called for stand-alone professional development for classroom management (Landau, 2001), whereas others have argued that this skill is better learned within simulated or authentic contexts, such as observing videos or participating in field experiences in school or sport settings (Emmer & Stough, 2001). One study found that using technology to facilitate data collection and management (e.g., grading, taking attendance, tracking student progress) was among the top trends and issues discussed by health and physical education professionals (Krause, Franks, & Lynch, 2017). Thus, given the challenges associated with classroom management, it is well worth exploring how technology can help us succeed in this key aspect of physical education, health education, and coaching.

a one-stop shop for course and team management in the form of the **learning management system (LMS)** or **athlete management system (AMS)**.

Learning Management Systems

An LMS is a software package designed for tracking, reporting, documenting, and delivering a course. Traditionally, such systems have been more popular in higher education—likely due to the high price tag for comprehensive versions—but K-12 schools and individual teachers are beginning to adopt these programs to help them organize and deliver their courses. In particular, an LMS can provide a teacher with opportunities to reinforce health and physical education content with their students (Kyriakidis & Papadakis, 2016).

A typical LMS includes many features that are helpful to teachers and students alike (figure 2.1). These features include *instructional tools* for presenting and sharing information, such as documents, audio and video files, and external web links; *communication and collaboration tools*, such as discussion boards, wikis, and journals; and *assessment tools* for administering and grading assignments and keeping records in a gradebook. In addition, a course calendar can help all parties stay abreast of what is due and what needs to be graded. Many LMSs also offer a corresponding mobile app that enables easy access by students and teachers and may even integrate with other tools and platforms, such as Google Drive, YouTube, PBS LearningMedia, and Infobase Health Reference Center.

Many K-12 schools have adopted an LMS to help teachers manage their courses, but even if your school has yet to do so, you can still use one for your own classes. Many LMSs offer basic individual packages for little or no cost. For example, Schoology offers a free basic package for instructors, students, parents, and advisors that includes features for classroom instruction (e.g., course material management and distribution, auto-graded tests, a gradebook, attendance tracking); classroom productivity (e.g., mobile app, messaging, calendar for managing assignments and activities); and classroom integration with external sites, games, tools, and resources. The enterprise version of Schoology is a schoolwide LMS that includes all of the basic features, as well as system-level administration and premium tools for instruction, communication, integration, and reporting. The cost varies based on the size of the organization. Many other LMS options on the market carry a high price tag, including Blackboard, D2L, and Canvas. If you are an individual teacher looking to try

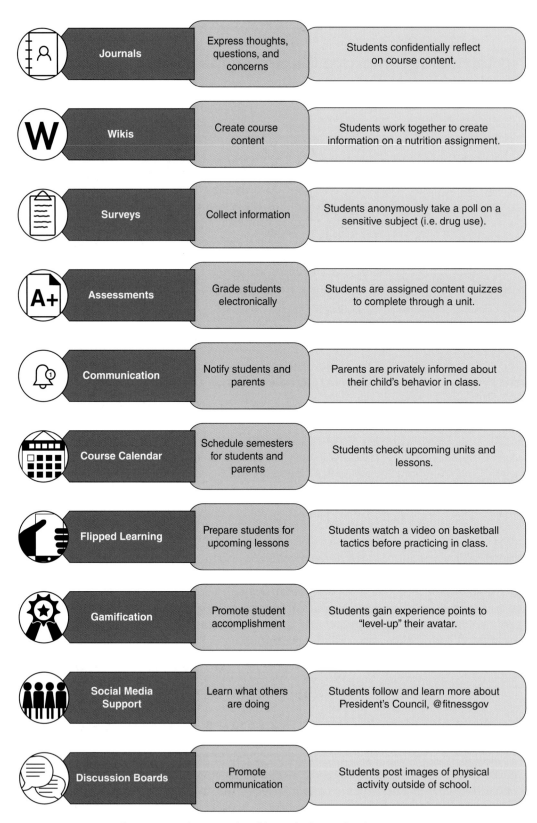

Figure 2.1 LMS features and uses in health and physical education.

Reprinted by permission from D. Cox, X. Fan, C. Brooks, and J. Krause, Top 10 Learning Management System Components for Health and Physical Educators. Poster presented at the Society of Health and Physical Educators Colorado Convention, Aurora, CO, 2018.

out an LMS for free or at low cost, other popular options include ATutor, Edmodo, Google Classroom, and Moodle.

Aside from budget constraints, using an LMS for physical or health education may also present some other challenges, including the need to find time for learning the features of the package (Hughes, 2018) and helping students negotiate their own learning curve. It may be worth the work, however, in order to obtain the advantages for course management and the ability to collect and analyze assessment data while engaging students in a unique way (Dietz, Hurn, Mays, & Woods, 2018).

Athlete Management Systems

Coaches who wish to manage their teams in one place can do so through an AMS, which is a software package for organizing and storing athlete and team information. Unlike LMSs, AMSs vary considerably, and an appropriate system should be selected based on the needs of the individual sport. Most AMSs offer certain basic features, such as calendar planners, messaging with athletes and parents, and questionnaires about wellness. One example, Teamstuff, offers a basic version (free of charge) and a pro version ($5.99 per year), and includes features related to games, training, scheduling, duties, payments, team and profile pages, schedule management, emergency information, and more.

TEACHING AND COACHING TIME AND TASK MANAGEMENT

It is critical for teachers and coaches to establish an environment in which learning can occur readily. In particular, two key aspects of the environment affect the dynamics of what can happen in a given lesson or practice: time and tasks.

Time Management

Time management is a basic yet critical component of any lesson or practice. The time dedicated to each task, and to transitions between tasks, should be planned and implemented strategically. Several technological tools can help with tracking and managing time in physical education, health education, and coaching. The most basic aid is a timer. In the years before modern technology appeared, common timing tools such as simple clocks, watches, and stopwatches were used to track time for lesson or practice segments, individual tasks, and transitions. Now, time management can be facilitated by a number of tools and apps designed to either simplify or magnify the process.

For example, before the emergence of smartphones, a coach might use a stopwatch to regulate the time spent by athletes on a particular drill. And indeed, a stopwatch is a simple, affordable piece of technology that is easy to transport and use. However, a mobile device such as a smartphone can also serve as a timer or stopwatch without requiring the coach to carry extra equipment if the device is already in his or her pocket. A digital device may also offer other capabilities that a typical stopwatch does not. For example, coaches can use an app such as Interval Timer Pro (small fee) to customize sets, high- and low-intensity intervals, and rest times for their athletes. Similarly, a physical education teacher could use the Team Timer app (free of charge) to record laps completed by multiple students at the same time. And a health teacher could use the Giant Timer app (free) to display a countdown clock for students working on a task in groups.

In addition to timer apps, teachers and coaches can regulate activity by managing the starting and stopping of music. This strategy has long been used by physical educators to indicate to students when to begin a task (i.e., when the music begins) and when to stop performing the task (i.e., when the music stops). Now, with the emergence of advanced audio systems, gone are the days of needing to walk over to a stereo system to press a

Figure 2.2   Bluetooth technology.

Play or Stop button; instead, the teacher can simply carry a remote control. Even greater convenience is made possible by **Bluetooth** technology, which uses radio waves to create a short-range wireless connection that allows teachers to play music from a mobile device (e.g., smartphone) through a speaker system (figure 2.2) and control it from anywhere in the gym. To take it a step further, smartwatches (e.g., Apple Watch) can connect to a smartphone via Bluetooth, thus enabling teachers to control the music from their wrist.

Technology can also help practitioners present information and facilitate learners' performance of tasks. For example, projectors, screens, and monitors can display directions and instructions for learners to view, either upon arrival or throughout a lesson or practice. In addition, teachers can use **Quick Response (QR) codes** at stations set up around the learning space for students to scan in order to access dynamic content, thus saving instructional time when various tasks need to be completed. A QR code is a bar code linked to web-based content, such as a specific website or video. Teachers and coaches can easily generate custom QR codes that lead to specific websites in order to aid in delivery of content to students or athletes. Once a QR code is created, the practitioner can print it and hang it in the activity space. Learners can then use a QR code reader on a mobile device, or the mobile device's camera app, to scan the code and engage with the content that appears on the screen. Instructions for creating a QR code can be viewed on the web resource for this text by scanning the QR code in figure 2.3; the web resource also includes more ideas for using QR codes in teaching and coaching.

Task Management

Coaches are often tasked with managing schedules, team statistics, and even the details of contests. Several technological tools are available to help with these tasks so that coaches can spend less time managing and more time coaching. For example, TeamSnap software allows coaches to manage teams and tournaments and includes features for managing roster lists, schedules, payments, team chats, real-time game sharing, statistics, lineups, and more. The program comes in several versions, which vary in their features and range from free of charge to roughly $20 per month.

Figure 2.3   Instructions for creating a QR code.

For coaches and teachers who want to put together a tournament, an app such as Bracket (free of charge) can help create brackets for up to 16 teams; set up single-elimination, double-elimination, and consolation rounds; and easily track wins and losses. In addition, scorekeeping during contests can be simplified with apps such as Scoreboard (free), which can be used on a mobile device and displayed for the group by mirroring the device on a large screen or monitor.

STUDENT AND ATHLETE MANAGEMENT

Once your teaching or coaching space is well organized and manageable, it is time to consider how you will manage your students or athletes. For instance, tracking attendance and managing contact and medical information are crucial tasks for a successful program. Could you simply print the roster of your class or team on a sheet of paper and check off who is present or absent every day? Absolutely, but that type of documentation can be tedious to maintain and cumbersome to use when needed in the moment. Fortunately, technology can facilitate your record keeping in several ways. As discussed earlier, an LMS can track student data (e.g., attendance), and some systems offer the option to keep notes about students (e.g., medical or parent contact information). If you do not have access to an LMS, fear not—many other simplified apps exist for managing information related to students and athletes.

Attendance and Rosters

Tracking student or athlete presence is important for many reasons. Tracking attendance patterns can help you with grouping and daily planning and provide you with important information if an issue arises with a possible link to attendance by a particular student. Attendance records can also affect safety, because teachers and coaches are accountable for all students or athletes during class and practice time. For example, knowing who was present at the start of class may be crucial information if a fire alarm sounds and you need to report on any missing students. Class or team rosters can help you access essential medical information (e.g., dangerous bee-sting allergy) at a moment's notice, and a roster can also include information about parents and guardians for easy reference when needed.

Taking attendance can eat up precious activity time if it is not handled efficiently. Even so, some schools require attendance to be taken at the start of every class and entered into a schoolwide computer system. Because physical education does not always allow for a computer to be kept in the learning space (e.g., gym, field), teachers often take attendance by writing on paper and then transferring the information onto a computer in a nearby office. However, if a teacher has access to a mobile device, the information can be entered at once without leaving the teaching space, thus saving time for everyone. Several apps are available for this purpose; they may also be able to store other content related to students (e.g., parent information, student photos), and some offer features to help with student grouping and assessment. These apps tend to be relatively inexpensive, and many are offered free of charge (with some in-app purchase options). Table 2.2 summarizes a few of the many options for teachers and coaches.

In addition to mobile apps, teachers can use scanning tools to check students into class as they arrive. For example, the Plickers app allows you to generate questions, scan unique bar codes, and record individual student responses for free. It also enables you to scan all students' Plickers cards during the class, either for direct attendance taking or through an alternative assessment question that you can then use to determine who is present. Chapter 10 provides more information regarding the use of Plickers.

Group Management

Selecting individual learners or groups of learners for teams can be time consuming if you want to be conscientious and strategic in your selection. For example, if you wanted to divide the group into teams for an upcoming 3v3 basketball tournament, you would need to think

Table 2.2   Sample Attendance Apps for Practitioners

App	Price	Availability	Key features
Easy Attendance	Free (with in-app purchases)	App Store, Google Play	• Manually entered or imported courses and rosters • Student photos, parent contacts, recorded observations • Option to produce random student groups • Exporting of attendance reports for groups or individuals
iDoceo	$11.99 (one time cost)	App Store	• Option to use offline (with no Internet required) • Unlimited classes • Schedule creation • Option to add files from other sources • Teacher gradebook • Student seating plans with photos • Time-stamped notes linked to students and classes • Random student selector
Teacher Kit	Free (with in-app purchases) or $3.99/month (premium version)	App Store, Google Play	• Importation of student roster • Class organization • Attendance logging • Creation of seating charts • Behavior notes • Grades

about your goals for the event. Are you a coach who wants to ensure that you have the best team in the tournament? If so, then you need to put your most highly skilled players on a team together. If, on the other hand, you are a physical education teacher planning the tournament for a high school class and are more concerned about equal opportunities for practice and success, then you might create teams with an even mix of skill levels and heights; you might even consider other factors, such as competitiveness, leadership, and other personal characteristics. Alternatively, you could be a health teacher who wants to create a random set of student groups for an upcoming project on body systems, with no set boundaries for individual groups other than separating certain students who don't work well together. For any of these scenarios, the process of creating appropriate teams goes well beyond simply counting off by fours, and it can take a lot of time to complete.

Fortunately, several applications are available that, with a little upfront work, can facilitate the process of selecting students and creating teams. One of the most popular apps for group selection is an inexpensive one called Team Shake (figure 2.4), which allows teachers and coaches to choose teams in any of multiple ways. For instance, team selections can be made by gender and skill ability (for more balanced teams or teams separated by skill level) and by the desired number of teams or team size. You can also pick a single random person from a list of participants. Rosters can be imported or entered manually, and additional features include rating user strengths from 1 to 5 (e.g., basketball skill level, academic achievement, leadership ability), ignoring absent students, and setting certain individuals to always or never be on the same team. Many other group management apps are also available for accomplishing similar tasks—for example, Who's Next, Team Maker (Pro or Lite), and Random Picker.

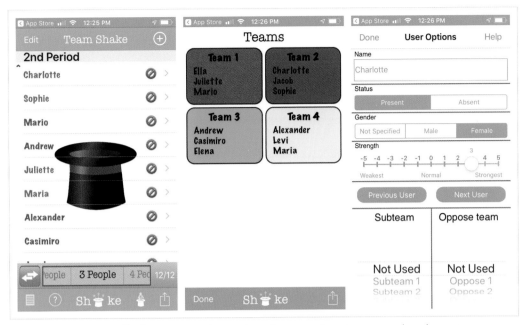

Figure 2.4   Team Shake app used to select four random teams and make notes on specific students.

Reprinted by permission from Team Shake app. Developed by Rhine-o Enterprises LLC.

Behavior Management

Managing student behavior is a crucial part of keeping order and maintaining a productive learning environment. Even a slight disruption from a student or athlete can throw off an entire lesson or session if not handled appropriately. Behavior management can range from creating a climate that promotes positive behavior and prevents problems to disciplining students who violate the rules. Basic behavior management techniques include modeling ideal behavior, establishing and displaying rules, instituting routines, reinforcing positive behavior, and consistently implementing established discipline procedures. For new teachers, behavior management is arguably one of the most difficult teaching skills to master, so they typically need all the help they can get! Happily, technology can help teachers and coaches with behavior management through a variety of web-based programs that allow them to track learners' behavior and communicate results to students, parents, and colleagues.

Individual Behavior Management

One of the most effective behavior management strategies is to promote and reinforce positive individual behavior. Several programs are available that allow teachers and coaches to track and reward students for positive behavior. For example, students who have individual plans for behavior issues may benefit from using the iRewardChart app (free, with optional in-app purchases) to help them with self-control and self-awareness. This app sets up a reward system keyed to performance and behavior and gives stars when the student exhibits good behavior or accomplishes certain tasks. For each child, categories can be customized based on desired actions and activities, such as cooperating with classmates or following directions. These categories can be established by an individual teacher, a group of teachers, an individualized education plan (IEP), or a behavioral intervention team. Stars can be earned or lost, and accumulating a specified number brings an appropriate reward determined by the teacher.

Group Behavior Management

Although apps such as iRewardChart are great for individual students, teachers and coaches also need to track and reinforce behavior with groups of students. One of the most popular and comprehensive programs for doing so is ClassDojo (figure 2.5). This web-based app offers not only behavior management but also other essential classroom management options, such as attendance taking, selection of groups or random individual students, classroom music, classroom noise monitoring, timer functionality, display of classroom directions, and digital portfolio creation.

In terms of behavior management, ClassDojo allows the teacher to create lists of "positive" and "needs work" skills that can be tracked for each student. Several options are already included in the program (e.g., on task, working hard, bullying, unprepared), and teachers can also create customized skill entries based on what they would like the student to achieve or minimize. Each skill is worth either one point (positive) or negative one point (needs work). Throughout a lesson, the teacher can easily open the class list, select a student, and mark the displayed behavior as either positive or needing work. The student's point total is updated, and a total score is displayed next to the student's name throughout the class. The teacher can also share the score with the student throughout class, either as a positive reinforcement strategy or as a warning to curb undesirable actions.

Although tracking is complete once the lesson is over, communication regarding student behavior has just begun. In this vein, ClassDojo allows the teacher to share results with other stakeholders (e.g., students, parents, other teachers), who can each create an account of their own. Students can log in to their account to see their own progress, and parents can log in to the child's account to view the point total throughout the day; you can also send reports directly to parents who have signed up. ClassDojo can be used by a single teacher or on a schoolwide basis. You can share your class with co-teachers and other teachers in the school, and they can award points, share updates, and review student progress.

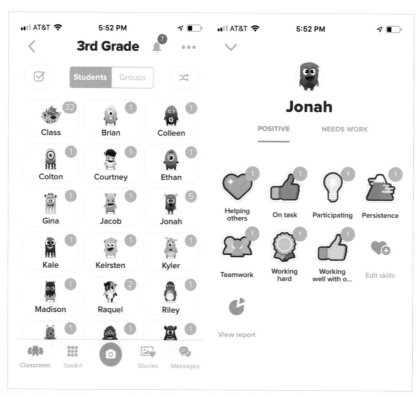

Figure 2.5 ClassDojo app: whole-class and individual student views.

Created by using ClassDojo communication platform.

BUDGET AND EQUIPMENT MANAGEMENT

Purchasing and tracking equipment and supplies are part of the job for teachers and coaches. If you are fortunate enough to have a budget allocated for new equipment or supplies for your classes or teams, then you will need to know how to manage it. This process can be facilitated by the use of basic technology, such as a spreadsheet tool (e.g., Microsoft Excel or Google Sheets) that allows you to create line-by-line accounts of items and their associated costs; these tools also allow for easy calculations to help you make the most of your budget.

Once you have purchased the necessary equipment and supplies, you'll need a way to keep track of it in an organized fashion. Documenting your inventory allows you to know what and how much equipment you have available and to keep track of it if you share it with others. Some programs even invite other members of the school or community at large to use equipment, in which case it is doubly important to create an easy yet effective system for keeping track of everything. Here again, a spreadsheet tool such as Excel can be used to list equipment by type, number, and condition. You can also make use of check-in and checkout features that include contact information for individuals using the equipment.

If your program checks out equipment to others on a regular basis, you might consider going beyond a spreadsheet and using an app geared toward equipment inventory and checkout. Many of the top inventory programs are cost prohibitive for a physical education or youth league professional, but a number of free and low-cost options are also available. AssetTiger, for example, is free if you have fewer than 250 assets (i.e., pieces of equipment). You can order bar codes to attach to the equipment or to an equipment list and then use the associated app to scan the codes when checking equipment in or out, thus updating the equipment's status in the system.

DOCUMENT MANAGEMENT

Historically, teachers and coaches have had piles upon piles of paperwork, including lesson or practice plans, instructional aids, student assignments, and more—all of which has typically been kept in desk drawers, binders on shelves, and filing cabinets. Nowadays, of course, the ease of digital document creation has greatly reduced the amount of paper and increased the number of electronic files! Thus it is important to organize these files into digital folders and be able to share them easily with others. The most basic way to do so is to create your documents by using word processing software (e.g., Microsoft Word, Microsoft Excel) and save them on a flash drive and a computer hard drive. It is extremely important to save files in more than one location, in case one of those locations is compromised (e.g., your dog ate the flash drive with the final exam!).

Alternatively, the emergence of web-based applications, such as Google Drive, has made it possible and relatively easy to create, edit, save, and share documents with others in a form that is accessible from anywhere with an Internet connection. Other options include OneDrive, Dropbox, and Box. When it comes to managing and sharing documents with students, an LMS offers a useful way to post important files and assignments, and students can submit their files to you and others through the assessments tool or through private messaging. Students can also share Google Docs files with one another in order to collaborate or provide access to the teacher for viewing.

TECHNOLOGY TIPS FROM THE FIELD

Using Technology to Help Students With Disabilities in Physical Education

Andrea Taliaferro, PhD, CAPE
Associate professor, College of Physical Activity and Sport Sciences
West Virginia University

What is your background and role at WVU?

I am an associate professor and teach adapted physical education/activity classes for preservice physical education teachers, coaches, and other preprofessionals. I also direct a physical education/activity program on-site for K-12 students with disabilities, where we often use technology for instruction, assessment, and management.

What types of technology do you use for class or behavior management with students with disabilities?

I use, and teach my students how to use, a variety of technologies for behavior management, communication, and instruction. One type of technology that I teach my preservice physical education teachers how to use involves apps on the iPad. There are a few behavior management apps that are useful for working with students with disabilities in physical education. I also use video recording for video modeling to assist with communication and instruction. Preservice students get experience learning about how to make picture schedules and reward systems with and without apps. Apps tend to be easier to manage since they are all in one place, where you can have multiple token economies and picture schedules on one device. There are various apps for token economies, such as My Token Board and iReward. Some apps, such as First then Visual Schedule allow the instructor to take pictures of the stations so that the participants can visualize what they will be doing at each station. To help with behavior management, timer apps are great. For example, the Time Timer app is useful for students to learn how to wait or understand how long they stay at one station/activity. The Calm Counter app helps students who get a little more stimulated, and the Wait Timer Visual Timer Tool app is useful to promote waiting for a turn.

What is your main objective for teaching about these tools for students with disabilities in physical education teacher education?

My main objective for teaching about these tools is to give my preservice teachers and professionals a variety of tools in their toolbox to meet the needs of students with various disabilities, because every person is different. The key is that there is not going to be a one-size-fits-all strategy, so the more I can teach them about various technologies that help to engage or motivate a student, the better prepared they will be to teach students.

What do you like about these behavior management tools?

I like that these tools can be tailored to each specific student fairly easily and quickly. They are practical for use by teachers because they are pretty easy and intuitive to learn how to use. They are also fairly inexpensive. You can use no- or low-tech options, but the apps are also very affordable. They are a great tool to learn to use with any student, whether they have a disability or not.

What are some challenges with using this technology for behavior management?

In our teaching setting, we sometimes don't have Wi-Fi, and that can be a struggle if the apps need it to work properly. Cost is always a factor, such as the tablets or iPads, and since the PE setting can sometimes be unpredictable, there is the risk of breaking or damaging a technology device. Another challenge is that these devices can sometimes be burdensome to carry around or keep track of during activity.

What suggestions would you offer physical and health education teachers and coaches who work with children with disabilities in terms of using technology for management?

I would suggest that they talk with the other teachers and service providers to see what other tech the student uses. It would be wise to replicate that same tech in the PE/health/coaching setting, since the student would already know how to use it and would be familiar with its use. I would also suggest that they collaborate with other individuals on the IEP team, such as parents, occupational therapists, physical therapists, and teachers, as they are good resources for other technologies.

DATA AND ASSESSMENT MANAGEMENT

Teachers and coaches generate and evaluate a variety of data on the individual and group levels. The data can be used for many purposes, such as informing practitioners and students about student achievement and the need for content progression, informing parents about their children's progress, and informing administrators about student achievement in a given content area. Coaches also use data continuously in order to determine game and player statistics that inform strategic decisions for upcoming contests.

In educational settings, an LMS (e.g., Moodle) can be used to host student data in the form of a course gradebook, where students are able to view their grades for individual assignments and for the course as a whole. Educators without access to an LMS can use spreadsheet software (e.g., Microsoft Excel) to record and calculate student grades, which can then be shared with students by other means. In addition, several mobile gradebook apps are available for teachers, some of which are embedded into other programs mentioned elsewhere in this chapter. GradeBook Pro, for example, can be used not only to record scores but also to track attendance and student performance. It allows for weighted and standard point-based scales, customized grading scales, categorized assignments, extra credit awards and penalty points, student averages, highest grades, total grade scores, and categorization of classes by overall and category-specific grades. It can also export grade reports and create summary reports for the class or for an individual.

One word of caution about student data: Privacy is of the utmost importance. The **Family Educational Rights and Privacy Act (FERPA)** protects student data by prohibiting it from being shared publicly (U.S. Department of Education, 1974). You run the risk of exposing student data if you use any app that is not supported by your school or organization for the purpose of hosting student data, especially if it is a web-based application. Check the privacy policy for any application, and gain permission from your administrators before using any outside app for student data. In addition, if you use any program outside of the organization's supplied options, minimize the amount of student information you store there; for instance, use students' first names only.

Conclusion

This chapter discusses how a variety of technological resources and tools can enhance management for physical educators, health educators, and coaches. Management constitutes an essential component of any educational or athletic program—including management of your class or team; of individual students or athletes and their behavior; and of space, tasks, time, and documents. Practitioners can facilitate this work by making effective use of appropriate technology.

Key Terms

athlete management system (AMS)— Software for organizing and storing athlete and team information.

Bluetooth—Method for achieving short-range wireless interconnection of electronic devices.

Family Educational Rights and Privacy Act (FERPA)—Federal law that protects the privacy of student education records and applies to all schools that receive funds through an applicable program of the U.S. Department of Education.

learning management system (LMS)— Web-based software (also referred to as a *course management system*) that helps instructors administer courses, deliver learning content, document and track student progress, and facilitate online course interactions with and among students (e.g., Blackboard Learn, D2L, Moodle, Canvas).

management—In education, process and techniques used to keep teaching and learning organized and to keep everyone on task and productive.

quick response (QR) code—A two-dimensional square bar code that can store encoded data and link to websites, text, or other data by scanning with a QR reader or mobile device camera links, text, or other data.

Review Questions

1. What are the advantages of using technology for management?
2. List three types of technology that can be used for management in physical education, health education, or coaching.
3. Describe some ways in which practitioners (teachers or coaches) might use technology to help manage their programs.
4. How might you use technology to manage behavior in a classroom?

Discussion Questions

1. Describe a common management issue that you might face as a teacher or coach, then describe how would you incorporate technology to help you address this issue.
2. How have you managed attendance (or rosters), grades, or other data in the past? How might you incorporate technology to facilitate these management tasks?
3. Design a typical lesson for health or physical education—or design a sport practice—and note where technology could help you with transitions, behavior management, and management of students and space.

Communication Technology

Chapter Objectives

When you have completed this chapter, you will be able to do the following:

1. Differentiate between a variety of technological tools for communication.
2. Describe several ways to share digital files with students and athletes.
3. Identify ways to communicate with students through various forms of video technology.
4. Identify barriers to and benefits of using technology to enhance communication.

Hero Images/Getty Images

Professionals in physical education, health education, and coaching tend to work with a variety of individuals on a daily basis. Although face-to-face communication is important for community building, it is not always the most practical way to meet your students, families, co-workers, and other community members. Fortunately, distance does not need to stifle the communication that is essential to teaching and learning; to the contrary, effective communication can often be facilitated through a variety of technology-based platforms.

OVERVIEW OF COMMUNICATION TECHNOLOGY

In education, the practitioner plays an active role in helping learners acquire information and experience activities that enhance learning (Moțățăianu, 2018). The process of teaching and learning is complex and involves helping learners gain access to information, process it, and demonstrate understanding of it. The process also involves assessing and correcting their knowledge and understanding as needed through feedback. Using **technology-mediated communication** in teaching and coaching allows students and athletes to engage in their learning through a variety of unique platforms by engaging in discussion forums, sending electronic mail, posting comments on social media, and collaborating to create cloud-based documents. These types of technology allow for learning that involves multiple members of the community, such as peers, teachers, parents, guardians, and experts in the field (Moțățăianu, 2018). Effective **communication** with purposefully selected tools helps practitioners engage students, athletes, and families in experiences that optimize learning; in particular, communication technology allows learning to extend beyond the traditional school setting by encouraging all members of the learning community to participate in the process. Technology can also streamline your communication, which in turn can help your learners experience academic and athletic success.

Outside of the school setting, access to communication technology is growing throughout the United States. As many as 90 percent of student homes are now connected to the Internet (Porterfield & Carnes, 2014), and increased access to mobile phone technology enables students to connect more readily with both you and their peers beyond the confines of the typical schedule for school or athletics. Technology-mediated communication can also break language barriers by providing families with translations in the language they use at home; examples include Facebook Messenger and GroupMe, both of which use the Google Translate tool. In addition, although traditional forms of communication on paper can still be effective, technology-mediated communication offers families instant information and feedback. In fact, instant communication is becoming more and more the norm in our increasingly technology-focused society (Porterfield & Carnes, 2014).

Along with its many benefits, communication technology can also involve some barriers; for example, communication via text message or email can lack the emotion immediacy of face-to-face interaction (Moțățăianu, 2018). Even so, you should focus your time on considering the benefits for you and your learners. For instance, your role as a future practitioner empowers you to build trusting and open relationships with families and youth. As part of this process, setting an open and sound communication policy, or method for providing youth and families with immediate feedback, will help you earn the respect you need from all members of the community you serve (see the sidebar titled Benefits and Barriers in Using Communication Technology). Establishing a solid platform for communication technology will benefit your learners and their families. Keep in mind that these tools should be used purposefully for one or more specific objectives and should be handled with fidelity (i.e., sticking to one or two tools rather than engaging in an overwhelming number).

Generally speaking, if you use technology-mediated communication in your program, then you are responsible for implementing the six steps for success detailed in table 3.1.

Table 3.1   Six Tips for Successful Implementation of Technology

Practitioner responsibilities	Dos	Don'ts
1. Follow the district's **acceptable use policy (AUP).**	Research the school's AUP. Typically, schools and districts adopt policies that outline how the Internet and media should be used by students and staff.	Don't use technology without express permission. You could face legal action if you violate district rules for technology use or acceptable communication.
2. Teach your learners and their families how to obtain and use the technology.	Find or create a tutorial video to walk all users through the technology you expect them to use. Spend time in a class setting or an in-service to walk all users through the process of obtaining the needed software or service.	Don't tell students and parents to download or obtain a technological tool without detailed instructions for doing so. Users bring various levels of comfort with technology, which can lead to marginalization.
3. Check in with all users and help as needed with troubleshooting.	Send out a sample assignment, text, or reminder to check that everyone has properly set up the required tool. Immediately troubleshoot any errors you find. Allow time for everyone to adjust to the technology. Be available to help with minor troubleshooting.	Don't assume that all users understand the tool immediately and that there will be no hiccups in using it.
4. Provide resources for additional troubleshooting.	Provide all of your users with a web link, phone number, or other resource to help troubleshoot errors that you are not equipped to address. Support your users as much as you can, then provide additional resources for complex issues.	Don't require your users to "figure it out" if there is an error that you cannot fix.
5. Offer solutions for families who may not have access to the technology.	Provide alternative assignments or tools for learners who do not have access to the preferred technology. If a student does not have access to a computer at home, allow time for going to a computer lab. Seek out technology resources at school; students can often check out resources for a semester if needed. Send home a list of important dates for families with limited access to technology (or who simply prefer a paper copy). Work with families to support learning however you can; do not leave families disadvantaged or marginalized.	Don't assume that everyone will have access to preferred resources or demand that everyone purchase tools regardless of cost.
6. Follow through by making purposeful use of the technology.	If you require learners to obtain a communication tool and teach them how to install and use it, then follow through and put it to good use! Be respectful of families who put in the time and energy to understand it. Asking learners to download an app and then never using it is a waste of time and resources. Find a good balance by using the tool only when necessary—but do be sure to use it. Also, do your best to use a minimal number of tools. For instance, asking users to obtain multiple apps that have similar features can be confusing and frustrating, not purposeful or thoughtful.	Don't require everyone to obtain a communication tool and then not use it, thus wasting time and money.

BENEFITS AND BARRIERS IN USING COMMUNICATION TECHNOLOGY

POSSIBLE BENEFITS

- *Accountability.* Communication technology increases learners' accountability. If learners are reminded of important activities outside of class or practice time, then they may remember to take time to continue learning outside of the traditional environment. The lives of your students and athletes are dynamic and complex, and this technology may be part of what they need in order to succeed.
- *Advocacy.* Communication with family members can increase advocacy for your program. Strike a good balance by providing pertinent information without giving too much.
- *Trust.* Two-way communication that is open and honest can build trust between you, your learners, and their families.
- *Understanding.* Learners and families are more likely to share information if they feel listened to and understood by you and their peers.
- *Help with difficult conversations.* You will sometimes need to have difficult conversations with learners and families. These situations are easier to manage if you have already established an open line of communication by communicating about easier topics.
- *Increased comfort for families.* Many families do not know the best way to approach a teacher or coach, and communicating electronically may ease their concern and allow them to reach out.
- *Bridging of language differences.* Many communication tools allow you to communicate in the preferred language of the learner's family; thus access to communication technology can break language barriers.
- *Removal of physical barriers.* Communication technology enables students and athletes to learn throughout the day and enables information exchange beyond the confines of the classroom or a coaching session.

POSSIBLE BARRIERS

- *Access.* In order for communication technology to work, students, families, and practitioners must all be able to access it, whether by means of a laptop, tabletop, or mobile device. However, not all families have access to devices or to the Internet.
- *Attitude.* Barriers can be presented by either teacher or student attitudes toward new technology. Typically, practitioners need to address five concerns before adopting a new technology (Rogers, 1995): Does it provide an advantage? Is it compatible with existing practices? Is it easy to understand? Does the use of technology meet objectives? Can it be experimented with before full adoption?
- *Cost.* The cost of equipment, Internet access, and applications may present a barrier for you, your school, or your learners and their families. Therefore, it is essential to research the costs before asking families to commit.
- *Choices.* With so many communication tools available, you may not know where to begin. The best first step is to see what tools are used by your colleagues. Being consistent within a school or program prevents learners and families from having to learn multiple platforms. Also, check with your legal team to ensure that you are allowed to use the technology you are thinking of adopting.
- *Culture.* Any technological tool must fit with the culture of the community or society in which it is being adopted (Rogers, 1995).

- *Competence.* Like confidence, competence is diminished when a teacher or learner lacks applicable knowledge or experience with similar technologies (Pelton & Pelton, 1996).
- *Language.* Tools must be selected that allow for communication in the learner's preferred language. Communication is ineffective if some parties do not fully understand the information.
- *Privacy.* Technology should keep personal information secure and meet district requirements for safe use of technology. Personal information should be stored properly, and **encryption** may be required by the school district before adopting the technology.
- *School support.* If the school does not allow for adequate professional development, or does not support your choice to use communication technology, it will be difficult to implement.
- *Time.* It can be a time-consuming process to research tools, sign up for services, and learn how to use them. Implementation should not be rushed, and it can be challenging to find the necessary time to learn and use the technology.

Communication technology in this chapter is divided into the following categories:

- Electronic mail
- Text messaging
- Social media
- Cloud-based file sharing
- Scheduling tools
- Reminder tools
- Video calls and videoconferences

ELECTRONIC MAIL

Email is one of the most basic forms of electronic communication. In order to use it, of course, one must have access to a digital device (e.g., smartphone, tablet, computer) and an Internet connection. Email can be a great tool for answering questions, submitting assignments, sending reminders, "hooking" students into a new topic, providing supplementary materials, and communicating with families (Filippone & Survinski, 2016). Email communication with students is fairly straightforward if you teach in middle school or high school, because your students' school email addresses are likely stored securely for you in the school's **learning management system (LMS)**. An LMS platform typically gives you the option to send email to either a single student or a group of students; for instance, you might create one email group for students whose fitness goal is to improve cardiorespiratory endurance and another email group for students whose goal is to increase flexibility. If you are a coach, you may or may not have access to the school's LMS. If not, you may need to gather email addresses for your athletes and create your own email groups, or you can also use your athlete management system (AMS) if your school uses one.

If you teach in an elementary school setting, it is less likely that your students will have an email address; in this case, you will communicate primarily with parents or guardians. In fact, many children under the age of 13 do not have an email address at all, and it wasn't until 2017 that Google began allowing children under 13 to enroll for an email account (Magid, 2017). Moreover, because of the **Children's Online Privacy Protection Act (COPPA)**, parental **consent** is needed in order for a child under age 13 to use a site or online service that can collect personal information. Some email accounts are available for younger learners, but they carry an expense for parents. For instance, Google Family Link offers parent-monitored email addresses for children under the age of 13, but it requires a one-time 30-cent verification fee to ensure that an adult (over the age of 18) has approved the account (Magid, 2017). If you wish to communicate with students under the age of 13, a good solution would be to send communication to a parent or guardian who can pass the message along to the student.

Helping Others Set Up an Email Account

As mentioned earlier, an LMS typically allows you to access students' school email addresses. Some students may prefer that you send emails to their personal addresses, but if you are sending school-related emails, you should use the addresses provided by the school. Similarly, as a professional, you should use your work email for all school-related communication for several reasons:

1. So the email doesn't go into the recipient's junk folder
2. So the recipient can easily see who the email is coming from, since most school email addresses include the sender and institution name
3. For transparency, so that if there is ever an inquiry from the administration, they see you were professional and only communicated through your work email

If some of student families do not have an email account, you might offer a tutorial on setting up a free account with Google, Outlook, or another service provider. If you plan to share files via Google (which offers numerous tools for educators), it may be helpful to suggest getting a Gmail account because it can also be used to log in to Google Drive (which is discussed in more detail later in this chapter). One way to collect contact information from families is to ask for it at a school information night held before the beginning of the school year or season; this type of event can also provide a great opportunity to help families establish an email address on a school computer. Many schools help families find the nearest library that offers free access to a computer, and some even allow parents to use the computer lab on campus throughout the day. Be aware of your families' level of access to technology and help them set up proper communication channels if you wish to use this technology during the school year.

Email Etiquette

Communication through email can become formal fairly quickly. On the other hand, since it does not occur face-to-face, it is sometimes treated with the same informal protocols as an average text message. Therefore, when communicating through email, you must take care to do so with proper levels of etiquette. Poor email etiquette can result in miscommunication and even strained relationships between you and your students or athletes (Filippone & Survinski, 2016). Many learners and families prefer to communicate with you through email because it alleviates some of the stress that can occur when talking about difficult questions face-to-face. On the other hand, email also allows students to use an informal or blunt tone that they might not display in a face-to-face interaction (Hartman & McCambridge, 2011).

Therefore, you should clearly state your expectations for communicating through email at the beginning of the year or athletic season, and you should revisit the policy several times to ensure compliance. It is also acceptable to address expectations with one or two students on an individual basis if necessary.

When creating an etiquette policy, start by looking into policies that have already been adopted by your district or program. If there is no formal policy, consider using the following suggestions to create your own (adapted from Filippone & Survinski, 2016):

- *Formal email address.* Always send school-related email from a school-provided email address, not a personal address. If you do not have an email address associated with the school where you work, ask the administration to assign one to you, or ask the principal or athletic director about the email policy.
- *Subject line.* Include a meaningful and concise subject line; do not leave this space blank. Adding a subject line gives the recipient a point of reference for the email.
- *Formal address.* Address the recipient formally—for instance, Mrs. Armstrong or Coach Miller. After the first reply, it is no longer necessary to use the person's name when you reply. When addressing a group, you do not need to include all names (Ex. Mrs. Armstrong, Coach Miller etc. Instead, you can simply say, "Greetings Team," or "Hello All,").
- *Tone.* Be straightforward in your tone. Because tone is difficult to infer on email, do not engage in sarcasm or confrontational language. Do ask clarifying questions.
- *Content.* Do not use email to debate grades or ask questions that require lengthy, complex answers. Tone is often lost in an email, so it is best to ask clarifying questions and then set up a time to talk on the phone, meet face-to-face, or meet via **teleconference**.
- *Response time.* Set up a policy for response time—for instance, a 48-hour window for responding to emails. You do not need to be available 24-7 for your students, and it is reasonable for you *not* to respond in the evening. Select a reasonable response window and communicate it clearly.
- *Self-monitoring.* Practice self-control in your emails. Do not say things you wouldn't say in a face-to-face conversation. Although email conversations may seem informal, they serve as a written record of conversation and can be referenced in the future.
- *Grammar correction.* Avoid the urge to write an email in the same way you would write a text message. For instance, avoid slang, casual abbreviations (e.g., IDK, CU later), and emoticons. Writing in a clear, professional manner conveys respect for the recipient.
- *Editing.* Check your spelling, grammar, and sentence structure. After drafting an email, reread it before hitting Send. In fact, it is also helpful to wait several minutes before sending the message in order to ensure that you've covered everything you need to address. You can always save an email draft to send at a later time; therefore, you can always continue to edit after taking some time to think about the issue or situation.

File-Sharing Restrictions for Email

Sharing files through email is often quick and effective. For example, you can easily send your health education class an article to complement a lesson, send your team a playbook, or send your physical education class a video of a dance routine. Be aware that most email platforms limit the size of an attached file; as of this writing, for instance, Gmail limits email attachments to 25 megabytes. This type of limit will sometimes stop you from attaching multiple files to a document or from attaching photos or videos. One solution to this obstacle is to use a cloud-based file-sharing platform (discussed later in this chapter) and send recipients a link to a file. In this approach, instead of attaching large files to an email message, you upload the content to the sharing platform (e.g., Google Drive, Dropbox), then enable recipients to access it from the cloud. If you send a lot of videos, you can even upload your videos to YouTube and use email to send video links to your intended recipients. These platforms allow you to restrict access to certain people, thus retaining your desired level of privacy for the material.

TEXT MESSAGING

Text messaging is a preferred method of communication for many people. Given that more than 70 percent of U.S. teens now own a smartphone (Anderson, 2015), and more than 95 percent of U.S. households now own a cell phone (Pew Research Center, 2018), texting is a convenient way for teachers to communicate with many students, athletes, and families. Text messaging is the number one way in which teens prefer to stay in contact with their friends; more specifically, 58 percent of smartphone users state that texting is the main way in which they communicate with their friends, and the second most popular means is through social media (Anderson, 2015). Text messaging can be seen as a cost-effective way to communicate—one needs only a smartphone and a data plan. In fact, as more businesses offer free Wi-Fi, learners can often access messages without using their data plan.

Notwithstanding the convenience and cost-effectiveness of text messaging, you have quite a bit to consider before opening up this line of communication through your personal device. For instance, many learners under the age of 13 do not own a cell phone; therefore, if you work with kids under that age, then you will most likely be communicating with family members rather than the learners themselves. Do you want to give out your personal number to families, thus enabling them to contact you at all hours? Generally, it is better to consider using a messaging app that keeps your information confidential. For example, you can send messages from Remind or TeamSnap without sharing your personal phone number. This decision may come down to a personal choice, or it may be dictated by district policy. To ensure that you take a good approach, contact your administration and read your school's policies about using a personal phone number to communicate with learners and families.

Regardless of whether you decide to use your personal phone number or a messaging app, you have plenty to think about before sending messages to students and families. Here are some tips to consider (adapted from Reich, 2015):

- *Be mindful of legal limitations.* You must be aware of school policies regarding the use of text messaging, and the limits to which you can message students and parents.

- *Find a texting platform.* Many platforms are available for text messaging (e.g., WhatsApp, GroupMe, TeamSnap). A texting app offers the benefit that you do not need to use your personal phone number, and all messaging apps offer a variety of features. Some help you translate conversations into multiple languages. Others allow one-way texting, where you can send a text but the families cannot respond. Some platforms allow families to enroll quickly by downloading an app and typing in a unique code, whereas others require you to manually enter phone numbers. Do some research to find one that meets your needs.

- *Be consistent.* If your school or department has a preferred texting platform, be consistent with your colleagues and use it. It is quite a hassle for parents and students to download and learn multiple platforms. Be flexible and willing to learn what others are using.

- *Include actionable and immediate updates for parents:*
  - *Actionable.* Ensure that parents have something to do with the information (it is easy to ignore information if it doesn't seem purposeful). For example, you might text the following: Please pack running shoes for tomorrow's fitness testing.
  - *Immediate.* Text messages can easily be forgotten, so it is best to text about something immediate—not information for the future. For example, you might text the following: Please have your student talk with you about their week-long study plan for the midterm on Friday. What is their nightly plan, starting tonight?

- *Introduce yourself.* Briefly include your name at the beginning or the end of the message so that students and families know for sure who it came from. Identifying yourself also stops people from thinking that the message is **spam** and therefore blocking your number.

- *Personalize your messages.* If your platform allows it, you can personalize your messages by inserting the student's name and preferred gender pronouns rather than using the generic "your student." This feature allows for more of a connection with the family and the student and can elicit a positive emotional response that may increase the likelihood of bringing about the desired action.

- *Don't send too many messages.* Keep messages purposeful and infrequent. Sending too many messages reduces their effect. Some apps have a feature for scheduling delivery of messages so that you can even be consistent about the day and time when messages go out.

- *Keep messages brief.* As a general rule, keep messages under 160 characters; not all phone carriers allow messages that go over this limit.

- *Try to text in the family's preferred language.* Some apps have a built-in translation service; for example, WhatsApp and Facebook Messenger do so via Google Translate. Many school systems also offer free translation services in the district office—you can email a message to the office and get it back in the preferred language. This step is extremely important in order to avoid marginalizing any of your students or athletes.

- *Formulate a plan for reading responses.* After you send a message, you may receive messages back within an hour or two, depending on your platform. Make a plan to address the responses in a timely fashion.

Although you have plenty to consider before sending messages to students and families, remember the benefits of sending this type of message. Mobile phones are easily accessible to most of your students and families. With the notifications feature turned on in the phone settings, members of your learning community will have instant access to the information you share. Note that you should not send messages to students during school hours; indeed, many schools have a policy against phone use during school time.

SOCIAL MEDIA

It is hard to ignore the effect that social media have exerted as tools for communication technology. Facebook, Twitter, Instagram, and blogs have overloaded consumers with information at overwhelming speeds. In fact, it is highly likely that while you are reading this chapter, you are also interacting with others via a digital device. Social media are also highly effective at rapidly distributing information to learners and families, especially since many of them already use social media and are therefore familiar with the applications. In addition, if notifications are enabled in their phone settings, then they will receive immediate access to the information you send. Social media can be used to share schedule changes, remind students of important dates, create polls, upload videos and documents, initiate group discussions, set up fundraisers, and share articles that complement material covered in class or practice.

Remember your intended audience. If you are working with children under the age of 13, COPPA requires parent permission before they can sign up for a platform that allows them to share personal information, as is required by many social media platforms. It is also critical that you establish policies for proper use and lay out consequences for misuse. Social media have the power to spread either useful information or misinformation. Take time to understand your district policies for social media use and clearly establish your expectations for using these tools. Some districts allow you to freely post photos of students whose parents or guardians have signed a waiver, as long as they tag the school with the appropriate hashtag or symbol. Other districts prohibit the sharing of student images regardless of family consent. Before initiating communication through social media, answer the following questions (adapted from Porterfield & Carnes, 2014):

- What social media tool are you using? Why?
- What are your school or district policies?
- How will you adjust the privacy settings?
- What will be your social media policy for the account?
- Who will manage and monitor the account?
- Who will have permission to post on the account? What sorts of files will be allowed?
- How will you let your community know that you have an account?

CLOUD-BASED FILE SHARING

Traditionally, teachers have shared files with students through the learning management software (LMS; see chapter 8 for more) that is specific to their institution—for example, Blackboard, Google Classroom, or Moodle. Typical shared materials include videos, lecture slides, worksheets, quizzes, and assignments (Sadik, 2017). Goals for using an LMS typically include the following (Meishar-Tal et al., 2012):

1. Providing students with learning materials
2. Facilitating interactive learning activities
3. Managing the course and the learners, including communication access

LMS platforms enable students to communicate via discussion board features, emails, announcements, and even **videoconferences**. For instance, Google Classroom includes a feature called Hangouts Meet that allows the practitioner to facilitate video calls or video-conferences outside of school time. This feature is extremely helpful when, for instance, a student takes an extended absence or an injured athlete wants to interact with teammates while they are away at an event.

Although an LMS is a great avenue for facilitating course content, many practitioners now prefer the benefits of **cloud-based file sharing** services, such as Google Drive, OneDrive, and Dropbox (figure 3.1). Cloud-based file sharing also tends to be preferred by students because it allows them to communicate with teachers about documents in real time (Miller, 2008). Most cloud-based systems are fairly similar in that they allow you to share multiple types of files, work on documents collaboratively and remotely, and communicate in real time with others who have access to your work. Google Drive, in particular, has been highly integrated into classrooms and currently hosts more than two trillion stored files (Price, 2017). It has more than 800 million monthly active users and more than a billion accounts in the system (Price, 2017). Of that total, 30 million belong to teachers and students around the world (Gorton, 2013).

Imagine that all of your students are huddled around a computer, and only one person is typing. This scenario is now obsolete thanks to platforms such as Google Drive, which allows users to compose and edit documents on any of their devices and show changes and feedback to everyone immediately (Sadik, 2017). Students can work on a variety of materials—including

Figure 3.1 Screenshot of a Google Drive home page with course content.

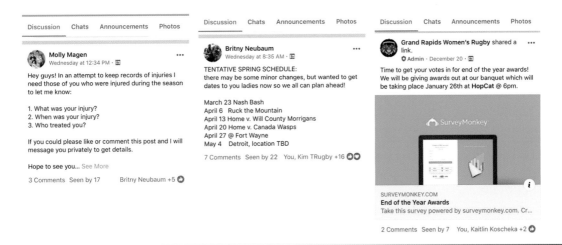

The Band app allows teams to communicate for a variety of purposes.

Reprinted by permission from Grand Rapids Women's Rugby.

verbal documents, spreadsheets, photos, and presentations—without having to purchase applications and install them on their computer (Sadik, 2017). The files are encrypted with the same security protocols used for Gmail and other Google services. In addition, documents can be shared with you instantly for feedback in real time. Whoever creates a document can give a certain level of access to all of the contributors or anyone else. For instance, you can create documents that are view-only, so that students can view the files but not comment on or edit them. You can also create documents that are available for viewing and commenting or for editing (figure 3.2).

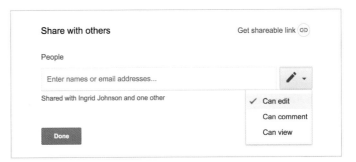

Figure 3.2   Screenshot of Google Drive sharing settings.

Because individuals can log in to Google Drive from any device, they do not need to carry paper copies, flash drives, or any other materials that might get misplaced. This convenience also eliminates the problems that arise if a hard drive gets full or a computer crashes.

In terms of communication, cloud-based file sharing offers different benefits depending on the content you teach or the files you wish to share as a coach. For instance, you might assign projects for students to complete or share your game schedule, event sign-up sheets, or goal-setting worksheets. Before using any of these platforms, obtain approval from your district's administration or technology support group. Some schools require teachers to use the schoolwide LMS, whereas others give teachers the option to use whatever tool best meets their students' needs.

Digital File Sharing for Health and Physical Educators

Digital file sharing can be used to complement course content in health and physical education. For instance, you might choose to assign group work to be completed during class or as homework. Such assignments can be worked on by all members simultaneously, with or without sharing a single device, and students can invite you to access their document.

All changes are saved immediately, so they are not lost even if a device loses power or an application closes suddenly.

By gaining access to students' files, you can see instantly who is contributing, when edits are being made, and whether students are understanding the assignment. You can gain access by simply asking students to type in your email and add you to the list; alternatively, your students can share a link that you can click to be directed to their work. On student assignments, you can give explicit directions about how you would like them to give you access to the file (figure 3.3). Allow students time to work independently while you circulate through the groups before joining in their shared document and providing feedback.

You have many options for collaborative projects that students can do. For example, SHAPE America's national standard 3 for K-12 physical education relates to understanding fitness concepts and encompasses quite a bit of cognitive knowledge based on grade level. In this vein, you could ask students to collaboratively develop fitness plans based on their goals from fitness testing or to create a project demonstrating skill-related knowledge versus health-related fitness knowledge. Or, in a health education class, students could upload photos of labels from their favorite foods at home, then complete a collaborative assignment based on MyPlate guidelines.

Digital File Sharing for Coaches

Coaches typically do not use a school's LMS. Some schools do structure their athletics as a course on the LMS so that coaches can work with the same platform, but most allow athletics to operate independent of the LMS. If that is your situation, then you could benefit from using cloud-based file sharing programs, such as OneDrive, Google Drive, and Dropbox. Cloud-based sharing benefits your program by giving athletes and families one location for accessing team materials. For instance, you can create a folder for the schedule, social events, fundraisers, and important forms (e.g., parent and athlete codes of conduct). You can also grant players access to the playbook and to discussion forums and goal-setting sheets specific to those users.

Cloud-based sharing also allows coaches to upload game footage and photos on a secure platform and share these files with players and families. These files are often too large to send via email or social media, so storing them securely in a convenient location helps all parties who need the information. You can limit access to certain people—for instance, the varsity squad but not the junior varsity squad—and set the security features so that users cannot share footage or files outside of the group. When sharing video and photo files, be sure that you have obtained waiver forms and are not in violation of the **Family Educational Rights and Privacy Act (FERPA)** before posting any materials on your platform. The waiver forms can also be made available in a folder on the platform.

SCHEDULING TOOLS

You may believe that your primary job as an educator is to teach or coach students, but in reality that is just the beginning. Your responsibilities also include planning and coordinating activities with learners, families, other staff, and the larger community (Näf, 2011). Scheduling meetings with individual learners, parents, and groups can seem like a daunting task, due in part to the challenge of finding a meeting time that works for everyone. In the past, scheduling such a meeting might have been handled by sending home slips of paper and asking students or families to select times that work. More recently, communication technology such as email and text messaging might have been used, but they still require you to track all of the availabilities in spreadsheet form. Fortunately, dedicated scheduling tools are now available to streamline the scheduling process, thus enabling you to devote more time to instructing youth.

Figure 3.3 PE metrics assessment project.

RATIONALE

According to SHAPE America's 2017 National Standards for Initial Physical Education Teacher Education (PETE), PETE students should be able to do the following:

4.e Analyze motor skills and performance concepts in order to provide specific, congruent feedback to enhance student learning.

5.a Select or create authentic, formal assessments that measure student attainment of short- and long-term objectives.

5.b Implement formative assessments that monitor student learning before and throughout the long-term plan, as well as summative assessments that evaluate student learning upon completion of the long-term plan.

DESCRIPTION

- You and a small group will be provided with a secondary assessment to administer from the PE Metrics manual. This assessment should be completed in a Google Docs file with your classmates, and you should allow your professor access to the document by making them able to edit the document. **Include MY email**.
- In class, determine who will complete the Plan, Performance, Discussion, and Hints sections; include this plan in the Google Docs file.
- I will provide feedback three days before the due date; address any feedback before submitting your assignment.
- Please address the following information in your Google Docs file:

Plan

- Describe what students and parents need to know before the test is administered.
- Describe the equipment needed for a class of 40 participants.
- Read and summarize the directions for performing the assessment.
- Create a map of the gymnasium setup that you would use for 40 participants.

Performance of the Assessment

- Assess classmates during class time.
- Make a video recording if necessary.
- Calculate the assessment score.
- Create an assessment report. (Give to student and parent—look up examples).

Discussion of the Assessment Tool

- Critique the tool's ease of interpretation and administration.
- Provide ideas and examples for using the tool in a real class. Please give concrete details.

Hints for Physical Educators

- Provide ideas for using the tool effectively with 40 students.
- What would you have done differently during class to make the assessment more successful?

Scheduling tools can also be used to handle volunteer sign-ups, gather important information from athletes who are signing up for a team, and collect other needed information that you would like to keep in a spreadsheet or calendar. One commonly used scheduling tool is Doodle, which allows you to create a poll for an event and sync the poll with addresses on your device (figure 3.4). When setting up a poll, you can vary the duration of the planned meeting and modify various poll settings. Doodle is free in its basic form, and a premium version is available with additional features. After creating a poll about availability for certain dates and times, you will be prompted to select poll settings. The four poll settings in the free version of Doodle are as follows:

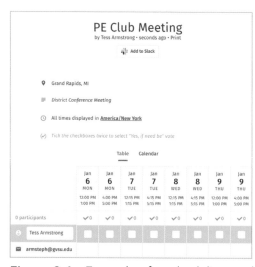

Figure 3.4   Example of a scheduling tool that can be used to facilitate meetings and other events and to collect information for storage in a spreadsheet.

- *Yes, no, if need be.* Participants can let you know if they absolutely can or cannot make a scheduled time.
- *Limited number of votes per option.* Once a time slot is taken, no one else can select it.
- *Single-vote limitation.* Participants must pick their top time, not multiple times.
- *Hidden poll.* Names, votes, and comments are confidential; they go only to you as the coordinator.

After participants select a date and time for which they are available, they are given the option to sync the appointment with their Google or Microsoft calendar, which will help remind them of the appointment they selected. If your goal is to find one time for everyone to meet, you can send a group email at the end of the process, letting everyone know the results of the poll. The benefit of using scheduling tools is that you no longer need to keep track of emails, messages, or pieces of paper in order to organize a meeting. In addition, participants can easily go back into the poll and change their responses, so they will not need to reach out to contact you. Table 3.2 presents a selection of scheduling tools, along with their benefits.

REMINDER TOOLS

Given their dynamic lives, your students and families often need to be reminded of important deadlines and schedule changes. It is certainly possible to do so via email or text, but streamlined apps make the process even easier. You can set reminders to go off on a regular basis and create short, effective instant messages if plans change. Reminding people of important events and changes through their phones is perhaps the best way to ensure that this important information gets to your students, athletes, and families in a timely manner.

One of the most highly recommended options for sending out reminders is the Remind app, which is fairly straightforward to use. The easiest way to set up a Remind account is simply to request that families download the app and provide them with a code to join your group. Your school might establish a Remind number for sending out schoolwide messages, and you might set up a unique code for each class you teach. If you use the app with students under the age of 13, their parents or guardians must give the child permission, and the family's contact information will be collected—not the student's (Smith, n.d.). Additional restrictions for children under 13 include a prohibition on participating in two-way conversations or responding to announcements.

Table 3.2   Examples of Digital Scheduling Tools

Tool	Cost	Website	Features
Doodle	Free with optional upgrades	www.doodle.com	• Customize dates and times for which you are available. • Limit responses using the built-in settings. • Sync with your contact list and calendar. • Use with iOS or Android. • Send invitations through email.
SignUp Genius	Free with optional upgrades	www.signupgenius.com	• Create sign-up sheets for event volunteers and supplies. • Customize templates. • Customize dates and times for which you are available. • Send invitations through email. • Use with iOS or Android. • Send email and text reminders.
Calendly	Free with optional upgrades	www.calendly.com	• Integrate with your preferred online calendar to create appointment slots. • Easily set up one-on-one and group meetings. • Send reminder notifications.
SignUp	Free with optional upgrades	www.signup.com	• Coordinate one-on-one meetings and group events. • Keep track of volunteer lists. • Access from any web browser.
Google Forms	Free	www.google.com/forms	• Use for scheduling. • Create questionnaires for parents and students and store responses in a spreadsheet. • Easily send one link to all participants. • Keep the form in your Google Drive so that participants can access it easily. • Use as an easy way for people to sign up for teams and groups. • Collect and store key information such as phone numbers, email addresses, and emergency contact information.

Here are some examples of messages that could be sent home via the Remind tool:

Elementary Physical Education

• Today in physical education your child learned the difference between a hop and a jump. Ask them to teach you the difference at home! — Mr. Stockton

• Tomorrow in physical education we will work on a tumbling unit. Be sure to pack shorts or tights for under skirts. — Ms. Nuñez

Middle School Health Education

• Today in class we talked about reading food labels. Remember, I would like you to find a food that you commonly eat and take a picture of the food label. Add the picture to our class Google Drive, and we will look at some examples in class. — Ms. Olsen

• Final projects in the Strategies for Coping With Stress unit are due on Friday. Please sit with your child and discuss their plan for finishing over the next few days. — Mr. Zeb

High School Athletics

- Parents, please note that the bus schedule has changed, and the JV team will return to school at 4:30 p.m. instead of 3:45 p.m. — Mr. Race
- The state track meet is two days away! Remind your outstanding athlete to continue to hydrate and meet the recommended 10 p.m. sleep curfew. — Ms. Johnson

Tools such as Remind can be used for either two-way or one-way communication. Therefore, if you like, you can allow people to respond to your message so that you can offer additional support or answer any questions. If you do so, make time during the following two hours to reply to any responses.

Be aware that reminders about what happened in class may seem redundant to some students and helpful to others. Be clear about your purpose in using the tool. Also, if you ask your learners and families to invest time in learning how to use a reminder tool, follow through and use it! If at some point you decide not to continue using it, inform your families that they can delete it or unenroll from the service. The frustration of being asked to download an app and then seeing no value in it is highlighted in the following interview with a middle school student-athlete.

Reminder functions are also included in many great tools that also offer other features (see table 3.3). For instance, the digital portfolio tool Seesaw enables you to organize and highlight the learning that occurs in your classroom. It also allows you to message families to remind them of upcoming assignments and other important dates. This comprehensive communication tool will likely appeal to practitioners who prefer to use one inclusive system. Another comprehensive tool is the Heja app, which is typically marketed to coaches. As with Seesaw, Heja provides multiple options, and reminders account for only a small part of what it offers. Depending on your communication needs, and your level of comfort with technology, you might choose a specific tool such as Remind (simply to send out messages) or a more comprehensive tool such as Seesaw (to meet a variety of communication needs).

As always, when you consider using any app or website with your students, athletes, or families, take the time to read the terms and conditions in order to ensure that the tool is COPPA compliant. If you are unsure, check with your administration or your district's legal team.

VIDEO CALLS AND VIDEOCONFERENCES

Video calls and videoconferences both use audio and video simultaneously to connect at least two people in different geographic locations (Rayler, 2010). Video calls allow two people to communicate with each other, whereas videoconferences allow three or more to meet at once. Both video calls and videoconferences are traditionally **synchronous**, meaning that all parties are present during the meeting. The combination of video and audio features allows participants to construct a unique learning environment in which students learn from both the practitioner and each other in ways that go beyond the confines of a typical face-to-face interaction.

These technologies are useful not only for online and distance education teachers. They also lend themselves to many applications that extend beyond communication—for example, teaching content, going on virtual field trips, and leading seminars (Rayler, 2010). This chapter, however, focuses on ways to use these options in order to enhance communication. In its simplest form, a video call requires you and a learner or family member to set up a time to call each other using any electronic device that includes both a camera and a microphone. This interaction can be facilitated through the video feature on an app such as Google Hangouts, Skype, or Facebook Messenger. A video call could be used to hold virtual office hours or provide additional support for students who need help with homework or upcoming assignments. It can also serve as a great tool for reaching out to a

Table 3.3   Sample of Reminder Tools and Multifunction Tools With Reminder Capabilities

Tool	Cost	Website	Description	Recommended content area
Remind	Free	www.remind.com	• Send announcements and other information to learners and families. • Ask students to sign up for small-group activities. • Create alumni groups for communication. • Complies with COPPA and FERPA.	Health, physical education, coaching
Heja	Free	https://heja.io	• Manage sports and teams. • Send messages. • Start group chats. • Set up is easy for administrator and families. • Offers multiple features, not just reminders.	Coaching
Class-Dojo	Free	www.classdojo.com	• Enables students to create digital portfolios. • Message parents in 30 languages. • Share videos and photos. • Complies with COPPA and FERPA. • Create reminders.	Health, physical education
Seesaw	Free	https://web.seesaw.me	• Build student portfolios to highlight learning. • Start group chats. • Set up is easy for administrator and families. • Offers multiple features, not just reminders. • Enables peer-to-peer feedback and collaboration. • Complies with COPPA and FERPA.	Health, physical education
BAND	Free	https://band.us/home	• Schedule practices. • Message or call groups. • Share digital files. • Set and send reminders.	Coaching

TECHNOLOGY TIPS FROM THE FIELD

Interview with Neve Johnson About Using Communication Apps

Neve Johnson
Eighth-grade student
Kenowa Hills Middle School, Walker, Michigan
Track-and-field and cross country athlete

What types communication technology do you use?
The Remind app.

How do you use it?
Coaches and teachers use it to tell us about practice times and changes or what is going on in class that day.

What do you like about this technology?
I don't like it, and I don't dislike it. I feel like it's not always important to use it.

What suggestions do you have for physical and health education teachers and coaches in using this technology?
It is not necessary for teachers to use it if they have already told us in class. It should only be used if there is a change in the plan.

student or athlete who is on an extended absence without having to negotiate the logistics of meeting face-to-face.

Videoconferencing can be used if the audience you need to speak with is larger. Everyone involved in the conference can meet by means of their own personal device; alternatively, a group can meet face-to-face and connect with another group via the communication technology. Staging a videoconference may require more complex equipment than a typical personal device. For instance, you may need external microphones, high-quality cameras, and relatively large projection screens. Even so, with the evolution of videoconferencing technology, you may be able to use the same app that you would use for a video call (e.g., Google Hangouts, Skype, Facebook Messenger). Using such an app offers the benefit of seeing multiple people on the screen at once, muting your microphone if you don't want to be heard, and, for the facilitator, controlling the audio to prevent people from talking over each other.

Here are some situations in which a videoconference might be helpful:

• Checking in with your class during a sick leave or other extended absence
• Holding a meeting for all families at the beginning of a season or school year
• Checking in with students during a stretch of snow days
• Working on a project with a small group
• Introducing yourself in real time to students in an online course
• Updating fans during the bus ride home from an away game

This virtual face-to-face interaction allows for personal connection with students, athletes, and families and helps everyone feel that their time and needs are valued. As a result, geographic distance should generally not pose an obstacle to education in general or to the

Videoconference.

communication that plays a role in effective education. The main challenges with video calls and videoconferences involve obtaining access to proper equipment and establishing a strong network to process the audio and video (Anastasiades, 2010a).

Proper Equipment and Infrastructure

In order to create a functional environment for video calls and videoconferences, schools and programs must obtain and set up the proper equipment. Although some forms of video communication require little more than a personal device, sound and image quality play a large role in this form of communication, which means that the value of the experience depends in part on the equipment (e.g., microphones, speakers, cameras) and the infrastructure (e.g., **bandwidth**, connection speed) (Anastasiades, 2010b). The most important feature for successful communication is high-quality audio. You may be able to tolerate momentary visual freezes, but hearing fellow participants is essential to the learning process (Anastasiades, 2010b). Audio technology may take a simple form, such as a phone, tablet, or computer connected to a headset or equipped with a microphone and speaker. For larger audiences (e.g., a large class), microphones may be set up on the teacher's desk or hung from the wall or ceiling around the room.

In a videoconference, whoever is speaking should stay within a reasonable distance of the microphone for best results (Anastasiades, 2010b; see figure 3.5). In some instances, you may be able to wear a Bluetooth microphone that attaches to your shirt in order to transmit consistent sound for the videoconference.

Once your sound quality is assured, consider image quality. Better image quality enhances the learning environment by enabling students to learn without visual distractions. For one-on-one video phone calls, you may be able to use the standard camera on a phone, tablet, or computer. If the audience is larger, and you are videoconferencing, then you may need an external camera that provides better image quality. Your equipment needs will also depend on

Figure 3.5   Students participate in a videoconference call.

your learning objectives. For instance, if you do not use video phone calls or conferences frequently, you can typically use your personal computer and built in speaker to talk. If you are conducting video conferences frequently, it would make more sense to purchase a speakerphone that is meant to clearly capture everyone's voices, or a larger monitor to hook up your computer or camera to make the video large enough for everyone to see. Before purchasing expensive equipment, ask whether any appropriate equipment is available for checkout at your institution or can be set up in your classroom.

To ensure the best experience during your video call or videoconference, you also need to confirm that you have sufficient bandwidth (i.e., capacity to transmit and receive content) *and* fast enough speed (i.e., rate of data transfer). If either is subpar, you will be unable to transmit your video and audio properly, thus leading to frustration and a poor experience for your students.

Asynchronous Video Communication

Whereas video calls and videoconferences are often used in a synchronous manner (i.e., with all parties communicating at the same time), other options make **asynchronous** video communication possible as well. Essentially, these options allow you to give students a prompt (written or on video) and ask them to respond by means of video. One example is FlipGrid, which functions like a small social networking site for a class or

WHAT DOES THE RESEARCH SAY?

Effective Communication Can Lead to Future Sport Participation

Research supports the idea that communication between coaches and athletes not only enhances the learning process but also can enhance athletes' motivation and satisfaction (Cranmer & Sollitto, 2015). Specifically, athletes who perceive their coach as communicating effectively with them tend to be more satisfied with the coach, feel higher self-worth, and feel more supported in their athletic experience. This same research supports the notion that effective communication from one coach can positively influence an individual's subsequent sport participation and quality of sport experience. Therefore, effective communication can serve a purpose that is larger than the immediate transfer of information: For some, it can lay a foundation for future sport participation.

team. It enables learners to post videos as part of assignments and allows the practitioner and fellow learners to watch each other's videos and post comments. All communication is housed within what is called a "Grid" within the FlipGrid application. This form of video communication offers benefits similar to those of synchronous discussion—specifically, establishing a positive learning environment and allowing students to express their thoughts and learning without writing their thoughts down. Asynchronous video communication can also help learners and families understand your tone, which is often lost in text messaging. This form of video communication also frees you of the need to coordinate a time for all participants to meet; instead, everyone can work around their own extracurricular activities.

Conclusion

Access to technology outside the home, especially in the form of mobile phones, provides practitioners with opportunities to communicate with learners and families in a variety of ways. In fact, ongoing communication is promoted by the Appropriate Instructional Practices document from SHAPE America, which advises health and physical educators to ensure that "clear goals and objectives for student learning and performance are communicated to students, parents/guardians and administrators" (Society of Health and Physical Educators, 2009). This communication can be organized and disseminated with the aid of current technology more readily than is possible through traditional paper-based methods. Before committing to a certain communication technology, determine your objectives and check with your administration or school legal team to ensure that you are authorized to use the technology you are considering. If you work with learners under the age of 13, ensure that the tools you select meet COPPA regulations for child privacy and realize that you may be communicating directly with families rather than with your learners themselves. Communication technology should streamline the practice of teaching and learning—not complicate it. Give yourself plenty of time to learn and practice the technology before asking learners and families to commit to learning it.

Key Terms

acceptable use policy (AUP)—Policy adopted by a school or district to outline how the Internet should be accessed and used by students and staff.

asynchronous—Nonsimultaneous, as when students work at their own pace through a variety of methods and are not required to meet face-to-face (F2F) or at a specific time with peers or the instructor or to be online at any specific time but instead send messages at various times over an extended period.

bandwidth—Transmission capacity, or amount of information that can be transmitted over an information channel per second.

Children's Online Privacy Protection Act (COPPA)—Law requiring operators of websites and online services geared toward children under 13 years of age to provide a detailed privacy policy and collect consent from a parent or guardian before supplying any personally identifiable information.

cloud-based file sharing—Web-based service that allows participants to use a specific amount of space on a server in order to store and share information via the Internet.

communication—Process of exchanging information and meaning between people in a variety of settings.

consent—Grant permission; agree.

encryption—Process of encoding a message or information so that only the intended audience can see it (e.g., YouTube video encoded so that only specific users can access it and the link cannot be shared by anyone other than the creator).

Family Educational Rights and Privacy Act (FERPA)—Federal law that protects the privacy of student education records and applies to all schools that receive funds under an applicable program of the U.S. Department of Education.

learning management system (LMS)—Web-based software that aids management of the learning process by helping the instructor administer the course, deliver learning content, document and track student progress, and facilitate online interactions between classmates and the instructor (also referred to as *course management system*, or CMS).

spam—Slang term for unsolicited electronic mail, also known as "junk mail."

synchronous—Occurring at the same time, as in a scheduled online meeting with an instructor or peers through a video call or videoconferencing (with instructor or peers leading classes in real time for remote students, thus allowing them to ask a question and get an immediate response).

technology-mediated communication—Communication via a web-based platform that allows learning to extend beyond the traditional school setting, encourages all members of the learning community (e.g., student, athlete, practitioner, family) to participate in the learning process, and can be used to schedule or remind families of important dates or events, thus facilitating organization and accountability.

teleconference—Communication involving audio that services two individuals who can be in different geographic locations.

video call—Communication involving video and audio that services two individuals who can be in different geographic locations.

videoconference—Communication involving three or more participants across long distances with both video and audio features.

Review Questions

1. Why should you care about communicating with students and athletes? How does communication enhance learning?
2. What are the advantages of using technological tools to communicate?
3. What are some barriers to using communication technology?
4. What special considerations must you address when communicating with children under the age of 13?

Discussion Questions

1. What type of communication tool is best for you in your future profession?
2. How would you convince a wary parent to use communication technology?
3. Describe a time when you used communication technology or a time when you wish you had done so.
4. What would you do if a family did not have access to communication technology? How would you ensure that all students are given equal opportunities?

PART III

Technology
for Instruction

4

Technology for Health Education Classroom Instruction

by Matthew Cummiskey, PhD
Contributing Chapter Author

Chapter Objectives

When you have completed this chapter, you will be able to do the following:

1. Describe the WSCC model, explain each of its components, and identify technological tools for promoting each component.

2. Explain how the technologies presented could be adapted and applied in the health education classroom.

Klaus Vedfedlt/DigitalVision/Getty Images

3. Identify how technology can be used to promote learning for students with disabilities.

4. Discuss how technology can enable an interactive classroom with real-time input and formative assessments.

5. Identify technology-driven assessment tools that go beyond traditional pen-and-paper techniques.

6. Describe how smartphones can be incorporated into instruction in ways that promote meaningful learning.

7. Describe tools for accessing resources that connect users with information, services, and people.

8. Identify tools for creating web pages, blogs, videos, wikis, online formative assessments, WebQuests, and cloud docs.

Health educators can implement a wide range of technology applications to enhance student learning and long-term health. Because health education is taught in a traditional classroom, there are more technology options available than in an activity space. Health education is moving toward a skill-based approach, in which students not only learn content knowledge but also apply it in order to build health-enhancing skills (Connelly, 2018). This trend aligns well with technology because many computer applications are experiential in that they give students opportunities to build and apply knowledge. For example, students might create a narrated video addressing safety hazards found in the home. In this type of work, students apply the information learned in class to a practical use, thus building health-enhancing skills.

Although the technology presented in this chapter focuses on health education, many of the tools can also be applied to other aspects of the whole-school model (Association for Supervision and Curriculum Development, 2014) (figure 4.1). The model includes 10 components: health education; physical education and physical activity; nutrition environment and services; health services; counseling, psychological, and social services; social and emotional climate; physical environment; employee wellness; family engagement; and community involvement.

The overall purpose of this chapter is for you to learn about technological tools and develop the ability to apply them concretely in your own classroom. The chapter's subtopics were chosen for their relevance to promoting student learning and achievement of learning standards. The content has been subdivided into the following sections: displays, Microsoft applications, Google applications, student

Figure 4.1 The Whole School, Whole Community, Whole Child (WSCC) model.

Reprinted from ASCD, Whole School, *Whole Community, Whole Child: A Collaborative Approach to Learning and Health* (Alexandria, VA: ACSD, 2014).

feedback and involvement, apps, video integration, learning management systems (LMSs), and websites and technology management.

DISPLAYS

Displays may seem to make for a mundane topic, but they matter because today's students tend to be visually oriented (Marzano & Haystead, 2009). They have more access to technology and spend a large percentage of their day viewing screens, most often on a smartphone. Therefore, in order to engage students, classroom displays must keep pace, which means mirroring the functionality and excitement of the screens to which students are accustomed.

To that end, **interactive whiteboards** (Thomas & Schmid, 2010) combine traditional aspects of a whiteboard with specialized computer applications (figure 4.2). They allow users to project a computer desktop onto a screen and interact with it using specialized pens to swipe, draw, drag, and type (Smith,

Davidf/E+/Getty Images

Figure 4.2 Traditional interactive whiteboard with multiple colored pens stored in tray.

Higgins, Wall, & Miller, 2005). Other interactive features include the ability to highlight, create virtual flipcharts, create notes, conduct quizzes, and poll students. For example, students could be asked to categorize foods by dragging an item to the appropriate MyPlate category (Betcher & Lee, 2009), label major organs of the human body, or fill in nutritional pie charts corresponding to ingredient amounts on a food label.

Educators are beginning to see more **interactive touch screens** (Martinelli, 2015). These devices can be thought of as a large tablet computer or all-in-one device that does not rely on a separate computer or a projection system. It can be connected to other devices and the internet via Bluetooth and Wi-Fi and allows all class materials to be accessed online and displayed, thus reducing or eliminating reliance on a photocopier.

Both interactive whiteboards and interactive touchscreens have been shown to affect students positively. According to Decker (2010), students in classrooms with interactive displays reported higher motivation to learn and achievement. Students also demonstrated a more favorable impression of the subject area, more ability to interact with one another, increased learning, and greater enjoyment.

Interactive displays allow teachers and students to share their individual screens with the entire class. To do so, users download a program to their smartphone, tablet or computer and connect to the interactive display via Wi-Fi. For example, students could create a public service announcement video related to tobacco and share it via Chromecast, Solstice, or another casting software. This approach eliminates the need to transfer a file to another storage medium. It also negates possible program incompatibilities since the source file never leaves the device of origin; only the screen output is cast to the display.

MICROSOFT APPLICATIONS

Microsoft is nearly ubiquitous in the United States due to the prevalence of Microsoft Windows and Microsoft Office (Hunt, 2005). However, even though most users are familiar with Microsoft products, they may be unaware of many tips and tricks that allow teachers and coaches to achieve more—and with greater efficiency.

Microsoft Office is termed a productivity suite, meaning that it is used to produce information (Microsoft, 2018a). Its most recognized products include Word for word processing, PowerPoint for presentations, Excel for **spreadsheets**, and Outlook for email. Depending on the specific package purchased, Office may also include Publisher (desktop publishing), OneNote (information gathering and collaboration), and Access (database management). To create a uniform look and feel, Office products feature a standard ribbon along the top (figure 4.3).

The ribbon includes several tabs (e.g., File, Home), and each tab is subdivided into groups that include individual functions. For some groups, the bottom right corner includes a dialog box launcher that pops the group out into a separate window containing additional functions. Users can customize the groups available on each tab by right-clicking anywhere in a group and selecting Customize the Ribbon. This feature allows users to put the functions used most into a condensed format; only whole groups can be removed— not individual functions within a group. To hide the ribbon entirely, right-click on it and select Collapse the Ribbon; doing so frees up more space for viewing information. To make the ribbon reappear, right-click on the tabs and deselect the collapse command. A shortcut for both options is to double-click the tab titles.

Over the tabs is an area known as the Quick Access Toolbar, where users can store their most frequently used functions. To add a function, right-click on it in the ribbon and select Add to Quick Access Toolbar. To remove a function, right-click on it in the toolbar and select Remove from Quick Access Toolbar. To open a separate window in order to add or remove multiple functions, select Customize Quick Access Toolbar. These ribbon steps can save you considerable time and energy over the years for which you are likely to use Office products.

Keyboard shortcuts also save time and effort by circumventing use of the mouse or touch pad. To use a keyboard shortcut, you simply depress certain keys simultaneously, thereby activating a function (Microsoft, 2018b). It may seem like a daunting task to remember various keystroke combinations, but the more you use them, the better you will remember them. Most shortcuts involve hitting two keys simultaneously, usually by holding down the Control button (Ctrl) and then another key. Table 4.1 presents a list of common keyboard shortcuts for Microsoft Office, and more can be found at the Computer Hope website (www.computerhope.com/shortcut/word.htm).

Of all the Microsoft Office applications, teachers and coaches are most likely to use Word, PowerPoint, and Excel. Because the basic functions of these programs are gener-

Figure 4.3 The standard ribbon in Microsoft applications.

Table 4.1   Keyboard Shortcuts for Microsoft Office

Keystroke combination	Function	Keystroke combination	Function
Ctrl+A	Select all contents of a page.	Ctrl+W	Close the open document.
Ctrl+B	Bold highlighted selection.	Ctrl+X	Cut selected text.
Ctrl+C	Copy selected text.	Ctrl+Y	Redo the last action performed.
Ctrl+F	Open Find box.	Ctrl+Z	Undo the last action performed.
Ctrl+H	Opens Find and Replace box.	Ctrl+<left arrow>	Moves the cursor one word to the left.
Ctrl+I	Italicize highlighted selection.	Ctrl+<right arrow>	Moves the cursor one word to the right.
Ctrl+J	Align selected text or line to justify the screen.	Ctrl+Del	Delete word to right of cursor.
Ctrl+K	Insert a hyperlink.	Ctrl+Backspace	Delete word to left of cursor.
Ctrl+L	Align selected text or line to left side of screen.	Ctrl+End	Move cursor to end of document.
Ctrl+N	Open new, blank document window.	Ctrl+Home	Move cursor to beginning of document.
Ctrl+O	Open the dialog box or page for selecting a file to open.	Ctrl+1	Single-space lines.
Ctrl+P	Open the Print window.	Ctrl+2	Double-space lines.
Ctrl+R	Align selected text or line to right side of screen.	Ctrl+5	Apply 1.5 line spacing.
Ctrl+S	Save the open document.	Function + F7	Spell-check and grammar-check selected text or document.
Ctrl+U	Underline selected text.	Ctrl+Enter	Insert page break.
Ctrl+V	Paste copied text.	Ctrl+Alt+Del	Open login screen or Task Manager.

ally well understood, the following paragraphs focus on specialized tips and suggestions for each one.

Microsoft Word

Instead of starting with a blank document, use a **template** (Microsoft, 2018a). Templates preformat some details (e.g., colors, images, backgrounds, fonts) but allow you to customize the text and layout. Since templates are professionally created, they are often superior to a document format that an average user could create. As of this writing, Microsoft Word offers 238 educational templates, along with others for topics such as Back to School (24), Graduation (19), Certificates (18), Schedules (6), and Sports (6). To create a document using a template, click the File tab, click New, and then, instead of selecting a blank document, click a template category such as Education (or search the templates available online).

Office also includes a tool called the **Accessibility Checker**, which is designed to improve the experience for individuals with disabilities (Microsoft, 2018c). This feature alerts authors to common accessibility issues and provides alternate suggestions. Thus it helps educators and coaches to provide equitable learning experiences for all students and athletes. The accessibility checker is located on the Review tab. Here is a list of the most common accessibility issues and how they can be prevented:

1. *Alternate text.* When a screen reader encounters an image in a document, it reads aloud the alternate text associated with the picture. This text should convey the same essential information as the picture, and all pictures should use alternate text or be marked as a decorative image. To do so, right-click an image and select Edit Alt Text.

2. *Hyperlinks.* Attach hyperlinks to text words instead of listing a URL. This approach provides two kinds of help to students who use a screen reader. First, the words convey the meaning of the link; second, students are not subjected to a long list of characters that may not include a context. For example, if students in health education are analyzing risky behavior, your assignment might include a hyperlink keyed to the words "Youth Risk Behavior Survey" instead of the URL "www.cdc.gov/healthyyouth/data/yrbs/pdf/2017/ss6708.pdf."

3. *Text format.* To help students with vision issues, differentiate text by using observable characteristics other than colors. For example, use bold and underlined text instead of red text. If using colors, choose ones that permit a high degree of contrast between text and the background. Although teachers and coaches may prefer various colors, some can hamper readability for students with low vision.

4. *Headings.* Headings can make it easier for individuals who use a screen reader to organize information by importance and fit it into the context of the overall document. Most screen readers announce a heading. For example, the title of a book is often treated as a level 1 heading, each chapter title as a level 2 heading, and chapter subsections as level 3 headings. This structure helps users understand when a new section begins, as well as its importance and significance in the overall document. If possible, use at least two head levels per document and three or more for longer documents. Select Heading Format from the Styles group on the Home tab.

5. *Lists.* Lists may help students organize information better than a long paragraph does. Ordered lists, such as this one, use numbers or letters and convey a sense of importance for items listed earlier. When sequence or importance is not an issue, consider using unordered lists marked by bullets or dashes.

6. *Tables.* If using tables, keep them simple and include column headers. A screen reader begins in the top left corner, then moves right to left and then down as if reading the page. If possible, do not merge or split cells. For example, the table of keyboard shortcuts presented earlier (table 4.1) has four columns throughout, along with column headers at the top.

When creating a long document such as a curriculum, student-athlete handbook, or collection of football plays, you can enable users to move around quickly by including a table of contents with hyperlinks. This way, readers do not lose time searching for pertinent information. You may be familiar with creating a hyperlink by using the Existing File or Webpage option, but hyperlinks can also be used within a document. To do so, create a table of contents in a format similar to the one shown in figure 4.4. In the example, the National Health Education Standards begin on page 9. To create the link from the table of contents to the standards, go to page 9 and insert a named bookmark. Then go back to the table of contents, highlight "National Health Education Standards," and insert a hyperlink. In the succeeding window, select Place in This Document and the

Introduction 3
Contributors... 5
Mission and Vision Statement... 7
National Health Education Standards 9
Whole School, Child and Community 15
Skill-based Health Education... 23
Units of Instruction
    a. Social and Emotional Well-Being.. 26
    b. Alcohol & Tobacco Prevention.. 35

Figure 4.4 Hyperlinks in a document are offset by a blue underlined font, whereas nonlinking text is formatted as usual. For each entry, a dot leader tab allows readers to easily read across to the relevant page number.

appropriate bookmark. At the end of each section, create a hyperlink back to the table of contents. Users may also click ctrl + home to return to page 1.

Microsoft PowerPoint

PowerPoint is so widely used that it hardly needs an introduction. Its basic purpose is to present information by means of a series of digital slides (Microsoft, 2018a). It is both loved and maligned, the latter because it is often used incorrectly. The most frequent criticism is applied to presenters who subject an audience, such as a classroom of students, to a long, noninteractive lecture in which they stare at one slide after another until, mercifully, class ends—thus the phrase "death by PowerPoint." To help you avoid this fate, the following list offers tips for delivering an effective presentation (Sommerville, 2017):

1. *Lecture segments should last no more than 15 minutes.* Use various teaching methodologies, preferably ones that get students actively involved with the learning objectives and with one another.

2. *Use an appropriate number of words per slide.* Although this may sound like a simple concept, the appropriate number depends to some extent on factors such as the audience, the presenter's goals, and the complexity of the material. Putting fewer words on each slide causes the audience to focus more on the presenter, but the document itself is less useful without the instructor being present (figure 4.5*a*); in addition, the presenter may forget some information. Using more words, on the other hand, increases the likelihood that viewers may ignore the presenter and read the words out of context, but it increases the utility of the PowerPoint document outside of class (figure 4.5*b*). General guidelines call for using no more than six bullet points per slide and no more than four words per bullet, but you will need to find an appropriate number of points and words for your philosophy and context. A compromise approach for figure 4.5*b* would be to show only the underlined words at first, then present the additional information orally and display the remaining text.

3. *Avoid backgrounds that are too busy or reduce the visibility of the information.* Viewers should be able to focus easily on the material—not the background.

4. *Consider your audience when selecting slide transitions and animations.* The traditional rule of thumb is that too many visual effects distracts the audience. However, younger audiences are more accustomed to varied and repeated visual stimuli and may be unengaged if they are completely absent (personal communication, PETE conference 2018).

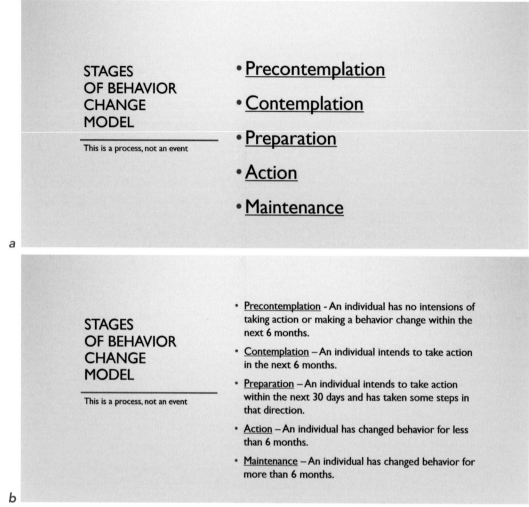

Figure 4.5 Choose an amount of text that works for your audience and teaching style. Consider experimenting with both and gauging the effectiveness of each.

5. *Leave clip art in the past.* Clip art consists of stock images typically bundled with a computer program. These images tend to be somewhat cliché and low in visual quality, especially when contrasted with the high-definition images that are familiar to students and athletes today. Therefore, you should use higher-quality images when available.

6. *Avoid using entrance animations in which one line appears at a time.* Such animations slow down the presentation. Use them only if absolutely necessary.

7. *Use the slides as triggers for what to say.* Avoid simply reading your slides. Doing so reduces eye contact and engagement with your audience. Besides, audience members can read the slides well enough for themselves!

8. *Be mindful of text size.* It's a good idea to test font size by displaying the smallest size used and then attempting to read it from the back of the room. Any illegible font sizes should be increased.

9. *Insert material only in the top two-thirds of a slide.* This restriction prevents your material from being obscured by the heads and shoulders of audience members. You may be able to use more of the slide if the display is mounted higher on the classroom wall or if the room uses stadium seating.

Instead of using PowerPoint throughout, break the class period into multi-modal learning formats. PowerPoint is a valid tool but should not be overused.

When creating a new presentation, you can select a template provided within PowerPoint (Microsoft, 2018a) or choose from a multitude of free and fee-based templates available on the web. When creating specific slides, you can select from several preloaded layout options. The two most commonly used options are Title Slide and Title and Content, which are shown in figure 4.6 along with other options. You can customize slides either one at a time, which is time consuming, or by using the Slide Master to ensure that each new slide generated includes certain customizations. To edit the Slide Master, click the View tab, click Slide Master, choose the desired layout, make the desired adjustments, and then click Close Master View.

Using images in a presentation can make it more attractive and engaging to viewers. It can be challenging, however, to arrange multiple images on a slide in a coherent fashion. To align images consistently, you can use gridlines, which are small dotted lines that appear when editing a slide but not during the presentation itself. Another way to improve viewability is to use the **Design Ideas** function available on the Design tab (Microsoft, 2018d). This feature provides suggestions for arranging a slide. For example, in figure 4.7, the coaching image was inserted into a blank Title and Content layout, after which Design Ideas was selected. Several options were provided, four of which are shown. The first two rearrange the title and content boxes and change the color, whereas the third uses the image as a background. The feature works best with preloaded PowerPoint templates; it works inconsistently with non-Microsoft templates.

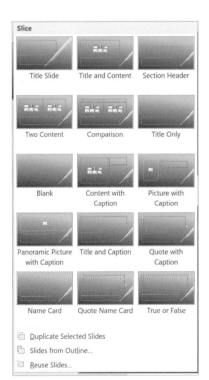

Figure 4.6 Templates help you create professional-looking slides more easily.

61

You can use PowerPoint to facilitate formative assessment by setting up a Jeopardy-style quiz. In years past, teachers painstakingly made their own quizzes, but Microsoft now offers a template called Quiz Show Game. Simply search for that template and insert your questions on the appropriate slides.

One disadvantage of PowerPoint is that students may tend to lose focus during a presentation. To minimize this pitfall, use a guided-notes handout that gives students some of the text but calls for them to fill in the missing information from the PowerPoint presentation. You might also pose questions in the document and check students' copies for completion before dismissing the class.

Many of the same keyboard shortcuts used in Word can also be used in PowerPoint, but there are some differences. Here are some shortcuts that can be used during a PowerPoint slide show:

- *Advance slide:* letter N, left click, space bar, right or down arrow, Enter, or Page Down
- *Go to previous slide:* letter P, backspace, left or up arrow, Page Up
- *End slide show:* Escape
- *Black out screen:* Letter B
- *White out screen:* Letter W
- *Use red pointer (without stopping slide show):* Ctrl+P (Ctrl+E to erase)
- *Highlight:* Ctrl+I

Figure 4.7 The Design Ideas function can be used to add visual interest and variety to a slide or set of slides, thus helping you capture and hold students' attention.

Excel

Microsoft Excel is the least commonly used Office program addressed in this chapter. Many of the functions for which teachers and coaches formerly used it are now embedded in learning management software (addressed later). Its functionality is still crucial, however, in certain circumstances.

Spreadsheet programs such as Excel are ideal for storing, organizing, and analyzing data in a tabular format (Selwyn, Henderson, & Chao, 2015). Columns are assigned letters, and rows are assigned numbers, thus creating a unique designation for each cell. You can use a spreadsheet to manipulate and analyze data by means of formulas, which must begin with an equal-sign and are typically followed by a range. For example, the formula =*average(A1:A10)* calculates the average of the numbers in cells A1 through A10. Here are the most common types of formulas:

- *Average:* =average(range1:range2)
- *Sum:* =sum(range1:range2)
- *High score:* =max(range1:range2)
- *Low score:* =min(range1:range2)
- *Standard deviation:* =stdev(range1:range2)
- *Number of scores:* =count(range1:range2)

Excel is a powerful yet complicated program with a longer learning curve than the other two Microsoft programs. Therefore, this segment of the chapter focuses on two narrow applications of the program for teaching and coaching. You can learn about the full gamut of Excel features from any of a multitude of videos and handbooks available online free of charge.

When designing an assessment, teachers often assign point values to each question, but these values seldom add up to 100. Therefore, figuring a percentage of correct answers requires some use of mathematics. Say, for example, that a test has 44 questions worth one point each and a student answers 38 questions correctly. The percentage of correct answers can be calculated easily with help from a spreadsheet. In column A, type the numeral 1 in cell A1, the numeral 2 in cell A2, and so on up to the maximum number of incorrect answers. Then in cell B1, type the formula $=(44-a1)/44$. Paste this formula all the way down column B, and a percentage score will be shown for all incorrect answer totals. This technique is faster than scoring tests by hand and faster than calculating the percentage based upon number correct for each student's assessment.

You can also create small Excel documents for which students input data that is automatically calculated. For instance, health educators often teach about the cardiovascular system, since heart disease is the number one killer of Americans (Fryar, Chen, & Li, 2012). The Technology Differentiations inset (figure 4.8) shows a spreadsheet that automatically calculates target heart rate range using the Karvonen technique based on a person's age, resting heart rate, and desired aerobic training zone. Spreadsheets can also be used for many other purposes—for example, to track attendance, record completion of assignments, store contact information, create equipment inventories, record grades, and create seating charts.

As of this writing, Microsoft is offering Office 365 free of charge for teachers and students. To pursue this offer, search online for the appropriate link, since the address may have changed or the promotion may have been discontinued. Teachers and coaches who are not provided with Microsoft Office as part of their employment may find another alternative in the form of Open Office (www.openoffice.org/), an application that is free of charge and installs locally on a given device. It includes word processing, spreadsheet, presentation, and database programs and allows files to be saved in Open Office, Microsoft Office, PDF, and other formats.

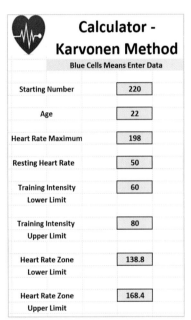

Figure 4.8   Students insert values into the blue-shaded cells, and Excel automatically calculates the target heart rate range.

GOOGLE APPLICATIONS

Google provides a dazzling and ever-growing array of products. To understand the scope, visit the Google products webpage (www.google.com/intl/en/about/products/), which lists more than 200 offerings. In particular, G Suite for Education is a collection of collaborative learning tools that includes Google Docs, Sheets, Slides, Forms, Drive, Hangouts, and Classroom, as well as with other applications (Google, 2018a). According to Google, more than 80 million faculty and students use G Suite, and more than 40 million use Google Classroom.

Google Classroom includes Docs for word processing, Sheets for spreadsheets, and Slides for presentations (Google, 2018b). All of the programs are free of charge and delivered online via a web browser. Files are automatically saved, and users can revert to previously saved versions; they can also collaborate either synchronously or asynchronously. For example, you might divide the class into groups of four and assign each group to present a classification of drugs, such as inhalants, opioids, or tobacco. Students could create their presentations by using Slides and create a one-page summary for distribution to classmates by using Docs. Each presentation could identify the drug classification, administration and effects, dangers and health problems, legal aspects, patterns of use, and portrayal in popular culture. Groups could assign each member a portion of the assignment to produce and then work simultaneously on the same document, all while seeing each other's edits in real time.

Meanwhile, teachers could access the document and provide feedback before it is formally submitted. To share a document, students can simply provide a link and give the teacher permission to view and edit it. Another option is to share a specific Google Drive folder in which the document is stored.

Another popular use of Google Docs is to conduct peer workshops. To do so, students create and store an assignment in their Google Drive, then share it with the entire class. On the last page of the document, other students post comments and suggestions. The originator might then be asked to reply to at least two of the peer comments. This process is similar to that of a traditional class discussion but eliminates the need for separate document and discussion formats. To help students act responsibly in the workshop, teachers should provide comment guidelines.

Google Docs can also facilitate do-now activities, also referred to as **bell-ringers** or welcome work, in which students begin working on a posted item immediately upon entering the classroom (Boettner, 2011). Such activities promote learning and on-task behavior. For example, students might access a certain Google Docs file and answer questions about an assigned reading from the night before.

Teachers can also design activities in which students compete against one another while applying learned information. For example, you might split the class into 10 groups, distribute a Google doc listing 15 major muscles of the human body, and task each group with identifying an exercise that works a muscle but does not duplicate a response from any other group. Once the activity has been completed, the class can examine the document for correctness and discuss the results.

One of the inherent problems with group assignments is that the workload will not always be distributed evenly. To address this concern, you can ask students to evaluate their peers by using Google Forms (more on this later) or tell them that you will examine the revision history of the documents submitted. The revision history keeps track of what changes are made, by whom, and when. You can also promote equitable contributions among group members by simply setting guidelines for group projects—for example, requiring that each person contribute roughly an equal amount.

Two other features that you may want to try are Voice Typing and Chrome extensions. Voice Typing converts spoken words to text with a high degree of accuracy and works well when using a virtual tablet keyboard (with which typing may be slower). The Chrome offline extension allows users to edit files without an Internet connection. Files are saved locally for the time being and then updated online when a connection is established. This extension works only with the Chrome browser—not Firefox or Internet Explorer.

Google Forms can be used to collect information on virtually any topic (Google, 2018a), whether by means of surveys, polls, user profiles, or assessments. For example, suppose that a teacher wants to measure how much students have retained from a lesson about MyPlate. The teacher might begin class with a 10-question Google Forms assessment that is limited to five minutes, allows one attempt per question, shows the correct answer, and displays a final score. Students access the form via an email link, a website, or social media. The teacher then views the responses in Forms or Sheets and discusses the results immediately. Google Forms also provides other analytical tools and can save time compared to traditional grading.

As you may recall, Google started out primarily as a web search company. Of course, teachers and coaches often search for information, which can be a daunting task given the volume of content available on the web! The go-to source for most searches is Google, but wading through the results can be time consuming. In such cases, consider conducting an advanced Google search, which allows you to specify variables such as exact phrasing, omission of certain words, language, file format, and date (Google, 2018c) (figure 4.9).

Another Google **app**, Translate, may be helpful to teachers and coaches who work with students or athletes who have limited English proficiency. This free translation app works with about 60 languages and can translate the spoken word as well as webpages and documents (e.g., assignments). In addition, users can either say or type a phrase into Translate and have it converted to another language and read aloud. In effect, this function allows teachers to "speak" with parents and students in their native language, thus breaking down barriers and promoting effective communication. Even teachers who are semi-fluent in another language can benefit from using Translate to learn or confirm proper pronunciation. When using Translate, always include a disclaimer noting that fact and acknowledging that some inaccuracies may appear.

Another product that lends itself to dynamic applications in schools is Google Cardboard (figure 4.10). Cardboard is a virtual reality viewer that uses the high-resolution screens of most conventional smartphones to create a 3-D experience (Miller, 2016). Inexpensive models made of—you guessed it—cardboard are available for as little as $10. Download the app from Google Play or the App store and secure your smartphone inside the apparatus. Uses of Cardboard depend on what apps are installed.

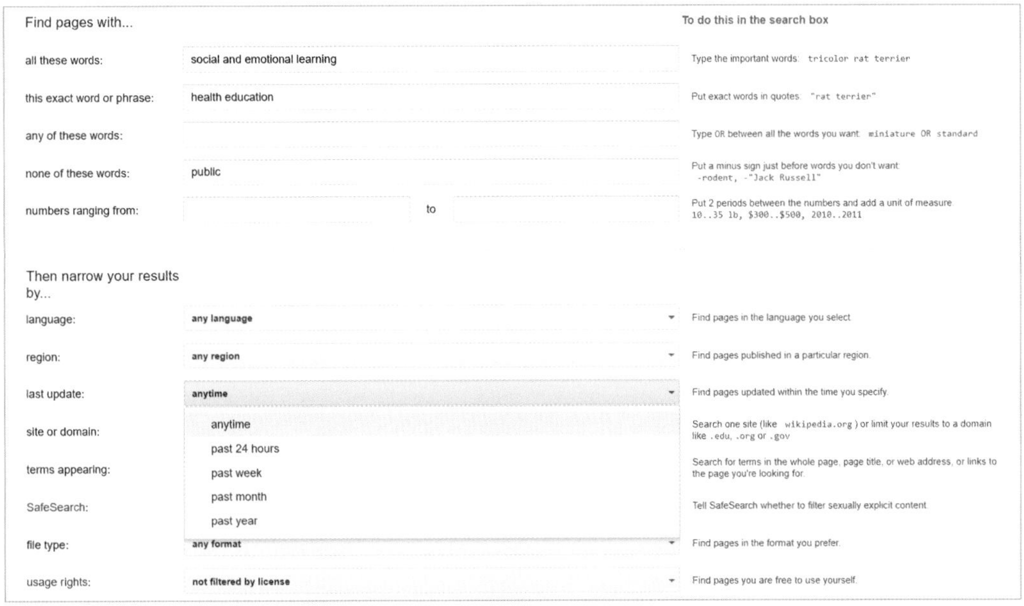

Figure 4.9   An advanced Google search allows you to customize a variety of parameters in order to gather more focused results.

Figure 4.10 To use Google Cardboard, lay a smartphone on the open flap, then close the flap to create a virtual reality experience that is unique, accessible, and affordable.

"Google Cardboard 2" by Maurizio Pesce is licensed under CC BY 2.0.

Here are a few recommended apps, along with possible uses in school:

1. *Expeditions.* Go on virtual field trips to more than 500 destinations.
2. *InCell VR.* Explore the microscopic anatomy of the cell and how to save it from viruses.
3. *Wizard Academy VR.* Fight germs and other pathogens.
4. *Cleanopolis VR.* Examine one's ecological footprint and how to reduce CO_2 emissions; includes quizzes.
5. *Walk the Streets.* Use Cardboard and Google Maps to walk the streets of any mapped neighborhood around the globe.
6. *YouTube app.* Watch YouTube videos in 360 degrees.
7. *Cardboard Camera.* Create movie projects using still photo or smartphone video; use as part of an assignment or a VR experience.
8. *Role Playing Apps.* Role-play with a video instead of with another person; for example, demonstrate refusal skills when offered drugs.

Most teachers have heard of **blogs**, but incorporating them effectively into instruction is another matter. A blog is a website characterized by frequent, informal text posts about a given topic; some blogs also include pictures (Kuo, Belland, & Kuo, 2017). In health education, students could blog about a required assignment to interview a health care professional. One in-class option would be to post at least one question for a guest speaker. Another creative application would be to assign one student per class to serve as the scribe on a rotating basis. That person would be responsible for taking notes about the topic presented and what should be learned and posting them in the blog. This work should be guided by a rubric to encourage a consistently high-quality blog.

Teachers can also use blogs to encourage students to stay abreast of current health information. Start by creating a Google Form that asks students what health topic they would most like to learn about. Based on their responses, create a blog where they post relevant information. All posts must include a source URL and avoid duplicating other posts. Blogs can also be used to gauge whether students have learned key information, which of course is an important part of teaching. You can use blogs for this purpose by means of a technique known as Best Summary. With five minutes remaining in class, assign students to groups and ask them to summarize the major learning objectives in a 100-word blog *without* referring to their notes. At the start of the next class, ask students to return to the same groups, choose a member to read their blog aloud, and then use learning management software to rank the posts. Students may not vote on their own blog.

Health educators often enjoy inviting guest speakers to class; these guests bring outside expertise, and students enjoy hearing fresh perspectives. The potential pool of guest speakers is nearly limitless and can include police officers, victims of sexual assault, individuals with eating disorders, nutritionists, doctors, nurses, and countless other professionals. The challenge lies in getting presenters to the school and making them available for all scheduled health classes. To meet this challenge, one alternative to traditional guest speakers is Google Hangouts, which is a free videoconference service that can accommodate up to 10 speakers from anywhere around the globe (Google, 2018a) (figure 4.11). If a presenter has limited availability, the teacher can record the presentation by means of a screen recording program (more later) and play the recording for students.

Teachers can also use Hangouts for various other purposes—for instance, to host meetings with students or parents who cannot be physically present. This approach is preferable to a simple phone conversation because videoconferencing allows for face-to-face communication and all of the nonverbal nuances it entails. Videoconferencing can also be useful for professional development when some or all of the colleagues involved are not local (McCrea, 2013). For example, a teacher who wants to meet other professionals could do so by using Google Hangouts, thus saving both time and money. These factors are important because time away and professional development money are often in short supply.

Finally, Hangouts allows for collaboration between groups or classrooms. For example, health classes in two high schools could collaborate on a drunk driving prevention campaign at a local mall during the holiday season. The classes could use webcams to meet during health education class in order to become familiar with one another and plan the event. The classes could also be divided into groups based on specific interests, such as visual displays, handouts, refreshments, and community outreach. Each group could meet with its counterpart in the other class by using the webcam embedded at the top of the display on most laptops.

Google also provides Google Duo, which is customized for smartphones and tablets. In addition, videoconferencing services can be accessed through non-Google apps, such as Zoom and Any-Meeting.

Google Drive is a free cloud storage service that allows users to upload and save files to servers connected via the Internet (i.e., "the cloud") (Google, 2018a). Cloud storage offers several advantages over local storage, in which files are saved in the

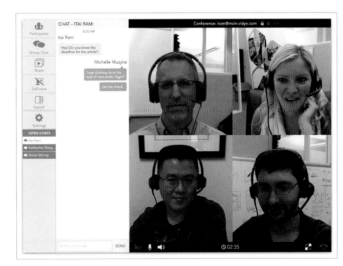

Figure 4.11 Google Hangouts permits multiple guest speakers from around the globe to speak to classrooms via videoconferencing through the Internet.

memory of a laptop, tablet, or smartphone. Users can access cloud-based files from various devices, which means that if you leave your work laptop at school you can access your files from a different device at home. Thus there is no need to email files to oneself or use a portable storage device (e.g., flash drive, hard drive). In addition, files stored in the cloud are more secure and less likely to be lost. Most users know the panic of being unable to access a file when it is needed—usually at the worst time! Not only are cloud-based files more secure, but also they can be shared on a per-file or per-folder basis, thus ensuring that all collaborators are accessing the most current version. Access and editing permissions can be revoked if an individual is withdrawn from a group. A shared folder can also function as an online portfolio, and students can upload artifacts to demonstrate mastery of learning standards and share the relevant folder with the teacher.

Here are two other useful Google-related products:

- *Scholar.* Search for and save journal articles to a customized library. Google automatically returns the most relevant and most frequently cited sources. Scholar includes a Cite button that delivers a citation in APA, MLA, and other formats. Users can also access several advanced search options (e.g., author, source, publication date) by clicking the pull-down arrow to the right of the search field.

- *Alerts.* Monitor the Internet and detect content aligned with specified search criteria, then deliver results to a specified email address (figure 4.12). This option is a great way for teachers to stay abreast of content in a certain field, such as immunotherapy or Alzheimer's research. Simply insert a topic into the search field and specify how often to receive updates (e.g., as it happens, once a day, once a week), from what sources (e.g., blogs, news sites), and how the information should be delivered. For example, a health education teacher could create a new alert for each class unit and have it forwarded automatically to students once a day. This approach could help students appreciate the dynamism of health knowledge and health-related skills while also acclimating them to sources of information besides the classroom. Coaches could create alerts related to their team or other teams in a school or district.

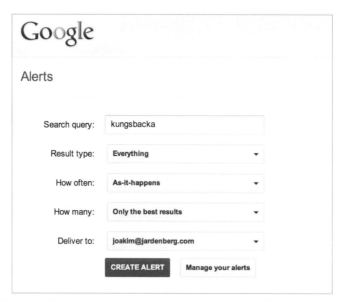

Figure 4.12 Google Alerts makes it easier to stay abreast of developments in the ever-changing field of health education. Users can customize the frequency, type, and amount of information to match their needs.

STUDENT FEEDBACK AND INVOLVEMENT

When teachers use a skills-based approach, the learning environment tends to be interactive, experiential, and assessment driven (Connelly, 2018). In contrast, a lecture-based approach, also known as "sage on the stage," is effective at disseminating information but less effective at building higher-order skills and promoting long-term retention. With a skills-based approach, the degree to which students build skills and master content knowledge should be checked frequently to inform midstream corrections. Thankfully, technology can play a role in both collecting student feedback and involving students in the learning process.

Poll Everywhere

Poll Everywhere is an excellent example of an interactive technology application that engages students, promotes learning, and provides teachers with firsthand knowledge of performance (Bates, Huber, & McClure, 2016). This versatile app allows you to collect information and view results instantaneously (figure 4.13). Table 4.2 presents some types of polls that can be created, along with a corresponding health education example for each. Additional poll types include open-ended, donut chart, spotlight, retrospective, team, discussion, map, short answer, bulletin board, and 2 × 2 matrix.

Due to the versatility of Poll Everywhere, it can be used in several ways in health education. One application is to conduct a diagnostic assessment at the start of a class or unit in order to determine students' existing knowledge (Institute for Teaching, Innovation, and Learning, n.d.). The resulting information enables you to minimize boredom and frustration while tailoring instruction to students' educational sweet spot. Another option is to create a continuous open-response mechanism through which students can ask "backchannel" questions for you to answer either as received or at regular intervals. Because these responses are anonymous, shy students and those who fear embarrassment are more inclined to participate. Polls can also be used at the end of a lesson to summarize major points or answer specific questions. Doing so involves students and uses a more engaging format than traditional closure questions. Finally, polls can be used collaboratively. For example, you might ask student groups to reach consensus before answering a poll, thus giving them a chance to share and defend their own ideas while also seeking to understand other points of view. If warranted, all poll responses could include a rationale.

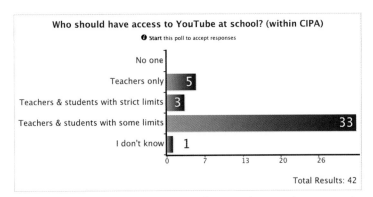

Figure 4.13 Sample Poll Everywhere output that can be used to springboard classroom discussions.

Table 4.2   Poll Everywhere: Selected Types of Polls

Type of poll	Description	Example in health education
Multiple choice	Respondents choose the best option that answers the question. You can add options and include images.	Use as a formative assessment of what students have learned: "Which of the following best exemplifies an I statement?"
Word cloud	Create an image composed of text words whose size corresponds to the frequency of submission.	"When I say marriage, what words come to mind?"
Q&A	Pose a question and ask students to write an anonymous response.	"What questions about contraceptives do you have that were not asked today?"
Clickable image	Display an image overlaid with shaded box regions, each of which is a possible answer.	"On the muscle figure, which region corresponds to the trapezius?"
Survey and competition	Combine multiple question types and ask students or groups to compete against one another.	Create 10 questions measuring students' comprehension of over-the-counter and prescription drugs.
Icebreaker	Use to start a conversation, focus a discussion on a theme, or reduce inhibitions.	"Tell me about a time that you failed and why that failure was the best thing for you?"
Upvote and downvote	Allow audience members to submit responses and then upvote or downvote responses.	"If fruits and vegetables are so important to your diet, why are they so drastically underconsumed? Limit your response to five words."
Leaderboard	Ask respondents to vote for their favorite.	"Which group's skit best exemplified the assigned conflict resolution strategy."
Emotional scale	Allow students to pick one of five faces on a continuum ranging from full smile to full frown.	"How would you rate your ability to administer CPR to an unconscious adult victim?" "How would you rate my lesson today?"
Brainstorm	Allow respondents to submit an idea and then vote for the best ideas.	"What is the best way you can personally address climate change?"
Ranking	Use in similar fashion to Leaderboard but allow students to rank options instead of simply voting for one.	"Which of following drinks contains the most alcohol?" "In your view, why do some students bully others?"

Since polls are anonymous, they can be used to gather sensitive information. For example, if you ask how many students have tried marijuana or had intercourse, they might be surprised by how low the percentage is and feel less pressured to engage in risky behaviors. You can also use the Presentation Feedback tool in Poll Everywhere to enable students to receive feedback from each other as well as from you. To prevent hostile feedback, preview open-text responses or use instruments with limited capacity to offend, such as ranking the most effective segments of a presentation.

A free Poll Everywhere account limits the number of responses per poll to 40, which is sufficient for an average-sized class. Teachers can also purchase an upgraded account, which includes computer scoring of assessments, automatic censoring of offensive language, and the ability to individually approve each response for display. Alternatively, a school or school district can purchase a site license, which includes additional functionality.

Gamification: Pros and Cons

Game-based learning in the classroom offers multiple advantages, including greater participation, alignment with students' digital learning styles, increased motivation to participate, customization options (e.g., avatars, badges, points), and usefulness for formative assessment (Furdu, Tomozei, & Kose, 2017). It also comes with some distinct disadvantages, including greater emphasis on lower-order thinking skills, inability to correct unsuccessful attempts, inability to provide customized feedback, and lack of clear consensus among educators about whether gamification improves student learning.

Kahoot

Gamification is the process of introducing gamelike elements into education with the intent of making learning fun and motivating ("Gamification," n.d.). Kahoot employs gamification by turning student smartphones or computers into a classroom response system (Ismail & Mohammad, 2017) that allows you to create a quiz, typically using multiple-choice and true-or-false questions. The quiz is projected onto a display, and students answer each question in real time on their device. For each question, the correct answer is then displayed, along with the five leading contestants; individual scores are displayed only on each student's device. Students tend to enjoy Kahoot activities and typically engage in friendly banter throughout the activity. Remind students to use appropriate names to identify themselves—or, better yet, specify a naming format, such as first name and last initial. Click on any inappropriate names to remove them from the listing. To prevent students from seeing inappropriate names at all, do not project the Kahoot screen until the sign-in process has been completed.

Kahoot is commonly used as a pretest, formative assessment, or lesson exit ticket (Plump & LaRosa, 2017). Teachers can include image-related questions, such as, "Which of the following bike riders is wearing her helmet correctly?" After a Kahoot activity, download the spreadsheet report to examine how individual students performed or to analyze response statistics for each question. Based on the results, you might choose to meet with students who performed poorly. For homework, you can assign students to create and administer a Kahoot activity on a rotating basis to their small group, table group, or seating row. This type of assignment prompts them to interact with the learning material in a higher-order fashion while also employing technology. Besides traditional Kahoot activities, some new game options are available:

- *Jumble Kahoot.* Students arrange choices in order. For example, you might say, "Arrange the following decision-making steps in correct order."
- *Team Mode.* Students use one device to submit their answer after five seconds of "team talk" to formulate a response.

Instead of creating a Kahoot activity from scratch, you can also search for and use already existing ones. A recent search for "health education" yielded nearly 20,000 possibilities on such topics as smoking, the endocrine system, and how climate change affects our health.

Other Options for Feedback and Student Involvement

Another excellent strategy to promote involvement in the learning process is the **WebQuest**, which is an assignment for students to search the web in order to answer questions (Strickland, 2005). For example, a high school class could be divided into groups and tasked with presenting on a stage of pregnancy and fetal development. Instead of giving the students total freedom to scour the web, the teacher indicates a group of websites from which students will gather information. For the first stage, conception, you might list five websites, such as that of the Office on Women's Health of the U.S. Department of Health and Human Services (www.womenshealth.gov). The project culminates with a Google Slides presentation developed collaboratively in the cloud.

Alternatively, instead of selecting every resource for the WebQuest, teachers may require students to find appropriate websites independently. This approach allows students to practice National Health Standards 3.12.1 ("evaluate the validity of health information, products, and services") and 3.12.5 ("access valid and reliable health products and services"). It is important for students to meet these performance indicators because distilling fact from fiction on the web is not easy.

When designing a WebQuest, you can promote higher-order thinking by prompting students to construct new understandings through a scaffolded learning process (March, 2000). As much as possible, use problems based in the real world to engage students and motivate them to participate. WebQuests typically contain the following five components but may have fewer or more, at your discretion:

1. *Introduction.* Build interest and provide background information and rationale.
2. *Task.* Describe what students must complete or produce.
3. *Process.* Provide clearly written steps that include resource websites that may be linked to questions.
4. *Evaluation.* This component most often takes the form of a rubric that sets expectations and provides an objective method for measuring student performance.
5. *Conclusion.* Summarize the experience and provide a mechanism for students to share their experience or provide feedback.

Another option for student involvement is the Nearpod website, where you can download free and fee-based lesson plans, including handouts, pictures, and presentation files. Lessons can be customized using interactive features such as polls, videos, assessments, virtual reality, and interactive objects (Delacruz, 2014). Nearpod lessons are streamed to all student devices in a classroom, and students work through a given lesson at their own pace, either individually or in small groups (figure 4.14). You can control the delivery of the lesson, monitor student progress individually or collectively, and interject questions. All students are required to participate actively and to collaborate at times in order to move through the lesson.

GoNoodle is the technological equivalent of a brain booster or brain break. It uses short, interactive activities and videos to get students moving, sometimes by means of an interactive whiteboard. Brain boosters help make learning fun, break up lessons, and refocus students after a brief bout of physical activity. GoNoodle activities can be done while students are either seated or standing beside their desks. The site is designed for K-5 learners and includes a large dose of silly and fun activities.

Book Creator moves project-based learning away from the usual suspects, such as reports, presentations, and videos. Instead, students create their own e-books by incorporating text, images, and even audio and video into one seamless online product. Available book options include interactive stories, safe routes to school, anti-bullying posters,

Figure 4.14   Students work in pairs on a Nearpod-based interactive assignment.

"Students respond to a Nearpod question" by Wesley Fryer is licensed under CC BY 2.0

body system reports, instruction manuals for various body systems, comic adventures in the immune system, and other fun formats. All created products can be shared online with teachers and parents. Many of the features of Book Creator are also available in Padlet but in a more collaborative format. For example, students can all make a collage or scrapbook of physical activities that they plan to do over summer break.

Health educators who play videos may require that students answer questions to promote attention. However, students who inadvertently miss a question may get out of sync with the video and distract others. This problem can be solved by using Edpuzzle, which allows you to easily add text questions and audio to a video, along with pauses for question-and-answer periods. You can overlay audio on an entire video or only on selected segments. You can also use Edpuzzle if a video's audio quality is poor, if segments are unclear, or if inappropriate language is present.

APPS

Who would have guessed, when Steve Jobs introduced the first iPhone in 2007 (YouTube, 2013), that people today would carry what amounts to a minicomputer in their pocket, capable of browsing the web, running programs, recording video, taking pictures, playing games, connecting with other people, and, of course, making phone calls. Smartphones have revolutionized the ways in which people live, and it is possible that someday they will entirely replace the personal computer. Even the display may become full-sized with the introduction of foldable screens.

At present, smartphones and tablets run on different **operating systems** than computers do. An operating system (OS) consists of the basic set of commands that allow a device to run programs, execute tasks, and control peripheral devices such as a keyboard or printer ("Operating system," n.d.). Most computers use either Windows or Mac OS, whereas smartphones and tablets rely primarily on Android or iOS. Most programs are designed to run on a specific operating system, and smartphones and tablets run miniprograms or applications, which are typically referred to simply as apps. Applications designed for Android devices do not work on an iOS (Apple) device, and vice versa. Apps designed for Android are typically downloaded from Google Play, whereas apps designed for iOS are downloaded from the Apple App Store.

Schools generally embraced tablets, such as the Apple iPad, from the beginning. Typically, they were purchased and controlled by the school district and offered distinct advantages over traditional computers. The introduction of smartphones has proven to be more complicated (Kowalski, 2016). Initially, many schools viewed them negatively due to nonacademic distractions such as gaming and social media. Today, however, due to the ubiquity of smartphones at the secondary level, as well as the educational advantages they offer, most schools permit students to carry them.

More than two billion apps are available for download from both Google Play and the Apple App Store (Clement, 2018). The challenge involves finding ones that enhance student learning, engagement, and motivation. There are three ways to find educational apps: search for an app by name or function using the search field; browse apps by category; and search the web at large for recommendations. Two relevant categories in Google Play are Education and Health and Fitness. Table 4.3 presents some apps relevant to health education that are available in Google Play (Google, 2018d); they are available free of charge and were selected based on their utility, popularity, and ratings.

VIDEO INTEGRATION

School-age students operate in a more video-saturated environment than did previous generations (Ryan & & Reid, 2015). The ubiquity of screens includes TVs, smartphones, tablets, and computers along with video delivery platforms such as YouTube, Hulu, Netflix, Amazon Video, and Instagram. Students are comfortable with videos and respond well when they are used in class (personal communication, PETE conference).

The use of video is well suited to a **flipped classroom**, in which students explore and learn from online resources first and then apply information learned in the classroom (Persky & McLaughlin, 2017). This approach allows students to progress through the material at the own rate using a familiar medium. The key to a successful flipped classroom is to guide students through the process. To do so, create a series of prompts or assignments that connect students to what they should be learning. For example, you might require that students watch a YouTube video on vaping, answer the following questions, and complete an online LMS quiz.

1. What is vaping?
2. What substances are in the vapor?
3. How is vaping regulated?
4. How does vaping compare with traditional cigarette smoking in terms of addiction and health consequences?

This relatively independent work allows students to continue learning at a higher level during the next class period. A more interactive option would be to form small groups, ask each group to decide on and share a consensus answer, and then ask students to vote on the best response via Poll Everywhere. Of course, videos can still be used in the traditional mode in which the entire class watches a video together. But you can make this process interactive by asking students to answer questions at their desks by tweeting responses or posting them to Poll Everywhere.

Table 4.3   Sample Apps for Health Education

Name	Rating	Use
Anatomy Learning—3D Online Anatomy Atlas	4.5	Provides 3-D models of multiple body systems. Includes ability to label, slice, and animate images; assemble puzzles; create transparencies; and quiz students.
Awesome Eats	4.3	Students sort fruit, vegetables, and whole grains to earn points, learn healthy eating habits, and shoo away crows while advancing through a series of levels.
Blood Pressure Evaluation	4.3	Evaluates the health of systolic and diastolic blood pressure using colors. Does not measure actual blood pressure; be careful of apps that claim to do so.
Bodimojo	N/A	Uses a virtual coach to teach about emotional intelligence and stress management. Includes mood tracking, daily intervention tips, and activities such mini-meditations and quizzes.
Brain Pop	N/A	Several related apps provide animated educational videos on a variety of topics, including health and fitness. Also provide activities, games, and quizzes in a friendly and playful format.
Carbon Footprint ACP	4.1	Teaches how daily activities such as waste, transport, electricity, food, and emissions contribute to one's carbon footprint and to climate change.
ClassDojo	4.4	Serves primarily as a classroom management app for tracking behaviors and providing encouragement. Can share positive news and photos with parents and send instant messages. Other tools include random group generator and background music.
Crazy Children's Dentist Simulation	4.2	Play the role of dentist. Make your own toothpaste and perform cleanings, cavity fillings, extractions, and placing of dental braces. Includes several minigames.
Eat This Much	4.3	Billed as a personal diet assistant, this app allows you to input user goals, food preferences, and budget and schedule information and to generate personalized meals. Features include calorie tracker, preset diet plans (e.g., paleo), allergy tracker, and nutrition targets.
First Aid—American Red Cross	4.5	Provides first aid advice and techniques for emergencies and in-class training. Includes videos, quizzes, and step-by-step instructions. Works without an internet connection.
Fooducate	4.4	Scans barcodes and identifies more than 250,000 items. Users can grade food items (A through D), list ingredients, track meals (calories, fat, protein, carb), get personalized meal suggestions, and identify unhealthy contents (e.g., added sugar, trans fat).
Gulp—Hydrate & Track Water	4.6	Tracks water consumption and updates progress toward hydration goal. Displays reminders and water consumption history throughout the day.
HitCheck: Sideline Concussion Test	4.2	Provides age-specific concussion tests for sideline administration. Includes baseline, post-injury, and recovery testing, along with performance reports.
Immune System—Wiki Kids	4.3	Presents information and videos about the immune system, including major functions, cells types, immunity, antibodies, and infections.
Medgic—AI for Skin	4.6	Use app to snap photo of skin and analyze moles; includes skin tips.

(continued)

Table 4.3   *(continued)*

Name	Rating	Use
Nights Out—BAC Calculator	5.0	Estimates blood alcohol content (BAC) based on number, size, type, and timing of drinks consumed while accounting for sex and physical size. Tracks drink history, projects BAC, and calculates time until sobriety returns.
OD_Bike_Safety	5.0	Provides instructions for helmet use, testimonials from riders whose safety practices saved them, rules of the road, and techniques for advanced tricks.
Pacifica—Stress & Anxiety	4.4	Manage stress through audio exercises, including deep breathing, muscle relaxation, visualization, and meditation. Also provides self-help audio paths, mood tracking (thought recording, journaling), community sharing, and tracking of anxiety triggers.
Period Tracker	4.5	Predicts upcoming menstruation based on three-month period history. Calculates ovulation and fertile days. Allows users to input notes about mood and symptom.
Pregnancy Tracker	4.6	This app is based on the What to Expect When You're Expecting book series. Allows students to track growth and development of a fictitious baby over several months. Sends weekly updates about baby's development, including videos. Also offers tips, articles, and parenting news.
Quizizz	4.3	Provides more than 10 million gamified quizzes on various subjects, including health. The app can read questions out loud and is integrated into Google Classroom.
Real Time CPR Guide	4.4	Uses audio and video to guide a person through the steps of performing CPR. Includes loud ticking sounds to guide speed of compressions.
Recycle Coach	4.5	Create a customized recycling calendar and look up individual items. Provides automated reminders, local disposal instructions, and news about community events (e.g., pickups for computers, hazardous materials).
Safety for Kid 1	4.7	Teaches prevention and procedures for addressing potential safety issues, such as stranger danger, getting lost, fire, and earthquake. Includes 12 animated games and an attractive interface.
Safety for Kid 2	4.6	Adds scenarios related to dangers in the home (kitchen, bathroom, garden) and common settings (street, school, cinema). Teaches how to recognize and respond appropriately to safety issues.
Seesaw	4.7	Students can create a portfolio, post video and pictures, overlay audio, display best work, and reflect on creations. Parents can view progress online and leave comments or encouragement. Includes many seesaw-ready activities.
Smoking Cost Calculator	N/A	Discover the cost of smoking on an annual basis by entering the number of cigarette packs consumed per day and the cost per pack.
Solve the Outbreak	4.5	Users analyze data to solve 12 outbreak scenarios. Response options include quarantine, interviews, and lab tests. Users learn about common diseases, transmission methods, disease prevention, and the immune system.

Name	Rating	Use
Standard Drinks Calculator	5.0	The app calculates the standard drink (i.e., containing 1.2 tablespoons of pure alcohol) for any beverage based on size and alcohol percentage, thus allowing users to easily compare drinks.
Super Hero Toilet Time Bathtub	4.2	Teaches when and how to properly wash hands. Includes hygiene games and tooth-brushing tips using a fun superhero motif.
Sworkit Kids	4.7	Uses videos to guide students through a customized workout based on goals, difficulty, time available, impact level, and targeted body regions. Combines interval training with randomized exercises and allows routines to be shared with others.
TeacherKit	4.2	Performs many routine administrative tasks of teaching, such as attendance taking and behavior logging. Allows you to import photos to help learn students' names.
WiFi Presentation Remote	4.4	Control a PowerPoint presentation using your smartphone. Includes options to escape; move forward and backward; and start from the first slide or current slide.

Regardless of how you use videos, select ones that balance education with entertainment. There is a tendency in teaching to eschew "edutainment," or the combination of education and entertainment. However, these two endeavors are not mutually exclusive, and it is beneficial, when possible, to choose activities that do both.

YouTube is a highly popular platform for finding and posting videos. For example, you might create YouTube channels to organize videos related to health education, thereby improving access for students. One danger with YouTube is that videos are sometimes removed, which is especially troubling when you find the *perfect* video for class but it is suddenly gone. To guard against this risk, download and save important videos to local or cloud storage. You can do so by using any of several apps, and the easiest option is simply to edit a YouTube URL by replacing the "www" with "ss" in the address bar. For example, the URL www.youtube.com/watch?v=HaLBXHgeIGo would be changed to https://ssyoutube.com/watch?v=HaLBXHgeIGo. Then, on the succeeding page, click the Download Video in Browser link. Using saved videos also ensures that a video is available when the Internet is not.

Flipgrid is a popular video platform that enables students to record and post 90-second videos of themselves in response to a teacher-provided prompt (Green & Green, 2018). For example, students could be given a homework assignment to view and analyze the sales strategies used in 10 TV commercials. The name *Flipgrid* is a mash-up of the word *flipped*, as in flipped classroom, and the word *grid*, in reference to the grid of videos produced when using the platform. To introduce Flipgrid, create a video prompt with a length up to three minutes; non-video prompt options include text, attachments, and images. You might choose to require that students reply to another person's video, as in a discussion. You might also consider using the moderation option, which allows you to preview the videos before they are posted to the grid. Begin the next class by playing selected videos and highlighting what students have learned. You can track usage by the number of views and the total hours of engagement. Flipgrid can also be used for end-of-course reflections, advice to next year's class, class debates, demonstrations of knowledge, exit tickets, and brainstorming (Green & Green, 2018).

Instead of using videos created by others, you may wish to create, edit, and save their own. For instance, you might use video for an open house to showcase your curriculum and what students will learn, to make a presentation to the school board about the need for more allotted instructional time, or to illustrate how the school's wellness team works together to promote health for the whole child. This approach can also work for students, who might, for example, create a video instead of writing a paper. Be sure to clearly state the requirements of the assignment, such as the necessary number of video clips or special features (e.g., inserted audio, still pictures, title screens, video effects, video transitions).

Video editors fall into one of two classifications: ones in which the app is installed on a local computer (e.g., Windows Movie Maker, VirtualDub, iMovie) and online editors (e.g., Vimeo, Kizoa). Many free options are available from Download.com. Finished products can be uploaded to a learning management system or posted on YouTube. All YouTube videos should be unlisted and accessible only via a provided link. For more on creating and editing digital videos, see chapter 11.

As teachers know, not every student "gets" something the first time it is taught. With this reality in mind, one advantage of using videos is that they allow students to progress through material at their own rate and to go over it again if necessary. Therefore, if you are teaching a particularly challenging topic, you might consider creating a screen recording, which is a video of a computer's desktop. For example, if students in past years have struggled when learning about the cardiovascular system, you might screen-record an entire presentation and share the video so that students can watch it as many times as needed to understand the material. Some school districts facilitate this approach by providing teachers with software such as Camtasia. Alternatively, you might try Screencast-O-Matic, which allows you to record selected areas of the screen, record via a webcam, or do both simultaneously. The latter option is excellent because it allows students to see the screen and an inset of the teacher simultaneously. An optional, low-cost subscription allows you to record unlimited videos and higher quality audio.

LEARNING MANAGEMENT SYSTEMS

Learning Management System (LMS) software creates an online learning environment for the administration, organization, tracking, and delivery of education-related activities (Walker, Lindner, Murphrey, & Dooley, 2016). Numerous LMSs are available, including Google Classroom, Schoology, Edmodo, Brightspace (D2L), Blackboard, and Moodle. Many users are familiar with the basic functions of an LMS, which include posting content, administering assessments, taking attendance, sending communications, posting surveys, and facilitating discussions.

The discussion format can be used to reserve topics and create a picking order. For example, student groups could be assigned to pick a fast food restaurant and create a healthy meal for lunch and dinner. You could create a discussion that opens at a specified time and enables students to identify their group members and pick a restaurant from a list of choices you provide. As a result, the process uses no class time, you have a clear record of what was selected, and the process is fair because it is first come, first served.

One of the best LMS features is the ability to design and administer assessments that are graded automatically—thus less paperwork! See figure 4.15. Assessments can be handled in a traditional manner by asking students to each use their own device to complete a quiz or test online (Walker et al., 2016). Another option is to ask students to complete an open-notes assessment before coming to class, thus using the flipped classroom approach discussed earlier. To reduce the likelihood that students will collaborate on an assessment, you can randomize the order of the questions and answer choices.

When an assessment is over, you can take advantage of the analytics offered by an LMS (Wang, 2017). For example, you can examine the questions with which students struggled the most. Which incorrect choice was selected mostly frequently? Was the low percentage of correct answers due to inadequate instruction by the teacher or failure to learn by the

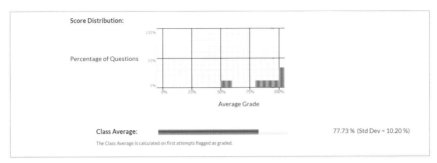

Figure 4.15 This LMS output visually directs teachers to questions on which students scored poorly and also indicates two questions with a negative discrimination index.

students? Available statistics include the standard deviation, or spread of the scores. A large standard deviation essentially means that some students "got" the information while others didn't. The LMS may also provide the discrimination index, which indicates the degree to which a question distinguishes between high and low performers on a scale of -100 percent to 100 percent. Higher values indicate more effective questions (D2L, n.d.).

WEBSITES AND TECHNOLOGY MANAGEMENT

Traditional, single-purpose websites still play a valuable role in the classroom. Here are some examples, along with ideas about how they might be used in health education:

1. *BlockPosters.com.* Allows users to create a poster or bulletin board display using a traditional printer and letter-size paper. When you upload an image, it is divided digitally into printable segments that can be stapled to a bulletin board in a manner that creates a seamless poster. The trick is that all white margins are obscured by another sheet.

2. *PDFcandy.com.* Converts various file types to PDF format; can also split, merge, rotate, protect, and unlock PDFs.

3. *ClassroomScreen.com.* Should be a favorite on any teacher's toolbar. Offers several functions, including a sound meter, QR scanner, drawing tool, work symbols, text box, timer, and clock.

4. *RandomLists.com.* Generates a random list from input data, such as words or email addresses. To generate random groups in class, paste student names into the form field, select a group size, and click rerun. To randomly select one student from class, reduce the group size to one.

5. *BouncyBalls.org.* Allows users to adjust the total amount of noise permitted, the sensitivity of the microphone, and the visual theme.

One drawback of educational technology resides in the potential for digital distraction. For example, the same device that allows students to complete a WebQuest in class might also allow them to refresh sport scores on the ESPN website, update their Facebook feed, or text their friends. The best solution for digital distraction is to create engaging, varied, interactive lessons and activities while carefully monitoring students' use of technology (Seemiller, 2017). Students also need to be able to function without digital technology, using only pen and paper and face-to-face communication; in other words, they need both technology-based skills and nontechnological skills.

To promote on-task behavior during technology-free periods, implement the following steps: Include the school's computer or Internet policy in the syllabus and make an announcement about the use of technology at the start of the term (Wood, n.d.). Remind students that multitasking has been proven to lower course grades (Uncapher et al., 2017). Treat all material taught in whatever format as potential exam material. Present information in chunks; avoid long paragraphs and use ordered lists whenever possible. As Levy (2014) said, "Come on, admit—you know you groan and/or navigate elsewhere when you open up a webpage and encounter a wall of unbroken text!" Continually move around to various locations in the classroom; don't forget to stand in the back where you can see all screens firsthand. Consider making some material available only in person for one time only; do not post it online.

If students will be using the Internet independently of you, remind them of the rules of the road, such as withholding personal information, using reputable sources, and reporting cyberbullies. Limit web searches for younger students to kid-friendly engines, such as Yahoo! Kids or KidRex (by Google).

Conclusion

Technology can be used in health education in many expansive ways. In fact, the range of possibilities can be intimidating, especially for a beginner. If that is the case for you, begin with a few applications that fall within your comfort zone, then gradually seek to develop your expertise. The goal of using technology should be to advance students' learning and mastery of content laid out by the relevant national standards; in this way, it is no different than traditional chalk and a blackboard. Avoid using technology for its own sake—use it only when it provides discernable benefit to students. Seek and use technological tools that make learning fun, interactive, and meaningful while also preparing students for the increasingly technology-immersive future into which we are heading.

Key Terms

Accessibility Checker—Feature in Microsoft Office that provides a list of potential accessibility issues for individuals with disabilities, as well as suggestions for addressing them.

app—Computer application, or program, especially one that runs on a mobile device's operating system (e.g., iOS, Android).

bell-ringer (do-now)—Activity that students begin working on immediately upon entering a classroom.

blog—Journal or column characterized by frequent text posts about a topic written in an informal style.

Design Ideas—Feature in Microsoft PowerPoint that provides layout and formatting customizations to improve the appeal of slides.

flipped classroom—Instructional approach in which students explore and learn from online resources first and then apply their learning in classroom activities.

gamification—Process of introducing gamelike elements into education in order to make learning fun and motivating.

interactive touch screen—Large tablet computer or all-in-one device that displays information without the need for a separate computer or projection system.

interactive whiteboard—Touch display created via a projector that allows users to interact with the content.

keyboard shortcut—Combination of keystrokes that provides quick access to a program function.

operating system—Set of basic commands that allow a device to run programs, execute tasks, and control peripheral devices (e.g., keyboard, printer).

responsive formatting—Formatting that adjusts and manifests well on a variety of devices, including both mobile and traditional operating systems.

spreadsheet—Document that stores and organizes data in a tabular format

template—Preformatted document or presentation file that specifies details such as colors, images, backgrounds, and fonts while also allowing for customization.

WebQuest—Assignment in which students use the web to search for and answer questions.

Whole School, Whole Community, Whole Child Model (WSCC)—Collaborative approach to student well-being that involves various aspects of school and community.

Review Questions

1. Identify the components of the Whole School, Whole Community, Whole Child model and provide at least one example of how technology can be used to improve student health for each component.
2. Describe ways to use displays to engage visually oriented learners.
3. Identify ways to customize Microsoft Office applications to enhance productivity for teachers and students.
4. Describe how productivity software can benefit students with disabilities and identify some common accessibility issues encountered by students.
5. Identify five strategies to create engaging PowerPoint presentations and avoid "death by PowerPoint."
6. What is G Suite for Education, and how can its applications be used to promote collaboration among students?
7. A blog is a relatively traditional yet flexible educational tool. What are some creative ways in which teachers can incorporate this technology?
8. Describe at least five possible educational uses for Poll Everywhere and similar software packages.
9. Describe three technologies that can be used either to incorporate or to produce educational videos.

Discussion Questions

1. What are some advantages and disadvantages of each student having a personal Chromebook or similar laptop in health education? How can teachers minimize the disadvantages?
2. Technology allows health educators to connect with individuals and resources around the globe, but ultimately students must make their own healthy choices. How can health be both global and local?
3. Health education focuses on helping students build health-enhancing skills—for example, being able to refuse an illicit drug or create a healthy meal. What are some technological tools that are well suited to building skills in an interactive, engaging fashion?
4. Is gamification a valuable use of class time, and is it equal to or better than traditional methodologies? Give reasons for your answers.

David Brewster/Star Tribune via Getty Images

5

Technology for Motivation

Chapter Objectives

When you have completed this chapter, you will be able to do the following:

1. Explain how technology can stimulate situational interest and motivation.
2. Discuss various types of motivational technology used in physical education, health education, and coaching.
3. Explain how motivational technology can assist in meeting objectives for lessons and training sessions.
4. Describe how motivational technology can be effectively incorporated into a lesson or training session.

Motivation is an inner state that initiates and guides a person's actions and behavior; thus it directly affects the intensity and direction of an individual's efforts. From the perspective of teaching and learning, motivation affects a learner's willingness to be taught and commitment to practice.

Motivated can be either intrinsic or extrinsic. **Intrinsic motivation** directs a learner's behavior through intangible internal rewards, such as having fun or feeling competent as a result of successfully completing an activity. **Extrinsic motivation**, on the other hand, drives behavior by means of external rewards, such as getting an A on a test, receiving praise from a coach or teacher, or winning a trophy. Because both types of motivation affect behavior and performance, we need to maintain a healthy balance between them in order to create a positive learning environment.

A learner's motivation and chances for success are affected by interaction between the individual's characteristics (e.g., goals, needs, interests), the task (i.e., what is being taught), and the environment (i.e., the setting in which the learning takes place). Many theories of motivation have been put forward—for instance, self-determination, self-regulation, cognitive evaluation, hierarchy of needs, attributional beliefs, expectancy–value, and goal setting—and a survey of these theories lies beyond the scope of this text. However, there is little doubt that increasing one's interest in a task enhances one's motivation to engage in it; indeed, interest in a task can motivate attention, persistence, and, eventually, the acquisition of knowledge or skill.

RichLegg/E+/Getty Images

Interactive video cycling can motivate users to exercise and provide activity-specific feedback.

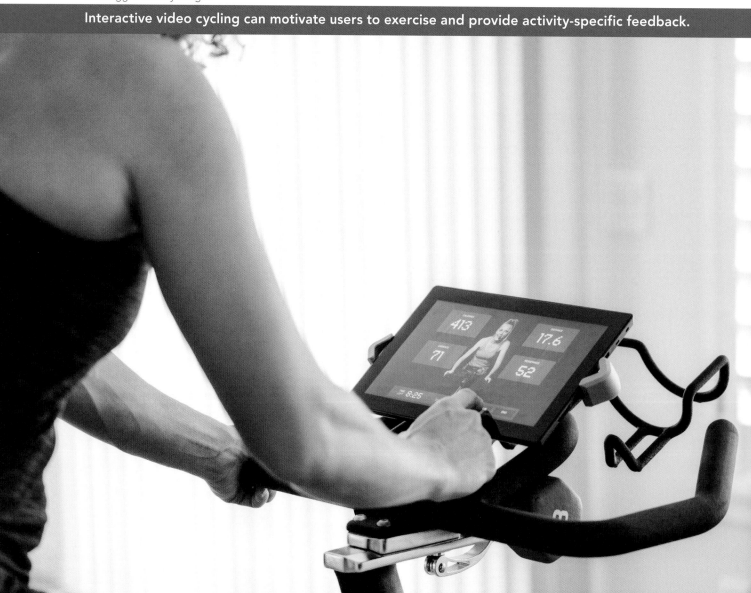

This chapter can help you facilitate intrinsic motivation among learners by using specific types of technology to trigger situational interest that enhances learning and hopefully evolves into personal interest. More specifically, the chapter addresses how to motivate students and athletes through music, video games, augmented and virtual reality, interactive video, and other activities that integrate technology. The chapter also provides teacher-tested pedagogical tips for implementing these types of technology.

MOTIVATING WITH TECHNOLOGY

Motivation and interest can be linked directly to certain styles of teaching and coaching; moreover, learning can be enhanced if the learner enjoys a specific approach (Larkin & Belson, 2005). For many learners, this connection may involve teaching styles that incorporate effective use of technology. One survey reported that 74 percent of the 503 sampled teachers (pre-kindergarten through 12th grade) felt that technology motivates students to learn (Mills, 2013). Another survey found that 62 percent of some 500 nationally representative P-12 school-based leaders (e.g., principals, assistant principals, deans) believed that digital technologies improve student engagement "quite a lot" or "a great deal." One reason is that technology frequently gives learners greater control over the educational process by facilitating interactive, hands-on learning.

The effectiveness of technology may also relate to the simple fact that most of today's learners are comfortable with it. In 2018, the Pew Research Center reported that 95 percent of U.S. teens aged 13 to 17 years have access to a smartphone, 88 percent have access to a laptop or desktop computer at home, and 45 percent claim that they are "almost constantly" online.

Interest Development

In both teaching and coaching, there are two types of interest: situational and personal. **Situational interest** consists of momentary interest spawned by environmental factors, such as how a task or skill is presented and whether and how a learning activity seems relevant to the learner's life. Situational interest is always motivating, but that motivation may or may not sustain over time. In contrast, **personal interest** derives from an individual's somewhat-underlying psychological disposition, which guides one's personal preference to participate repetitively in a specific activity or to reengage with a particular content area over time.

As shown in table 5.1, it has been proposed that interest develops in four phases (Hidi & Renninger, 2006). In this model, the first two phases involve the development of situational interest. During the first phase, an environmental factor initiates situational interest in an activity or subject; in the second phase, that situational interest is maintained. If the interest is sustained over a longer period, then a third phase brings the emergence of personal interest through questioning and activity participation, which can be facilitated by others (e.g., teacher, coach). In the fourth phase, this personal interest becomes well developed.

The personal interests of individual learners can vary widely, and they often lie beyond our control. As a result, you may find it easier, and perhaps more effective, to stimulate situational interest on the group level. However, as long as all content relates to the desired objectives, you can use differentiated approaches in an effort to meet the personal interests of all learners. Of course, it is easier to do so when working with smaller classes and teams.

For example, increased situational motivation in physical education has been linked to an increase in self-reported effort and persistence among students (Gao et al., 2012), increased intensity during class as measured by heart rate (Jaakkolo, et al., 2008), pursuit

Table 5.1   Four Phases of Interest Development: Using Technology to Trigger Interest in Rock Climbing

Type of interest	Situational interest (SI)		Personal interest (PI)	
Phase	Phase 1: triggered SI	Phase 2: maintained SI	Phase 3: emerging PI	Phase 4: well-developed PI
Phase traits	*Sparking of interest*	*Focus, persistence*	*Deepening of interest, meaningfulness*	*Increased value and knowledge*
Instructor behaviors	• Instructor incorporates a virtual rock climbing video game in physical education. • Instructor teachers basic climbing skills.	• Instructor permits learners to play the video game again during recess or study hall. • Instructor helps learners make connections between climbing and current skills, knowledge, and experiences.	• Instructor provides learners with information about a local climbing gym. • Instructor provides feedback and answers questions posed by learners.	• Instructor continues to encourage learners' climbing activities, provide feedback, and answers questions.
Corresponding learner responses	• Learners' interest in rock climbing is triggered by video gaming experience in physical education.	• Learners begin to develop positive feelings toward rock climbing and considers trying it in "real life." • Learners begin to value content knowledge related to rock climbing.	• Learners ask parents take them to the climbing gym. • Learners begin to demonstrate climbing skills and knowledge gained from prior experiences. • Learners experience positive feelings toward rock climbing.	• Learners independently reengage in climbing. • Learners actively seek feedback and continue to ask questions. • Learners demonstrate self-regulation and perseverance relating to climbing activities.

Adapted from Hidi & Renninger (2006).

of after-school physical activities (Chen et al. 2014), increased levels of moderate to vigorous physical activity as measured by pedometers and accelerometers (Ning et al., 2015), and increased motivation overall in physical education (Roure & Pasco, 2018).

Stimulating Situational Interest With Technology

The goal of many teachers and coaches is to stimulate situational interest in a topic with the hope that personal interest develops and is sustained over time, thus resulting in intrinsic motivation for that activity or topic. To help build situational interest, technology can be used to design enjoyable learning tasks, which may motivate long-term personal interest. Various forms of technology can be used by practitioners to facilitate both intrinsic and extrinsic motivation.

For instance, research has shown that situational interest and student motivation can be stimulated in physical education by using classroom-based digital games (Rodríguez-Aflecht et al., 2018), mobile and Internet communication technology (Rau et al., 2008), and digital feedback—which also increases exercise levels (Nation-Grainger, 2017). In coaching environments, particularly in youth sport, motivation related to content (in this case, sport-specific activities) is likely higher than it is in school-based education, if the athlete chooses to be there and if instruction incorporates the types of fun activities touted in coaching manuals (Martens, 2012; Society of Health and Physical Educators, 2005). Thus, integrating activities that are purpose based and laden with technology can help coaches stimulate situational interest and build athletes' motivation.

MOTIVATING WITH MUSIC

As discussed in chapter 2, music can be used to aid classroom management by cueing students to start, stop, or transition to a new activity. It can also be used to create a motivating environment. If you have ever been pumped up by a song blaring on the loudspeakers as you started your warm-up exercises for an early morning sport practice, or energized by a favorite song while exercising on a cardio machine in a fitness center, then you understand the motivating power of music. Specifically, what you have experienced was an increase in arousal and a type of "psyching up" effect. Research has shown that music can increase motivation and physical activity rates in physical education and sport at health management centers (Brewer et al., 2016; Garbana et al., 2015; Karageorghis et al., 2013; Lee et al., 2017). In part, music can be used as a distraction to desensitize awareness of the intensity of physical activity as the listener gets "lost" in the music.

Today, many physical educators and coaches who work outside use a portable, wireless speaker that is battery operated, water resistant, and equipped with **Bluetooth** technology (see figure 5.1). This setup allows them to control and play music from a smartphone, often streaming it via a music service app (e.g., Amazon Music, Apple Music, Google Play Music, Pandora, Spotify). For practitioners without Wi-Fi access or unlimited wireless data, a good option may be an MP3 player (e.g., Apple iPod). Such devices compress digital sound files (e.g., songs), thus permitting very large storage capacities (i.e., 1,000+ songs). Almost all newer music playing devices can be either hardwired to speakers with an audio cable or controlled wirelessly. Health teachers might complement in-class activities with

Seth Jenny

Figure 5.1 A youth coach uses a portable, battery-operated, wireless speaker on wheels with a luggage-style handle to motivate students in an afterschool fitness program. The music is played via Bluetooth from his smartphone. This speaker can also be integrated with a microphone for making announcements or giving instructions to the group.

music via a computer or MP3 player with speakers and various free music websites (e.g., YouTube Music). Figure 5.2 provides teaching tips for integrating music into instruction, as well as suggestions related to music equipment and song selection.

MOTIVATING WITH VIDEO GAMES

To say that video gaming is very popular would be a massive understatement. United States consumer spending on video gaming in 2018 exceeded $43 billion in 2018 (Entertainment Software Association, 2019). Moreover, 90 percent of U.S. teens aged 13 to 17 years (97 percent of boys and 83 percent of girls) play video games of some kind, whether on smartphones, computers, or consoles (e.g., PlayStation, Xbox), and 84 percent (92 percent of boys and 75 percent of girls) have access to a video gaming console at home (Pew Research Center, 2018). In addition, a survey of more than 4,000 U.S. households found that 60 percent of Americans play video games daily, 64 percent of American households own a device used for playing video games, 45 percent of gamers are female, and the average age of gamers is 34 years old (Entertainment Software Association, 2018).

Video games are also being used more and more in both the classroom and the gym as a way to stimulate interest and convey instructional content in an enjoyable manner (Jenny, Schary et al., 2017). The games are commonly played with computers, smartphones, mobile devices (e.g., iPad, tablet PC), and off-the-shelf gaming consoles (e.g., Xbox, PlayStation). **Traditional video games** are sedentary in that they often involve seated game play while manipulating a computer keyboard and mouse (PC gaming) or handheld game controller (console gaming). These games primarily involve fine motor movements of the arms, hands, and fingers.

In a study involving 212 fifth-grade students, a classroom-based math video game successfully triggered and maintained situational interest as well as strengthened individual math interest in the majority of the participants (Rodríguez-Aflecht et al., 2018). However, the researchers concluded that practitioners should not use video games only for motivation; rather, they should use games that also help players attain clear and validated learning objectives. In this vein, sport video games may help physical educators and coaches fulfill cognitive learning objectives.

Sedentary Sport Video Games

Sport video games (SVGs) simulate sport action and are primarily sedentary, as players use handheld controllers to manipulate on-screen characters. Many SVGs not only involve playing the sport but also incorporate strategies and tactics. Popular examples include FIFA Soccer (EA Sports), Madden NFL (EA Sports), NBA 2K (2K Sports), MLB The Show (Sony Interactive Entertainment), UFC (EA Sports), and NHL (EA Canada). Although more research is needed, some empirical studies have found that SVGs can increase development in the cognitive and affective learning domains.

For example, in a sample of international college students who were unfamiliar with American football, playing two 30-minute sessions of Madden NFL per week for four weeks increased overall American football knowledge as compared with a control group, as well as motivated intention to watch or play real-world American football (Jenny & Schary, 2014). Similarly, in a sample of American college students who were unfamiliar with cricket, playing two one-hour sessions of Don Bradman Cricket (Big Ant Studios) per week for two weeks significantly increased overall cricket knowledge as compared with a control group, as well as motivated intention to watch or play real-world cricket (Jenny, Chung et. al., 2017). In addition to enabling simulated sport game play, both of these SVGs (and many others) incorporate a simulated live television broadcast with in-game broadcasters providing auditory commentary on game action. Thus, SVGs may be

Figure 5.2   Music: teaching tips, equipment, and selection.

MUSIC TEACHING TIPS

- Consider how you might use changes in volume or starting and stopping of the music, respectively, as stop and go signals to help you with classroom and behavior management (see chapter 2); for instance, cuing to rotate to a new station or addressing overall class misbehavior might result in temporary pauses of the music.
- Be wary of permitting students or athletes to use headphones or earbuds during activity; doing so can hinder their ability to listen to instructions and in some situations may be unsafe.
- Music can be used to aid time management during circuit training and station activities; for example, insert silence between songs to signal when it is time to rotate or change exercises.
- Ensure that your music system is protected (i.e., caged) or placed in a safe location so that it does not get hit by people or sport equipment.
- Music played in a consistent location can be used as a sound beacon to aid students with visual impairment (see chapter 7).

MUSIC EQUIPMENT

- Wireless speaker (smartphone- or MP3-compatible) with features such as the following:
  - 50- to 100-watt amplifier
  - AM/FM radio
  - Wheels and carrying handle similar to those for carry-on luggage (or accompanying lockable audio-visual equipment cart with wheels)
  - Battery-powered operation for easy transport inside and outside (typically with a 75-hour rechargeable battery)
  - Bluetooth compatibility (permitting short-range wireless connection with smartphones and other electronic devices) to stream music wirelessly
  - Inputs for a microphone or other audio source
  - Water resistance
  - Microphone options (e.g., wired, wireless, microphone headset)
  - USB port for mobile device charging
  - Cost of about $100 to $250
- Mobile device (e.g., smartphone, iPad) with audio app or MP3 player
- CD player and discs (with possible disadvantages of having to change discs and replace scratched discs)
- For battery-operated equipment, sufficient charge to last an entire school day

(continued)

Figure 5.2 *(continued)*

MUSIC SELECTION

- Screen all songs to ensure that they are appropriate for your learners' ages and learning environment; for instance, check for inappropriate language or sexually explicit lyrics.
- KIDZ BOP offers compilation albums of contemporary popular songs performed by children with inappropriate lyrics screened out; this music is most appropriate for elementary and middle school students
- The music genre should match the preferred majority of the class or team—not of the teacher or coach!
- Song tempo (beats per minute) should match the desired intensity of activity.
- Consider the possible legal issues related to music copyright (see chapter 15).
- Specific songs can be used to cue specific physical activities or dances, such as the Cha Cha Slide and Watch Me (Whip/Nae Nae); see the web resource.
- Song content can also be related to specific activities—for example, using Van Halen's or Kris Kross' "Jump" during a jumping unit or Jack Johnson's "The Sharing Song" during a cooperative games unit.
- Consider songs relevant to upcoming holidays, particularly for elementary students—for instance, "Jingle Bell Rock" at Christmas or "Mexican Hat Dance" near Cinco de Mayo.

Adapted from Hams and Ryan (2012).

used as a tool for increasing learners' sport knowledge and stimulating motivation to engage in real-world physical activity.

Motion-Based Video Games

Motion-based video games (MBVGs) use sensors and software so that the player physically performs both fine and gross motor movements in order to play the game as the on-screen character (i.e., avatar) mimics the player's actions. Thus MBVGs combine video gaming and exercise and are also known as exergames, active video games, or interactive video games. These games employ various types of motion-sensing technology, including cameras (e.g., Xbox Kinect), handheld motion controllers (e.g., PlayStation Move), balance boards (e.g., Wii Fit), and motion-detecting dance platforms (e.g., Dance Dance Revolution), and some systems integrate multiple motion-detection technologies. MBVGs have been found to benefit children's motivation and physical activity levels as compared with sedentary video games in an educational context (Sun & Gao, 2016).

For instance, interactive video game cycling has been shown to result in significantly greater energy expenditure, maximum oxygen uptake reserve, and enjoyment as compared with traditional stationary cycling (Monedero et al., 2015). Typically, interactive video game cycling allows the user to compete against computer-generated riders while sitting on a bike and pedaling to move an on-screen bike avatar on the gaming display located in front of the rider. In addition, left and right movements of the handlebars correspond to in-game movements, and music and mechanical sounds are coupled with visual and

COMPETITIVE VIDEO GAMING: ESPORTS

Like it or not, competitive video gaming, also known as esports or electronic sports, is growing rapidly on a global scale. Esports are most often played via a computer, mouse, and keyboard and streamed online, but it can also be played via a gaming console and handheld controller. The global esports market generated $1.5 billion in 2017 and is expected to grow 26 percent by 2020 (Superdata, 2017). Moreover, major sporting venues such as Madison Square Garden in New York and the Staples Center in Los Angeles have hosted massive esports events attracting some 20,000 spectators, and esports-specific arenas continue to be built in the U.S. and around the world (Jenny et al., 2018). Just to give you an idea of how popular esports have become, League of Legends had 101 million monthly active players in 2017 and racked up more than 1.6 billion hours watched by spectators; meanwhile, Dota 2's professional tournament prize purse reached $37.1 million (Superdata, 2017).

In addition, esports have garnered the attention of high school and collegiate athletic departments (Keiper et al., 2017). For example, in 2018, esports were added to the New Mexico Activities Association's (NMAA) high school calendar, and its season now concludes with a state tournament (Yodice, 2018). At the collegiate level, some 159 colleges and universities are members of the National Association of Collegiate Esports (2019). All of these member intuitions recognize esports as a varsity sport; in addition, many offer esports scholarships, and some of the teams are housed in the institution's athletic department. Moreover, sport science research into esports is in its infancy, but past video gaming researchers have noted that playing at the elite level requires considerable fine motor skills (e.g., eye–hand coordination, reaction time, accuracy), communication and teamwork (for team esports), visual and spatial processing, strategic thinking, and intentional decision making (Jenny, Manning et al., 2017; Lipovaya et al., 2018).

However, the purpose of mentioning esports in this chapter is not to weigh in on whether it constitutes a sport. Other publications provide an overview of that debate (Baltezarević & Baltezarević, 2018; Jenny, Manning et al., 2017). In any case, practitioners must be cognizant of the massive surge in popularity of esports and know that more and more people view competitive video gaming as a sport in itself. Although popular esports primarily involve sedentary gaming, some video gaming systems use large amounts of gross motor movement, thereby increasing the participants' physical activity levels.

audio feedback as part of the gaming experience. However, due to the cost and equipment required, this technology may fit best as an option in a fitness or recreation club or an exergaming lab.

Sheehan and Katz (2010) have proposed that MBVGs and other forms of interactive video technology may satisfy six Cs that are essential for intrinsically motivating physical activity in children (see table 5.2). These characteristics include control, challenge, curiosity, creativity, constant feedback, and competition.

Preservice physical education teachers tend to perceive MBVGs as fun and believe that they can increase student motivation during class (Jenny, Hushman, et al., 2013). These perceptions are supported by research showing that MBVGs can motivate previously unmotivated students in physical education to display a positive attitude and demon-

Table 5.2   Six Cs of Motivating With MBVGs and Interactive Video Technology

Characteristic	Means of motivation
Control	Providing learners with individualized attention
Challenge	Allowing learners to select an appropriate difficulty level
Curiosity	Stimulating interest through varying games and game levels
Creativity	Allowing learners to express themselves in how they play the game
Constant Feedback	Providing continuous, concurrent, augmented feedback via the video display
Competition	Providing competition against either the game or other players

Notes: Adapted from Sheehan and Katz (2010).

strate willingness to collaborate with classmates (Finco et al., 2015). However, evidence also exists that participating in a sport (e.g., rock climbing) in the real world motivates future activity more than playing the MBVG version of the sport (e.g., Kinect Sports Rivals Rock Climbing) (Jenny & Schary, 2015). Still, at least in the short-term, MBVGs appear to increase enjoyment and motivation (i.e., situational interest) more than traditional physical education activities do for some students (Moholdt et al., 2017).

Teaching Motor Skills With MBVGs

For physical educators and sport coaches, one of the most important questions about MBVGs is whether they help teach sport-specific motor skills. In other words, do they require the same correctly executed motor movements that are needed in the authentic or real-world sport or activity? For example, does a track-and-field MBVG that involves

Mordolff/E+/Getty Images

Virtual reality boxing video game.

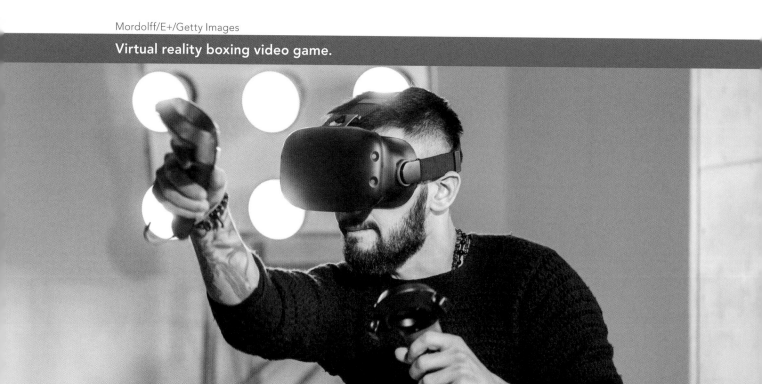

MBVGs and Energy Expenditure

Much of the early research on MBVGs focused on energy expenditure in clinical settings. As compared with traditional sedentary video games, MBVGs can contribute significantly to overall moderate levels of daily physical activity (Kakinami et al., 2015; Sween et al., 2014). In addition, a systematic review and meta-analysis concluded that MBVGs produce a small effect of improving body mass index (BMI) in overweight or obese children (Ameryoun et al., 2018). Of course, the amount of energy expended will vary depending on the particular MBVG being played; for example, a game that requires only arm movements (e.g., Kinect Sports Rivals Target Shooting) requires less energy than does a fighting game (e.g., Fighter Within) that requires kicking and punching. Unsurprisingly, studies that compare the same physical activity in the real world with activity in an MBVG environment have found that the real-world version expends more energy (Garn et al., 2012; Warburton et al., 2007). However, evidence exists that time spent playing MBVGs outside of school does not replace sedentary activities or other forms of physical activity (Simons et al., 2015). Overall, then, MBVGs appear to help users expend more energy than they do in sedentary gaming or other forms of sedentary screen time (e.g., watching television), but authentic or real-world versions of sport typically expend more energy than MBVG versions.

hurdling require the user to use proper hurdling technique, with a lead leg and a trail leg, or does it simply require the user to execute a standard two-footed jump straight up and down?

One study found that although MBVGs are perceived by preservice physical education teachers as a fun way to increase student physical activity and heart rate, they do not always mimic the fundamental motor movements used in real-world sport (Jenny, Hushman et al., 2013). For example, one experimental study found that the Kinect Sports Rivals Rock Climbing used similar arm movements to authentic wall or rock climbing but that the leg movements (arguably the most important part of climbing) were totally different (Jenny & Schary, 2016). Another study compared NCAA Division I tennis players performance of the forehand, backhand, and serve in a MBVG versus in an authentic environment (Jenny, Noble et al., 2017) and found that all three strokes were performed significantly differently in the MBVG. More broadly, a literature review on the effectiveness of teaching motor skills with MBVGs concluded that

> MBVGs may be beneficial with novices in teaching basic sport concepts or with individuals with special needs who might otherwise not be able to participate in the full authentic version of the sport. However, empirical evidence is lacking which supports the effective use of MBVGs in accurately teaching authentic sport-specific motor skills. (Jenny, Schary et al., 2017)

Therefore, based on current technology, the majority of MBVGs should be used to encourage physical activity, and using them to teach motor skills should be performed only with caution. Even so, activity-specific cognitive and affective learning (e.g., sport rules, strategy, terminology, enjoyment, cooperation) may be accomplished through the use of MBVGs. See figure 5.3 for a recommended gym setup involving multiple MBVG systems.

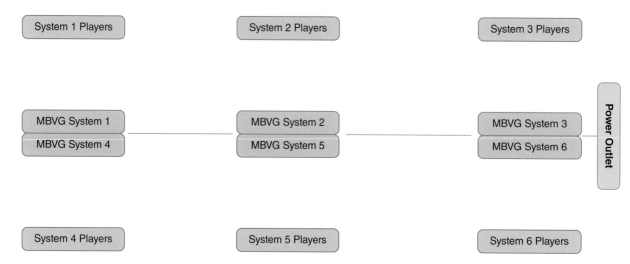

Figure 5.3 Sample gym setup with multiple MBVG systems.

Note: This setup would require three carts with two MBVG consoles (e.g., Xbox Kinect) and two back-to-back flatscreen televisions strapped down on each cart. The televisions and MBVG consoles are positioned back-to-back because people standing behind the game players may accidentally be picked up by the motion-sensing cameras. The extension cord should be covered with tape or a mat so that students do not trip on it. Many MBVGs permit as many as four players to participate simultaneously.

Dance Dance Revolution

We would be remiss if we did not mention one of the oldest MBVGs, which is still popular: Dance Dance Revolution (DDR). Participants stand on a motion-sensing platform marked by four colored arrows in a cross formation. Users are judged on the timing and accuracy with which they tap with their feet on the prescribed arrows in a rhythmic fashion using auditory musical and visual on-screen cues. Performing well makes available new songs and greater difficulty levels. DDR first gained popularity in the arcade but now thrives in many physical education classrooms in the form of Dance Dance Revolution Classroom Edition, which permits up to 48 students to play at the same time through wireless dance mats that interface with the gaming console. All students' scores are tracked on-screen. A less expensive version of the game uses plastic mats with the DDR arrows printed on them and only one authentic DDR mat interfaced with the game. Students follow along on the fake mats, but the score is tracked only for the student on the authentic mat. This approach appears to work well at the elementary level. Many mainstream MBVG systems now include knockoff games such as Dance Central and Just Dance. Figure 5.4 provides more teaching tips for integrating motion-based video games into your teaching and coaching.

Video Games in Health Promotion and Health Education

Video games have also been used in health and wellness promotion and education. For example, they have been used to motivate preteens to get vaccinated for the human papillomavirus (HPV; Cates et al., 2018), to motivate children to make positive changes

Figure 5.4   Teaching tips and recommendations for motion-based video games (MBVGs).

MBVG TEACHING TIPS

- Consider the objective of the lesson. Why are you integrating video games into the lesson? What objective(s) do you hope that gaming will help your students attain? Is video gaming the best pedagogical tool for the purpose?
- Be aware of ratings from the Entertainment Software Rating Board (ESRB); most educational video games are rated E (meaning suitable for everyone).
- Some video games are not appropriate for all settings (e.g., fighting games, dance games with suggestive moves or inappropriate lyrics).
- Particularly in a gym with WiFi deadspots, console gaming is recommended over Wi-Fi gaming to alleviate potential Internet issues.
- The cost of setup and upkeep for gaming equipment always poses a concern; consider renting equipment for a short unit or look for funding sources (see chapter 16 for ideas).
- Another major concern with video gaming is that of time on task, given that gaming equipment (e.g., displays, consoles, controllers) is often limited. For this reason, many practitioners offer gaming as a stand-alone station.
- Ensure that your gaming system is updated before class begins; otherwise, you could end up using class time to download any required game updates (or choose the "play offline" option if it is available).
- Permit first-time players to learn how to play by viewing or playing the game tutorial.
- Consider creating a tutorial handout with instructions such as, "On offense, button A does (such and such); on defense, button A does (such and such)."
- Students who are new to gaming or to the specific gaming system being used may need more time to figure out where controller buttons are located compared to learning how to play the game itself—this increases cognitive load and difficulty in learning the game.
- Be aware that negative transfer may occur if your gaming system and the corresponding controller differ from what a student is used to using. For instance, the buttons on a PlayStation controller are not the same as those on an Xbox controller.
- Know that it is often important to hear the game's audio in order to receive in-game feedback. As a result, wireless headsets may be appropriate for gaming in a gym or large classroom where echoes are common and multiple activities are occurring.
- Ensure that all students are engaged and active—not passively watching video game play for long durations.
- If appropriate, create a cognitive worksheet for students to complete when they are not actively playing the game. To complete the sheet, they might track key statistics, analyze game strategy, or assess the accuracy of the sport biomechanics displayed in the game.
- Permit students to raise the difficulty level of the game in order to stay sufficiently challenged and engaged.

(continued)

Figure 5.4 *(continued)*

MBVG RECOMMENDATIONS

- Consider also using heart rate monitors or pedometers to track student effort and physical activity while playing MBVGs.
- MBVGs might be used as incentives or rewards for excellent student behavior.
- Consider using a whole-class MBVG (e.g., Dance Dance Revolution Classroom Edition).
- Set up a MBVG station during circuit training (i.e., as a station activity).
- Realize that the area needed to play MBVGs may be larger than you think.
- Consider renting MBVG equipment (e.g., from C'motion) for an MBVG unit.
- Consider hiring a company (e.g., Exergame Fitness) to create an exergaming lab, perhaps in an unused classroom or on a racquetball court.
- Some motion-sensing cameras will pick up movement from any nonplayers located behind the MBVG players. Consider traffic patterns behind the MBVG system and use a wall or partition if needed.
- MBVGs should be used to increase students' physical activity and to *supplement a physical education program—not replace it!*

in diet and physical activity (Baranowski et al., 2010), and to train health care professionals (Wang et al., 2016). In a review of game use to aid health, Baranowski and colleagues (2016) noted that early results are promising, additional research is needed, and key stakeholders should be involved in both game design and the process of motivating behavior change in order to mitigate potential adverse effects (e.g., gaming addiction, gaming-related health problems or injury, breach of privacy, online harassment). If this area of research interests you, we encourage you to peruse *Games for Health Journal*, which details many studies on the use of sedentary video games and MBVGs to improve health outcomes across varying populations.

MBVGs in Rehabilitation and Health Care Settings

MBVGs have been used in rehabilitation for various purposes, such as performing balance activities and aiding at-home exercise adherence, particularly with elderly populations and those who are recuperating from a fall or who have a disease or injury that affects balance. For example, when a player stands on the Nintendo Wii Balance Board, the gaming system interprets weight shifts and movements of the player's feet and provides visual feedback on a display screen (de Carvalho et al., 2018). Research has found that MBVGs can also help improve dynamic postural control, reduce pain sensitivity, and increase mobility in diverse populations, such as individuals with spinal cord injury, elderly females who have fallen, healthy older adults, and long-term care residents (Aguillar et al., 2018; Carey et al., 2017; Manlapaz et al., 2017; Rosly et al., 2017; Taylor et al., 2018). Collectively these studies show

Students playing motion-based video games via an Xbox Kinect with motion-sensing camera.

Courtesy of Zan Gao.

promise that MBVGs may improve health outcomes and can motivate clients in adhering to a self-facilitated at-home exercise protocol.

Gaming Disorder

Particularly for health educators, it would be irresponsible not to mention a mental health condition that has been newly recognized by the World Health Organization (2018)—namely, **gaming disorder**, which is defined as follows:

> a pattern of gaming behavior ("digital-gaming" or "video-gaming") characterized by impaired control over gaming, increasing priority given to gaming over other activities to the extent that gaming takes precedence over other interests and daily activities, and continuation or escalation of gaming despite the occurrence of negative consequences. (para. 1)

Diagnosis typically requires gaming behavior that is evident for at least 12 months and severely impairs one or more areas of typical functioning (e.g., personal, social, educational, occupational). Practitioners must stay abreast of potential negative effects of integrating video gaming into instruction.

97

MOTIVATING WITH AUGMENTED REALITY AND VIRTUAL REALITY

Augmented reality (AR) technology overlays digital elements onto the physical environment, often by using the camera on a mobile device (e.g., iPad, smartphone), thus creating a new blended reality on the digital display. A popular example is the app Snapchat, which superimposes comical AR objects (e.g., funny glasses, crazy hair styles) within the camera function so that it looks as if those items were actually present when a photo was taken. Studies have reported that AR technology can motivate physical activity while facilitating academic learning in physical education (Hsiao, 2013). It can also provide immediate, concurrent feedback during physical activities, thereby assisting in instruction—for example, medical procedure training (Herron, 2016).

Pokémon Go is a massively popular AR game and MBVG for mobile devices that was released in July 2016. It accumulated 20 million active users in the United States within one month of release, and 500 million downloads of the game worldwide within four months (Smith, 2016). Health and physical educators have been attracted to it because it incorporates exercise. Players use AR and **Global Positioning System (GPS)** technology as they travel physically (e.g., walk, bike, run) along streets in the real world to reach specific destinations (e.g., landmarks, buildings) in order to collect AR treasures (i.e., Pokémon) placed on a virtual map—all while avoiding in-game dangers (e.g., traps). The player's movements are mimicked by an on-screen character. The purpose of the game is to collect as many Pokémon as possible while accumulating experience points through other features of the game. Although the popularity of Pokémon Go has dropped significantly, studies have reported that it motivates short-term increases in physical activity (Althoff et al., 2016; Ni et al., 2019) and can be integrated successfully into recreation programs (Jenny & Thompson, 2016).

High amounts of physical activity are also encouraged by another example of an AR game app, which is called Monsuta Fitness (The PE Geek Apps, 2017). You can use the app to superimpose AR monsters on a real-world map (e.g., around your practice area, your whole school, or even your town as a whole). Your students or athletes travel physically to find a monster and then "battle" it by physically performing exercises (e.g., burpees, push-ups) specific to each monster in order to earn points. You can determine the number of sets and reps for each exercise.

Unlike AR, **virtual reality (VR)** completely shuts out the physical world and provides the user with a totally immersive digital experience, often through the use of VR goggles. As participants experience this virtual world, they can turn 360 degrees and move around. Some VR systems also incorporate handheld implements (e.g., PlayStation Move controller). In one large-scale example, fans at the 2018 Major League Baseball All-Star Game participated in a VR home run derby using the Sony PlayStation VR system while swinging actual baseball bats during VR game play (Kostka, 2018).

Many media reports also describe professional and collegiate football teams using VR to help players learn—in particular, to help quarterbacks learn to read defensive formations and to permit injured athletes to train mentally (Cortez, 2018; Cronin, 2018). One case study of American football quarterbacks ranging from seventh grade to collegiate juniors demonstrated a 30 percent improvement after three days of VR training in the ability to make presnap defensive reads by correctly identifying which receiver to throw the ball to on passing plays (Huang et al., 2015). As technology continues to evolve for AR and VR apps that incorporate real-time, interactive sensory activities, new modalities for teaching and learning will develop across many domains. Though it may sound corny, the possibilities will be limited only by the practitioner's imagination.

MOTIVATING WITH INTERACTIVE VIDEO PROJECTION

Some creative physical educators have begun motivating their students during lessons by incorporating **interactive video projection (IVP)** in the gym. IVP involves using a digital projector to display images on a wall or other surface as students perform skills or activities in response to those images. Advanced interactive video technology can even detect touches to the display or screen and then elicit further responses from the user.

For example, IVP is often integrated into lower elementary lessons on throwing and aiming. In these activities, digital images are displayed on a wall, often by means of PowerPoint animations, while students try to hit projected moving objects with an item (e.g., ball). Physical educators have also used the old Nintendo Entertainment System (NES) video game Duck Hunt for this purpose as students throw yarn balls at the ducks flying across the display (Dayton, 2013). Some practitioners have also integrated IVP into math lessons by displaying a multiple-choice question along with possible answers and asking students to throw a ball to hit the correct answer (Gilchrist, 2018). This type of cross-curricular activity can be used with multiple age groups and can address virtually any subject area.

Another example of IVP involves a rock-wall obstacle course (PE Central Videos, 2018), in which shapes such as a cross are projected on an indoor climbing wall and students climb by using only the handholds and footholds found within the displayed images. Shapes of varying difficulty can easily be swapped out between students to provide differentiated instruction. See figure 5.5 for more teaching tips related to stationary and interactive video projection.

MOTIVATING WITH GAMIFICATION AND TECHNOLOGY

Although some researchers apply the term *gamification* only to the integration of video games into instruction, others give it a much broader definition. In this text, we define **gamification** as the integration of common game-playing elements (e.g., rules, competition, point scoring if appropriate) into traditional nongame contexts with the aim of increasing student or athlete engagement and motivation. For instance, you have experienced gamification if you have ever been motivated by playing McDonald's Monopoly or gained reward points through a credit card or airline company. In coaching and health and physical education settings, many gamified activities integrate technology; a few examples are provided in figures 5.6 and 5.7.

One option that integrates gamification and AR is the smart ball product line from Dribble Up. These products can be used by athletes to practice at home while being monitored by a coach; they can also be used to increase skill and build situational interest at an activity station in a physical education class. When paired with a mobile device's video camera and a television or other projection device, the user can dribble a Smart Soccer Ball between AR-generated virtual cones or dribble a Smart Basketball at designated AR target heights displayed. Meanwhile, the ball wirelessly sends assessment data, such as the number of dribbles or juggles, crossover speed, ball control accuracy, and pattern consistency.

In this approach, the user is motivated by concurrent visual and verbal feedback while performing, and drills are included for various skill levels. The Smart Medicine Ball, which weighs either 6 or 10 pounds (2.7 or 4.5 kg), includes a virtual trainer with AR targets

Figure 5.5   Teaching tips for stationary and interactive video projection.

- Remember the lesson objective(s): Is the video projection activity meant to achieve physical activity (expend energy) or physical education (teach skills)?
- Consider integrating teacher, peer, or self-assessments into the activity so that goal achievement is assessed (e.g., cooperation, skillful throwing).
- Remember that projected images will be seen more easily if the activity area is darker.
- Consider using a digital video projector with a high lumen count so that the images are not too light or unclear.
- Extremely large images or difficult-to-remove shadows may require projection overlap through multiple projectors to make the image brighter.
- Consider student traffic patterns so that individuals do not move in front of the projection and that implements do not hit or damage the projector.
- If an item is being thrown off the wall, consider the bounce. A yarn ball may work better than a bouncier ball (e.g., tennis ball) by minimizing both the risk of players being hit and the time required to chase after balls.
- If you mount your digital projector on a gym ceiling or wall, considering encasing it in a metal security cage to protect it from theft and flying projectiles.
- Here are some ideas for things you may want to display with stationary projection:

  - Class procedures or rules
  - Lesson schedules, directions, and safety reminders
  - Skill demonstrations (via videos or GIFs)
  - Activity layout (e.g., stations, traffic patterns)
  - Skill or assessment cues

Some ideas adapted from Mast et al. (2015) and Support Real Teachers (2018).

and gives the user instructions across varying drills. Gamification is employed across all Smart Ball apps, and users can compare statistics against others' by means of a leaderboard.

TECHNOLOGY-INTEGRATED ACTIVITIES THAT MOTIVATE MOVEMENT IN THE CLASSROOM

In addition to providing a high-quality health and physical education program, all classroom teachers should consider integrating short physical activity breaks (30 seconds to five minutes) into lessons in order to motivate students, increase attention, stimulate learning, and increase overall physical activity levels. Cognitive functioning can be improved by physical fitness, physical activity programs, and even single sessions of physical activity (Donnelly et al., 2016). More specifically, cardiorespiratory fitness positively correlates with academic achievement across the majority of academic subjects while also negatively correlating with body mass index (Chu et al., 2016). Other research has found that classroom physical activity can increase students' time on task (Szabo-Reed et al., 2017). Despite these benefits, some traditional classroom-based teachers may be hesitant to include physical activity in the classroom for various reasons. For instance, they may not know that physical activity is beneficial, may not know what or how to incorporate physical activity into

Figure 5.6 Choreographed YouTube plank challenges.

DESCRIPTION

- Also known as an abdominal bridge, a plank is a bodyweight isometric core-strengthening exercise that encompasses holding positions similar to a push-up with back straight: head, shoulders, hips, and ankles aligned. While generally the body weight is held by the hands, sometimes the forearms are used for planking.
- Students attempt to follow along with an exercise video that incorporates choreographed movements that correspond to the beats of the song, based on the plank position. The video could be displayed on a television or digital projector with audio.
- Examples of plank challenge videos can be found on YouTube (simply search for the name of the below song with "plank" or "push-up" after the name of the song):
  - Cha Cha Slide
  - The Cupid Shuffle
  - Bring Sally Up
- Movements to the song include, for example within the Cha Cha Slide, walking plank to the left when the song's lyrics state: "Slide to the left."
- Many students like these videos because it incorporates music and rhythmic dance, and they do not have to hold a static plank for a long duration of time.

OBJECTIVE

- Demonstrate coordination and muscular strength and endurance by mimicking the choreographed plank exercises performed within the video.

TIPS

- While planking can be appropriate for any age group, consider shorter videos or pausing the video at times for younger students.
- Challenge the students to track the time elapsed on the video and have them try to see how many seconds or minutes they can go before losing form or needing to rest. Subsequently, they can try to beat their previous best time.
- Consider having students create their own choreographed routine of planking or other body weight exercises to a different song. Then perform it for others or post it to YouTube with appropriate approvals (see chapter 15).

AN EXAMPLE OF A YOUTUBE PLANK CHALLENGE

- Cha Cha Slide: https://youtu.be/x_YFkVSp34s

the classroom routine, and may feel that there is not enough time to include physical activity due to an emphasis on core academic content (Armstrong & Jenny, 2018).

The following subsections offer ideas for incorporating technology into physical activities that can be performed in a classroom. Typically, the only kinds of technology required are a computer (or mobile device), a digital projector, a screen, an Internet connection, and audio speakers. As with any physical activity, safety is always paramount. Consider carefully the arrangement of students, desks, or chairs, as well as any other safety concerns (e.g., slippery floors or rugs). Also make yourself aware of any medical conditions affecting any of your learners that could make the activity unsafe for them (consider checking with the school nurse). These activities can also be used outside of a classroom as long as you have access to the necessary technology.

Figure 5.7 Simultaneous video chat challenges and performances with other classes or teams.

DESCRIPTION

- In this activity, learners connect with another class or sport team via video chat and either challenge each other in the same activity or watch the other class or team perform. The video chat is projected on a screen for each group simultaneously (possibly in the gym).
- Examples of video chat apps include Skype, FaceTime, and Google Hangout.
- Needed equipment consists of a video chat program, a webcam, a digital projector, a screen or projection surface, audio speakers, and a microphone.

OBJECTIVE

- Increase motivation, build confidence, and appreciate other students' performances by connecting with another class or team via video chat while participating in a physical activity.

EXAMPLES

- Challenge idea: Two physical education classes start the FitnessGram PACER test at the same time so that students in each group compete against each other and against those in the other group. This arrangement adds another layer of friendly competition, which may facilitate improved performance.
- Performance ideas: As a unit-culminating activity, one class performs a rehearsed routine (e.g., dance, gymnastics, basketball skills) while the other class watches via video chat. Then the other class performs. Of course, such performances require practitioners to plan ahead with their classes.

Sworkit

The Sworkit website hosts an extensive digital library of workout videos for people of all ages. Sworkit offers customized training plans and personalized workouts for an annual or monthly subscription fee. It also offers several free apps for mobile devices (with in-app purchase options)—for example, Sworkit Kids, which provides follow-along strength, agility, and flexibility workout videos and games for children. For a practitioner's example, see the Technology Tips From the Field sidebar.

GoNoodle

Geared toward students in kindergarten through fifth grade, GoNoodle provides brief follow-along physical activities designed for the classroom environment. A free account is required to access the website content. For a fee, GoNoodle Plus provides more content, including cross-curricular, interactive learning games aligned with learning standards for health and other subjects.

TECHNOLOGY TIPS FROM THE FIELD

YouTube Dances and Sworkit

Adam Mullis
Health and physical education teacher; football, basketball, and track coach
Crayton Middle School, Richland One School District, Columbia, South Carolina

What types of technology do you use with YouTube Dances and Sworkit?
I use four Dell laptop computers with external speakers, YouTube, iPad Air, and the Sworkit app.

How do you use it?
During a dance unit, rather than teaching all students the same dance at the same time, I created a YouTube playlist of dances students can follow. I set up four to five laptop computers (four to five students at each) and allow students to vote on what dances they would like to do.

Sworkit is often used to give students a choice during warm-up times. Students are put into small groups and are allowed to pick which type of exercise they would like to do.

Students get into groups themselves. Students will be pick a song of their choice off of the playlist for the allotted time.

What is your main objective for using this technology?
I want students to explore and learn basic dance skills. When using this technology, I am trying to appeal to student interest, rather than me teaching a dance I think they want to learn. Students are now more in control of the lesson.

What do you like about this technology?
I like that this technology gives students a choice. Also, students who don't like to dance are more likely to participate because they are in smaller groups. Sworkit gives students a choice in what they would like to do; thus they are more willing to participate in it.

How might the technology be improved (or what don't you like about it)?
Depending on the space, it can be difficult to hear the music playing. Also, the advertisements on YouTube can be inappropriate. Students' accounts do not permit access to YouTube; thus, I have to log into five different computers.

What suggestions do you have for using this technology?
I suggest starting small. Demonstrate at one group first as they try the YouTube dances or Sworkit. Then allow all groups to start after the demonstration.

Students from Crayton Middle School in Columbia, South Carolina, mimic dance moves via YouTube and a laptop computer with Wi-Fi access in a physical education class.

Homemade Videos for Classroom-Based Exercise

You might also consider creating your own developmentally appropriate videos with follow-along exercises to integrate into your classes. If you are not qualified to do so, you might consider involving your certified physical education teacher in this project. With appropriate approvals, you might also consider including students from your school in these "brain break" videos to spark even more interest and motivation. Younger students may be extremely motivated by following along with exercises performed by high school athletes or other older students from their school district. For recommendations about making digital videos, see chapter 11.

MOTIVATING WITH TECHNOLOGY-RELATED EXTRINSIC REWARDS

Although the ultimate goal is to facilitate intrinsic motivation, extrinsic rewards can be used to instill situational interest, which may develop into intrinsic motivation over time. The key is to use extrinsic rewards sparingly and only when the reward is warranted. Rewards can also be used just for fun! Many teachers and coaches provide certificates for exceptional behavior or sporting performance, either immediately after class or more formally at an end-of-year or end-of-season awards banquet.

Award Certificate Templates

Creating your own printable award certificates may help you save money. Many free programs are available online for making printable certificates—just Google it. Several award certificate templates are also available in Microsoft (MS) Word. Simply click File, click New, type "certificate" in the template search bar, and hit Enter; many options will appear.

Digital Badges

As technology continues to permeate modern society, some practitioners and employers have turned to digital badges to recognize accomplishment rather than the traditional paper certificates. Like an award certificate, but in digital form, a **digital badge** recognizes achievement, skill, competence, or an assessment result. It can be displayed, accessed, and verified online. Younger generations may be more motivated by digital badges if they have the capability of easily sharing them via their social media accounts (e.g., Instagram). Digital badges may be incorporated into learning management systems (e.g., Edmodo Award Badges, 2017). As younger generations continue to integrate technology into daily life, digital versions of traditional products may be the direction of the future.

Conclusion

This chapter discusses technology-related ideas intended to motivate health and physical students and athletes. Technology can stimulate situational interest, which may facilitate learner engagement and learning, and possibly the development of an intrinsically motivated personal interest. All of the technology-integrated activities discussed in this chapter carry the potential to motivate. However, teachers and coaches must always be cognizant of the fact that technology should *not* replace traditional learning and physical activities but should augment them. Similarly, motivational activities involving technology should not be performed merely for fun but should help meet lesson or training session objectives and educational curricular standards.

Key Terms

augmented reality (AR)—New, blended reality created on a digital display that overlays the real-world environment with digital elements, often by using the camera of a mobile device's (e.g., smartphone) and an AR app (e.g., Snapchat).

Bluetooth—Short-range technology used for exchanging data wirelessly (i.e., by remote control) between electronic devices (e.g., mobile phone, computer, wireless speaker).

digital badge—Digital certificate that recognizes achievements, skills, competencies, or assessment results and can be displayed, accessed, shared, or verified online.

esports—Organized competitive video gaming (i.e., electronic sport).

extrinsic motivation—Motivation focused on external rewards (e.g., earning an A on a test, receiving praise from a teacher or coach, winning a trophy).

gamification—Integration of common game elements (e.g., rules, competition, point scoring if appropriate) into typically nongame contexts in order to increase student or athlete engagement and motivation.

gaming disorder—Pattern of gaming behavior in which the gamer has lost self-control in regard to gaming, thus prioritizing gaming over other interests and daily activities and continuing with game play even after negative consequences have resulted.

Global Positioning System (GPS)—Digital device that integrates satellite triangulation technology that tracks exact changes in geographic location, providing user data like distance, speed, and pace.

interactive video projection (IVP)—Use of a digital projector to display images on a wall or other surface as students perform skills or activities responding to the projected images.

intrinsic motivation—Motivation focused on intangible, internal rewards (e.g., having fun, feeling competent) that are naturally enjoyable.

motion-based video game (MBVG)—Video game that uses motion-sensing equipment and software that requires the player to perform fine and gross motor movements, which are often mimicked by an on-screen character.

motivation—Inner state that initiates and guides actions and behavior.

personal interest—Individual's somewhat underlying psychological disposition that guides personal preference to participate repetitively in a specific activity or to reengage with a particular content area over time.

situational interest—Momentary interest spawned by environmental factors (i.e., how a task or skill is presented) that facilitates motivation that may or may not be sustained.

sport video game (SVG)—Video game that simulates sport game play (e.g., Madden NFL, NBA 2K).

traditional video game—Primarily sedentary (i.e., seated) video game played while manipulating either a computer keyboard and mouse (PC gaming) or a handheld game controller (console gaming).

virtual reality (VR)—Digital experience in which participants are completely immersed (often through the use of VR goggles) and completely shut out visually from the physical world.

Review Questions

1. How can music motivate?
2. To what extent have video games been incorporated into education, health promotion, or sport?
3. What is the difference between augmented reality and virtual reality?
4. What is gamification, and how does it relate to technology?
5. Describe several technology-related activities that can be used to stimulate physical activity in a traditional classroom.
6. What are the benefits of short breaks for physical activity during a traditional classroom lesson?
7. What is a digital badge?

Discussion Questions

1. Should video games be incorporated into physical education, health education, and coaching? Why, or why not?
2. Do you think esports are a sport? Why, or why not?
3. What might happen if players do not receive feedback or assessment related to correct performance of motor skills during interactive video projection activities?
4. Does gamifying a lesson or training session undercut learning objectives? Explain.

6

Technology for Lifelong Health and Fitness

Chapter Objectives

When you have completed this chapter, you will be able to do the following:

1. Identify and define the three components of health.
2. Identify and describe types of lifelong technology to help optimize physical, mental, and social health.
3. Identify strategies to promote the use of technology for lifelong health in all domains.
4. Describe the limitations of using technology to optimize mental and social health.

Teachers and coaches play a strong role in preparing students for life beyond the pre-K-12 school years. While teaching and learning can be enhanced by using appropriate technologies in our school programs, we should also be aware of technologies geared toward lifelong health pursuits. These lifetime technologies are typically oriented toward adults who tend to participate in individual health-enhancing activities (e.g., meditation, joining a gym) rather than group or team activities (e.g., team sport, taking a health class). Therefore, your high school students will soon become consumers of personal health technologies, and you have the capacity to educate them about how these products can enhance their personal health beyond the pre-K-12 years.

To help you make the most of this opportunity, this chapter discusses technologies that can be used to promote lifelong health and wellness. Many of the devices addressed here are not ones that you would purchase for your program; you could, however, provide a sample of equipment for your students to try out or borrow. Please be mindful that this chapter merely introduces the topic, and your students may need to do their own consumer research in order to find technologies that support their individual health goals.

LIFETIME HEALTH TECHNOLOGIES

Technologies exist for improving all aspects of health, which is defined by the World Health Organization (WHO) as "a state of complete physical, mental, and social well-being" (World Health Organization, 2017). Each of these domains can be further detailed as follows:

- Physical health involves a person's biology, which can be influenced by the various components of health-related fitness—cardiorespiratory fitness, muscular strength, muscular endurance, flexibility, and body composition.
- Mental health involves a person's emotional health, intellectual health, and personal perceptions of well-being. Mentally healthy individuals tend to be more optimistic, appreciate their flaws and the flaws in others, and feel that they have a reasonable degree of control over their lives.
- Social health involves a person's ability to interact with others in a social environment, including friends, family members, and intimate partners.

Both students and student-athletes can be introduced to technologies that support all three of these components of health. Technological tools can be used to monitor health, assess or diagnose current health levels, improve health, and implement advice from other professionals (e.g., clinical dietitians, therapists, expert coaches). These tools are meant to enhance learning—not to replace personal interactions with field experts. In fact, using a variety of available technologies in conjunction with face-to-face interactions is becoming increasingly common in the field of lifelong health (Kleiboer et al., 2016).

PHYSICAL HEALTH

By maintaining a healthy physical body, one can enjoy the following benefits (Conkle, 2019):

- Weight control
- Improved blood flow and cardiovascular health
- Reduced stress and anxiety
- Increased self-esteem
- Increased muscular strength and endurance
- Injury prevention

People tend to engage in less physical activity as they age, and this decline can negatively affect health and overall quality of life. In contrast, enhancing or maintaining one's physical health is considered to be preventive medicine, and it often prevents injury due to falling, poor diet, or poor cardiorespiratory fitness. The best way to prepare students to be active for life is to teach them about fitness concepts and help them understand why it is important to work on all components of health-related fitness (Conkle, 2019). Along with teaching them the how and why, you can introduce them to technology that supports physical health in order to increase their confidence and ability to be active for a lifetime.

The stairway to lifetime fitness model (figure 6.1) provides a guide for preparing students to be active for a lifetime. If we want our students to move for a lifetime, we need to first prepare them directly in our classes, teach them to be active consumers of lifetime health and wellness options, and help them access tools and resources for becoming independent and monitoring their own lifestyle in the future. Fortunately, there is a huge push for technology that supports the needs of adults who wish to be active for a lifetime.

Wearable Activity Trackers

It is increasingly common for both youth and adults to purchase **wearable activity trackers (WATs)** for everyday, personal use. WATs can be used to monitor and change personal behavior and therefore can exert a positive influence on one's physical health. They are typically attached to one's wrist and provide a user-friendly way to generate health-related information (Shin et al., 2019). Information gathered from these devices is typically uploaded automatically to a mobile device or a website to enable tracking of physical health trends. Some analysts predict that the use of personal wearable devices will grow from 113 million units sold in 2017 to 222 million in 2021 (International Data Corporation, 2019). The top five brands for WATs are Xiaomi, Fitbit, Apple, Huawei, and Garmin. People purchase WATs for a variety of reasons:

- Recovery—monitoring physical activity after surgery
- Intervention—losing weight (in individuals with obesity or diabetes)

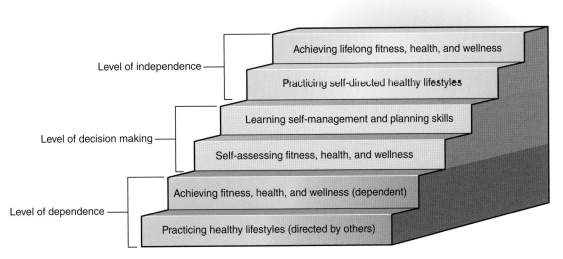

Figure 6.1   The stairway to lifetime fitness model highlights how practitioners can prepare students to be lifelong movers.

Reprinted by permission from C.B. Corbin, G.C. Le Masurier, and K.E. McConnell, *Fitness for Life*, 6th ed. (Champaign, IL: Human Kinetics, 2014), 34.

- Behavior change—achieving personal fitness goals through goal setting and self-monitoring
- Self-awareness—becoming more aware of one's lifestyle (active or sedentary)
- Fear of missing out—purchasing equipment because it is trendy
- Life optimization—collecting data and answering personal questions about oneself

The upward trend of WATs in the personal fitness industry has been accompanied by substantial research on attrition among users—specifically, the reasons for which people abandon the technology (Shin et al., 2019). Common reasons for abandoning WATs include the following:

- Privacy—concern about how one's data may be used
- Disappointment—misunderstanding of how a device works and disappointment when it doesn't meet the user's needs
- Design—discomfort, quality (e.g., lack of waterproofing), aesthetics
- Lack of accountability—decrease in motivation to use the WAT due to lack of a personal coach
- Lifestyle change—loss of interest in tracking personal fitness

Helping your students become aware of the benefits of WATS and the differences among them will help them meet future health goals on their path to becoming lifelong movers. You can help your students be active consumers and learn how to research the differences between WATs as part of a class activity or homework assignment. Among the huge number of wearable technologies on the market, this chapter focuses on three popular consumer products that can be purchased for a variety of purposes: **pedometers, heart rate monitors (HRMs),** and **global positioning system (GPS)** monitors.

Pedometers

A pedometer is a portable device that measures your daily step count. It may be attached to any of various body parts, such as your wrist, hip, or foot. Typically, adults set their daily step-count goal at 10,000, which is roughly equivalent to walking five miles (eight kilometers). This adult goal of 10,000 has been agreed on in several studies as sufficient to receive health-enhancing benefits (Conkle, 2019), though it may be either too difficult or too easy to reach, depending on one's current level of fitness.

Therefore, you should first determine and consider your baseline step count. For instance, if you are walking 1,500 to 2,000 steps per day, you might begin by setting a goal to increase your total by 1,000 steps per day for two weeks. Once you reach that goal, you might continue the process until you reach the 10,000-step target (Rieck, 2018). If, on the other hand, you can easily accumulate 10,000 steps per day, then you might try increasing by an additional 1,000 steps per day to stay motivated and enhance your fitness. Another approach is to wear a pedometer for either four days (for children) or eight days (for adults) and calculate the baseline average of steps per day. Then increase the daily step total by 10 percent every two weeks until you reach a level that is 4,000 to 6,000 steps beyond the initial baseline.

Pedometers are relatively low-tech devices that are fairly inexpensive; in fact, several minimalistic models are available for less than $10 each. These lower-end models are typically unable to sync with a phone or app; therefore, they simply provide you with a count of the steps you take on any given day (there is no tracking feature). Workplaces or fitness centers often incentivize employees or patrons with 10,000-step goals to earn rewards. For people not interested in calculating their target heart rate zones, or who are easily overwhelmed by fitness technology, a pedometer may be the best tech gadget for them. Wearing a pedometer on the wrist, as with a watch, can help most anyone easily

monitor daily step count. Some pedometers that are slightly higher tech can sync with a smartphone to enable monitoring of step progress over time. All of these fitness devices are great for people who are new to fitness technology or who want to start with small, simple goals.

Increasingly, some WATs are being designed specifically for children—for example, the Garmin vívofit jr. 2. This wristwatch primarily tracks daily steps and activity minutes but can also sync wirelessly with a mobile app so that parents can track the child's physical activity and chores, initiate reminder alarms, and award virtual coins, among other options.

Heart Rate Monitors

A personal heart rate monitor (HRM) is traditionally worn on the wrist and displays the user's heart rate. Depending on one's fitness goals, this information can either be used immediately to make judgments about intensity level or be saved for later use. Depending on your needs, you can purchase a basic HRM that provides information about sleep patterns, step count, and heart rate or a smart HRM that can send and receive phone calls or messages, make purchases, play music, and perform a variety of other functions. For a detailed description and analysis of HRMs, see chapter 9.

Personal Global Positioning System Monitors

For many consumers, a heart rate monitor is sufficient to provide basic daily tracking for personal health. However, users who wish to train with greater purpose and collect more training information may consider the benefits of watches with global positioning system (GPS) functionality. A GPS watch, typically worn on the wrist, uses **trilateration** based on satellite signals to determine your exact geographical location and determine the distance, speed, and pace at which you are moving. GPS watches are typically used not only by runners but also by other distance athletes (Steinheimer, 2017); specifically, some are designed to meet the needs of triathletes, cyclists, mountaineers, skiers, and paddlers.

The accuracy of a watch's calculations are affected by strength of the GPS signal. When determining which GPS watch to purchase, pay attention to reviews of accuracy so that you can get the information you need in order to guide your training goals. Also keep in mind that the best way to measure the course on which you are training is to do so manually with a measuring wheel, but that is not always realistic. The GPS network measures distance by using 29 satellites in orbit around the planet; at any time, most users are within range of four of those satellites, which enables determination of exact location (Hayes, 2014). The satellites send the watch's GPS receiver a high-frequency, low-power radio signal, which is reported as your exact coordinates in space (Hayes, 2014). Some GPS watches are also able to connect with the Global Navigation Satellite System (GLONASS), which provides another 25 or so satellites from which to receive signals. This increased signal allows for quicker and more accurate readings on the WAT, especially in built-up areas where GPS satellites may be obstructed (Angrisano et al., 2012).

Although GPS signals are typically easy to find, they may be lost in circumstances such as the following:

- Many tall buildings
- Significant tree cover
- Bridges or tunnels

Therefore, it is realistic to think that your GPS watch will sometimes lose its signal. When that occurs, most brands show you as having run a straight line from point to point and do not account for other pathways that may have been traveled (Team COROS, 2019). Watches can better account for the actual route traveled if they are equipped with an **altimeter**, **barometer**, or **gyroscope** (all defined in table 6.1).

GPS watches often cost more than an HRM does, and they are typically much more technically involved. Many people have written technically informed reviews of the watches, thus enabling you to become an informed consumer and to urge your students to do so as well. More specifically, according to SHAPE America's National Standards for K-12 Physical Education (Society of Health and Physical Educators, 2014), high school students should be able to do the following:

- Evaluate the validity of claims made by commercial products and programs pertaining to fitness and a healthy, active lifestyle. (S3.H2.L1)
- Analyze and apply technology and social media as tools for supporting a healthy, active lifestyle. (S3.H2.L2)

To this end, you can discuss with students the features of wearable technology, read reviews with students, and connect them with experts to learn more about how technology can help them with their fitness goals. Although some GPS watches are more basic and offer only standard features, others use algorithms to estimate how long you should rest before your next workout, estimate your running reserves, and even allow your friends and family to track you while you work out. Table 6.1 provides an overview of some features to look for before investing in a GPS watch.

Other Wearable Technology

This section on wearable technology could extend to the entire length of a textbook. Lifetime technologies have been developed for many sports and activities, and new technologies are being developed rapidly for a variety of reasons. Table 6.2 highlights several other forms of wearable technology for you to be aware of, based on a comprehensive

Table 6.1   GPS Watch Features

Feature	Description
Accelerometer	This feature can be used for multiple purposes, most commonly to count steps. It measures orientation and acceleration force to determine whether the device is horizontal or vertical and whether it is moving or not.
Altimeter	An altimeter uses either barometric pressure or GPS data to indicate how high above sea level you are. A GPS altimeter is much more precise than a barometric altimeter and requires no calibration. The altimeter feature comes in handy for navigation—it is easier to find your location on a map if you know how high above the sea level you are (Blaz, 2019).
Barometer	A barometer detects changes in atmospheric pressure, thus allowing you to predict the weather. If the atmospheric pressure is increasing, the weather will clear up; if it is falling, the weather will worsen (e.g., get cloudy or rain). A rapid drop in atmospheric pressure typically indicates a storm coming. This feature is especially good for mountaineers, hikers, and anyone who ventures into the elements for extended periods of time (Blaz, 2019).
Battery life indicator	Some GPS watches have a fairly short battery life in GPS mode, but the battery can last longer in a different mode. This variation can make a difference for, say, ultramarathons versus as compared with individuals who use the watch for significantly less time in a stretch.
Breathing guidance	Some devices include guided meditation features that walk you through breathing techniques for relaxation.
Built-in maps	Some watches offer built-in map features, whereas some others allow you to download maps.
Calorie management	Some units include an estimated calorie counter based on your minutes of activity.
Cellular service	Some devices allow you to directly send and receive phone calls.
Coach feature	A personalized coaching feature can walk you through body-weight exercises.
Email capability	Some devices allow you to directly send and receive emails.
Gyroscope	A gyroscope senses your movement in all planes and uses gravity to determine your orientation and direction on the earth.
Heart rate tracking	GPS watches typically include a personal heart rate feature for calculating resting and current heart rates.
Live tracking	This feature allows friends and family to live-track your runs.
Music integration	Stream or download playlists to your watch for use with a Bluetooth headset.
NFC payment capability	Near field communication (or NFC) allows you to make payments with your watch if it is near a payment receiving device. This feature requires you to sync your watch with a payment option, such as a credit card.
Pace calculation	This feature calculates your speed per mile or kilometer and can estimate your workout finish time.
Personalized maps	Some watches can calculate a running route for you after you type in the distance you wish to run. They may even tell you when to turn, thus saving you the trouble of stopping to look at your watch.
Personalized workout options	Some watches offer you a variety of workout choices, such as interval training and ab workouts.
Sleep tracker	Track your sleep habits, including time spent in light, deep, or REM sleep, as well with periods spent awake.
Smartphone apps	Accessing your apps on your watch allows you to do such things as stream music, make posts to social media, and pay for coffee.
Sport modes	Many watches track movement in a variety of exercises beyond running—for instance golf, HITT, yoga, badminton, swimming, biking, and surfing.
Step counting	Tracks your daily step count.
Waterproofing	This feature, of course, is very important for certain individuals, such as swimmers and water-sport athletes.
Wi-Fi compatibility	Built-in Wi-Fi capacity allows you to stream music and send and receive phone calls, messages, and emails (if those features are available on your device).

Table 6.2 Examples of Other WATs for a Variety of Uses

Device	Summary
Biometric headphones	These devices can provide information such as steps taken, distance traveled, and calories burned. Brands include Samsung, Under Armor, and Jabra.
Golf watches	In addition to features typical of other GPS watches, golf watches can also tell you the distance to the green, alert you to objects in the way, and even auto-recognize some golf courses. You can also track your score and analyze your swing based on feedback about speed, angle, and swing path.
Resistance training sensors	Resistance training sensors (e.g., Beast Sensor, Atlas Wristband, Gymwatch Strenx) show you rep by rep how much weight you are pushing when lifting weights, using a machine, or performing body-weight exercises. Some can even tell the difference between different types of push-ups.
Smart rings	Smart rings (e.g., Motiv, Oura) function similarly to HRMs and can track activity, sleep, and heart rate based on optical heart rate monitoring.
Smart shoes, inserts, and socks	Smart footwear is designed almost exclusively for runners and can measure foot and knee pressure and track distance, cadence, stride length, and calories used. Many use built-in sensors to collect the data and require you to have a phone or other device to display data during or after your workout.
Meditation and stress management options	These devices (e.g., Muse 2) can provide electroencephalograms (EEGs) and help you measure heart rate or state of mind by means of sensors placed on your forehead. The purpose is to help you become mindful of your body and reduce stress. Because this technology is obtrusive, it is typically used at home.
Wellness trackers specifically for women	Wellness trackers (e.g., Bellabeat) monitor and track sleep, step count, stress levels, physical activity, and reproductive health.

list found at the Gadgets and Wearables website (gadgetsandwearables.com). It is *not* your job as a practitioner to know all of the technology available, but you can help your students become conscious consumers by prompting them to research technological options for lifelong fitness.

You might also consider asking a college coach or community expert to speak with your athletes about beneficial technology for them to use after graduation. If you plan to coach in community programming, you might suggest or even require that your athletes purchase some sort of technology (like radar guns to measure pitching speed, or impact response systems in football helmets to measure the impact of a tackle) that meets the goals of your program. If you are a health or physical education teacher, you might ask your high school students to research a wearable technology that they might be interested in purchasing. For a sample worksheet, see figure 6.2. This activity would meet two of SHAPE America's grade-level outcomes for high school physical education and could help students better understand what is involved in becoming a conscious consumer of fitness products. Wearable technology may constitute a big investment for your students after graduation, and you can help them prepare to make good use of this growing market.

Geocaching

Geocaching is similar to going on an outdoor scavenger hunt by using GPS information. This recreational activity was created in 2000 and is now supported by several websites

Figure 6.2   Sample high school WAT assignment.

General Physical Education Fitness Unit for High School: Wearable Activity Tracker Assignment
Due: Friday, February 25
Value: 40 points
Rationale: According to Shape America's National Standards and Grade-Level Outcomes for K-12 Physical Education, high school students should be able to demonstrate the following capabilities:

- Evaluates the validity of claims made by commercial products and programs pertaining to fitness and a healthy, active lifestyle. (S3.H2.L1)
- Analyzes and applies technology and social media as tools for supporting a healthy, active lifestyle. (S3.H2.L2)

Description: By the end of the week, you should bring your final typed response to class. For the purpose of this assignment, assume that you have an unlimited budget.

PART A: RESEARCH

1. Go online and research personal, wearable heart rate monitors. Select your top two monitors and note their costs.
2. Create a chart to tell me the top three technological features (not mere appearance) that drew you to your selections. Describe your rationale in at least two sentences.

Next, go online and research two different types of personal, wearable fitness or wellness trackers (e.g., GPS watch, smart shoes, golf watch, meditation headset). Select your top two devices and note their costs.

3. Create a chart to tell me the top three technological features (not mere appearance) that drew you to your selections. Describe your rationale in at least two sentences.

Sample Chart

HEART RATE MONITOR 1: ARMSTRONG MONITOR ($87)	
Top 3 features	**Detailed rationale for the feature's importance**

PART B: DISCUSSION

1. What types of research did you use (e.g., written, video)? How many sources did you consult? Why do you think you could make an informed buying decision based on the sources you consulted?
2. State your top personal fitness goal for the immediate future. What technology could help you reach this goal? Could you reach the goal without using the technology?
3. How will cost affect your ability to purchase the technology you want?
4. In at least three sentences, tell me why you think people purchase wearable activity trackers but then stop using them.

that contain databases indicating the locations of hidden caches (Hödl & Pröbstl-Haider, 2017). Geocachers hide caches around the globe in the form of a small trinket, a logbook, and a writing utensil enclosed in a waterproof container. One can locate a cache by logging onto a geocaching website (e.g., geocaching.com), creating a profile, and then going on a hunt based on the GPS coordinates for a given cache. Once you locate the cache, you record your name and date in the logbook, log back into the geocaching website, and report your find. Many caches are located in plain sight, whereas others are more difficult to find. The rating scale ranges from 1 to 5, where 5 indicates a cache that is extremely hard to find due either to hazardous terrain (e.g., requiring scuba equipment) or to a serious mental challenge (such as solving a riddle) that must be met in order to open the cache (Hadl & Probstl-Haider, 2015).

It is easier to participate in geocaching now that most people have access to a smartphone. You can also participate by using a GPS watch or simply a compass. Many teachers and coaches already teach GPS skills as survival skills, but geocaching can turn GPS use into a lifelong recreation activity as well. Consider setting up your own geocaching activity at your school site at a beginner level and then extending the activity for students and parents to participate in together outside of school (Schlatter & Hurd, 2005). When promoting geocaching for use beyond school, make sure to emphasize safety. Encourage students to participate in the activity with other people, to be cautious about going into or near abandoned buildings, and to pay close attention to their surroundings.

Augmented Reality (Pokémon Go)

Pokémon Go and other augmented reality (AR) games are typically played by using a mobile device, such as a phone or tablet; however, unlike traditional video games, they involve interacting with one's physical environment (Rouse, 2016). Specifically, AR games use GPS signals to integrate visual and audio content with the user's immediate environment in real time. These games use many features of a person's phone (e.g., camera, gyroscope) to project virtual images onto a representation of the environment shown on the screen. The Pokémon Go app itself was downloaded nearly six million times (by both

Geocaching quick guide.

Geocaching.com screenshots copyright Groundspeak, Inc. DBA Geocaching. Used with permission.

3 steps to begin your adventure

1. Create an account

Create an account online or through the Geocaching® app to view a map of geocaches near you.

2. Find a geocache

Use the app to navigate to a geocache nearby. Don't forget to bring a pen!

3. Share your experience

Once you find the geocache, sign and date the logbook. Place the geocache back where you found it and log your experience online.

youth and adults) on its first day of release in the United States (Iqbal, 2019). Since then, use of the app has declined, but this novelty effect is quite common, and the potential remains for new AR games to come to market and help promote physical activity among individuals who are normally reluctant to engage (Althoff et al., 2016).

If you decide to integrate a pop culture trend into physical education, Bruno (2018) suggests using the following strategies:

1. *Integrate technology that students love.* Students often relate readily to current trends. Using trendy technology could integrate well with SHAPE America's National Standard 5 for physical education, as part of that standard relates to self-expression and enjoyment.

2. *Facilitate positive, productive computer use outside of school.* Teach students to use the technology safely outside of school. For instance, they should play the game only while supervised and should remain aware of their surroundings so they do not enter unsafe buildings, cross heavy traffic, or experience any other environmental hazards (such as cliffs or fast-moving rivers).

3. *Allow students to use pop culture to present topics.* Assign homework projects based on the AR unit and use it to foster excitement about engaging in physical activity outside of class.

4. *Address health media literacy.* Teach students where they can find credible information online; foster positive use of media outside of class time.

Fitness Center Machines

Once your students graduate from high school, they are more likely to join a gym or fitness center than to play on a sport team; some may also want to purchase a cardio machine for personal use at home. Therefore, as you prepare them for their future beyond high school or postsecondary school, remember that fitness center machines constitute a form of fitness technology. Knowing the basic features of these machines will help your students make good choices about them.

If your school is equipped with cardiorespiratory fitness equipment, teach students the features of the machines so that they fully understand how to use them in a way that benefits their health-related fitness. If you do not have access to such machines, encourage your students to go to the gym and use a variety of equipment; you might also take them on a field trip to a local gym or fitness center. As students gain experience in using exercise equipment, they develop greater **self-efficacy** for using all of the features of these machines.

When preparing students to research at-home models, ask them to investigate the minimal features needed in order to reach their fitness goals. For example, do they need top-of-the-line monitors with personal coaches, or will a more basic model suffice? Table 6.3 offers a quick overview of the differences between a basic or lower-end machine and a more commercial or higher-end machine. Between these two poles lies a spectrum of features, which means that not all low-end or high-end machines are created equal, and many machines fall somewhere in the middle. Therefore, this list is not all-inclusive, and there are many more options that you can try at a fitness center (e.g., arm-only ergometers, stair-steppers, ladder-climbers, multifunction machines). It is highly recommended that you do the following:

Students using cardiorespiratory fitness machines during physical education class.

Boogich/E+/Getty Images

- *Teach students how the machine relates to the components of health-related fitness.* Does it work on cardiorespiratory fitness? What HR zone should students work in?

- *Teach students how to use the basic features.* How do they increase and decrease intensity? How do they raise or lower the seat?

- *Teach students how to monitor their fitness goals.* Does the machine have built-in HR monitors? How do students know if they are working at the correct intensity?

- *Allow students to explore a variety of equipment.* Not all equipment is created the same. For instance, try running on a flat treadmill versus a curved one. Take time to feel the difference in stride length between a fixed elliptical machine and one with variable stride length. Try a variety of fitness machines so that you are aware of both basic and advanced features.

- *Give students feedback about form and progression toward their goals.* Provide feedback on elements of overall form, such as foot strike and posture. Also find out students' goals and determine whether they are working at the correct intensity to meet those goals.

Try incorporating an assignment into your class that requires students to test three machines and perhaps find ways to track their heart rate while using the machines. Such an assignment can help you evaluate your students' understanding of the following grade-level outcomes from SHAPE America (Society of Health and Physical Educators, 2014):

Table 6.3   Features of Selected Cardiorespiratory Fitness Machines

Type of machine	Basic features	Top-of-the-line features
Treadmill	• Basic treadmills can be very affordable but lack the bells and whistles of top-of-the-line models. • Includes a lanyard for emergency shut-off. • Some require no motor. • Some have a built-in motor; if you want to run, choose a motor with at least one horsepower. • Even the most minimal treadmills offer a monitor for basic stats (e.g., distance, speed, calories used). • Lack incline features. • Some offer fold-away capability. • Provide little cushioning on landing. • Come with only a limited warranty.	• Top-of-the-line treadmills are often bought commercially (i.e., for the wear and tear of the gym). • Offer a variety of incline and resistance settings. • Monitors include live trainers and personal coaching. • Multifunction swivel displays allow for a variety of workouts off of the treadmill. • Speed and incline can be adjusted automatically based on a personalized workout plan. • Smart monitors display HR, time, distance, pace, speed, and calories used. • Heart rate monitor is built in with sensors or integrated with a chest strap or WAT. • Integrated map features allow you to virtually run courses all over the world. • The latest technology makes for smooth running and long-lasting motors. • Workout fans are integrated. • Fold-away capability minimizes needed space. • Bluetooth functionality is integrated. • Reading or tablet tray and water bottle holder increase convenience. • Large frames accommodate long stride length and heavier body weights. • Mobile apps can be used on the touch screen. • Safety features include a shut-off lanyard and side rails. • May be flat or curved. • Come with a lifetime warranty.
Traditional elliptical	• Basic ellipticals can be very affordable and can meet basic training needs • Some offer either manual or magnetic resistance. • Even the most basic models usually include a screen for display of distance, speed, and calories used. • Weight and height limits are relatively low. • Warranty is limited.	• Top-of-the-line ellipticals can also be used as step climbers and gliders. • Offer a variety of incline and resistance settings. • Include preset workouts. • Include personal coaching options. • Offer built-in heart rate tracking with sensors or WAT or chest strap integration. • Include built-in fans. • Offers Bluetooth and audio subscription options. • Include water bottle and book or tablet holders. • Auto-adjust to gait. • Include movable or stationary arm bars. • Offer LCD displays and a variety of resistance options. • Include Internet connectivity options and interactive course selections. • Include apps for advanced fitness tracking. • Come with a lifetime warranty.

(continued)

Table 6.3   *(continued)*

Type of machine	Basic features	Top-of-the-line features
Under-desk elliptical or pedal bike	• Basic under-desk fitness machines provide a great option for people with limited mobility, people looking to increase their physical output while at work, and students in a classroom. • Typically include LDC display of time, distance, and calories used. • Very basic models offer manual resistance with no output displays. • Some are less ergonomically designed.	• Top-of-the-line models are used for similar reasons as basic models but offer more data for users interested in tracking progress. • Include built-in Bluetooth capability to sync with apps on phone or WAT. • Offer quiet and compact designs. • Include a variety of resistance options. • Feature ergonomic range-of-motion designs.
Rowing machine	• Typically have an LDC display of time, strokes per minute, and calories used. • Can use a chain flywheel or arm bars to pull back for resistance.	• Feature ergonomic seats. • Include a chain flywheel feature. • Provide smooth and quiet resistance. • Include adjustable footrests. • LCD monitors include a variety of features (e.g., calorie count, strokes per minute, time, meters rowed). • Use air resistance. • Can connect to apps with Bluetooth to track HR.
Stationary bike	• Basic stationary bikes can be very affordable but lack the bells and whistles of a top-of-the-line model. • Seat height is adjustable. • Use magnetic resistance. • LCD screen displays basic stats (e.g., distance, speed, calories used). • Can be a little louder than higher-end bikes. • Often use manual resistance. • Warranty is limited.	• Top-of-the-line stationary bikes are often commercially bought (i.e., meant for the wear and tear of the gym). • Include adjustable seat and handlebars. • Controls are built into the handlebars. • Provide smooth resistance. • Include multifunction swivel displays that allow for a variety of workouts off the bike. • Offer a variety of resistance settings. • Monitors include live trainers and personal coaching. • Speed and incline can be auto-adjusted based on personalized workout plan. • Smart monitors display HR, time, distance, pace, speed, and calories used. • Heart rate monitor is built in with sensors or integrated with chest strap or WAT. • Integrated map features allow you to virtually bike courses all over the world. • Workout fan is integrated. • Bluetooth functionality is integrated. • Feature a reading or tablet tray and water bottle holder. • Allow use of mobile apps on touch screen. • Come with a lifetime warranty.

- Independently uses physical activity and fitness equipment appropriately, and identifies specific safety concerns associated with the activity. (S4.M7.8)
- Applies best practices for participating safely in physical activity, exercise and dance (e.g., injury prevention, proper alignment, hydration, use of equipment, implementation of rules, sun protection). (S4.H5.L1)

Online Coaching

Providing opportunities for people to be physically active is not always as easy as we think. Some people lack a safe environment in which to be physically active outside, others live in areas where extreme weather (heat or cold) limit outdoor activity, and others simply cannot afford a membership or transportation to their local gym or fitness center. Many individuals also experience concerns related to self-efficacy. They may lack the confidence and competence to go to a public facility for exercise; as a result, they may prefer to work out in the comfort of home.

Because of these obstacles to physical activity—and due to the increasing availability of technology—some people turn to online coaching platforms to facilitate their physical activity. These platforms allow people to follow a workout directly through a TV, computer, tablet, phone, or even smartwatch. Online coaching platforms can be either on-demand or live.

On-demand coaching opportunities are similar to workout DVDs. In the DVD model, users purchase a workout DVD to use at home at their convenience. The on-demand coaching model is similar but allows for greater variety than purchasing a DVD. Described as "the Netflix of Fitness" (Laczo, 2018), on-demand fitness apps use tablets, computers, TVs, and other electronic devices to provide access to a workout. They can typically be accessed anytime and anywhere as long as you have access to a wireless connection. Thus you can easily take your workout with you wherever you go. Users typically pay a monthly fee to gain access to a variety of workouts, ranging from yoga to HITT to meditation.

This fitness-on-demand model of personal coaching allows people to work out in the convenience of their own home, thereby overcoming some of the obstacles to physical activity. Examples of companies that offer this sort of subscription-based home workout service include Daily Burn, CorePower Yoga, and Peloton Digital. Two major benefits of using the on-demand model are cost and availability. These models are usually affordable, typically ranging from $10 to $30 per month. They are also available anytime, so working out at 4:00 a.m. is always an option. On the other hand, one potential pitfall of using on-demand models is the possible lack of accountability. As with WAT options, the novelty of working out at home can fade over time, especially with limited accountability. Although different users have different personal needs, it has been found that greater external support typically leads to better adherence to the program (Shin et al., 2019).

To combat lack of accountability, some apps and services offer you the ability to live-stream a workout with an actual trainer or class. In either case, users can receive immediate feedback and motivation from classmates and the instructor. Examples of companies that offer live-stream options include Peloton and ClassPass live. This type of more personalized program is typically more costly and may require you to purchase WAT so that the instructor can monitor your fitness data (e.g., HR) in real time. In addition to streaming live classes, many people engage with personal trainers remotely. An online personal trainer can offer customized workout routines, customized meal plans, daily motivation, and even immediate feedback if you have the option to video-chat for assistance with exercise form. For instance, coaching by Born Fitness allows users to sign up for personal training through the service's website; it also provides meal coaching and weekly one-on-one meetings. Remote coaches vary in terms of their offerings, and options include the following, among others:

A smartphone and WAT may sync together to monitor fitness data.

Andrey Popov/iStock/Getty Images

- Personalized meal planning
- Video feedback
- Motivation via text message

Potential weaknesses of on-demand, live-stream, and remote coaching include the following:

- Lack of camaraderie
- Lack of instant feedback on proper form when using some platforms
- Lack of access to equipment
- Lack of commitment to a daily routine

Lifetime Sport Technologies

Up to this point, much of the technology discussed in this book has focused on individual fitness technology. Although that type of technology constitutes a booming industry, a variety of lifelong technologies are also available to complement most any sport you might like to pursue. Whether you participate in an invasion sport (e.g., rugby, soccer, lacrosse), a net or wall sport (e.g., volleyball, tennis, badminton), an outdoor pursuit (e.g., hiking, camping, fishing), a target sport (e.g., archery, golf), or a water sport (e.g., rowing, kayaking, sailing), there is most likely a technology to help you improve your game. Examples range from slow-motion smartphone apps (e.g., Hudl Technique) that enable you to compare your form with that of the pros, to smart rackets that calculate force and analyze your swing, to solar-powered stoves that enable you to cook meals on a hiking adventure.

ONLINE INSTRUCTING

As you read this section, you may develop an interest in using an online platform to offer remote personal training or coaching services. Indeed, this approach is gaining popularity as a way for coaches to supplement their income. To become an online coach, begin by researching companies for which you might like to work. Find out what certifications they require; many personal training courses are offered online, and you can research them online, compare their benefits, and determine whether they are accepted by the company for which you wish to work. The following companies offer certification courses to become a certified personal trainer:

- American Council on Exercise (ACE)
- American College of Sports Medicine (ACSM)
- International Sports Sciences Association (ISSA)
- National Academy of Sports Medicine (NASM)
- National Strength and Conditioning Association (NSCA)

As an online coach, you have the capability to work remotely with athletes from around the globe and easily share your knowledge and passion for sport, nutrition, and wellness. See chapter 8 for more information.

We highly recommend that you highlight some of these technologies in your program in relation to the sport units that you teach. For instance, in an outdoor pursuits class, you might ask students to use GPS devices, solar-powered stoves and lamps, water filtration systems, and Bluetooth-enhanced fishing bobbers or fish finders. You can also invite volunteers from local sporting goods stores to highlight the newest technology available for lifelong fitness pursuits and give your students the opportunity to research ways in which they might like to stay active and relevant technological tools they might like to purchase. You can also connect with coaches at your school or at a local institution of higher education and invite them to speak to your class about the types of technology they use in their programs.

Nutrition Tracking Technology

Eating a healthy diet requires a certain amount of understanding. Many people are generally aware of "good" and "bad" foods, but recommendations about what to eat can seem confusing. One source of such recommendations, the **dietary reference intakes (DRIs)**, were introduced in 1997 by the National Academies' Food and Nutrition Board to help people know what to eat in order to promote optimal health (Murphy, 2008). These recommendations specify the level of nutrients that people should consume daily and offer ranges of acceptable nutrient intake.

Another set of recommendations for making healthy food choices can be found in the **Dietary Guidelines for Americans**, which are published by the U.S. Department of Agriculture (USDA) and the U.S. Department of Health and Human Services. When you use these guidelines to teach youth about recommended daily food choices, you will most likely present them in the form of MyPlate, which helps students understand the benefits of eating foods from all of the food groups. If you are a coach, you might talk with your athletes about optimal pre-workout and post-workout meals or use research-based methods to discuss which foods and drinks to avoid during the competition season (for national standards relating to nutrition in physical education and coaching, see table 6.4). Whatever related content you are required to teach in your program, your overall goal should be to help your students make healthy nutrition choices for a lifetime. Understanding how and why to make healthy food choices can help your students avoid illnesses such as type 2 diabetes and heart disease, which can be caused by poor diet.

To optimize overall health, we need to be aware of our daily dietary intake and determine whether we are getting the recommended daily levels of nutrients. Although not everyone has access to a nutritionist or clinical dietitian, it is increasingly common for people to use nutrition tracking technology to either establish a baseline for their nutritional intake or change their eating habits. People may want to track their nutrition intake for a variety of reasons. Some people may monitor their diets to identify a food intolerance, others may look to gain or lose weight, and still others may want to maintain their current weight.

Regardless of the reason, people who are beginning a nutrition plan may face obstacles similar to those encountered when beginning a fitness plan. Some consumers are overwhelmed by the wealth of available nutrition information, whereas others are enticed by fad diets. The best recommendation is to start by talking with a professional, then supplement that face-to-face support with nutrition tracking. Registered dietitians often recommend using nutrition-tracking apps such as Fitbit and MyFitnessPal (Griffiths et al., 2018)—and doing so with advice from an expert.

According to current research, 58 percent of people with a smartphone have downloaded a health app, most often for the purpose of tracking nutrition intake (Griffiths et al., 2018). The top five free apps for nutrition tracking downloaded from the Apple App Store are as follows:

- MyFitnessPal
- Fitbit
- Lose It!
- MyPlate
- Lifesum

Table 6.4 Selected Professional Standards Related to Nutrition

SHAPE America's National Standards for K-12 Physical Education	**Develops strategies for balancing healthy food, snacks and water intake, along with daily physical activity. (S3.M17.7)**
	Designs and implements a nutrition plan to maintain an appropriate energy balance for a healthy, active lifestyle. (S3.H13.L1)
	Creates a snack plan for before, during and after exercise that addresses nutrition needs for each phase. (S3.H13.L2)
	(Society of Health and Physical Educators, 2014)
SHAPE America's National Standards for Sport Coaches	**Standard 19: Model and encourage nutritional practices that ensure the health and safety of athletes.**
	Sport coaches use sound nutritional practices (i.e., research-based, proven safe and effective) with their athletes and in their own lives to promote a healthy lifestyle. They will promote a diet that fuels the athlete in a safe and healthy manner and encourage a healthy body image. Sport coaches are proactive in identifying potential eating disorders and referring athletes for appropriate professional assistance.
	(Society of Health and Physical Educators, n.d.)

Reprinted by permission from SHAPE America, *National Standards and Grade-Level Outcomes for K-12 Physical Education* (Champaign, IL: Human Kinetics, 2014); Reprinted by permission from SHAPE America, *National Standards for Sport Coaches* (Reston VA: SHAPE America 2018).

Nutrition tracking apps need users to frequently input data about their daily meals, including portion sizes and brands of food, drink, and any supplements. Information can be inputted manually or in some cases by scanning the barcode on the label of the food or drink consumed. If a food is not included in the app's database or scanner, then you can input the information yourself from the food label. Once you input the needed information, the app evaluates your intake to the extent of its capabilities.

A comparison of the top five apps shows that they typically estimate calorie and macronutrient intake fairly well but may underestimate the intake or vitamins and minerals (Griffiths et al., 2018). As a result, it has been recommended that you use caution if you are getting all of your nutrition advice from an app rather than a clinical dietician. Still, these apps are often free and can be accessed in one's free time. Moreover, ongoing advancements in technology suggest that nutrition apps will continue to improve. Therefore, such apps are recommended for use as a supplement to one's overall health and wellness efforts; of course, one must take care to maintain a healthy relationship with

TECHNOLOGY TIPS FROM THE FIELD

Practitioner Interview

Rachel Laughlin
Registered dietitian, Aquinas College adjunct professor
Grand Rapids, Michigan

What type(s) of technology do you use for lifelong health and fitness?
A variety of phone apps and computer programs.

What is the name of one example of this technology?
Recovery Record.

How do you use it?
You simply free-write the food items you ate and/or take a picture of your plate (e.g., 1 cup oatmeal, 2 tbsp brown sugar, 1/2 cup skim milk, 1/2 cup orange juice, and include a picture of your breakfast table). It will also ask you questions about your hunger before and after the meal, your mood, exercise, and mindfulness of the meal.

What is your main objective for using this technology?
To make people aware of how their body feels before and after their food choices and quantities.

What do you like about this technology?
It is easy to use; if they want, they can simply take a picture of their meal.

What suggestions do you have for PE and health teachers or coaches who use the technology?
I think the technology should be used in conjunction with a health care professional (e.g., registered dietitian).

Can you provide any activity or assignment directions for the technology you use with your students and athletes?
Yes. For instance, they would keep track of the number of colors in their day or meal.

food. To this end, you can frequently check the MyPlate guidelines, which are updated every five years. If you or a student has a serious medical condition, consult an expert for additional guidance.

Hydration Trackers

In addition to eating well, it is recommended that people drink about eight cups of water per day for optimal hydration. As a result, a growing market exists for hydration trackers to help people monitor whether they are meeting their daily goal. These trackers typically come in the form of smart bottles that vary in their capabilities. Some can sync directly with your WAT to notify you if you need to increase water consumption in order to meet your daily goals. Some can also sync directly with your phone to give you notifications, whereas others simply rely on the bottle to flash lights or display other visual signals when you need to drink. Additional features may include water filtration, water cooling, and built-in buzzers to remind you to drink. Modeling this technology for your students or athletes can help them understand its potential benefits.

Hydration level can also be tracked through apps. In fact, many nutrition and fitness tracking apps include a category for you to log your daily water consumption. For instance, many Fitbit models allow you to specify a hydration goal and manually input your daily water intake. This option is much less expensive than a smart water bottle, which typically costs upward of $80.

MENTAL HEALTH

Mental illness affects nearly 20 percent of people in the United States, and depression is the leading cause of disability worldwide (World Health Organization, 2017). Common barriers to seeking treatment for mental illness include stigma, lack of appropriate facilities, cost, and lack of awareness that treatment is necessary or possible (Mojtabai et al., 2011). Many people feel embarrassed about seeking help for mental illness. Their embarrassment, fear, and struggle to feel supported could be resolved by erasing the stigma associated with mental illness and providing lower-cost options for help.

Until such measures are taken, one alternative is to make use of **eHealth** options. Given the widespread use of technology and its potential applications, the term *eHealth* was coined to address anything related to the combination of computers and the field of medicine (Eysenbach, 2001). In addition, given the increasing access to mobile technology (e.g., smartphones) around the world, the term **mHealth** was coined to refer to health-related content built specifically for mobile devices. Both eHealth and mHealth resources can be used to reach billions of users, and they provide convenient options for people experiencing mental illness (World Health Organization, 2011).

The best initial treatment plan begins with a trained mental health care provider and includes supplemental technology to support and enhance professional advice. EHealth and mHealth technologies can reduce global spending on health care because of their ease of use and low cost. Although they do not replace the critical value of face-to-face interactions, they do serve as part of the solution for addressing the mental health concerns across the globe. From video games to specially designed apps, people can use these resources to supplement face-to-face treatment plans on their journey to a more positive mental state.

As a practitioner, you carry the responsibility to address mental health. To help you understand this challenge, table 6.5 summarizes some national standards related to mental health.

Table 6.5   Selected Professional Standards Related to Mental Health

SHAPE America's National Standards for K-12 Physical Education	Identifies stress-management strategies (e.g., mental imagery, relaxation techniques, deep breathing, aerobic exercise, meditation) to reduce stress. (S3.H14.L1)
	Applies stress-management strategies (e.g., mental imagery, relaxation techniques, deep breathing, aerobic exercise, meditation) to reduce stress. (S3.H14.L2)
	(Society of Health and Physical Educators, 2014)
National Health Education Standards	**Standard 3:** Students will demonstrate the ability to access valid information and products and services to enhance health.
	3.12.1 Evaluate the validity of health information, products, and services.
	3.12.2 Use resources from home, school, and community that provide valid health information.
	3.12.3 Determine the accessibility of products and services that enhance health.
	3.12.4 Determine when professional health services may be required.
	3.12.5 Access valid and reliable health products and services.
	Standard 7: Students will demonstrate the ability to practice health-enhancing behaviors and avoid or reduce health risks.
	7.12.1 Analyze the role of individual responsibility for enhancing health.
	7.12.2 Demonstrate a variety of healthy practices and behaviors that will maintain or improve the health of self and others.
	(Joint Committee on National Health Education Standards, 2007)
SHAPE America's National Standards for Sport Coaches	**Standard 27: Incorporate mental skills into practice and competition to enhance performance and athlete well-being.**
	Sport coaches incorporate mental skills training at all age levels as a means to increase learning and performance, but also as part of the holistic development of the athlete. They train mental skills (e.g., goal-setting, arousal regulation, attentional control, imagery/visualization, self-talk) through a periodized model that will allow athletes to progress in their development of these skills and peak at appropriate times during the season. Sport coaches help athletes develop a mental competition plan that includes pre-competition preparation, contingency plan for errors during competition, and managing stress.
	Standard 42: Maintain work-life harmony and practice self-care to manage stress and burnout.
	Sport coaches develop strategies to manage the stress experienced in coaching and develop strategies to preserve work-life harmony. By being physically and mentally healthy, coaches can be the best for themselves, their athletes, and their social communities.
	(Society of Health and Physical Educators, n.d.)

Reprinted SHAPE America (2014); Reprinted from the American Cancer Society (2007).

App-Based Technologies

More and more apps are being developed to support mental health. In a recent study, 7 percent of the 165,000 health-related apps identified were targeted toward mental health (Ameringen et al., 2017). People choose to use apps for mHealth for a variety of reasons. Although no app should serve as a replacement for face-to-face treatment, appropriate apps can be used for supplemental purposes when access to a professional is not an option.

Some apps are specific to one mental health disorder (e.g., social anxiety, post-traumatic stress disorder), whereas others offer a variety of features to help with a variety of needs. Here are some popular reasons for which people use mHealth apps:

- *For screening.* Many apps offer questionnaires or scales to help people determine whether they have a mental health disorder, such as depression, post-traumatic stress disorder (PTSD), social phobia, or anxiety. For example, PTSD Coach is a multifunction app that offers screening tools as well as tools for tracking and managing symptoms. Although mHealth screening tools are appealing for users who want quick answers, not all such tools are validated (Ameringen et al., 2017). Therefore, it is best to consult with a professional for screening purposes, though with ongoing rapid advancements in technology, it would be no surprise if some apps were soon as valid as the research-based assessments provided by health care professionals.

- *For tracking and monitoring symptoms.* Many people use mHealth apps to monitor and track their symptoms. Some apps allow users to track and monitor their own progress, whereas others collect information that can be shared instantly with a health care provider. Apps that track symptoms can collect data either passively or actively. Passive tracking requires the user to carry out a typical day while the app tracks a variety of inputs (e.g., phone use, GPS location, heart rhythms). For example, the Purple Robot app uses a variety of passive inputs to generate a report on the user's predicted depressive state. Other apps require users to input their data actively by manually recording information about mood, sleep, and daily behavioral patterns (Ameringen et al., 2017). This active tracking can make users more aware of their patterns and allows them to share data with health care providers at a later date.

- *For treatment.* Treatment apps for mHealth give users the opportunity to manage their symptoms, thereby alleviating some of the burdens caused by a shortage of trained professionals (Ameringen et al., 2017). Users simply open the app, choose the treatment option that best suits their needs, and begin instant therapy. These apps vary greatly and may offer options such as the following:
  - Hypnosis
  - Music or nature-sound therapy
  - Exercise therapy
  - Spiritual or faith-based therapy
  - Positive affirmations
  - Cognitive behavioral therapy

And here are some popular treatment apps:

- *Calm.* Helps calm anxiety, bring about mindfulness, and promote positive sleep.
- *Talkspace.* Helps with depression and can connect the user with a professional for a live talk.
- *MindShift CBT.* Helps with anxiety and depression and provides calming solutions.
- *Quit That!* Helps with addiction and shows how much money the user is saving by quitting the addiction.
- *My3.* Helps manage suicidal urges.

A quick search of the Google Play app store will bring you to the most popular mental health apps, but professional input is highly recommended. Many of the apps mentioned here are multipurpose, and many are also available free of charge. Bringing awareness to these apps in your school-based program could open the conversation for students who are afraid of looking for available resources or who have been unaware that these resources exist. Remember that one in five of your students may be suffering from a

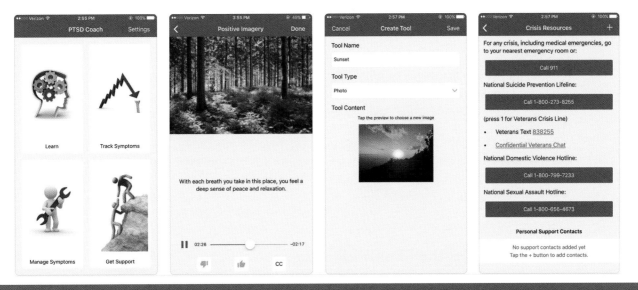

A mental health app and sample features.

From US Department of Veteran Affairs.

mental health disorder now or may experience one in the future. You might give your students an assignment in which they research three mHealth apps that target different populations (e.g., one each for anxiety, PTSD, and OCD) and then compare them based on factors such as purpose, cost, and ease of use.

Therapeutic Video Games

The National Institute of Mental Health (NIMH) has called for experts to develop novel interventions to help treat correlates of depression due to findings that many existing treatments manage symptoms but do not treat underlying causes (Insel & Wang, 2009). This call for new interventions seems to have led researchers to study the use of video gaming for therapy. Given that nearly 40 percent of Americans played video games in 2017 (Brown, 2017), video gaming has the potential to reach a large range of people. Researchers who study video games for therapy divide them into two groups: those that are specifically geared toward health-based interventions and those that are commercial off-the-shelf games not created specifically to improve mental health (Colder Carras et al., 2018). Some experts see the promotion of video game therapy itself as a public health concern because they fear that any benefits may be accompanied by negatives such as violence, obesity, and addiction (Colder Carras et al., 2018); still, there is potential for video games to improve mental health outcomes.

Specially Designed Therapeutic Video Games

Some video games are designed specifically to serve a therapeutic purpose. For example, SPARX is an online, government-funded eHealth tool created in New Zealand. This game is geared toward youth who are experiencing mild to moderate anxiety or depression. It relies on **cognitive behavioral therapy (CBT)**, which is a known intervention tool for improving mental health. The benefits of SPARX have been highlighted in many studies (Merry et al., 2012; Shepherd et al., 2018), so it is encouraged for practitioners to highlight these tools in their programs, in addition to advocating for face-to-face meetings with school counselors or other mental health professionals.

Studies have also found that mental health outcomes can be improved through the use of virtual reality (VR) exposure specifically geared toward therapy. Health care practitioners may use virtual reality exposure therapy as an intervention to help participants cope with PTSD or reduce symptoms of depression (Li et al., 2014). As a pre-K-12 practitioner, you should *not* implement such interventions with your students or athletes, but you can use basic knowledge of these resources to help your students. Specifically, you can help students become aware of this treatment option by sharing relevant videos or arranging visits by experts in using VR therapy.

In addition to making your students aware of therapeutic gaming technologies, you can connect them with therapeutic gaming organizations. Nonprofit organizations such as Stack-Up (providing support for veterans with PTSD) and Rise Above the Disorder (challenging communities to end stigma related to mental health) provide spaces where students can learn about mental health problems, find support or assistance, and interact with others either in person or online.

Commercial Off-the-Shelf Video Games

Unlike therapeutic games, commercial off-the-shelf (COTS) video games (e.g., Pac-Man, Candy Crush Saga) are not created specifically to benefit mental health. A number of studies have been conducted on the use of COTS as part of an intervention to address a variety of mental health disorders. The results have been mixed, but it is worth sharing with your learners that video games may offer benefits for people experiencing a mental health disorder. For instance, traditional handheld video games have helped children facing surgery to reduce their levels of anxiety (Patel et al., 2006), and several games with puzzle elements have been shown to reduce depression and stress and to prevent flashbacks after trauma events (Russoniello, 2009; Iyadurai, 2018). Video games that include online elements can also offer social support for people who need to feel connected—for instance, those who struggle with suicidal thoughts or behaviors (VanOrden et al., 2010). It is worth sharing about the potential benefits of certain COTS video games with your students, some of whom may be looking for tools to complement their ongoing treatment plans.

Help your students understand that you are not prescribing video games but that many games may offer mental health benefits. Video gaming should be coupled with positive physical and social health habits to facilitate optimal overall health benefits.

SOCIAL HEALTH

The third component of health—and possibly the most important for longevity—is social health. A recent TED Talk addressed a 75-year study that found the most important contributing factor to happiness is the presence of healthy, genuine relationships (Waldinger, 2016). People who are more socially connected live happier and healthier lives, whereas those who are isolated live shorter, less satisfying lives (Aylett, 2017).

Social health involves one's ability to form satisfying relationships with others. Social relationships involve interactions with a variety of people, including friends, acquaintances, family members, co-workers, and intimate partners. Social health also relates to one's ability to adapt comfortably to different social situations and to act appropriately in a variety of settings. Healthy relationships include the following key components:

- Strong, two-way communication
- Empathy toward each other
- Mutual respect

One factor in social health that has risen consistently is loneliness, which is reported more frequently among youth than among elderly persons (Kim, 2017). One contributing factor to social disconnection comes in the form of access to electronic communication tools and social media. As people become increasingly connected through social media, they are also becoming more disconnected from face-to-face (F2F) interactions. Therefore, although this section of the chapter promotes the use of technology to build social connections, we also know that the best way to improve social health may be to engage in more F2F interactions. This solution may seem straightforward, but some people find F2F interaction to be terrifying. When people are inhibited in regard to F2F interaction due to social anxiety or perceived lack of social skills, technology may serve as a helpful mediator (Kim, 2016). Another contributor to social isolation is declining mental and physical health. As people age, they tend to see a decline in various areas of health, which makes them less able to seek social support (Garattini et al., 2012).

As a practitioner who works with youth, you will most likely interact F2F with your students. You will also be charged with demonstrating how to create and maintain positive social interactions. To this end, table 6.6 highlights selected standards related to social health in physical education, health education, and coaching.

Table 6.6   Selected Professional Standards Related to Social Health

SHAPE America's National Standards for K-12 Physical Education Standards	S5.H4 The physically literate individual recognizes the value of physical activity for health, enjoyment, challenge, self-expression and/or social interaction.
	Identifies the opportunity for social support in a self-selected physical activity or dance. (S5.H4.L1)
	Evaluates the opportunity for social interaction and social support in a self-selected physical activity or dance. (S5.H4.L2)
	(Society of Health and Physical Educators, 2014)
National Health Education Standards	Health Education Standard 4: Students will demonstrate the ability to use interpersonal communication skills to enhance health and avoid or reduce health risks.
	4.8.1 Apply effective verbal and nonverbal communication skills to enhance health.
	4.8.3 Demonstrate effective conflict management or resolution strategies.
	4.12.1 Use skills for communicating effectively with family, peers, and others to enhance health.
	4.12.3 Demonstrate strategies to prevent, manage, or resolve interpersonal conflicts without harming self or others.
	4.12.4 Demonstrate how to ask for and offer assistance to enhance the health of self and others.
	(Joint Committee on National Health Education Standards, 2007)
SHAPE America's National Standards for Sport Coaches	Standard 9: Acquire and utilize interpersonal and communication skills.
	Sport coaches develop their interpersonal skills to build positive relationships with all stakeholders. These interpersonal skills include learning to engage in conversation, actively listening, understanding another's perspective, navigate personality styles, negotiating, maintaining self-control, and resolving conflicts. Sport coaches also make concerted efforts to develop positive coach–athlete relationships that are based on trust, commitment, clear expectations, appropriate interactions, constructive feedback, and support. Sport coaches work to develop their oral and written communication skills to concisely and clearly communicate information, elicit community support, and advocate for the program.
	(Society of Health and Physical Educators, n.d.)

Reprinted SHAPE America (2014); Reprinted from the American Cancer Society (2007).

Standard Forms of Tech-Based Communication

Chapter 3 focuses on ways of communicating with students and their families. These communication forms include the following:

- Mobile phone
- Email
- Social media
- Communication apps

The majority of these forms of communication allow people to connect instantly, regardless of time and distance. In some instances, people can even engage in media-facilitated F2F interactions by using apps such as FaceTime or Messenger. In most cases, video-calling apps require people to connect to Wi-Fi, whereupon they can enable instant communication with anyone around the world free of charge.

Many forms of communication can be facilitated by the use of a smartphone, tablet, or computer. One benefit of tech-based communication for students is that it is often low in cost and most students already have access to an appropriate device. You can also encourage students to find places in the community (e.g., libraries), where they can access email and social media free of charge. Access to tech-based communication may be more difficult for elderly persons, but many tech companies recognize this potential obstacle and are creating tech gadgets specifically to help older persons stay connected. For instance, the Jitterbug phone features large buttons, a large screen, an extra-loud speaker, and a limited menu. Similarly, the GrandPad tablet allows users to make calls, send emails, check the weather, and play games. Although these forms of technology can bring people together, there is still a component of meeting up that should be encouraged in order to facilitate positive social connections.

Another way in which traditional communication technology has the potential to bring people together is through social media. For example, Facebook often advertises social events in a given local area, and online dating apps (e.g., Bumble, HER, OKCupid) are extremely popular with various age groups because they allow people to find an intimate partner after creating a digital profile. In another example, the Meetup app allows users to search for special interest groups nearby.

To help prepare your students for the future, you might ask them log in to Meetup and look for local groups that they might want to join after graduation. To extend this assignment, ask students to find a city where they would love to live and then investigate Meetup groups to create new social connections in the chosen city. Remember to acknowledge that people are often lonely and disconnected but that resources are available to help meet others. Many of your students may feel lonely and disconnected, and you can validate that their feelings are important and can be addressed with the help of tech-based ways to find high-quality interactions.

Therapeutic Video Games

Therapeutic video games may also contribute to positive outcomes in terms of social connection. Specifically, these games may help users build rapport and develop positive social skills. Family members or loved ones may also be able to help by playing noncompetitive and nonviolent video games together—an experience that fosters positive parent–child interactions (McNeil & Hembree-Kigin, 2010). Playing together as a family can also help create social connection between grandparents and grandchildren, which can positively affect the health of older adults (Zhang & Kaufman, 2016).

Many video games offer multiplayer options that allow users to interact with people from around the world, either anonymously or by using a web camera to virtually meet other players. The gaming community is very large and often holds F2F conventions where gamers meet in person. Although gaming can help people with autism, social anxiety, and other social challenges, F2F interaction should also be given priority. A therapist or counselor might use electronic communication, apps, or gaming as an initial treatment but will likely work toward a plan that facilitates in-person interactions.

Conclusion

As health educators, physical educators, and coaches, we all work in the field of preventive medicine. Specifically, we work together to help our students find ways to be active and move for a lifetime. Preparing our students to be lifelong movers requires us to educate them about ways to monitor their health in all aspects: physical, mental, and social. Bringing awareness to technologies that can support their ongoing pursuit of health goals will increase their awareness, self-efficacy, and access to the resources they will need in the future. Creating health goals in all three areas—and creating plans to improve or maintain health in all three areas—should be your emphasis as you prepare students to become increasingly independent.

Key Terms

altimeter—an instrument used to determine the altitude of an object, which is the distance above sea level.

barometer—an instrument used to measure air pressure, which can help with both measuring weather, and determining altitude.

cognitive behavior therapy (CBT)—this form of short-term psychological treatment focuses on helping people understand the thoughts and the feelings that influence their behaviors.

Dietary Guidelines for Americans—evidence-based nutrition information to help people make healthy choices about the foods and beverages they consume.

Dietary Reference Intakes (DRIs)—a set of reference values used to help people plan and evaluate whether they are meeting the daily number of nutrients recommended by the Food and Nutrition Board and the Institute of Medicine.

eHealth—the use of technology (both information and communication) for health-related purposes.

global positioning system (GPS)—a system that uses satellites to determine a person or an object's exact location.

gyroscope—an instrument that uses gravity to measure orientation and direction in space. In a fitness device, it is typically used to determine direction, and is used for navigation.

heart rate monitor (HRM)—a device used to measure a person's heart rate in beats per minute (BPM).

mHealth—the use of a mobile device or other wireless technology to deliver medical information.

pedometer—a device used to measure a person's step count.

self-efficacy—a person's belief that they are going to be successful in a specific situation. A person's self-efficacy varies from task to task.

trilateration—when 3 satellites are used to pinpoint the specific location of a GPS receiver.

wearable activity tracker (WAT)—an activity tracker that is small and wearable, that works to track some sort of fitness data.

Chapter Review Questions

1. Based on the definition from the World Health Organization, what are the three components of health?

2. Compare three types of wearable technology that one could purchase to support pursuit of lifetime health goals.

3. Why are we responsible for teaching students about technology that they could purchase outside of school? What are two potential benefits for your students?

4. Describe how commercial video game technology might benefit or harm one's overall health.

5. What is the best way for human beings to interact socially? How can that interaction be facilitated through the use of technology?

Discussion Questions

1. How do you think technology will help you pursue your future health goals? What types of technology might you purchase, and what features would you look for? Why?

2. What do you think is the biggest barrier to living a physically active life in the future? How might you overcome that barrier through the use of technology?

3. In great detail, describe why people with a mental health disorder might be hesitant to seek treatment. How might it benefit your students to hear a mental health expert talk about using technology to support diagnosis, management, and treatment?

4. Look back at this chapter and find the table that addresses national standards for physical education, health education, and coaching. Create an assignment for your future students to complete outside of class time that meets one of the standards related to social health.

Meeting Special Needs and Abilities Through Technology

Chapter Objectives

When you have completed this chapter, you will be able to do the following:

1. Define assistive technology (AT) and delineate its three levels.
2. Use mid- and high-tech AT devices with individuals who have physical disabilities or impairments in vision, hearing, or cognition.
3. Analyze apps commonly used by individuals who have disabilities and evaluate each app's purpose and intended population.
4. Implement video gaming with individuals who have disabilities and use appropriate equipment and pedagogical accommodations.

Steve Nagy/Getty Images

In chapter 1, we defined *technology* as a manner of accomplishing a task using technical processes, methods, or knowledge. We also noted that technology applies science in order to solve problems. The beauty of technology is that it often affords opportunities or alternatives that are not otherwise possible. This is certainly true for individuals with **special needs** in health education, physical education (PE), and sport settings.

More specifically, the term **assistive technology (AT)** refers to services, tools, applications, equipment, and devices that help individuals compensate for disabilities by maintaining, enabling, or improving functional abilities. AT aids learning and quality of life by enabling capability and independence while also improving self-esteem. Examples include using a guide rope with a student who is blind, using an **ability switch** with a person who has a cognitive or physical impairment, and using a beep ball to play baseball with an athlete who has visual impairment.

In one taxonomy, AT has been divided into the following 13 categories (RehabTool, 2004):

1. Communication aids
2. Computer access aids
3. Daily living aids
4. Education and learning aids
5. Environmental aids
6. Ergonomic equipment
7. Hearing and listening aids
8. Mobility and transportation aids
9. Prosthetics and orthotics
10. Recreation and leisure aids
11. Seating and positioning aids
12. Support services (e.g., AT training, functional evaluations)
13. Vision and reading aids

This classification illustrates the wide array of AT available but can be quite confusing. Therefore, in this chapter, we use a simpler classification that divides AT into just three categories (table 7.1).

This chapter provides a sampling of digital technologies that practitioners can use in sport or health and PE settings with individuals who have a disability, impairment, or activity restriction. Therefore, it focuses on mid- and high-tech AT. Certainly, additional technologies discussed in other chapters can also be used in working with individuals who have special needs and may also be helpful in providing differentiated instruction for gifted students. For example, an adapted physical education (APE) expert might observe or supervise a general PE teacher who is implementing inclusive AT remotely by using digital video technology covered in chapter 8. Similarly, a health teacher might monitor individualized education plan (IEP) goals and benchmarks by using management or assessment technology discussed in chapters 2 or 10, respectively. This chapter focuses on digital technologies for meeting special needs and abilities of individuals with disabilities across the psychomotor, cognitive, and affective learning domains.

The scope of this book does not extend to detailed information about specific types of disabilities; advanced pedagogy recommendations; or low-tech accommodations in APE, adapted sport, or special education classroom instruction. However, we suggest that you participate in continuing professional development opportunities in special education and APE (for more on professional development, see chapter 12). In addition, specifically for movement practitioners, we suggest consulting the APE National Standards (APENS)

Table 7.1   Three Levels of Assistive Technology (AT)

AT level	Defining characteristics	Examples
Low-tech	• No battery needed • Minimal or no training needed	Bowling ramp, manual wheelchair, gripping gloves, lower volleyball net, guide rope, handles, straps
Mid-tech	• Electronic and/or battery needed • Minimal training needed • Minimal-step processes (i.e., uncomplicated)	Beep ball or box, simple ability switch, simple talking device (e.g., pedometer, watch, jump rope), audio book, laser pointer
High-tech	• Electronic and/or battery needed • Specialized training needed to use multistep processes • Individualized programming possibly needed	Mobile smart device or computer (e.g., iPad) with communication app, powered wheelchair, motion-based video game, electronic prosthesis, beep baseball kit

Adapted from Hodge, Lieberman, and Marata (2012); and McNamara (2018).

textbook provided by the National Consortium for Physical Education for Individuals with Disabilities (NCPEID, 2020) and perhaps earning the Certified Adapted Physical Educator (CAPE) certification (Adapted Physical Education National Standards, 2008). APE professional development is also provided in the form of on-site workshops and online webinars by SHAPE America (Society of Health and Physical Educators, 2019a). Furthermore, a six-session online webinar and Certified Inclusive Fitness Trainer certification (CIFT) are offered by the American College of Sports Medicine (ACSM; 2019) in concert with the National Center on Health, Physical Activity, and Disability (NCHPAD) for practitioners who work with individuals who have health risks or physical limitations. Finally, the ACSM and Exercise Connection (2018) offer an Autism Exercise Specialist certification.

In summary, practitioners must possess pedagogical content knowledge about how to use AT and make appropriate modifications in the context of standards-based programs (Laughlin et al., 2018). As examples, table 7.2 presents four APENS topics that are addressed briefly in this book.

This chapter addresses sample digital technologies commonly used by students and athletes with visual, hearing, or cognitive impairments, as well as physical disabilities. Many of these individuals have multiple types of disabilities. The chapter begins by discussing disability and related legal mandates, then provides recommendations related to using AT in your teaching or coaching. Next, it reviews sample AT devices and apps, as well as other technology-related activities and equipment frequently used in APE, health education, and sport settings. It also covers practical applications of these AT devices.

DISABILITY AND LEGAL MANDATES

Disability is an umbrella term for **impairments**, **activity limitations**, and **participation restrictions** that substantially limit one or more major life activities (e.g., seeing, hearing, walking, learning, concentrating, communicating). Globally, more than a billion people have a disability, which accounts for 15 percent of the world's population (World Health Organization, 2018). In the United States, in 2014, more than 85 million people had a disability, thus accounting for more than 25 percent of the population (U.S. Census Bureau, 2018). Disability rates continue to rise worldwide due to various factors, including increases in chronic health conditions and the ageing of the population (World Health Organization, 2018).

Table 7.2 Adapted Physical Education National Standards Related to Technology

INSTRUCTIONAL DESIGN AND PLANNING	
Technology applications	"Knowledge of communication systems sanctioned by the American Speech-Language-Hearing Association" (p. 153).
Assistive devices	"Knowledge of adaptation of assistive devices to enhance participation in physical education" (p. 154).
Mobility devices	"Knowledge of various mobility aids to enhance participation in physical education" (p. 156).
CONTINUING EDUCATION	
Technology	"Use technology as a technique to disseminate information pertaining to physical education" (p. 198).

Reprinted from NCPEID (2020).

Disability has been framed in various ways. In a structural, social perspective, individuals with disabilities are perceived as being disabled not by their bodies but by society—that is, by an adverse interaction between an individual with a health condition (e.g., blindness, Down syndrome, autism spectrum disorder) and that individual's environmental and personal factors (e.g., lack of access to equipment or facilities, limited social support, negative attitudes) (World Health Organization, 2018). To prevent this mismatch from occurring in teaching and coaching settings—all of which include **diversity**—educators and coaches must strive for inclusion by using differentiated pedagogical techniques in environments that afford **accessibility**. More specifically, we must employ appropriate equipment for people of varying skills and abilities. In this way, AT can help us meet the unique needs of special populations.

In the United States, and in other countries with similar laws, it is required to provide individuals who have disabilities with necessary **accommodations** in order to comply with federal laws. Example laws include the Individuals with Disabilities Education Improvement Act (IDEIA, 2004) and Section 504 of the Rehabilitation Act of 1973—now the Americans with Disabilities Act (ADA; 1990) and the American with Disabilities Act Amendments Act (2008). Section 504 of the ADA prohibits **discrimination** based on a person's disability and requires federally funded entities to provide equal opportunity to individuals with disability if opportunity is afforded to individuals without disabilities, including PE and extracurricular sporting activities. These accommodations and services may be detailed in a **504 plan**. Similarly, as long as PE is offered to his/her peers, IDEIA requires a student in **special education** to receive inclusive general PE unless the student with the disability is enrolled full-time in a different facility or the student's **individualized education plan (IEP)** prescribes adapted PE.

An individualized education plan is a written document addressing special education and related services to be provided in order to meet the unique needs of a student with a disability in accordance with IDEIA (2004). Often, students with disabilities are served through the process of **inclusion**, which provides them with individualized services and adaptations (e.g., technology-related adapted equipment) in a mainstream environment (e.g., general PE class or sport team) rather than in a separate isolated setting. Effective practitioners who work in environments marked by great variation in skills and abilities often incorporate the **universal design for instruction (UDI)** model—a planned yet flexible instructional approach that uses accommodations (e.g., differentiated activities, adapted rules or equipment) to provide customized opportunities for all students to learn and achieve standards, goals, and outcomes (Lieberman & Houston-Wilson, 2009). Moreover, assistive technologies are often used as recommended accommodations in IEPs for both educational and sport settings.

Adapted physical education (APE) includes educational services and accommodations aimed at meeting the unique needs of each student with a disability in PE. This approach could be taken within an inclusive general PE class or in a separate PE class for students with relatively severe disabilities. Similarly, sport coaches often serve an athlete who has special needs, or may coach in an environment that provides a specific sporting competition for athletes with disabilities, such as the **Special Olympics**, **Paralympics**, or **Deaflympics**. Movement practitioners may also even include or coach **adaptive sports**, which are designed specifically for people with disabilities. One example is goalball, which uses a ball equipped with bells so that it can be heard and therefore located by players who have visual impairment.

Academic institutions are continuing to close the gap between special education and general education as school cultures shift and inclusion becomes more common in health education, physical education, and sport. For instance, the Special Olympics (2019) and SHAPE America (Society of Health and Physical Educators, 2019b) promote social inclusion, as well as attitude and behavioral change among individuals with and without disabilities. They do so through purposeful school and community programs that use sport as the catalyst—for example, the Unified Champion Schools and Unified Sports initiatives. Primary aims include eliminating **bias**, **prejudice**, and **stereotypes**. AT can help practitioners achieve these goals, and it works best when it is appropriate, sustainable, affordable, and accessible (World Health Organization, 2011).

BRIEF RECOMMENDATIONS FOR AT IMPLEMENTATION AND PEDAGOGY

When making decisions about any technology, we must go beyond simply using technology for its own sake; specifically, we must consider its purpose and how it will be used with a particular individual. Zabala (2005) recommends that IEP teams consider the SETT framework, which addresses the following considerations indicated by the acronymic name: the student's individual abilities, interests, and needs; the environment in which the AT will be used (e.g., school, home, community); the tasks that are performed in the environments and how AT might facilitate them; and the tools available to meet the individual's needs, including potential AT devices, services, and pedagogical strategies.

Moreover, Laughlin et al. (2018) note that the IDEIA (2004) requires services that evaluate the student's needs; obtain necessary AT and customize it if needed; harmonize its use with other services or therapies; and train the student, teachers, and other professionals to use it effectively. You should also investigate whether your institution or school district provides an AT expert liaison (e.g., assistive technology specialist) who can perform individualized evaluations and recommend specific AT services for each student with special needs. You may also have access to instructional technology resource teachers (ITRTs). Finally, consider using the Self-Evaluation Matrices for the Quality Indicators in Assistive Technology Services (QIAT Leadership Team, 2012) to evaluate all facets of using AT throughout the process of developing, implementing, and reevaluating an IEP.

MID-TECH AND HIGH-TECH ASSISTIVE TECHNOLOGY

The following sections present examples of mid- and high-tech AT and other digital technologies for individuals with a physical disability or impairment in vision, hearing, or cognition. Again, please remember that low-tech AT may also be available to serve the same purpose, but this chapter focusses on digital AT. Table 7.3 provides a sample of websites that sell products related to AT, APE, and adaptive sport.

Table 7.3 Sample Product Sources for AT, APE, and Adaptive Sport

Company	Website
AbleNet	www.ablenetinc.com
Adaptive Tech Solutions	www.adaptivetechsolutions.com
Amazon	www.amazon.com
American Printing House for the Blind	http://shop.aph.org
Beyond Sight	www.beyondsight.com
Enable Mart	www.enablemart.com
Enabling Devices	https://enablingdevices.com
FlagHouse	www.flaghouse.com
Gopher Sport	www.gophersport.com
Gym Closet	www.gymcloset.com
Independent Living Aids	www.independentliving.com
Innovative Products	www.bowlingramps.com
MaxiAids	www.maxiaids.com
School Specialty	www.schoolspecialty.com
Spinlife	www.spinlife.com
Sportaid	www.sportaid.com

Note: Also consider searching your mobile device's app store.

Blindness and Visual Impairment

The following subsections provide a concise discussion of sample digital technologies commonly used by individuals who are blind or have visual impairment (VI).

Talking Devices

A wide variety of talking AT devices are geared toward individuals with VI; these devices are not to be confused with speech-generating communication devices intended to help nonverbal individuals. Instead, these devices report data to the user by means of a digital voice, often prompted by the push of a button; for example, a student who is blind might use a talking pedometer in PE in order hear her current step count. Some talking devices also offer multiple language options. Many also vibrate to provide the user with an additional physical cue (e.g., for an alarm). Figure 7.1 lists a variety of examples that can be used across various settings, from fitness to health care to education to daily living.

Another high-tech talking product is the Cone Coach (FlagHouse, 2019). This digital device, used for voice playback, can be hung from the top of a cone and is often used in station activities. The practitioner first records auditory instructions into the device, which,

Figure 7.1   Sample talking AT devices.

- Alarm clock
- Body-weight scale
- Calculator
- Color identifier
- Computer or smart device with screen reader software
- Cooking items (e.g., liquid measurer, microwave oven, kitchen scale, cooking thermometer)
- Global Positioning System (GPS) device

- Glucose and blood pressure meters
- Heart rate monitor
- Jump rope
- Pedometer
- Pill organizer
- Reading pen
- Thermometer for body temperature (ear or forehead)
- Thermometer for outside temperature
- Timer
- Watch

thanks to motion-sensing technology, are then played back to students as they approach the cone. Clearly, this product could be used to good effect in both APE and general PE.

Electronic Magnification and High-Visibility Hardware and Software

Beyond a low-tech magnifying glass, individuals with VI may use electronic magnifiers that increase the size of text or objects for easier viewing. Electronic magnification options range from handheld digital devices of varying sizes to desktop setups with a tray to support the viewing material, a built-in digital camera, and an enlarged viewing monitor. Some devices also include audio text-reading software.

Students with VI may also benefit from using a high-visibility computer keyboard with bright keys that are enlarged and feature bright contrasting colors. Likewise, the Kinderboard (FlagHouse, 2019) is intended to help individuals with VI by incorporating oversized, color-coded keys for distinguishing vowels, consonants, and punctuation marks. Individuals with VI can also change the display settings of a computer or other smart device in order to modify the size of the text, cursor, app icons, and other displayed items, as well as the display brightness and color.

Digital Beep Balls

A **beep ball** emits a loud beeping sound from an embedded digital device within the ball, thus allowing individuals with VI to track the ball's movement. The imbedded sound module is typically replaceable and often requires a replaceable 9-volt battery. The most common beep balls are multipurpose foam balls that can be used for throwing, catching, and kicking. Some individuals with autism may also benefit from using beep balls because the auditory stimulation may help them stay focused on the ball-related activity. Digital beeping devices can be integrated into almost any sport implement, including sport-specific balls, birdies, and pucks. Some products, such as the waterproof Disc Jock-e Musical Flying Disc (FlagHouse, 2019), incorporate Bluetooth connectivity so that music can be streamed through the product's wireless speaker via your smart device. For those working in a pool setting, water-safe floating digital toys or balls may be used to prompt individuals to move toward the sound. However, the purpose may be served just as well by the low-tech alternative of simply equipping a ball with embedded bells that make noise with movement.

Digital Sound Beacons

Sound beacons are closely related to beep balls and are often sold with them. **Digital sound beacons** are stationary electronic sound-making devices that emit either continuous or intermittent sounds to help individuals with VI navigate their surroundings. You may have heard such a sound beacon at a crosswalk that provides an auditory cue indicating when it is safe to walk; it may also provide a sound source to target on the other side of the street. In PE, sound beacons can be used to signify locations such as boundaries, targets, and bases.

One example of a digital sound beacon is a beep box, which is a targeting device enclosed in a padded case and placed near a target, net, or goal. For instance, a beep box might be used to help locate an archery target or the headpin when bowling. Beep boxes are often controlled by a wireless remote and may include hook or loop fasteners so they can be hung. Similarly, wireless beep sets for specific activities such as baseball, softball, and tennis may include both sport-specific beep balls and sound beacons for placement at a base or near the net, respectively. One alternative commonly found in APE involves simply using a radio or wireless speaker to play continuous music in a certain location (see chapter 5); a digital metronome can also be used as a sound beacon, for instance behind a basketball rim (McNamara, 2018).

United in Stride

United in Stride uses the Internet and computer technology to connect runners who are visually impaired with sighted guides. The networking website permits registered users to search (free of charge) for either sighted guides or runners with visual impairment via a zip code database or an interactive map search. User profiles include a description of the runner, degree of experience, and average running pace. Users can send private messages to potential partners to set up a training run.

Deafness and Hearing Impairments

The specific scope of this text precludes a discussion of the various types of digital hearing aids that may be prescribed by an audiologist or otolaryngologist. However, the following sections provide a few examples of digital technology that can be used with individuals who have a hearing impairment (HI).

Amplifying Sound Devices

As long as they are not too disruptive to other students, aids for independent daily living may also be useful in the classroom—for instance, various digital AT devices that amplify sound for individuals with HI. Some audio-amplifying products can wirelessly connect electronic devices (e.g., mobile phone, portable audio player) directly to a hearing aid. Amplified Bluetooth headphones or earpieces can connect to any Bluetooth-enabled audio device (e.g., iPad, smartphone) to magnify sound for the user. In addition, digital wireless communication systems enable an individual with HI to hear the teacher or coach more easily; in this approach the practitioner wears a microphone and transmitter and the student listens via a receiver and earbud.

Alternative Visual Digital Notification Devices

Sports that involve starting guns, whistles, or buzzers (e.g., track and field, swimming, cycling, skiing) traditionally use auditory cues to start the event (e.g., beep, starting pistol) or to stop the action. However, these signals are inaudible to some athletes who have

Using Digital Technology in Adapted PE

Robert Waugh

Elementary Health and Physical Education Teacher and Unified Sports Head Bocce Coach

Pleasant Valley Elementary School, Knoxville, Maryland, and Williamsport Elementary School, Williamsport, Maryland

What types of disabilities do your students have, and do you teach these students in an inclusive PE class?
I have had students with many different special needs including, Down syndrome, autism, spina bifida, and many more. All of the students I have taught have been in an inclusive PE setting and not in an isolated APE class.

What type(s) of digital technology do you use with students who have special needs?
First, the most obvious use of technology in my classroom would be the music that I play during activities. We use it as a cue for when to start and when to stop activities. I also use a projector and screen in order to enlarge anything of importance that I would like to go over during class.

The other main way I use technology for students with special needs is with the use of an Apple iPad and various iPad apps. I use various fitness and yoga apps that the students use when at fitness stations. The apps I have used the most have been Daily Cardio, Daily Legs, and Daily Yoga, but there are quite a few apps that can be used with students in the PE classroom. Most of my students have and use iPads or tablets at home and they feel very comfortable with them. The fitness apps will be playing when the students arrive at a station, and they will perform the exercise that is playing on the iPad.

I've also projected apps such as Temple Run and Subway Surfer on the big screen and had my students act out the game as it is played. My students who enjoy a lot of stimulation tend to like these activities. One student will play the game, and if the player in the game is running, we run in our spots. If they jump, we jump; if they duck, we duck; and so forth.

Finally, I have had students use the video recorder function on the iPad for activities. For example, as a class we created an exercise video. One student with special needs was uncomfortable being on camera performing our exercises, so that student was our camera operator. We also have used the iPad video camera for self-assessment. When learning to throw a Frisbee, I had the students get into groups of three. One student threw the Frisbee, one student retrieved it, and one video-recorded the throwing motion so that we could see what cues we were missing after the throw. This helped tremendously with some of my students.

What is your main goal for using this technology?
I want my students to be engaged and enjoy the technology, as well as use it to be successful during various units throughout the school year.

What do you like about this technology?
The technology was easy to use, most students are comfortable with it, and most students really enjoy incorporating it into the PE classroom. I thought the technology worked great for our uses and doesn't need any improvements.

(continued)

Using Digital Technology in Adapted PE *(continued)*

What suggestions do you have for others in using this technology?

Don't be afraid of it. Many of us, especially those who have been teaching for many years, can get set in our ways. However, technology can be a great tool when working with students with special needs. Many of our kids are more fluent in the technology than we teachers are, so many times we just need to get them started and get out of their way. Incorporating technology into PE and using it with all students is much easier and much more beneficial than many teachers would think.

Students in an adapted PE class follow along with exercises displayed via an iPad app; *used as 45 to 60 second stations during warm-up or a fitness unit.*

Courtesy of Robert Waugh.

HI. Certainly, an official's hand or flag signals can also be used, but signal systems with flashing lights are also used in these sports for individuals with HI. Similarly, rather than using a stopwatch with an auditory alarm, individuals with HI may use a wristwatch that vibrates. Practitioners who work with individuals who have HI must replace safety devices that emit only an auditory warning with ones that also provide a visual warning—for instance, a smoke and carbon monoxide detector that provides an auditory alarm coupled with a strobe-light warning.

Computer and Digital Video Considerations

Individuals with HI who use a computer should consider adjusting several settings, such as the computer's volume, closed captioning options, and visual (rather than auditory) notifications. These topics and many others are covered in the accessibility guides provided by both Microsoft and Apple. Many options are also available in the form of digital devices, software, and mobile device apps for transcribing speech to text. **Closed captioning**(i.e., subtitling) involves converting the audio portion of a video (e.g., dialogue and sounds) into text that is displayed concurrently on the screen. If you are using a video for instruction, you should include closed captioning or provide a script of the video to individuals with HI, particularly for online instruction (see chapter 8).

In addition, videoconferencing apps such as Skype and FaceTime (again, see chapter 8) enable people to communicate through sign language. Another possibility might be to employ **video remote interpreting (VRI)**, which is often used in medical settings. VRI enables communication between a person who is deaf or has HI with a hearing person through the use of a live off-site interpreter connected via videoconferencing.

Finally, a picture can be worth a thousand words, and movement practitioners should provide not only verbal explanations but also visual demonstrations of physical movements. This consideration is extremely important for individuals with HI, and we must make sure that any individuals with HI can see the demonstration unobstructed. If demonstrations cannot be performed face-to-face, they can be prerecorded by the practitioner and provided to students or athletes via a digital video or a photo sign—a technique often used with station activities.

Cognitive Impairments

This section provides a brief overview of sample digital technologies commonly used by individuals with cognitive impairment or multiple disabilities. Using such technologies with these individuals may not only help you provide more effective instruction but also often improves quality of life for your students or athletes outside of school or sport.

Digital Message Communicators

Digital message communicators fall into the category of augmented and alternative communication (AAC) devices, which aid communication by producing speech for the user, typically through the simple push of a button. The digital speech might derive from a message recorded by a teacher or caregiver or be digitally synthesized on demand. Message communicators aid independence by enabling users to attract others' attention and communicate feelings, requests, preferences, and rejections of things not wanted. A low-tech alternative could involve using laminated flip cards with pictures that convey messages. Message communicators can be used by anyone who struggles with speech or communication, which might include individuals with autism spectrum disorder, cerebral palsy, Down syndrome, aphasia, amyotrophic lateral sclerosis (ALS), paralysis, or recovery from stroke.

Digital message communicators can be either single- or multi-message devices and offer various features in terms of activation methods, message recording times, device size, portability and mountability, power options, and total number of possible saved messages with accompanying buttons. Some units can also be worn on a wrist strap. Single-message communicators play one message at the push of their one button. One of the more popular single-button communication switches is the BIGmack, which also acts as an ability switch (described later in this chapter) (AbleNet, 2019), thus permitting users to directly record and play back an audio recording up to two minutes long.

Some single-message units are designed to be mounted on a wall so that simple messages can be initiated in specific locations (e.g., request to use a computer or drinking fountain). Many multi-message units permit users to insert picture cards into slots, thus enabling varied responses or messages. Users often start with a single-message communicator and move to a multi-message unit as their comfort and skill levels increase. The decision about which type to use may also be made by an expert such as a speech therapist. A wide variety of communicators is available from companies such as Enabling Devices (2019) and FlagHouse (2019). The same purpose can be fulfilled by message communication apps for mobile devices, which are described in the Apps for Individuals With Disabilities section later in this chapter.

Digital Sensory Stimulation

Individuals with cognitive or multiple disabilities may benefit from sensory stimulation activities. **Digital sensory stimulation** involves assimilating multiple sense modalities (e.g., visual, auditory, tactile) into an activity and producing at least one modality by means of digital technology. For example, for a throwing and catching activity, a practitioner might consider using sensory stimulation balls that emit light or sound or have a special feel (e.g., gel core, fur, multiple ridges, soft spikes, spaghetti strands). As the practitioner tries to advance an individual's sensory–perceptual motor development, the added stimuli may help direct the learner's attention to the activity. This sensory-integrative approach

Many practitioners interacting with individuals who have cognitive impairments may use various tablet or iPad apps to assist with communication.

FatCamera/E=/Getty Images

may prove beneficial for individuals with cognitive impairments and learning disabilities, but practitioners must consider the learning environment and what works best for each individual (Hodge et al., 2012). For instance, some individuals (e.g., some students with autism) may not react well to overstimulation or to an environment in which things appear to be out of order.

Occupational, recreational, and physical therapists may also use special sensory rooms (e.g., comfort room, sensory gym) for individuals who have special needs (e.g., autism, attention deficit/hyperactivity disorder [ADHD], sensory processing disorder, mental illness, chronic pain) at school, in a therapy clinic or hospital, or in a long-term care setting. **Sensory rooms** are specialized spaces designed to deliver immersive multisensory inputs, either passively or actively, and are often used for relaxation or to treat cognitive or learning disabilities (Scanlan & Novak, 2015). In schools, sensory rooms could be used as spaces for regulating emotions (i.e., "time out" area), facilitating communication, or stimulating multisensory exploration across cognitive, affective, and psychomotor learning domains.

Many of these inputs include low-tech items for tactile, olfactory, or visual stimulation, such as textured or brightly colored balls, seats, floors, walls, toys; swings or rocking chairs; weighted blankets; and scented items. At the same time, many components also involve mid- or high-tech digital features, such as electronic self-massagers, relaxing digital lights, music or other sounds, digital images or videos projected around the room, and adapted electronic switches for easy user control. A specific type of relaxation-orientated sensory room that relies heavily on digital technology is the Snoezelen Multi-Sensory Environment (2019). For example, Sensory Magic (FlagHouse, 2019) integrates Snoezelen principles in using wireless touch screen software and adaptable switches to permit users to control their multisensory environment. The control includes the colors of the lighted devices (water bubble tubes, fiber optic hanging strands, interactive wall panels), wall-projected videos and images, and corresponding sounds, thus collectively creating adjustable, sensory-divergent, self-selected themes (e.g., sunset, beach, sunrise, skiing, autumn). This product includes more than 80 themes categorized into education, relaxation, or stimulation with the capability to create a profile for each user, as well as upload your own pictures or music to further personalize the experience.

Much like a sensory room, a shallow-water sensory pool often integrates digital technologies such as varying colored lights and sounds as users are delivered a unique hydrotherapy experience. Finally, practitioners who work in concert with a certified therapist may also consider creating a mobile sensory cart that contains items for multisensory stimulation to engage individuals who might benefit from it when a dedicated sensory room is not feasible.

Wearable Focus and Physical Activity Tracker

One product geared toward helping individuals who find it difficult to focus and stay on task—such as individuals with autism or ADHD—is a wearable device called the Revibe Connect: Vibration Reminder Watch, which is accompanied by a mobile app (Re-vibe

Technologies, 2019). ADHD is characterized by restlessness, nearly constant activity, and difficulty with concentrating and controlling impulses. To help, Revibe Connect provides quiet vibrations and prompts users to ask themselves, "Am I doing what I'm supposed to be doing?" and to respond with a "tap-back report" about whether they were on task or off task. Over time, the software adapts the frequency of prompts according to the user's history. The watch also connects wirelessly to a mobile device that enables teachers or parents to track the individual's focus, attention span, participation, and step count by means of an app. The watch also provides positive reinforcement messages and icons to support behavior improvement. More research is needed to determine this new product's effectiveness while also taking into account characteristics of individual users.

Physical Disabilities

This section discusses sample digital technologies and AT devices often used with individuals who have a physical disability or multiple disabilities.

Ability Switches

Designed for individuals with severe fine motor limitations or multiple disabilities, an ability switch allows the user to independently operate electronic switch-adapted AT devices. Examples include communication devices, computers, appliances, battery-powered toys, and sensory stimulation devices. Ability switches are typically used to turn on or turn off a switch-enabled device through the push of a button with any body part. They often enable communication when paired with a digital message communicator (described earlier in the chapter).

As evidenced in figure 7.2, ability switches come in many types and with various features. Most use a circular button connected to a switch-enabled device by means of a wire. Some are wearable or can be mounted on a wheelchair, desk, or wall. For example, a cushioned pillow-textured switch might be connected to a bendable gooseneck mount

Figure 7.2   Varying styles and features of ability switches.

- Switch activation sensitivity (i.e., how much pressure is needed to activate the switch button), including micro-touch options for individuals with limited strength
- Switch size, up to 7 inches (18 cm) in diameter to permit easier activation
- Switch shape
- Switch texture (e.g., cushioned, soft, hard, gel, smooth, tactile, bumpy, spiky, shaggy)
- Switch button color
- Light-up switches to motivate user engagement
- Length of switch cord (from device to activation button)
- Wireless (e.g., Bluetooth) connectivity from switch to device
- Mount-enabled switches (for connection to wheelchair, desk, table, wall)
- Wearable switch connected via wrist-mounted touch-fastener strap
- Single switch, or multiple switch buttons for multiple devices
- Pull-string switch (for limited strength or limited finger or hand mobility)
- Switch connectors to control battery-operated items
- Switch connector plug size, typically 1/8-inch (3.5 mm) mono or 1/4-inch (6.35 mm) phono connector plug (or adapter)

attached to a wheelchair so that an individual with limited mobility can activate a switch-enabled device or digital message communicator by applying pressure to the switch with the forehead or a cheek. Ability switches can also be made wireless simply by using a wireless switch transmitter and receiver plugged into a switch-adapted device, thus eliminating possible complications such as the risk of wires getting caught in a wheelchair.

Varying styles of switches can help individuals increase their fine motor skills—for instance, palmer and pincer grasping. Some individuals may be averse to tactilely distinctive switches, preferring a smooth surface instead. Some switches are compatible with computers, such as a large trackball with oversized switch buttons that can replace a computer mouse. Some switches are even designed specifically to initiate the roll of a bowling ball down a ramp for individuals who lack the strength or mobility to roll or push the ball (Innovative Products, 2019).

Pool Entry and Exit Lifts

The ADA mandates that all public and semi-public swimming pools and spas be fully accessible, including for entry and exit, by individuals with disabilities (Lepore et al., 2007). Pools with universal design features may satisfy this requirement simply by including a low-tech, sloped-ramp entry with handrails (i.e., a wet ramp). As a mid- or high-tech alternative, a lift consists of a mechanized seat that can be lowered or raised independently by a person who is injured or disabled in order to get into and out of the pool. Some lifts are portable, whereas others can place an aquatic wheelchair directly into the water. Pool lifts should permit one-hand operation, should not require tight grasping (i.e., no more than 5 pounds, or 2.3 kilograms, of force), and should permit operation with a closed fist (Lepore et al., 2007). Overall, pool lifts provide a great example of how technology can provide access to a fitness facility for individuals with disabilities, and practitioners who work in aquatic environments must be informed and must advocate for these inclusive features.

Powered and Sport-Specific Wheelchairs

Some individuals with acute or chronic physical impairments due to illness, injury, or disability use a manual (i.e., self-propelled) wheelchair or a power-operated vehicle (e.g., scooter). Wheelchairs enable mobility and are often outfitted with specialized seating adaptations and individualized controls. Individuals who have more severe physical impairments may use a high-tech, electric-powered wheelchair that uses batteries and motors and is often controlled (by the user or a caregiver) through push-buttons or a joystick. If the user cannot operate the traditional controls integrated into a powered wheelchair's armrest, some advanced AT adaptations permit independent use by means of chin-, head-, or tongue-operated switches or sip-and-puff air pressure controllers. Furthermore, "smart" wheelchairs—which further reduce the physical, perceptual, and cognitive skills necessary to operate a power wheelchair—may integrate touch-display controls and include sensors with collision-avoidance software to help users avoid accidents. Often, medical insurance covers the cost of a power-operated wheelchair if a doctor prescribes it and it is deemed medically necessary. In addition, low-tech products—such as flexible and rigid mounting devices and adjustable mounting clamps that attach to a wheelchair or table—permit these individuals to more easily access and use computers, view monitors, and operate mobile smart devices (e.g., smartphones, tablets).

In addition, **paramobile devices** are typically powered, four-wheeled powered carts designed for an individual with paraplegia to facilitate an upright posture. Originally designed to permit an upright golf swing, paramobile carts and wheelchairs can be customized to almost any stationary upright leisure or sporting activity—for instance, archery, fishing, and baseball batting-cage swinging.

Soft forehead ability switch connected to an adjustable gooseneck arm mounted to a wheelchair via a clamp.

Reprinted by permission from Enabling Devices, Hawthorne, NY; enablingdevices.com. 800-832-8697.

Practitioners who work with individuals who have disabilities must stay informed of the variety of specialized and sport-specific **adapted physical activity (APA)** equipment available. If they do so, then they may be able to inform these individuals and their caregivers of additional exercise opportunities. For instance, though not high-tech according to our definition (see table 7.1), it would be hard to argue that a carbon fiber sport-specific racing wheelchair is not high-tech. Although racing wheelchairs are not electric, wheelchair racers may use global positioning system (GPS) or cycling computer technology (see chapter 9). Many elite marathons and other running-related events now include wheelchair racing divisions, and some offer prize money in this category.

Another option involves adaptive performance wheelchairs, which are made for a runner to push someone with a disability in order to promote inclusion during recreational activities and athletic competition (e.g., Hoyt Running Chairs, 2019). Other **adaptive sports** (i.e., disability sports or para sports) use advanced sport-specific mobility devices or wheelchairs, such as sit skis or skates for snow and ice sports, Powerchair Football (i.e., Power Soccer), and other wheelchair sports (e.g., basketball, rugby, tennis). Finally, several wheelchair training para-treadmills have appeared on the market; they are similar to a traditional treadmill but target manual arm-propelled wheelchair users (e.g., Invictus Active, 2019; Wheelers' Paramill, 2019). Practitioners may consider hosting fundraising events to support these athletes in purchasing these types of accessible equipment.

High-Tech Prosthetics

A **prosthesis** is an external or implanted artificial device that replaces a missing or defective body part, whether due to a congenital disorder or lost to trauma or disease. Artificial limbs are engineering marvels that incorporate microprocessors into materials such as titanium and carbon fiber in order to enhance ambulatory movement, anatomical mobility, and movement versatility. Sport-specific prosthetics, for example, allow individuals who have lost one or more limbs to run on a track, ride a bike, swing a golf club or baseball bat, ski down a slope, or skate on ice. Again, movement practitioners must become aware of such options, advocate for them, and help individuals obtain more accessible equipment that promotes physical activity and independence.

From the perspective of elite sport performance, many celebrated South African 400-meter runner Oscar Pistorius as he became the first double-leg amputee to participate in the Olympic Games in 2012. However, some questioned whether the use of his J-shaped, carbon-fiber Flex-Foot Cheetah running "blades" gave him

This paramobile device acts as a powered cart designed for an individual with a physical disability to facilitate an upright posture for golf.

Anthony Netto inventor of Pargolfer Paramoblile made by Ottobock of Germany. Golf professional.

an unfair advantage (Eveleth, 2012). Although the topic of high-tech prosthetic versus human limb is still being debated, athletes with disabilities who compete against other athletes with disabilities in the Paralympics are governed by specific rules for equipment technology set forth by the International Paralympic Committee (IPC, 2011). These rules state that adapted equipment used in IPC-sanctioned competition must be safe (for the user, for others, and for the field of play), fair (each sport's rules must regulate equipment in detail), and universally available to all athletes (including in terms of cost and scale of availability). They also require that sport performance be a result of human physical prowess, rather than as a result of technology or equipment. The policy continues by reiterating that "equipment that results in sport performance not primarily being generated by the athlete's own physical prowess but being generated by automated, computer-aided, or robotic devices is prohibited in IPC-Sanctioned Competitions and Events, and at Paralympic Games" (International Paralympic Committee, 2011, p. 2). Practitioners who work in this environment must know these regulations. In most settings, however, the aim is to provide access for independent daily living activities and physical exercise abilities through prostheses.

APPS FOR INDIVIDUALS WITH DISABILITIES

Apps fall into many categories that may be used with individuals with disabilities. Although apps are specific to a given operating system (e.g., Google's Android, Apple's iOS), many are designed to work with mobile smart devices (e.g., iPads, tablets, smartphones). In addition to the plethora of apps discussed in other chapters of this text that may prove useful with this population, table 7.4 provides several apps geared toward individuals who have one or more disabilities.

The majority of the apps summarized in table 7.4 are geared toward individuals who have learning disabilities or cognitive impairments. However, many can also be used with typically developing children and adults. Finally, consider low-tech alternatives to these apps. For example, flip cards with printed pictures might be able to help express emotions in much the same way that a digital app might. Likewise, laminated visual

Table 7.4 Sample Apps for Individuals with Disabilities

App	Description	Need addressed
ABA Flash Cards & Games—Emotions	Helps users identify, understand, and respond appropriately to human emotions via digital flash cards and interactive games	Cognitive impairment
BrainWorks	Customizable app provides structured, timed sensory activity breaks specific to the setting (school, home, community, desk) and the user's current sensory feelings (just right, slow and sluggish, fast and stressed, or fast and hyper)	Cognitive impairment
Choiceworks	Multipurpose app facilitates independence, helps establish daily routines with a visual schedule planner, improves patience, and regulates emotions	Cognitive impairment
ExerciseBuddy	Autism-friendly visual exercise system includes videos, exercises, worksheets, and a healthy history tracker	Autism or other cognitive impairment
First Then Visual Schedule	Visual picture scheduling app intended to lower anxiety and increase independence throughout activity transitions	Behavior management
My Token Board	Customizable token economy visual reward system intended to motivate desirable behavior and task completion	Behavior management
Pedius	Allows users with HI to communicate by mobile phone without a third-party intermediary; Users type in a message, and the app translates it into speech, thus enabling the person who was called to hear the message. Then, when this person responds verbally, their speech is translated back into text so the user can read it.	Hearing impairment
Prism (ETC)	Aims to help those who do not have autism gain an understanding and cultivate empathy for those who do have autism	Autism
Proloquo2Go	Symbol-based AAC app provides a visual vocabulary for communicating needs and messages	Communication challenges
Special Education Dictionary	App that includes special education terms and definitions; It was developed by the National Association of Special Education Teachers (NASET)	Special education
The Mood Meter	Tool that helps users reflect on and manage emotions while building emotional intelligence	Emotional regulation
Time Timer	Provides a visual representation to help learners understand time, display patience by waiting their turn, or stay at a given activity	Behavior management
Touch and Learn—Emotion	Teaches users how to recognize other's emotions and body language	Cognitive impairment

Note. AAC = augmented and alternative communication.

schedules or printed exercise pictures may be a more accessible option in a swimming pool or gym compared to a mobile device app. Consider what might work best for your students or athletes in your environment.

VIDEO GAMING FOR INDIVIDUALS WITH DISABILITIES

In chapter 5, we discussed how to use video games for motivation. As you may recall, motion-based video games (MBVGs), or exergames, use cameras, sensors, and software to track the gross motor movements required of the player, thus motivating physical activity. Individuals with disabilities are often less physically active than their peers without disability due to lack of opportunities and other types of barriers (e.g., environmental, physical, mental, emotional) (Hodge et al., 2012). Thus, it has been suggested that MBVGs provide a safe and motivating option for increased physical activity for those with special needs (Jenny et al., 2013).

Of note, MBVGs don't always require the correct sport-specific movements; moreover, they typically require less expenditure of energy than do the authentic version of a sport. Even so, they can be used as pedagogical tools for teaching basic sport concepts and strategies to individuals who would otherwise be unable to participate in the real-life version of the sport due to injury or disability (Jenny & Schary, 2016; Jenny et al., 2017). Ultimately, for example, MBVGs may allow someone in a wheelchair to participate more easily in a boxing match, climb a rock wall, physically navigate a wake rider, or play tennis all in a virtual world—where strength, balance, mobility, and other motor skills may not be as rigorous compared to authentic environments. Companies such as US Games (2018) sell a variety of MBVGs geared toward group fitness and physical education classes.

WHAT DOES THE RESEARCH SAY?

Health Benefits of Video Gaming for Individuals With Disability

Video games have been shown to facilitate several positive lifestyle-related health behaviors and health outcomes among individuals with disabilities. For instance, various MBVGs have been found to help elicit positive social initiation behaviors among children with autism spectrum disorder (Malinverni et al., 2017), to provide a motivating and safe exercise intervention for individuals with Huntington's disease (Kloos et al., 2013), to facilitate increased motor function and performance of activities of daily living among individuals with chronic stroke (Lee, 2013), and to stimulate moderate-intensity exercise among persons recovering from spinal cord injury (Rosly et al., 2017).

Virtual reality (VR) MBVGs totally immerse the user in a digital world, typically through the use of VR goggles, and have been found to improve balance ability in individuals with chronic stroke (Lee et al., 2017) and in adults who have moderate intellectual and developmental disabilities (Lotan et al., 2018). In addition, Wilcox et al. (2016) found that a specialized therapeutic video game controller helped facilitate enjoyable, repetitive, and goal-directed wrist range of motion activities in children suffering from wrist impairments. Finally, studies involving participants with VI have reported high levels of enjoyment among youth when being physically active through various MBVGs (Bofolli et al., 2011), energy expenditure equivalent to moderate levels of physical activity while playing a VI bowling game (Morelli, Foley, & Folmer, 2010), and moderate to vigorous physical activity while playing two versions of a VI tennis game that provided tactile or audio feedback or both (Morelli, Foley, Columna, et al., 2010).

Beyond physical activity, some video games are intended to improve other health outcomes. For instance, although research is needed to validate its effectiveness, a new free self-help mobile game called Shadow's Edge (Resonance House, 2019) aims to take teens and young adults who have an illness through an emotional healing process ultimately geared toward improving mental health.

Esports

Video games offer an inclusive environment where people with disabilities can play side by side with and against individuals without disabilities. As noted in chapter 5, esports (i.e., electronic sports) involves organized competitive video game play. The most popular esports are primarily sedentary console or PC video games played online, but the popularity of VR is seeping into competitive video gaming, and many of these games are MBVGs.

Some see esports as a sport in itself, due to the physical skills (fine motor skills, reaction time, eye–hand coordination), cognitive skills (decision making, strategizing, emotional control, in-game knowledge, anticipation), and teamwork skills (communication, adherence to a position or role) required for elite performance (Besombes, 2018; Fanfarelli, 2018; Lipovaya et al., 2018). Esports is now providing an inclusive platform in which players with disabilities or who are female are competing on the same team with players who do not have disabilities or who are male. For example, the Susquehanna Soniqs (Susquehanna Esports, 2019) are a co-ed professional esports team. In addition, Dayton "Wheels" Jones, who uses a wheelchair due to spinal muscular atrophy type 2, is a highly competitive professional esports player who has placed in the top 10 at many international esports tournaments (Martin, 2017). Although the lack of gross motor physicality in many seated esports is seen as a major disadvantage, this characteristic of traditional esports gives many individuals with disabilities an opportunity to compete in an environment similar to that of traditional sport. As Hans Jagnow (as cited by Hofmann, 2019) has noted, making esports accessible to all is technically feasible, but social visibility is elusive for many esports participants, manufacturers, associations, and policymakers. Even so, esports may be the new wave of accessible "sport."

Video Game Accommodations

Some video games, or the gaming environment itself, may require individualized adaptations in order to meet the unique needs of individuals with disabilities. For example, Gasperetti et al. (2011) discuss several ideas for equipment and pedagogy accommodations for practitioners using the popular MBVG Dance Dance Revolution (DDR), which is discussed in detail in chapter 5. DDR involves the player(s) rhythmically stepping on four directional arrows placed on a motion-sensing platform where performance is based on the timing and accuracy of one's steps, which should correspond to the music and on-screen visual dance characters. Gasperetti and colleagues (2011) recommend modifications for individuals with VI who play DDR —for example, using a digital projector with a large screen to enlarge the game display (rather than using a small television), reducing the room lighting to enhance the projected display contrast, moving the dance pad(s) closer to the game display, slightly angling the dance pad so that an individual's "better" eye is directed toward the center of the display, using a high-quality external speaker system to enhance the volume and tonal quality of the in-game audio, reducing the difficulty level of the game (e.g., slower music and accompanying steps), having the instructor provide directional and step-timing verbal cueing in sync with the music (e.g., "right, step;" "back, step"). Such ideas can be applied to many games; the key is to know your students and accommodate their individual needs and abilities.

Several resources address accommodations for video gaming. First, the Game Accessibility Guidelines (2019) provide categorized motor, cognitive, vision, hearing, speech, and

High school students in James Gunther's adapted physical education class participate in a bowling video game equipped with an ability switch.

Courtesy of James Gunther.

general recommendations for accessible game design. In addition, AbleGamers (2018) is a U.S. nonprofit organization whose mission is to "bring inclusion and improved quality of life for people with disabilities through the power of video games" (para. 1). AbleGamers accessibility experts offer individualize assessments to determine custom gaming setups, including modified controllers (e.g., mouth controllers, eye gaze, customized controllers) and special AT. Similarly, CapGame (2018) is a French nonprofit that facilitates access to video games for individuals with disabilities by providing consulting, offering hardware and software solutions, and providing accessibility reviews of games.

Several adaptive video game controllers are available for both console and PC gaming. The Xbox Adaptive Controller (Microsoft, 2019) can integrate multiple external AT gaming devices (e.g., ability switches, joysticks) and couple them with compatible specialized mounts for things like wheelchairs or body parts (e.g., leg, arm, abdomen), thus creating a customized gaming experience for an individual with special needs. Sample adaptive controllers, most of which assimilate with the Xbox Adaptive Controller, include the QuadStick (2019) hands-free game controller made for individuals with quadriplegia, the PDP One-Handed Joystick (Microsoft, 2019) and Rock Adapted Joystick (AbleNet, 2019) for one-handed game control, and the 3dRudder (2019) Foot Controller for in-game foot-powered control. Other ability switches, such as foot pedal switches, may also be used to perform additional game-specific features.

Finally, several video games have been designed specifically for individuals with disabilities as they work in concert with simple ability switches (discussed earlier). For example, Switch In Time (n.d.) software company offers accessible, switch-enabled video games for baseball, bowling, and music. Similarly, HelpKidzLearn (2017) offers many single-switch accessible games, such as the track and field game Hurdle Champion, and the curling game New Age Kurling. Tar Heel Gameplay (n.d.) offers several speech-enabled games that integrate with a touch screen or one to three ability switches and provide an additional area for creating switch-enabled games and videos via the website. Overall, MBVGs and esports may provide the equalizing, inclusive medium for adapted sport and physical activity in the future.

Conclusion

This chapter covered digital technologies that can be used by health and physical education teachers and sport coaches with individuals who have an impairment, disability, or activity restriction. In particular, it highlighted mid-tech and high-tech assistive technology that is electronic or uses a battery to function aimed at accommodating individuals with a visual, hearing, or cognitive impairment or physical disability. It also discussed sample apps designed for individuals with disabilities and reviews video gaming possibilities for individuals with disabilities.

Whatever the disability may be, instruction must be differentiated and individualized, because any given type of AT may work for one individual but not for another. In addition, practitioners should focus not on disabilities but on abilities. Because highly specialized digital tools can be pricey, it is advisable to consider low-tech AT options as well.

While the Technology Tips sidebar provided a practitioner interview with an APE teacher who uses digital technology with his students with disabilities also, see chapter 2 for an APE-focused practitioner interview with a teacher who uses various behavior management apps with students who have disabilities.

Key Terms

ability switch—Device engineered to help individuals with physical disabilities interact more easily with electronic devices (e.g., computers, digital message communicators, toys).

accessibility—Approach and environment (i.e., curriculum, facilities, equipment, pedagogy) geared to provide opportunities for success to individuals across a diverse spectrum of abilities and special needs.

accommodation—Modification of equipment, curriculum, environment, or teaching strategies (e.g., lowering the height of a basketball hoop) to permit an individual with a disability to complete a task or access content.

activity limitation—Inability to perform physical tasks or engage in social or recreational activities without the help of special equipment or another person.

adapted physical activity (APA)—Activity that provides accommodations to individuals with disabilities so that they can participate in physical activity for recreation, fitness, or sport.

adapted physical education (APE)—Educational services that provide accommodations geared to meet the unique needs of each student with a disability in physical education.

adaptive sport—Traditional recreational or competitive sport that includes modifications for people with disabilities (e.g., wheelchair basketball) or sport designed specifically for and played by individuals with disabilities (e.g., goalball, for individuals who are blind); also known as *disability sport* or *parasport*.

assistive technology (AT)—Tools, applications, equipment, and devices that help individuals with disabilities compensate for limitations by maintaining, enabling, or improving functional ability.

beep ball—Ball that emits a loud beep sound from an embedded digital device so that individuals with visual impairment can track the its movement through auditor cues.

bias—Stereotyping, prejudice, or discrimination that involves differential evaluation or treatment of a group or of an individual based on group membership (e.g., individuals with disabilities).

closed captioning—Conversion of the audio portion of a video (e.g., dialogue, sounds) into words displayed on the screen; also known as *subtitling*.

Deaflympics—Elite sporting competition sanctioned by the International Olympic Committee for athletes who are deaf.

digital message communicator—Type of augmented and alternative communication (AAC) device that either plays a prerecorded message or produces digitally synthesized speech on demand.

digital sensory stimulation—Stimulation that integrates multiple sensory modalities (e.g., visual, tactile, auditory) and produces at least one of them digitally. Examples include digital lights or sounds and self-massagers.

digital sound beacon—Stationary electronic sound-making device (e.g., radio, beep box) that helps people with visual impairment to navigate their surroundings by providing either continuous or intermittent signals, often to signify boundaries, targets, or bases.

disability—Umbrella term for impairments or restrictions that substantially limit at least one major life activity, such as seeing, hearing, walking, learning, concentrating, communicating, caring for oneself, etc.

discrimination—Unjust treatment based on membership in a certain group, such as people with disabilities.

diversity—Presence of differences that are socially meaningful (e.g., in mental or physical ability).

504 plan—Education plan that includes accommodations, modifications, or other services for a student who does not qualify for an IEP but has a disability that substantially affects learning or participation.

impairment—Any loss or abnormality in one's anatomy, cognition, or physiology that impacts or diminishes typical functioning (e.g., inability to bear weight on one's feet).

inclusion—Provision of services and adaptations (e.g., of equipment) to students with disabilities in a mainstream environment (e.g., sport team, general physical education class) rather than in a separate setting.

individualized education plan (IEP)—Document addressing special education and related services to be provided in order to meet the unique needs of a student with a disability in accordance with the Individuals with Disabilities Education Improvement Act (IDEIA, 2004)

Paralympics—Global Olympic-style sporting event staged specifically for elite athletes with a wide range of intellectual and physical disabilities.

paramobile device—Powered cart or wheelchair, typically four-wheeled, designed to help individuals with paraplegia assume an upright posture and customizable to facilitate almost any stationary upright leisure or sporting activity (e.g., golf, archery, fishing, baseball batting).

participation restriction—Problem (e.g., physical limitation) experienced by a person that restricts a daily life activity (e.g, driving).

prejudice—Preconceived opinion about a certain group or about an individual based solely on membership in a certain group.

prosthesis—Artificial device, either external or implanted, that replaces a missing or defective body part.

sensory room—Specialized space designed to deliver immersive multisensory inputs, either passively or actively, that is often used for relaxation and to treat cognitive and learning disabilities.

special education—Differentiated instruction that includes accommodations to meet individual differences and needs of each student with a disability.

special needs—In the context of education and coaching, accommodations required due to an individual's disability or difficulty with learning, behavior, or emotions.

Special Olympics—Global sport organization that provides year-round training and competition for individuals with intellectual disabilities.

stereotype—Preconceived belief about a particular group's skills, traits, or attitudes.

universal design for instruction (UDI)—Planned but flexible instructional approach that uses accommodations (e.g., assistive technology, equipment, differentiated activities) to provide customized opportunities for all students to learn and achieve desired standards, goals, and outcomes.

video remote interpreting (VRI)—Service that enables communication between a person who is deaf or has hearing impairment with a hearing person through an off-site interpreter connected via videoconference.

Review Questions

1. What is assistive technology (AT), and what are its three levels?

2. What digital AT devices are commonly used by or with people with visual impairments?

3. What digital AT devices are commonly used by or with people with hearing impairments?

4. What digital AT devices are commonly used by or with people with cognitive impairments?

5. What digital AT devices are commonly used by or with people with physical disabilities?

6. What are some apps that are commonly used by practitioners when working with individuals who have disabilities?

7. What are some common video game accommodations for individuals with disabilities?

Discussion Questions

For the following questions, first describe your setting and the age of your participants, then respond separately to each question.

1. What are your experiences with assistive technology (or the experiences of someone you know)? Describe the AT in detail. For what purpose was the technology used? Did it work? What suggestions would you offer others for using it effectively?

2. Describe a mid- or high-tech piece of assistive technology, then explain in detail whether a low-tech device or accommodation could replace it. Indicate why, or why not.

3. In great detail with examples, describe how you would implement assistive technology in a sport practice or competition, health education lesson, or physical education activity.

4. Describe a specific disability and detail how you would accommodate it using assistive technology.

5. Would you encourage (and, if needed, help) an individual with a disability to play recreational video games or esports? Why, or why not?

8

Online Instruction and Remote Supervision

Chapter Objectives

When you have completed this chapter, you will be able to do the following:

1. Discuss advantages and challenges of online instruction.
2. Apply best practices in designing online, hybrid, and flipped instruction courses.
3. Create a screen recording video for online course delivery.
4. Describe the necessary equipment and offer recommendations for effective remote supervision via synchronous videoconferencing.

Odds are that at some point you have taken an online or hybrid course, or at least completed professional development or training via the Internet. Perhaps you have completed, are working on, or are considering an online degree. You may even be using this textbook in an online or hybrid course.

Like it or not, online instruction continues to pervade education and coaching. This trend may be most apparent in higher education, where a 2017 report from the U.S. Department of Education found that over 15 percent of undergraduate and graduate students were enrolled exclusively in **distance education courses** (Ginder et al., 2018). Moreover, during the 2015-2016 academic year, almost 45 percent of undergraduate students reported taking at least one online course (including over 45 percent of those studying education or health), and more than 10 percent reported that their entire program was online (U.S. Department of Education, 2018). During the same time frame, 45 percent of graduate students reported taking at least one online course (including nearly 60 percent and more than 45 percent, respectively, of those studying education and health), and more than 25 percent reported that their entire program was delivered online (U.S. Department of Education, 2018). Another recent report found that almost all (99 percent) of the sampled higher education administrators perceived that the demand for online education has either remained strong or increased, and nearly 75 percent reported deciding to offer fully online programs primarily based on the growth potential for overall student enrollment (Venable, 2018).

At the K-12 level, it is more difficult to determine exactly how many students are taking online courses. **Virtual schools** have emerged on the K-12 learning landscape, particularly in rural and homeschool education. During the 2016-2017 fiscal year, state virtual schools served more than 420,000 K-12 students through nearly a million supplemental online course enrollments (Digital Learning Collaborative, 2018).

State virtual schools provide statewide services for **online learning** for both students and teachers (e.g., supplemental online courses, teacher and staff professional development, educational programming) that are created, facilitated, and/or funded by a state. A state virtual school program may be managed by a state education agency, a contracted charter school, a 501(c)(3) nonprofit organization, higher education institution, or other organization. State virtual schools do not award diplomas and are not required to meet common K-12 school responsibilities, such as counseling, state and federal reporting, and administration of state-level standardized assessments. With some exceptions, most states require that enrollment in a state virtual school course be approved beforehand by the student's school district, and all districts must still provide counseling and mentoring to all students. Many of these virtual schools also set up physical drop-in centers where students can meet with teachers **face-to-face (F2F)** for tutoring.

During the 2016-2017 fiscal year, state virtual schools operated in 23 states (and Washington D.C.). The average student took 1.2 online courses, 9 percent of all courses were categorized as "health/fitness," and participating students were distributed across levels as follows: 80 percent grades in 9 through 12, 14 percent in grades 6 through 8, and 6 percent in grades K through 5 (Digital Learning Collaborative, 2018). According to a 2016 SHAPE America report, 31 states permit the use of online physical education courses to satisfy required physical education credits (Society of Health and Physical Educators, 2016).

Coaching has also moved online. In sport, online coaching is more prevalent among individual lifetime sport athletes, particularly in less technical activities where immediate concurrent feedback about form and mechanics is not paramount (e.g., distance running, triathlon, swimming, cycling). Online coaching has also developed a strong presence in health and wellness, where it is offered by many certified health/wellness coaches.

Despite all of these developments, online teaching and learning still encounter some strong resistance, and this is particularly true among traditionalists in academia. However, as distance education has gained traction, past perceptions that online instruction is always inferior to F2F instruction have begun to shift, especially among students and employers (Venable, 2018). Faculty are paramount in implementing successful **digital learning** technologies, yet both administrators and faculty report that such endeavors often lack sufficient resources (Lammers et al., 2017).

This chapter provides you with ideas and resources for initiating and facilitating effective online, hybrid, and flipped instructional techniques. It also provides specific discussions centering on physical education, health education, and coaching, as well as best practices for remote supervision of teachers and coaches via videoconferencing. You can use the online instruction and remote supervision methods covered in this chapter to augment your current instructional practices and perhaps also earn additional income.

ONLINE INSTRUCTION

An **online course** is delivered almost completely online (i.e., via the Internet), including all content, student–teacher interactions, and assessments. In some cases, additional student–teacher interactions may be conducted by telephone, but such courses typically involve no F2F meetings, with the possible exceptions of office hours or a proctored final exam. Online delivery may be used for a single course or for an entire program. Online education comes with many advantages and disadvantages, as shown in table 8.1.

Online courses often utilize a **learning management system** (LMS), which may also be referred to as a *course* (or *content*) *management system*. An LMS uses web-based software to help the instructor administer the course, deliver learning content, document and track student progress, and facilitate online course interactions between classmates and with the instructor. Examples include Blackboard Learn, D2L Brightspace, Moodle, Canvas, Absorb, and Schoology.

Online and Blended Course Structures

Online course delivery formats include synchronous and asynchronous, whereas blended instructional techniques include hybrid, web-facilitated, and flipped instruction. Although a **synchronous online course** involves no F2F class meetings in a brick-and-mortar building, students still attend scheduled classes led by the instructor through videoconferencing with chat text features. In other words, the instructor in this virtual classroom leads classes in real time via the Internet by means of video and audio functions. Students can also ask questions and get immediate responses from the instructor through either audio or instant messaging. During an online lesson, the instructor may use LMS features to set up discussion or chat groups that function much like small groups in a traditional classroom.

An **asynchronous online course** takes a student-centered approach in which learning content is delivered online, typically via email and a learning management system (LMS), without the constraints of time or place. Although assignments may require student interactions, students typically work at their own pace through **learning modules** and are not required to meet F2F or be online at any specific time (except for possibly a proctored final exam). Throughout the course, the instructor interacts with students and facilitates student exchanges through email and LMS functions (e.g., **discussion boards**, assignment feedback).

Some courses, known as **massive open online courses (MOOCs)**, are geared toward a very large or even unlimited enrollment (i.e., 100 or more students) and operate on an open-access basis (i.e., are free to anyone). These online courses are typically asynchronous and self-paced and use an LMS or **courseware** that enables auto-graded assessments (e.g., multiple-choice exams) with minimal instructor-to-student interaction. A detailed discussion of MOOCs lies beyond the scope of this text.

In **blended learning**, at least a portion of the content or some of the opportunities for interaction are delivered online and F2F. This approach typically affords students

Table 8.1 Potential Advantages and Disadvantages of Online Education

Potential advantages	Potential disadvantages
Schedule flexibility for students and instructors since coursework is completed on students' own time, which is particularly beneficial for students with busy schedules (e.g., due to jobs, sport involvement, or family responsibilities)	Need for computer or digital mobile device with reliable Internet access at home or elsewhere (e.g., library, public Wi-Fi, friend's home)
Convenience for students and instructors because coursework and grading can be completed anywhere with Internet access	Depending on course structure, student perception of a sterile learning environment with inadequate social interaction (particularly in some poorly designed asynchronous courses)
Possible career advancement (e.g., online degree attainment by working professionals who lack time or flexibility for a F2F program)	Potential difficulties with communication and collaboration among classmates (particularly in asynchronous courses that involve group problem-solving and brainstorming activities)
Promotion of lifelong learning (particularly among post-traditional students)	Delayed communication with the instructor and student dissatisfaction (e.g., not receiving an immediate answer to a question posted or emailed as part of an asynchronous online course)
Self-pacing, as students complete coursework at their own pace within a framework of deadlines established by the instructor	Possible lack of institutional support for students (e.g., LMS or other technical assistance)
Facilitation of developing self-discipline through self-paced course formats	Potential for higher course drop-out rates compared to F2F courses in higher education (Allen & Seaman, 2015), though perhaps due to student factors (e.g., trying online due to work or family commitments) rather than the nature of online courses per se
Student-to-instructor and student-to-student communication is possible at any time of the day (though perhaps delayed)	Student accountability and self-regulation issues due to more flexible course structures (e.g., some students may prefer to be told when to come to class and engage with the learning content)
May facilitate more individualized and immediate student feedback, particularly as compared with large F2F classes	Technical issues for students or instructors (e.g., loss of Internet access, LMS problems, device–software incompatibility, course navigation)
Easy review of course content (multiple times if needed) to aid student understanding	Time required to learn the LMS or online learning environment while taking or creating an online course for the first time
Benefits for some students with special needs (e.g., lecture subtitling for students with hearing impairment)	Depending on course structure and activities, fewer student opportunities for practical hands-on experience with immediate instructor feedback, especially as compared with hybrid and F2F courses
Financial benefits for students and instructors (e.g., reduced travel costs, ability to maintain a job during typical business hours)	Online pedagogy and technical LMS-specific knowledge required of instructors
Time savings and potential reduction in transportation-related stressors (e.g., parking) for both students and instructors since no commute is required to and from campus	Possible lack of institutional support for online instructors, such as lack of training and inadequate financial compensation for creating new online courses (typically $1,000 to $2,500 per credit in higher education)
Real-world technology skill development for both students and instructors	Some online instructors report that the time investment is greater than that of F2F courses, particularly for course preparation, grading, and providing student feedback (Zhang et al., 2018)

Potential advantages	Potential disadvantages
Connection of students to a global learning village (i.e., community of learners) with diverse perspectives and experiences as students may interact with others around the world to share ideas	Persistence of misconceptions about the quality of online learning on the part of some key stakeholders (particularly some potential employers, education administrators, and admissions representatives) that perpetuate the false idea that F2F instruction is always superior to online instruction
Potential for increased student choice of courses due to the alleviation of scheduling conflicts common with F2F courses, which may better align with career paths, particularly in terms of opportunities for professional development	Lack of specific research targeting online learning in health and physical education (particularly at the K-12 level) and in coaching
Useful for students to connect with certified teachers or experts in the field with a subject-specific certification and accompanying pedagogical content knowledge who do not have access to these experts locally	Difficulty involved in providing online learners in asynchronous formats with real-time feedback about their performance of motor skills (but could be taught through synchronous videoconferencing within online environments)
	Online education may not be appropriate for elementary students, particularly asynchronous instruction (SHAPE America, 2018)
Ease of differentiation of instruction or assessments for every student (e.g., individual student extended exam time within LMS)	Online physical education or coaching may not be appropriate for individuals who lack competency in basic movement patterns (e.g., elementary students, students with special needs) (SHAPE America, 2018)
Potential for decrease in instructor's midsemester workload after the majority of the course's learning content is developed before the semester	
Possible increase in student enrollment (particularly for summer and intersession courses)	
Increase in revenue for institutions and instructors through increased online enrollment and possibility of supplementing income through flexible-schedule online instruction	
More scheduling flexibility and reduced costs for institutional infrastructure (e.g., no physical classroom or office space required)	

Note: F2F = face-to-face; LMS = learning management system.

Some ideas adapted from Healy, Block, and Judge (2014); and Mohnsen (2012).

some control over time, place, path, or pace. It can take various forms. For instance, **hybrid courses**, which include blended learning practices, reduce the number of F2F class meetings in favor of delivering some content online. In contrast, **web-facilitated courses** meet F2F but are augmented by Internet-based **educational technology** that enables the instructor to do such things as post the syllabus online and receive student assignments through an LMS. A web-facilitated course is not a hybrid course, because it does not reduce the number of F2F class meetings. Another blended approach uses a format known as flipped instruction, which is discussed later.

WHAT DOES THE RESEARCH SAY?

What Is Best: Online, Hybrid, or F2F?

A recent study found that about 85 percent of online college students believe the value of their degree equals or exceeds the cost, and that those who have experienced both online and F2F courses view online learning as being equally good or better (Magda & Aslanian, 2018). Furthermore, a 12-year meta-analysis performed by the U.S Department of Education on 99 studies revealed that online instruction can result in meaningful student learning and that students in online or hybrid courses perform modestly better, on average, than students learning the same material in a F2F setting (Means et al., 2010). The study also indicated that hybrid instruction was more effective than either fully online or fully F2F instruction, and that learning was greatest when online instruction was collaborative or instructor-directed rather than focused on independent student learning. However, the authors advise caution about generalizing these results to K-12 settings or to any given academic subject (e.g., physical education), because the majority of the studies examined in the analysis involved older learners distributed across varying subjects. Overall, although more research is needed and individual environmental factors must be considered, in general it appears that online instruction can be effective and that the hybrid approach may be best.

Online Course Equipment and Software

Online and blended course design can be affected by multiple factors, such as the type of course (e.g., synchronous or asynchronous; fully online or blended), the length of the course, and the availability of LMS tools and other technology as well as the knowledge and willingness to use them. Typical equipment and software needed by online instructors and students include the following:

- Computer with speakers (mandatory for instructor) or digital mobile device (e.g., tablet, smartphone)
- Reliable Internet access
- Access to the learning management system (LMS)
- Types of commonly required software:
  - Email (typically provided by the educational institution)
  - Word processing (e.g., Microsoft Word, Google Docs)
  - Presentation software (e.g., Microsoft PowerPoint)
  - Up-to-date web browser (e.g., Firefox, Google Chrome)
  - Spreadsheet software (e.g., Microsoft Excel, Google Sheets)
  - Adobe Acrobat Reader (to open PDF files)
  - Web conferencing software provided by institution (e.g., Zoom, WebEx, Adobe Connect)
- Other possible items: scanner, webcam, external microphone, digital video camera, other course-specific items (e.g., textbook, heart rate monitor, pedometer, motion analysis software), screen-capture software (e.g., Camtasia, Screencast-O-Matic), digital video editing software (covered in chapter 11)

Online Course Design and Delivery

Even though online course design is affected by both the LMS used and the instructor's preferences, many online courses include similar components. Quality Matters (QM; MarylandOnline, 2019) and the Aurora Institute (formerly International Association for K-12 Online Learning[iNACOL], 2019) both provide commonly referenced standards and rubrics that can be used in designing and evaluating online courses in secondary education and higher education (see table 8.2). Online instructors should use these resources as guides for building and delivering high-quality online courses.

QM's rubrics for K-12 education (MarylandOnline, 2019b) and higher education (MarylandOnline, 2018) are subdivided into the following domains (each of which contains substandards): course overview and introduction, learning objectives (competencies), assessment and measurement, instructional materials, learning activities and learner interaction, course technology, learner and instructor support, and accessibility and usability. Similarly, iNACOL's standards for K-12 online courses are categorized as follows: online course content, instructional design, technology, student assessment, and course management. Of course, many of these standards and rubric areas are also applicable to effective F2F instruction.

QM also offers various other resources and online education professional development, such as a workshop on applying the QM rubric, an online teaching certificate for higher education and K-12 instructors, an option to have an online course be QM certified, and course design rubrics (higher education and K-12) for publishers (MarylandOnline, 2019a). Again, it is advisable for all online instructors to refer to the appropriate rubric and standards listed in table 8.2 when designing and delivering an online course.

For those who are unfamiliar with what an online course might look like, figure 8.1 provides a sample screenshot for an online course using the D2L Brightspace LMS. For additional examples, see the web resource (WR) that accompanies this textbook.

Common Components of an Online Course

When designing an online course, consider including the following common components. Some of these recommendations were adapted from QM's K-12 (MarylandOnline, 2016a) and higher education (MarylandOnline, 2018) rubrics.

- *Welcome-to-class email.* Send a welcome email through the LMS one month before the start of the course, another message one week beforehand, and yet another on the first day of class (for an example, see the WR). The most important thing is to initiate

TELEPHONE OPTIONS FOR ONLINE INSTRUCTORS

Students sometimes want to speak directly with the instructor, especially in asynchronous courses. If only audio is needed, then an office phone provides the best option. However, many online instructors work from home and may not want to give students their personal phone number. One alternative is to set up a business phone number to share with students that forwards any voice calls or text messages from that number to your personal phone by means of a Google Voice account (free Google account required). If you need audio, video, and screen-sharing capability, then you might use web conferencing software such as Zoom, Skype, Google Hangouts, Adobe Connect, or WebEx. Two other good options are Facetime and WhatsApp, but they may require you to share your smartphone number.

Table 8.2 Sample Standards, Rubrics, and Guidelines for Online Education

Type of resource	Source
Higher education online course rubric	• QM higher education rubric (6th ed., 2018)
K-12 education online course standards and rubrics	• QM K-12 rubric (5th ed., 2019) • iNACOL National Standards for Quality Online Courses (version 2, 2011)
Continuing and professional education rubric	• QM continuing and professional education rubric (2nd ed., 2015)
Online instructor skills set and teaching standards	• QM online instructor skill set (2016) • iNACOL National Standards for Quality Online Teaching (version 2, 2011)
Blended or hybrid rubrics	• iNACOL Blended Learning Teacher Competency Framework (2014)
Online program standards	• iNACOL National Standards for Quality Online Programs (2009)

Note: QM = Quality Matters (MarylandOnline, 2019a), and iNACOL = International Association for K-12 Online Learning (2019). Rubrics or standards by QM can be accessed at www.qualitymatters.org and iNACOL at www.inacol.org.

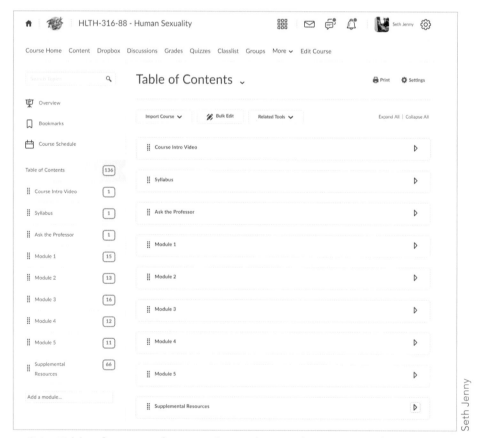

Figure 8.1 Table of contents for an undergraduate online course in human sexuality that uses the D2L Brightspace learning management system (LMS).

communication early with your students and give them time to acquire the textbook or any required course-related material (e.g., pedometer) before the course begins.

- *Welcome! Start here!* This message could be posted within the LMS and found easily by students when using the system to log in to the course. In some LMSs, this message could be posted in an Overview or Course Home tab. This posting and the syllabus will probably make up the most text-heavy area of the course. Although some of this information could also be included in the course syllabus or in an instructor-created course video introduction, be sure to include the following information for students:
    - Course purpose and introduction, with a course structure orientation (i.e., where to locate course components)
    - Expectations for student and instructor communication (e.g., email, discussions, phone contact, instructor response time)
    - Institutional and course policies (e.g., grading policy, late work policy, web link to institution's online student code of conduct)
    - Minimal technology requirements for the course (e.g., computer system requirements, videoconferencing capability) and where to locate or sign out needed technology
    - Prerequisites (e.g., course, technology-specific knowledge)
    - Instructor and student self-introductions
    - Measurable course-specific learning objectives and competencies
    - Instructor's plan for interactions with students (e.g., discussions, assignment feedback, preferred modes of communication for student questions)
    - Information about digital privacy and how to protect one's data
    - Where to find key student resources (see later item in this list)

- *Syllabus.* Some instructors use a syllabus quiz or course scavenger hunt as an initial assignment to check for student understanding of course structure and requirements.

- *Video introduction.* This video often includes a screen recording introduction of the instructor and an overview of the course structure; it may also highlight key areas of the syllabus and selected components from earlier in this list.

- *Video overview of assignments.* If students will work on a major project throughout much of the course, some instructors may also provide a video specifically about the project in order to prepare the student in stimulating early thoughts and ideas. This is especially true if students will self-select a topic or if several small assignments will build toward the major assignment; in that case, additional videos for each assignment can be embedded into each learning module.

- *Ask the Professor discussion board prompt.* Consider including an open digital forum (i.e., discussion board) where you can answer questions posed by students for the whole class to see (for an example, see figure 8.2). This approach spares you from answering the same question repeatedly through individual messages (i.e., emails) from multiple students and can enhance student understanding for the whole class. It can be used in online, hybrid, and web-facilitated courses. Student questions may also prompt you to modify or clarify course content or assignment directions.

- *Online student introductions.* The instructor's introduction is typically included in the course introduction video. Many instructors also require students to provide an online introduction to the class through a discussion board assignment during the first week of class (for an example, see figure 8.3). You might welcome students to the class individually by replying to their initial postings and asking a follow-up question about something they wrote in order to make a personal connection. This activity can help you cultivate a community of learners.

Figure 8.2 Example of an Ask the Professor prompt for a discussion board.

ASK COURSE-RELATED QUESTIONS HERE!

- If you have a question, then it is likely that one of your classmates does as well.
- Please do not email me privately (unless it pertains to something personal, such as your grade).

DIRECTIONS

- Click on the Ask the Professor discussion link, then click Start a New Thread.
- Type your question and then submit it.
- This approach allows everyone to read both the question and my answer. Thank you!

Note: If the LMS permits, it is recommended that students and instructors alike subscribe to this discussion board so that an email notification is sent automatically when anyone posts to the forum.

• *Learning modules.* Learning modules make up a sequenced collection of subject-related materials presented in a logical order to guide students through learning content and assessments. They can be used to support course goals or objectives, a group of concepts, or a theme. An online course is often divided into multiple learning modules, which may each center on one or more course objectives or chapters of the course textbook. This structure is often carried out through folders and subfolders in the LMS, where you can place text, files, web links, videos, discussion boards, assignments, and exams. For example, an 8-week online course might be divided into eight 1-week learning modules, whereas a 16-week course might be divided into eight 2-week modules or five 3-week modules with a remaining final exam/project 1-week module. Some instructors provide a screen recording video introduction for each learning module (for an example, see the WR).

• *Learning module content (i.e., learning activities).* This content should be current, varied (e.g., text, videos, multimedia materials), in compliance with copyright law (see chapter 15), supported by accurate references, and clearly correlated with objectives and competencies for both the module and the course overall. Although instructor styles may vary, and a program may require the use of a certain template, learning modules often include the following elements:

- Module schedule (including activity sequence with corresponding deadlines)
- Module learning objectives that are appropriate, measurable, and clearly correlated with the module's learning activities as well as course objectives and competencies
- Required readings (e.g., textbook chapters, articles)
- Instructor lectures and videos, which must go beyond simply posting publisher-created PowerPoint slides to include the instructor's own voice, perhaps in the form of screen recording instructional videos (detailed in the next section) with closed captioning for students with a hearing impairment
- Assignments and assessments (both discussed a bit later in this chapter)

Figure 8.3   Sample discussion board assignment for student introductions in a graduate course.

DIRECTIONS

- Click on the Online Introduction Assignment, then click on Start a New Thread.
- Introduce yourself to the class by answering the following questions.
- Number your responses and answer each in complete sentences (and please check your grammar and spelling).

For more information about me, [insert a web link to the biography page of your personal website, or answer the following questions yourself].

1. What is your name (including preferred first name)?
2. Where you are from (i.e., hometown)?
3. What was your undergraduate major (and minor, if any)?
4. At what institution did you earn your undergraduate degree?
5. What is your current graduate degree program?
6. What are your career goals or ambitions? If you are currently employed, please mention your current position as well.
7. [Ask a question about the specific subject of the course, such as the following:] What is your research or survey experience? What are your thoughts about taking a course that addresses [course subject]? What is your background in sport and coaching?
8. [Ask a question geared toward getting to know students personally, such as the following:] What was the best vacation you ever took, and why? Describe your perfect day. What is something that nobody knows about you at this school?
9. Please attach a picture of yourself (or of a movie character that represents you).

After posting your initial response, reply and comment on at least two classmates' initial postings (e.g., welcoming them to the course or asking follow-up questions). Refer specifically to something mentioned in that individual's initial posting. Make an effort to reply to any introductions that have no replies yet.

This assignment is due by 11:59 p.m. on Sunday of the first week of the course (date listed in syllabus).

Note: This example is set up for a graduate course, and some questions are not appropriate for K-12 settings (e.g., attaching a picture of oneself). Adjust questions according to your setting.

- *Student resources.* Useful resources might include descriptions, web links, or contact information for the following: technology and LMS support (e.g., IT help desk), accessibility services and policies, and academic and other student support services (e.g., bookstore, writing center, library, online tutoring, first-time online course introductory information or video, student handbook, reference style guidelines, counseling services, recreation services, career services, program director contact information, end-of-course evaluation information).

PRACTICAL TIPS FOR ONLINE INSTRUCTION PEDAGOGY

- Course instructional technology is varied, reinforces clear course and module learning objectives and competencies, and facilitates active student engagement and interaction.
- The instructor may consider providing students with flexibility, such as self-pacing opportunities and various options for attaining course objectives.
- At least weekly, the instructor should email the learning module schedule and overview (including upcoming activities and deadlines) as a reminder to students who may not be logging into the LMS as often as they should.
- The instructor provides students with frequent and timely assessment feedback—for instance, within a few days for smaller assignments or up to a week for a lengthy major assignment. Feedback may take the form of a grading rubric, written comments, or even audio feedback. It may be helpful to include information about how students can access assignment feedback through the LMS in the Student Resources section.
- Course content should be user friendly and accessible to diverse students across varying multimedia platforms and mobile devices (e.g., smartphones, tablets). It should include text, images, and videos that are easy to view and read in working files, LMS pages, and embedded web links.
- Consistent and purposeful instructor-to-student and student-to-student interactions are critical to building relationships and providing constructive feedback.
- The instructor should act as a source of continued guidance and support.
- The instructor and the institution should consider devising an alert system to aid in retention of online students who may be at risk. The instructor might initiate an alert after trying via email to contact a nonresponsive student (e.g., one who is missing assignments or not logging into the course). The system could automatically notify the student's academic advisor, a student success center, or the institution's retention team. Such a system could be used to help any student who is in jeopardy of not passing the course due to lack of attendance, lack of participation, or poor performance—if nothing else, by providing an opportunity to drop or withdraw from the course.
- The institution should use online communication modes to support online students similarly to how it supports on-campus students (e.g., through online academic advising, library services, tutoring, writing center services, disability services, career services, financial aid services).
- Instructional technology (IT) support should be available 24 hours a day.
- For synchronous online courses, record your videoconference class sessions and post the videos to your LMS so that students (especially any who were absent) can review the lesson later.
- Account for any potential differences in time zones between the instructor and all students, particularly when setting up online office hours, conference calls, and synchronous instruction.
- Some instructors restrict learning modules so that a given module's content is unavailable until that module's start date. This approach prohibits students from working far ahead which can, for example, cause some students to forget to interact within the current module's discussion assignments if peer responses are required. This decision is left to your personal preference.
- Consider using common online course shells across academic programs so that students are familiar with where to locate course features and how to navigate all courses across all program instructors.

Note. Many of these recommendations were adapted from QM's K-12 (MarylandOnline, 2019b) and higher education (MarylandOnline, 2018) rubrics.

- *Ancillary and supplemental material.* In addition to the required content for each module, you might also include additional "not required" resources (e.g., videos, articles, website links) to help students complete assignments and enhance their learning. Such resources allow students to dig more deeply into content of particular interest and can be organized by means of subfolders according to specific course topics or textbook chapters.

Creating Screen Recording Videos for Online Course Delivery

Online instructors often introduce a course or cover key course concepts by creating a **screen recording video**, or *screencast*, which is a digital video recording of a computer screen or mobile device output accompanied by voice-over narration. Whereas a simple screenshot creates a single still image of a screen, a screen recording video includes what appears on the computer display or device screen over a period of time. The equipment needed to create a screen recording video includes a mobile device or computer with speakers, a microphone for voice-over narration (external if not built-in or if higher quality audio is desired), a webcam (if the narrator is to be seen, perhaps in an inset box on the screen), and screen recorder software. Screen recording videos can be used in various ways, such as the following:

- Introducing an online course (e.g., purpose, objectives, competencies)
- Indicating where to locate course components (i.e., orienting students to the course structure)
- Giving mini-lectures that deliver course content
- Creating a tutorial for using a particular computer program or navigating a specific web-based resource
- Describing assignments in detail
- Discussing a work sample from a past student in preparation for an upcoming assignment
- Revisiting a key concept that appears to be misunderstood by several students

Screen recording videos can also help infuse your voice and personality into the course, which is particularly important in asynchronous courses. You should also provide closed captioning or a script of the video for students with hearing impairments. For an example of a screenshot from a screen recording video lecture, see figure 8.4.

There is no need, however, to reinvent the wheel if someone else has already made available an instructional video with the content you need (e.g., on YouTube, Vimeo, TeacherTube, Twitch), particularly if it was created by a reputable expert. For example, if you want to introduce physical education students to geocaching, you might simply do a web search for "What is geocaching?" and click on the video results. In a few seconds, you will find a plethora of high-quality instructional videos posted by Geocaching.com, including a YouTube channel (Groundspeak, 2019).

Figure 8.4 This screen recording video was created with the free version of Screencast-O-Matic and posted to YouTube. The presenter is wearing an external microphone headset and is included in the video by means of a webcam. The video can be viewed by students through inserting the video's YouTube web address into the LMS.

When evaluating an online video for instructional purposes, preview it in full. If some or all of it is inappropriate or irrelevant, check whether your LMS (if you have one) allows you to display only a selected portion. Other considerations that may help you quickly evaluate a video include the number of views, likes, and dislikes, as well as the date posted and any accompanying comments. Of course, views and likes do not equate directly to high quality or appropriateness, and newly posted videos have had less time to acquire either one. Ultimately, then, it is your responsibility to provide your students with excellent instruction, and the best option may be to create your own instructional video. For information about legal aspects of technology use in your courses, see chapter 15.

Example screen recorder software includes Camtasia, Screencast-O-Matic, Filmora Scrn, SnagIt, and Jing. Because these programs differ considerably, and new or updated versions continue to be released, we suggest that you find a web page with step-by-step directions or view screencast tutorials for the exact software and version you plan to use. For example, search for "Camtasia 2020 tutorial" or "How to use Jing" via either a search engine (e.g., Google) or the YouTube search bar. You can also search for answers to more specific questions (e.g., "How do I disable the webcam in Screencast-O-Matic?") or simply use the software's Help function, which often includes a search bar or a FAQ (i.e., list of answers to frequently asked questions).

If cost is a concern, you may be able to find free or reduced-price versions of screen-cast software in which certain advanced functions are limited (i.e., recording length, text embedding, partial-screen recording, on-screen drawing, zooming tools). We recommend that you read online reviews and do research to determine which features you want, but you may find a less expensive option that is adequate. If you are selecting a screencast app for a mobile device, verify that your operating system is compatible (e.g., iOS, Android). See the following lists for examples of uses, as well as recording and pedagogical tips, related to recording your own screen recording videos.

Screen Recording Video Tips

- If funds are tight, you may be able to borrow a webcam or external microphone (e.g., headset) from a library or instructional technology center.

- Limit your screen recording video to a maximum length of 2 to 15 minutes for the following reasons:

  - Shorter length helps students maintain attention.

  - A shorter video is easier to replace if some of the content becomes outdated.

  - Shorter videos make it easier for students to find material that they need to review; for example, if you are covering a textbook chapter, create a separate video for each major concept.

- Consider breaking larger concepts into subtopics that are covered in multiple short videos.

- For longer videos, consider including time stamps to indicate where key concepts are introduced and noting them in the description that accompanies the video (e.g., 1:35 Frequency of Training; 2:47 Intensity of Training).

- In general lectures and tutorials, avoid referring to specifics such as dates, days of the week, and exact assignment deadlines. This generality allows you to reuse the video in subsequent semesters without confusing your students.

- Drink some water during breaks while recording to avoid dry-mouth and improve voice quality.

- If you use notes or an outline, make sure that you also know the content well in order to avoid sounding like you are reading a script.

- Record in standard video dimensions (e.g., 480p, 720p) to avoid black bars upon playback within platforms such as YouTube.
- Provide clear titles for the videos when saving them.
- When finished, consider editing the video if needed (e.g., removing dead space, adding introductory or closing music).
- See chapter 11 for more tips about recording and editing digital video and audio (e.g., saving and disseminating digital video files).

Screen Recording Audio Tips

- Test the microphone to make sure it is working.
- Test the sound quality and be sure that playback is loud and clear enough to understand.
- Begin by briefly introducing yourself and the content to be covered (i.e., learning objectives).
- Speak naturally, but slowly.
- Make voice-over narration easy to hear and free from echoes and distracting background noises; if possible, record in a quiet, carpeted room.
- If playback sounds bad, consider obtaining a higher-quality external microphone (e.g., podcast microphone).
- Keep voice-over dialogue professional by using correct grammar and pronunciation while avoiding inappropriate slang, gender-exclusive language (e.g., "you guys"), and repetitive extraneous verbiage (e.g., "ah," "like," "you know").
- Keep your mouth consistently the same distance from the microphone (not an issue if using a headset).
- Consider ending with a summary and mentioning resources in which to find more information about the topic.

Video Screencast Recording Tips

- If the software allows, record only the portion of the screen that is relevant (rather than the whole screen). For example, you could record PowerPoint slides but not the "notes" pane, thus allowing yourself to use the notes as a type of script for the presentation but keeping it out of the finished screen recording video.
- Close all unnecessary applications and tabs when recording. This will help avoid recording irrelevant material or unwanted sounds, like the audible chime of a newly received email.
- If allowed by the software, use the cursor as a type of pointer to draw attention to key aspects of the screen when you are discussing them (while being mindful that excessive cursor movements can be distracting); also consider zooming in where appropriate if that feature is available.
- If the software allows, consider using annotation tools (i.e., drawing).
- When navigating while recording, consider using keyboard shortcuts for quicker transitions and always scroll smoothly.
- If you stumble, use the pause and rewind functions to rerecord a sentence rather than starting the video recording over entirely; also, a minor slip-up is okay!

Webcam Inset Video Recording Tips

- When aiming the webcam at yourself while speaking, avoid backlit recording conditions as much as possible; instead, ensure that some light shines on your face.

- Fill the webcam frame with your head and shoulders.
- Ensure that the webcam inset box does not cover important content on the screen (e.g., PowerPoint slide text).
- Make sure that the background behind the presenter is not distracting.

Saving Screen Recording Videos With PowerPoint Narration

You can also create videos from PowerPoint presentations with voice-over narration. In addition to a computer with PowerPoint and speakers, you also need a built-in or external microphone to record your voice. Several options exist for adding narration, and each version of PowerPoint is a little different, so we recommend using the application's Help function and searching for terms such as "adding narration in PowerPoint 2016" or "creating a video with narration in PowerPoint." You can also use similar search terms in a search engine or on YouTube to find video tutorials. These resources will give you step-by-step directions. One simple option is to add a separate voice-over narration file for each individual PowerPoint slide, then save the entire presentation as a compressed video file (e.g., MP4 or WMV format). The video will then display each slide with the inserted voice-over and automatically advance to the next slide after the current slide's audio narration is finished, thus compiling it all into one video. For more information about creating effective PowerPoint presentations, see chapter 4.

Online Course Assignments and Assessments

Learning module activities and assignments within online courses must include interactions both with the instructor and with classmates. These aspects may take the form of partner or group assignments but are most evident in discussion activities and in feedback provided by the instructor in response to completed assignments.

Online courses should include multiple assessments that are appropriate, varied, and logically ordered to clearly measure both whole-course and module-specific learning objectives and competencies. Grading criteria must be clearly stated for each assessment (e.g., in a rubric) and be connected clearly to the overall grading policy (i.e., how many points or what percentage of the grade each assessment is worth). Major course assignments can be explained in detail in instructional screencast videos, which may also include past student examples. Common online course assignments include discussions (i.e., forums), course-specific activities and projects, and quizzes and exams.

Discussions

Discussion assignments deliver an online forum for students to interact both with classmates and with the instructor as they provide written commentary or post content (e.g., files, web links, videos). Discussion questions or prompts are created by the instructor and should focus on a learning objective relating to the learning module's content. This type of activity is meant to replicate the discussions that take place in a F2F classroom, and many online tools for this purpose are available in LMSs (e.g., discussion boards, forums, blogs, journals, wikis). These activities are particularly important in asynchronous courses that do not include discussions via videoconferencing or instant text chats through the LMS. It is common practice to include at least one student-interaction activity (e.g., discussion board assignment) in each learning module. Figure 8.5 provides a sample template for online discussion board assignments, and table 8.3 presents a corresponding sample of a discussion board grading rubric.

Figure 8.5   Sample discussion board assignment template.

This is a multistage assignment with three separate due dates—all listed in the syllabus.

1. Be sure to look at the accompanying grading rubric [instructor-created in the LMS and made viewable to students].
2. Click the Start a New Thread option and use your name as the subject or title of the post.
3. Answer the following question and include the corresponding letter prompts in your response:

    a. [This should be an open-ended discussion question that stimulates higher-order thinking related to the content of the learning module. It may relate to concepts covered in the course textbook or an article posted in the module. You might also consider posing several questions and asking students either to respond to all of them or to choose one.]

    b. [This may be a second discussion question or prompt if you are requiring responses to multiple questions, or are giving students the option to choose from multiple questions. Again, for ease of grading and knowing what question the student chose to responded to, require the students to letter their response].

Due date for initial discussion response: first Sunday of the module by 11:59 p.m. (per syllabus).

4. Click Reply and comment as well as ask follow-up questions on at least two of your peers' initial responses (again, look at the grading rubric). Do not simply agree with others when making peer comments. Provide your own opinion (with examples) and include reference support in APA style. Then facilitate further discussion by asking them questions that relate to the content (this part is required and noted in the grading rubric).

Due date for peer comments and questions: second Wednesday of the module by 11:59 p.m.

5. **Due date for answers to all questions posed to you by classmates about your initial post**: last day of the module by 11:59 p.m.

Note: This example includes three deadlines across a two-week learning module: initial posting, peer comments and questions, and responses to questions posed by classmates about initial posting. Many online instructors structure discussion assignments without requiring students to ask peers follow-up questions or step five and list only one deadline, for both the initial response and the peer comments.

Course-Specific Assignments and Projects

Course-specific work should allow the student to practically apply course content in a meaningful way. You can post assignment directions and grading rubrics in the LMS, along with a link through which students can submit their work. The LMS should allow various types of computer files to be attached for submission.

Additionally, in an effort to increase revenue, some textbook publishers are now offering textbook specific web-based assignment and assessment platforms similar to an LMS. Examples include McGraw-Hill Connect and Pearson MyLab. Students must purchase an access key (even if using a preowned textbook) to log into the website. These systems

Table 8.3 Sample Grading Rubric for a Discussion Board Assignment

Criteria	Excellent (2 points)	Good (1.5 points)	Needing improvement (1 point)	Needing more effort (0 points)
Thoroughness of responses (using details and examples)	Responses demonstrate thoughtfulness and offer supporting details and examples. All parts of the responses are complete and well done.	Responses demonstrate some thoughtfulness and offer some supporting details and examples. All parts of the responses are complete.	Responses demonstrate little thoughtfulness and offer few details or examples. Most parts of the responses are complete.	Responses demonstrate no thoughtfulness and offer no details.
Relating concepts from text or other course content to responses	If relevant, responses consistently include concepts from course content or text(s) and consistently use APA reference style.	If relevant, responses occasionally include concepts from course content or text(s) and consistently use APA reference style.	If relevant, responses infrequently include concepts from course content or text(s) and inconsistently use APA reference style.	If relevant, responses do not include concepts from course content or text(s) and do not use APA reference style.
Interaction with peers (at least two follow-up peer responses)	At least two follow-up responses are made to initial postings by peers. Responses are made to all questions posed by other students regarding own initial post. Points from peer ideas are clearly built on or refuted with APA reference support.	Only one follow-up response is made to initial postings by peers. Responses are made to some questions posed by other students regarding own initial post. Points from peer ideas are clearly built on or refuted with APA reference support.	Responses are made to others but with no specific feedback or APA reference support (e.g., simple repetition of points made by peer). Does not respond to questions posed by other students regarding own initial post.	No follow-up peer responses are provided.
Peer response(s) facilitate continuing discussion	Peer responses promote interaction, ask provocative questions, and deepen the discussion. Enthusiasm for the topic and clear effort to keep discussion flowing are demonstrated with APA reference support.	Peer responses minimally promote interaction, but no questions are posed. Enthusiasm for the topic and clear effort to keep discussion flowing are minimally demonstrated.	Peer responses do not promote interaction, and no questions are posed. Enthusiasm for the topic and clear effort to keep discussion flowing are not demonstrated.	No follow-up peer responses are provided, or the response(s) discourage others from sharing ideas.
Organization and mechanics	Information is well organized in well-constructed paragraphs. The writing is free from errors in grammar, spelling, and punctuation.	Information is somewhat organized, and paragraphs are somewhat well-constructed. A few errors are present in grammar, spelling, or punctuation.	Information is disorganized in outlined paragraphs. Many errors are present in grammar, spelling, or punctuation.	Information and paragraphs are disorganized. Errors are consistently made in grammar, spelling, or punctuation.

may or may not integrate with other LMSs in order to effortlessly transfer assessment scores from one platform to another.

Online Quizzes and Exams

Online quizzes (also called exams in some LMSs) are often used as one way to assess students' understanding of course content. They come with several advantages and disadvantages (see table 8.4).

Depending on the LMS, instructors often have several options for quiz (i.e., exam) settings; when deciding on settings, consider the possibility of cheating. Options may include the following:

- Randomize question order or use a test bank that provides questions randomly to each student.
- Display one question per page; this setting is recommended as student responses will then be saved after each response, which can alleviate losing unsaved answers if internet connection is lost prior to submitting the entire quiz.
- Set exact number of points available for each question, including bonus questions.

Table 8.4   Advantages and Disadvantages of Online Quizzes (and Exams)

Instructor advantages	Student advantages
• Instructors can auto-grade quizzes in the LMS (assuming that all items use either multiple-choice, true/false, or matching questions) and automatically export grades to the gradebook. • Instructors can embed multimedia material (e.g., videos, pictures, audio) into quiz questions. • Instructors can provide students with automated feedback on specific question responses (i.e., rationale for the correct answer, reasons that certain responses are not correct). • Instructors can permit a specific number of attempts on the same quiz with additional features (e.g., student keeps the highest score). • Instructors can set specific availability windows (day and time) as well as time limits. • Most LMSs permit instructors to offer individual students specific accommodations (e.g., additional quiz time). • Many textbook publishers provide LMS-formatted chapter quizzes with questions that can be modified (thus saving time that would be spent in creating quizzes from scratch).	• Students can take a quiz on their own schedule (based on instructor's chosen settings). • Unless a quiz is proctored face-to-face in a computer lab (e.g., final exam), many instructors permit online quizzes to be "open book" (i.e., students can reference the textbook while taking the quiz). • Students can receive feedback on specific questions and overall quiz score immediately upon completion (depending on instructor-created quiz settings). • Students have the opportunity to take the quiz in a distraction reduced testing environment at home or elsewhere online.
Instructor disadvantages	**Student disadvantages**
• Grading open-response questions can be time consuming, which may encourage instructors to use only question types that can be auto-graded by the LMS. • Instructors must address technical issues that arise while students are taking a quiz (e.g., Internet connectivity problems, accidental auto-submission of a quiz when not finished, finishing the quiz but forgetting to click the submit button). • Instructors have to address cheating (e.g., taking a quiz with a helper, recording quiz questions and answers and providing them to others).	• Students may not have internet access at home (particularly K-12 students) • Students may experience technical issues while taking a quiz (e.g., losing Internet connection). • Students are likely unable to ask the instructor clarification questions while taking the quiz.

Note. The terms quiz and exam are synonymous in this table.

- Permit students to revisit a question (i.e., move backward within the quiz).
- Set viewing options for the content of post-quiz feedback (e.g., overall quiz score, questions missed, questions missed with correct answer displayed, quiz statistics for entire class) and the timing of that feedback (e.g., immediately upon finishing the quiz or at the end of the quiz availability period).

The following specific options are commonly available for online quiz questions:

- Choose the types of questions to use (e.g., multiple-choice, true/false, matching, open-response, completion, ordering).
- Set the number of response choices and points per question (including bonus questions).
- Provide students with feedback on specific questions.
- Randomize the response order for multiple-choice questions (do *not* do this for questions that include an "all of the above" option).

One concern, of course, is the prospect of someone taking a quiz or even an entire online course for another person. Another worry is that one person will copy the quiz text or take screenshots of questions and give them to others. An LMS may provide you with certain instructor options to forestall such problems—for instance, disabling the right-click function for copying quiz information, displaying only one question at a time, randomizing question order by using a test bank, including a time limit with auto-submission, locking the web browser to prevent printing or opening another window while taking the quiz, providing feedback on specific questions only when the quiz availability period has ended for all students, and viewing the Internet protocol (IP) address and exact LMS log-in date and time for each student. Instructors can also use companies and software geared toward reducing online cheating—for example, Biometrics Signature ID, Examity, Proctorio, ProctorU, LockDown Browser).

Some institutions also use remote online proctoring of online quizzes, which requires students to display their face, identification card, and testing environment and to be watched via webcam while taking the quiz. The future of online cheating prevention may lie in the use of biometrics, whereby students are identified through factors such as fingerprinting, retinal scanning, voice recognition, and keyboard stroke analysis (Ubell, 2017). At the same time, such measures may raise ethical concerns about collection of students' biometric data.

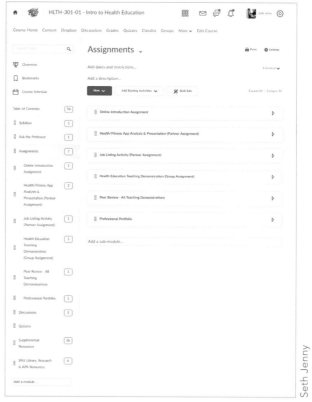

Seth Jenny

Figure 8.6 *Sample hybrid undergraduate course (Introduction to Health Education) using the D2L Brightspace LMS. The Assignments tab is visible on the right, and the left menu displays the other online components of the course. Also visible in the left menu are several other common online course components.*

Online Assignments in a Hybrid Course

Figure 8.6 provides a screenshot of a sample hybrid course that uses the D2L Brightspace LMS to post, collect, and grade all course assignments. The course was structured as a hybrid to deliver some content online, thus reducing the number of F2F class meetings. Using an LMS enabled this course to become a paperless classroom and incorporate many benefits of both online and F2F course structures noted in the Common Components of an Online Course section (e.g., syllabus, Ask the Professor, discussions, assignments, quizzes, supplemental resources).

FLIPPED INSTRUCTION

Many practitioners now use the pedagogical technique known as **flipped instruction** (also called *flipped learning*), which is a blended strategy that inverts the traditional classroom-based learning model. In this approach, a learning concept is introduced to students outside of the classroom (e.g., via an online instructional video), after which F2F class time is reserved for what would have been homework (i.e., application and problem-solving activities facilitated by the instructor to enable deeper understanding); see figure 8.7. This instructional approach is viewed as blended learning, and a course that uses it is viewed as web facilitated. A meta-analysis of various teaching strategies used by health educators found that the flipped instructional approach yielded significantly better student learning than did traditional teaching methods (Hew & Lo, 2018).

Because students are introduced to the learning content online at home, they come to class with a basic understanding of the content and can engage in application activities during class time, thus enabling the instructor to provide feedback, clarification, and reinforcement. In other words, instead of lecturing in class and then giving homework as in the traditional model, practitioners provide the lectures to students at home (e.g., in the form of an online video), thus saving class time that can then be used for students to engage with the content, check for understanding, and extend their learning.

For example, in physical education, this approach might involve students in learning the rules of a new game or activity online before class, then use class time to briefly address clarification questions before being physically active with the game or activity for the rest of the period. Practitioners who employ flipped instruction should make sure to provide their students or athletes with opportunities to access the content ahead of time and include mechanisms to assess content understanding (e.g., online quiz, short question and answer session). They should also ensure that in-class activities focus on active, higher-order learning. More details and suggestions related to flipped learning are provided in the following question-and-answer format.

1. What are the steps to flipped instruction?

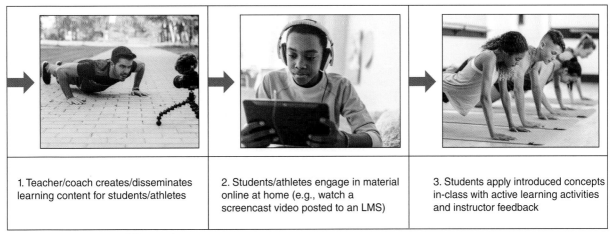

1. Teacher/coach creates/disseminates learning content for students/athletes	2. Students/athletes engage in material online at home (e.g., watch a screencast video posted to an LMS)	3. Students apply introduced concepts in-class with active learning activities and instructor feedback

Figure 8.7   Steps of flipped instruction.

2. How do students receive the learning content online at home?

Instructors find or create online-friendly content and post it to an LMS or email it to students. Videos could also be stored on specific app websites (e.g., Coach's Eye, Hudl Technique, Coach Note) or uploaded to online video storage sites (e.g., YouTube, Vimeo, Google Drive); the relevant link can be emailed or posted for students.

3. What are some examples of online-friendly content?

Previously posted online instructional videos; podcasts or vodcasts; video of PowerPoint presentations with narration; screencast videos; demonstration videos created by the instructor with a digital video camera and wireless microphone and then edited (as discussed in chapter 11).

4. What does a student typically need in order to access the material outside of class?

A computer or mobile device with audio capability and an Internet or Wi-Fi connection.

5. What are some possible benefits of flipped instruction?

For the teacher, it saves class time that would be spent on introducing content basics, increases activity and application time, helps differentiate instruction across student levels, provides learners with responsibility, and may allow more content to be covered in the course.

For students, it allows them to feel actively engaged in class as they apply learning content, extends learning as appropriate for the student's level, and allows students to learn at their own pace (e.g., by pausing, rewinding, or replaying online video content).

6. What are some examples of content that can be flipped?

- Sample content topics: historical content (e.g., origin of a sport, evolution of a disease), class or activity rules, game-play strategies and tactics, skill demonstrations and modeling, familiarization and practice with class technology (e.g., heart rate monitors, pedometers), learning of lesson terms (e.g., $\dot{V}O_2max$, BMI, components of fitness), demonstration of teaching progressions (e.g., phases of punting), health behavior change theories, review and preparation for tests
- Discussion boards that allow students to interact with each other and ask questions of the instructor
- Instructional videos
- Screencasts of lecture-based content
- Pre-assessments (online pretests using the LMS, Google Forms, or a motion-analysis app)

7. What are some general tips for flipping my first lesson?

- Try flipping just one piece of content (e.g., rules for a new game) with just one class and ask students for feedback.
- Keep the videos short (e.g., 5 to 10 minutes).
- Explore the technological tools relevant to flipping a classroom and sharing content with students. Give yourself time to learn a tool and see what procedures work best for you and your students.
- Be open-minded about what can realistically be flipped.

8. What if my students don't watch the videos before class?

- Require students to do something while viewing the online content (e.g., take notes) or some other form of accountability (e.g., take a short online quiz after). This requirement immediately informs you about who has viewed the content, and it could be graded.
- Consider setting up a remediation area in the corner of the classroom or gym with a mobile device or computer for students to view at the start of class for those who did not do so at home or who need clarification; consider providing headphones.
- Students may be able to pick up the missed content through peer teaching as the application activity begins in class. Encourage them to ask you questions if anything remains unclear.

9. What if some students don't have Internet access at home?

- Consider giving students several days to access the material (to offer flexibility).
- If possible, allow students to access the videos in your class at other times (e.g., lunch period, homeroom, study hall).
- Your students may be able to view the video elsewhere, such as a library, public place with Wi-Fi, or someone else's house.
- Save the content (e.g., video file) to a USB flash drive or DVD and provide it to students who lack Internet access.

10. What are some additional resources where I can learn more?

- Flip Learning (https://flippedlearning.org)
- Flipped Learning Worldwide (https://flglobal.org)

ONLINE PHYSICAL EDUCATION

Due to the physical activity involved in physical education (i.e., learning within the psychomotor domain), online physical education (OLPE) may receive more resistance from practitioners than is the case for online health education. Certainly, some skill-based sport and movement activities may be taught more effectively through F2F instruction. Even so, online instruction can play a meaningful role in physical education (Society of Health and Physical Educators, 2016, p. 18):

> Online physical education courses, if designed and implemented appropriately, may serve as an appropriate method of instruction for students who are unable to be in school-based settings, such as students located in remote geographical areas, students with special needs, or working students. Online physical education courses may be particularly advantageous for schools that lack certified teachers or have inadequate facilities and equipment.

In practice, OLPE courses are becoming more common in both K-12 and higher education. As mentioned earlier, nearly two-thirds (31) of U.S. states allow K-12 PE credits to be earned through OLPE, and 25 of these states stipulate that it must be taught by a state-licensed physical education teacher (Society of Health and Physical Educators, 2016). As the prevalence of K-12 online instruction increases, more states will soon need to decide whether to allow their students to be taught online by teachers who are certified in a different state. For example, Connecticut permits online teachers to be certified in any state (Mohnsen, 2012). Although the term *K-12 OLPE* is used loosely in the literature, SHAPE America does not support the use of OLPE with elementary students or with others who lack competency in basic movement patterns (Society of Health and Physical Educators, 2018).

Thus, major concerns about OLPE courses include the question of accountability and the potential lack of physical activity required, the possibility of insufficient emphasis on motor learning and competency, and the difficulty involved in providing online learners in asynchronous formats with real-time feedback about their performance of motor skills (Daum & Buschner, 2018; Society of Health and Physical Educators, 2018). However, these potential drawbacks can be overcome. It is strongly recommended that all OLPE teachers read SHAPE America's guidance document titled *Guidelines for K-12 Online Physical Education*, which also provides OLPE screenshots for sample learning modules centered on the national physical education standards (Society of Health and Physical Educators, 2018). Table 8.5 provides practical examples of using the standards for teaching and assessment in OLPE (Society of Health and Physical Educators, 2014), and the following lists offer practical pedagogical recommendations for OLPE. Many of the recommendations were adapted from Daum and Buschner (2018) and SHAPE America (Society of Health and Physical Educators, 2018).

Student Prerequisites

- Do not use OLPE at the elementary level. For OLPE at the secondary level, require competency in fundamental movement patterns and achievement of appropriate grade-level outcomes for physical education.

- Consider establishing formal prerequisites for OLPE (e.g., minimum GPA, skills testing), especially at the secondary level, and recommend or require students to complete a readiness self-assessment for online learning (e.g., Loyola University New Orleans, 2019).

Curriculum, Pedagogy, and Professional Development

- Address all learning domains—psychomotor, cognitive, and affective—and all physical education standards and objectives at the program, state, and national levels (see table 8.5).

WHAT DOES THE RESEARCH SAY?

Empirical research on OLPE is limited. In higher education, one study found that university students enrolled in wellness courses improved their cardiorespiratory endurance patterns significantly more in hybrid and F2F formats compared to fully online formats but that self-reported nutrition habits and weekly physical activity (i.e., strength and cardiorespiratory training) improved across all three formats (Everhart & Dimon, 2013). Moreover, a meta-analysis of 34 studies revealed that web-based programs geared toward behavior change can elicit small but significant increases in physical activity in adults (Davies et al., 2012).

A survey of 32 secondary-level OLPE teachers found that 75 percent of them focused on a fitness curriculum emphasizing cognitive learning and that 66 percent required physical activity on three or more days per week, 15 percent required it on one or two days, and 19 percent did not require it (Daum & Buschner, 2012). As a result, the majority of students were not required to meet the national guidelines of 225 minutes of physical activity per week. Overall, current OLPE courses tend to involve a fitness-based curriculum and to focus narrowly on the cognitive learning domain while deemphasizing psychomotor and affective learning (Daum & Buschner, 2018; Kooiman et al., 2017; Society of Health and Physical Educators, 2018).

Table 8.5   Sample Activities and Assessments to Meet Standards Through OLPE

Standard	Sample OLPE learning activities	Sample OLPE pedagogy and assessment tools
1. Demonstrate motor skill and movement pattern competency.	• Student submits still images demonstrating the critical elements of varying phases of a motor skill (e.g., preparation, swing, and follow-through of a tennis serve). • Student submits digital video of motor skill performance. This could include demonstration, execution, or the creation of new movement patterns.	• Asynchronous digital photo or video, which could be submitted through the LMS or a motion-analysis app (e.g., Hudl Technique) • Synchronous videoconferencing with instant instructor feedback
2. Understand and apply motor skill performance concepts and strategies.	• Students apply knowledge of motor skill tactics and strategies through analysis of a video recording of a motor skill performance (self- or peer assessment) as compared with established critical elements. • Based on a self-assessment, or instructor or peer feedback, students demonstrate corrected motor skill concept or strategy.	• Task analysis rubric and word processing evaluation of a digital video with clear demonstration of higher-order thinking skills • Tools similar to those listed for standard 1
3. Demonstrate knowledge and skills of fitness and physical activity.	• Students perform and analyze their own physical activity patterns and create or modify an exercise plan or practice schedule based on best practices and guidelines. • Students plan, perform, and analyze personal assessments of physical fitness across all components of fitness.	• Student performance of health-enhancing physical activity and analyses with help from wearable technology data (e.g., heart rate, step count, GPS data) • Student use of presentation software and online discussion boards to explore fitness assessment performance and results
4. Demonstrate responsible personal and social behavior.	• Students are facilitated through simulations or scenarios related to appropriate social behavior in fitness settings (e.g., personal safety, respect for equipment and others).	• Instructor- and peer-facilitated discussion boards, quizzes, digital presentations, video simulations, or videoconferencing
5. Value physical activity.	• Students keep a training log that includes reflections about their feelings toward physical activity. • Students compile a digital portfolio featuring accomplishments related to physical education.	• Discussion boards, digital presentations, self-assessment assignments, video, or videoconferencing

Note: LMS = learning management system.
Standards adapted from SHAPE America (2014); Some examples adapted from Juniu, Hofer, and Harris (2012); Mohnsen (2012); and SHAPE America (2018).

- Require physical activity in OLPE courses and make the weekly physical activity goals consistent with age-appropriate and developmentally appropriate national guidelines.
- If possible, give students an equivalent F2F alternative to OLPE; students should not be forced to take physical education in an asynchronous online format because feedback about their motor skills performance would be significantly delayed, potentially reducing learning gains.
- Many K-12 OLPE teachers use the *Fitness for Life* (Corbin & Le Masurier, 2014) or *Fitness for Life: Middle School* (Corbin et al., 2018) textbooks, which offer digital versions and include web resources.
- Revise curriculum regularly with input from formal peer and administrative observation as well as student evaluation feedback so that you are integrating the latest

technological and content-specific methods. For example, consider tapping into the recent fitness trend of virtual races (Casanova, 2019). Virtual races can be run at any pace, location, or even inside on a treadmill, but evidence must be provided that you have performed it (e.g., wearable technology data, picture of a treadmill display indicating distance and time). OLPE students may train for a culminating fitness activity (e.g., virtual race) and the instructor may award a digital badge or certificate upon validated completion.

- For OLPE at the secondary level, consider conducting synchronous one-on-one communication with each student on a weekly basis (e.g., via phone or web conferencing) and with parents and guardians at least monthly.

- If possible, consider structuring the course in a hybrid format where the majority of cognitive content is covered online and students meet with you periodically for F2F psychomotor learning supervised physical activity, instant feedback, and student performance of motor competency.

- Afford differentiated instruction for all students, including those with disabilities.

- Only permit certified physical education teachers to teach OLPE and require regular (e.g., yearly) professional development in online pedagogy, preferably subject-specific.

- Consider consulting your institution's legal counsel about any liability you might incur if an OLPE student becomes injured or dies while performing physical activity independently for an online class. Require a signed waiver (signed by a parent or legal guardian if the participant is under age 18) before joining the class (see chapter 15). Also consider requiring a signed Physical Activity Readiness Questionnaire (PAR-Q) and physician-signed sport physical.

- Ensure that you adhere to an age-appropriate rubric for online instruction, such as that provided by Quality Matters (MarylandOnline, 2019a) or iNACOL (International Association for K-12 Online Learning, 2019); see table 8.2.

Assignments and Assessment

- Try to involve learners' parents, guardians, households, and support networks (e.g., friends) into OLPE assignments—for instance, through collaborative physical activities and student-conducted interviews about physical activity preferences and patterns.

- When appropriate, give learners autonomy about where, when, and how to be physically active. Consider offering them category-based options, such as cardiorespiratory, strength, and mobility and flexibility.

- Include assignments where students design, monitor, and critique their own physical activities.

- Make a concerted effort to include assignments that move learners away from computers and mobile devices and into interacting with their environment and being physically active.

- Assignments should encourage students to meet national guidelines for physical activity (U.S. Department of Health and Human Services, 2018).

- Refer to objective measures of physical activity, such as those used by wearable technology such as heart rate monitors, pedometers, GPS watches, and smartphone apps. Such information can be collected through online training logs integrated with activity-tracking software (e.g., Garmin Connect, Strava, Polar Flow, Runkeeper) – see chapter 9. Do *not* rely only on self-reporting. To verify that physical activity has been performed, many K-12 OLPE teachers require weekly signatures from a parent, guardian, or coach.

- Evaluate motor skill performance through digital photography or video (e.g., video-conferencing, video analysis) – see chapter 10.
- Consider how you might integrate motion-based video games (i.e., exergaming) into OLPE – see chapter 5. Playing active video games against one another via the Internet has been found to produce moderate-intensity heart rate levels that are consistent with recommended physical activity guidelines for secondary students (Kooiman et al., 2016).
- Provide varied assignments and assessments geared toward meeting standards and outcomes for physical education at the program, state, and national levels (see table 8.5).

ONLINE COACHING

In this chapter, the term *online coaching* does not refer to the use of an artificially intelligent computer program for virtual self-coaching, which does not involve an interactive human coach. Nor does it refer to simply following an instructional exercise video posted on the Internet (e.g., performing a yoga routine while watching a yoga video on YouTube). Finally, we are not referring to online executive coaching geared toward helping business executives, often within corporate settings.

Instead, for our purposes here, we define **online coaching** (sometimes called *virtual coaching*) as a person-to-person coaching relationship geared toward helping an individual attain either sport and fitness benefits or health and wellness benefits through online means (e.g., videoconferencing, email, LMS) and in many cases additional phone-based communication (phone calls, texting). Many of the OLPE concepts and suggestions already discussed also apply to online coaching, and here we wish to briefly draw your attention to a few unique aspects of each type of online coaching. To that end, table 8.6 provides a sample of online or remote coaching services.

Online Health and Wellness Coaching

Online coaching for health and wellness is gaining traction, and many coaches now offer clients the remote options of videoconference or telephone coaching. **Wellness coaching** aims to guide and motivate generally healthy individuals who wish to improve or maintain overall health (e.g., smoking cessation, nutrition, weight management, physical activity behavior) (Huffman, 2016). **Health coaching**, on the other hand, was spawned by rising health care costs and is geared toward helping individuals with acute or chronic health conditions or health risks to modify their behavior in order to better manage their wellness, improve their health outcomes, and lower their health care costs (Huffman, 2016). Both of these types of coaching should use skillful conversation as well as behavior change theory rooted in evidence-based practices to help clients improve their overall health and well-being.

Health and wellness coaches are becoming more common as part of corporate wellness programs, medical providers, and health insurance companies where on-site or online (i.e., remote) coaching may be available to employees or patients. Evidence suggests that health coaching geared toward facilitating behavior change is just as effective when performed online as compared to F2F coaching (Bus et al., 2018). Mobile apps such as Vida Health (2019) offer person-to-person health coaching via video or phone consultation, as well as daily motivational messaging, educational resources, and tracking (of exercise, diet, sleep, and body weight). Certifications such as Certified Wellcoach (Wellcoaches, 2016), Health Coach (American Council on Exercise, 2019), and Certified Health Coach (National Society of Health Coaches, 2019) add further credibility to the profession of online health and wellness coaching.

Table 8.6   Sample Online and Remote Coaching Services

Sport or activity	Company	Website
Cross-country skiing	CXC Academy	www.cxcacademy.com
CrossFit	Invictus Fitness	www.crossfitinvictus.com
Cycling	Semi-Pro Cycling Tailwind Coaching	https://semiprocycling.com https://tailwind-coaching.com
Distance running	McMillan Running Runcoach	www.mcmillanrunning.com https://runcoach.com
Equestrianism	Artistic Dressage EquiFITT	www.artisticdressage.com https://equifitt.com
Esports	Gamer Sensei	www.gamersensei.com
Health and wellness coaching	Vida Health Wellcoaches Wellworks For You	www.vida.com https://wellcoachesschool.com www.wellworksforyou.com
Mountain biking	Ryan Leech Connection	www.ryanleech.com
Multiple Sports	CoachUp Peloton TrainingPeaks Without Limits	www.coachup.com www.onepeloton.com www.trainingpeaks.com www.iamwithoutlimits.com
Personal training	Central Athlete Strength Ratio	www.centralathlete.com https://strengthratiohq.com
Swimming	SwimSwam	https://swimswam.com
Triathlon	CTS Keep It Simple Coaching	https://trainright.com www.kiscoaching.com
Weightlifting	Juggernaut Project Lift	www.jtsstrength.com www.project-lift.org

Online Sport and Fitness Coaching

More research is needed to determine the effectiveness of online sport and fitness coaching. Despite this need, many online offerings have already been made available, especially in sport coaching. Online sport coaching often involves competitive athletes who participate in an individual sport. An asynchronous online approach is more appropriate for sports that do not require immediate feedback from a coach about the athlete's form or mechanics and with older, more experienced athletes who demonstrate mastery of the sport's specific movements.

Online sport coaching has become common in individual lifetime sports (e.g., distance running, swimming, cycling), and many companies are capitalizing on this new trend by appealing to individuals who have location or scheduling constraints and want access to motivation and training guidance to improve their sport performance (see table 8.6). Here are some sample customers for an online sport coach: an elite athlete who wants an elite coach but does not live near one; a high-performing high school athlete who desires advanced coaching and wants to earn an athletic scholarship; a recreational athlete who needs help with accountability, motivation, or planning a training program.

For example, CoachUp (2019) provides online coaching services such as written training plans, live synchronous video training sessions, online drills, and video analysis for a variety of individual and team sports. Another CoachUp (2019) option allows athletes to submit "game film" for review and receive "game notes and analysis". In another example, Artistic Dressage (2019) offers two equestrian online video coaching options via Skype or

Zoom: one, a VIP Lesson in which the rider wears a two-way Bluetooth headset while a second person video-records the riding performance and transmits synchronous video to a coach, who observes and comments via the Internet to the rider; and two, Video Coaching, in which the rider sends a digital video to a coach and schedules a synchronous videoconference to discuss it as they watch together online. Finally, apps such as Peloton (2019) offer a less personal option that hardly includes coaching but provides live instructors who lead studio-style classes in spinning, cycling, or treadmill running through a subscription service whereby the athlete simply follows along at home via synchronous video streaming.

As these examples illustrate, it is possible to receive feedback from an online coach via either asynchronous or synchronous video. Asynchronous video feedback is discussed in more detail in chapter 10, and synchronous videoconferencing is addressed in the next section of this chapter. It is also possible to use a hybrid structure in which the coach is physically present for key workouts, assessments, or competitions while the rest of the coaching is performed remotely. In addition, as noted in the discussion of OLPE, online sport coaches often analyze an athlete's online training logs (e.g., via TrainingPeaks, Garmin Connect, Strava, Polar Flow), which are typically integrated with data from the athlete's wearable technology, such as heart rate, pace, distance, cadence, and workout times. Other information may also be tracked, including food intake, sleep patterns, perceived recovery levels, and overall life stress.

Online fitness coaching (i.e., online personal training) is also becoming more popular. Online personal trainers typically provide comprehensive training programs that include strength, cardiovascular, biomotor, and flexibility training programs electronically to clients that are often accessed via mobile device. Clients can then perform their workouts at any time and in any location, which is ideal for those that have varied schedules or travel frequently. Depending on the coaching arrangement, sharing training results data and other communication between the coach and client may assist future training program development. When considering this option, make certain that the trainer holds a reputable certification through a legitimate organization, such as the American College of Sports Medicine or National Strength and Conditioning Association.

REMOTE SUPERVISION USING DIGITAL VIDEO TECHNOLOGY

In any teacher or coach preparation program, resources can be quickly drained by the supervision of field placements, internships, and student teaching. These resources consist primarily of the time, money, and staffing to handle as many as six or more placement visits for each intern (i.e., student teacher). These visits might include conferencing with the intern and the cooperating teacher or coach, as well as observing multiple teaching or coaching sessions led by the intern. Traditional F2F supervision challenges include:

- Monetary cost (e.g., transportation and parking expenses, additional staffing, etc.)
- Time (travel time to and from supervision sites; makes multiple site observations in the same day challenging)
- Distance from supervisor to intern placement (relating to time, but also limits placement options for students if supervision sites must be in close proximity to the supervisor)
- Consistency of and quality of feedback (due to time constraints of full-time faculty members, additional part-time staffing are often hired to supervise. While certainly not always the case, these part-time supervisors may not provide the same consistent feedback as full-time program faculty members who teach the theory-based courses, or the same quality of feedback as full-time program supervisors)

TECHNOLOGY TIPS FROM THE FIELD

Practitioner Interview: Online Remote Coach

Matthew Hammersmith

Without Limits Greenville (South Carolina) Head Coach and Director and Cofounder of Upstate Ultra Trail Events

- Websites: www.iamwithoutlimits.com/greenville and www.upstateultra.com
- Sports Currently Coaching Remotely: Track and Field, Cross Country, Ultra and Trail Running, Road and Marathon Racing
- Coaching Certifications: USATF Level 1, USA Triathlon Level 1, BS Degree in Physical Education and Health
- Years Coaching Overall (and Remotely): 12 (4)
- Number of Athletes the Company Currently Coaches Remotely: 75
- Age Range and Gender of Remote Athletes: 6 to 66 Years (50 Percent Female)
- Standard of Remote Athletes: Diverse Range From Beginners to U.S. Olympic Trials Qualifiers

Why do you coach remotely or online?
We feel that our knowledge and experience in the coaching field can meet the demand of athletes around the globe to better assist them in achieving their personal goals. We coach because we can help.

What are the main reasons your athletes have a remote or online coach?
Access to credible coaches with experience working with true runners or triathletes is limited. There is a large industry of personal fitness and wellness experts in the field, but the required skill/knowledge base it takes to facilitate endurance-based athletes is quite different.

How does remote or online coaching work with your company (i.e., what is the coaching process)?
We have done a great job promoting our services through our athlete base so when a new athlete approaches us we have them complete a short five-minute survey to get to know more about their personal history and their future goals. Once we have that, we schedule a 15-minute phone call to establish how Without Limits can assist them in their endeavors. If you are being coached online, we structure training to meet a specific goal. Our remote athletes that work with us are very self-motivated but require guidance, and a coach provides feedback and alterations to the training plan. Just because we have remote athletes doesn't mean we can't get them on-site occasionally for analysis too.

What technology does a remote or online coach need?
A smartphone with access to TrainingPeaks is always helpful. We also write 16-week stagnant training plans for certain athletes to follow. Specifically, with remote coaching, we find that a simple phone call can solve a lot of athlete questions in just a few minutes. Developing a personal relationship is the most important thing to an athlete's success, so technology is not always the forefront of what we aim for as a business leader.

What technology does a remote or online athlete need?
Access to TrainingPeaks, phone, email, Without Limits app, and Facebook groups.

How much does your online coaching cost?

We have various packages for our onsite coaching clients. But for our TrainingPeaks remote-coaching athletes we have a $165 monthly charge that includes individualized online training plans using TrainingPeaks software specifically geared for triathletes, runners, cyclists, or swimmers; weekly phone calls and emails; on-site location practices; initial 90-minute one-on-one phone consult; race planning; and nutrition advice. Additional upgrade options include video analysis, on-site swim-stroke or cycle-efficiency analysis, data analysis of power files, training stress score analysis, and more.

Please describe TrainingPeaks, the online training log software you use for remote coaching.

There is a free version, but with our number of athletes and the features that we want, we have a paid subscription to the program. It enables athletes to sync their training data to each day's designated workout for each coach to view and review to provide instant feedback. Our main objective using it is to communicate clearly the desired training objective of each workout. The features of TrainingPeaks are the best in the business for accomplishing this task.

Do your athletes use any wearable technology (e.g., watches, GPS) for remote coaching?

We do not have a single wearable device that we promote, but I personally use Garmin for my fitness tracking that syncs with TrainingPeaks, Garmin Connect, and Strava. I am a bigger advocate of "how I feel" when it comes to certain training because as a former collegiate Division I athlete, I competed at a high level, and the only piece of technology I had was "feel." I got a basic watch my sophomore year in college to track intervals, but as far as pace, heart rate, cadence, distance, etc.—we went off the perceived exertion level of effort.

Do you collaboratively write training plans with your remote athletes, or is this done alone by the coach?

I schedule calls with athletes before we begin a 12- to 16-week training plan to develop the best plan that suits the needs of each athlete. Remember, most of these athletes have kids, jobs, family responsibilities, and a life outside of endurance sports.

Overall, what are the benefits of online or remote coaching?

I always promote on-site coaching if available, but for athletes with busy schedules or locations that do not permit it, we always try to work with athletes to facilitate their success through our online TrainingPeaks premium coaching program.

What are the greatest drawbacks or negatives to online or remote coaching?

Instant feedback is invaluable. My athletes who attend practice receive feedback that can change or affect the end result of a training session, whereas the athletes who are training remotely might not receive that feedback until after the session is over—after assessing the training data. I believe in the "eye test," and I can tell if an athlete is overstressed, overpaced, and overworked where I can quickly make an adjustment during the training session. Online or remote athletes do not have that luxury.

What do you do to minimize these drawbacks or negatives?

Communicating clear and precise workout goals is very important. Setting the stage before a workout begins can help facilitate the athlete's success and deter any unwanted results from a workout.

Table 8.7 Advantages and Disadvantages of Remote Synchronous Video Supervision

Advantages	Disadvantages
• Less monetary cost (see above listed traditional supervision challenges) • Less time needed to travel to supervision site, which may enable more observation flexibility and more total observations • Easier accommodation of last-minute schedule changes (and avoidance of time wasted in traveling to a site if the lesson does not occur) • Increased opportunities for placement outside of the immediate area (even outside of the state or country); very helpful for island or extremely remote communities with limited transportation options • Possibility of increased consistency and quality of feedback if synchronous video-conferencing permits full-time program faculty members who teach the theory-based courses to also supervise remotely (see previously listed traditional supervision challenges) • Opportunity for supervisor to provide concurrent in-ear feedback to intern during the lesson via wireless headset • Increased ability for supervisor to hear what intern is saying via wireless microphone • Increased likelihood that intern will infuse technology into lessons during placement and after graduation (Krause et al., 2018) • Possibility of reducing disruption and distraction as compared with on-site supervisor visits (Krause et al., 2018)	• Cost of equipment • Limited or lost Internet connectivity in the instructional space • Limited camera angles of some video devices • Possible limitations on observation viewing by the supervisor (e.g., students or athletes standing in front of camera) • Possible sense by the intern of a lack of personability in virtual conferencing, which could limit the supervisor's relationship building with the intern (O'Neil & Krause, 2017)

Fortunately, it is now possible to supervise remotely due to advances in digital video technology. Still, practitioners must consider carefully whether the potential benefits outweigh the possible disadvantages (see table 8.7); success depends on both the supervising instructor and the student being supervised.

One option is to record digital video of a lesson and share it with the supervisor later. However, this approach comes with some inherent problems; for instance, the intern does not receive instant feedback from the supervisor, and if the lesson includes minors then written consent is required from a parent or guardian for each child. Both of these challenges could be avoided by using synchronous videoconferencing between the intern and the supervisor. **Synchronous videoconferencing (SVC)** involves live two-way communication in which both audio and video are transmitted online, thus allowing participants to interact with each other in real time. Common apps for SVC include Skype, FaceTime, and Google Hangouts. The necessary equipment is summarized in figure 8.8.

Figure 8.8   Remote supervision equipment.

INTERN:

- Computer or mobile device with internet access (or smartphone with unlimited cellular data plan—4G, LTE) and wireless microphone connectivity (e.g., Bluetooth)
  - *Note: If utilizing a mobile device, a tripod with corresponding mobile device tripod attachments is beneficial. Also, a wide-angle camera lens attachment can be utilized with some mobile devices.*
  - *If utilizing internet, connection to institution's secure wireless network is mandatory (i.e., do not connect to a public unsecured network). If instruction is occurring outside, a smartphone with unlimited cellular data should be considered.*

- Webcam (or built-in camera)
  - *Note: New options include 360-degree cameras where a view in every direction is recorded at the same time, increasing field of view compared to traditional cameras.*
- SVC software installed, same as supervisor (e.g., Skype, FaceTime)
- **Wireless microphone headset (with connectivity to computer/mobile device – usually Bluetooth) – long-range (300 feet) if intern will be moving around a large instructional area

SUPERVISOR:

- Computer or mobile device with internet access (or smartphone with unlimited cellular data plan – 4G, LTE)
  - *Recommended: desktop with hardwired internet connection along with 2 monitors—one to view word processing software to evaluate or take notes during observation and the second to observe the intern via the SVC software program*
  - *If utilizing internet, connection to institution's secure wireless network is mandatory (i.e., do not connect to a public unsecured network)*
- Webcam (or built-in camera)
- SVC software installed, same as intern (e.g., Skype, FaceTime)
- Microphone (built-in or external)
- Speakers or headphones

University supervisor   Intern

Note. SVC = synchronous videoconferencing.

PRACTICAL TIPS FOR REMOTE SUPERVISION

- Before you purchase any equipment, consider investigating whether your institution or community has an instructional technology center or library that loans out the needed items.
- If needed, install the same encrypted SVC software (e.g., Skype, FaceTime) on both SVC devices (e.g., supervisor's computer and intern's mobile device).
- View online video tutorials to learn how to use the SVC software and how to connect and use the wireless headset and microphone that will be connected to the intern's video device (typically via Bluetooth).
- Create and share user IDs (i.e., user names) for the SVC software account for the supervisor, intern, and cooperating teacher or coach.
- Perform a test run with the SVC equipment days before any lesson observations to determine whether any troubleshooting is needed. As part of the test, the intern should walk and talk across the entire instructional space to identify the best camera placement and determine the range of the wireless microphone.
- The intern, supervisor, and cooperating teacher or coach should discuss everyone's roles and expectations, as well as common technical issues and ways to resolve them.
- Ensure that all equipment (e.g., mobile device, microphone) is fully charged or that the batteries work the night before an observation. Bring fully charged spare batteries to the observation site for any device that uses them.
- Before making the video call, turn on the wireless microphone or headset and synchronize it with the laptop or mobile device.
- Place the intern's video device (i.e., camera) in a safe space that maximizes preferred viewing angles (e.g., elevated in a well-lit corner).
- Avoid public Internet connections to help minimize security threats.
- If you start with a bad connection (i.e., trouble with audio or video), end the call and reconnect; if the connection is lost during the observation, call back.
- Consider installing more than one SVC software (e.g., Skype and FaceTime) on each party's device so that you can switch if a problem is encountered.
- During the lesson observation, consider turning off the supervisor's camera or covering the intern's video device display so that learners are not tempted to interact with the supervisor (whose face may be visible on-screen).
- The cooperating teacher or coach should regularly monitor the SVC transmission and the Internet connection during the lesson.
- The observation in its entirety may include a 10- to 15-minute time for connection and pre-conferencing before the lesson, the lesson observation itself, and a post-conference immediately after the lesson (preferably during a planning period so the intern does not miss instruction time and so the cooperating teacher or coach can be included if desired).
- Consider using a private setting (e.g., cooperating teacher's office) for pre- and post-lesson meetings.

Some ideas adapted from Krause et al. (2018).

TECHNOLOGY TIPS FROM THE FIELD

Remote Supervision, Supervisor Perspective

Dr. Brandy M. Lynch

Assistant Professor, Physical Education Teacher Education, University of Central Missouri, Warrensburg, Missouri

What type of technology did you use for supervising remotely via synchronous video conferencing?
In my experience with remote supervision, we have provided the student teacher with an iPad and a Bluetooth earpiece. On my side, I use an iPad or computer.

What is the name or brand of the technology used?
We would connect using FaceTime or Skype. No specific type of iPad for the student teacher or computer for me. The student teacher's earpiece was a Motorola ELITE Sliver II Bluetooth Headset HZ770.

How do you use the remote supervision synchronous video technology?
Students are provided the iPad and microphone headset. They are responsible for charging the tech and gaining access to the school Internet. We do a test run before their first observation to make sure everything works and to see if there happen to be any dead zones or areas of poor connectivity in their teaching space. We find a spot for the iPad to sit where as much of the teaching space can be seen as possible. The cooperating teacher stays with the iPad in case there is a disconnection or it needs to be relocated. Then, we conduct our formal teaching observations the same way we would for face-to-face observations. There is a pre-conference with the student, then I perform the teaching observation, and finally we do a post-conference with the student teacher (and cooperating teacher if they are available).

What is your main goal for using this technology?
The goal is to provide teacher candidates, who complete student teaching in placement schools outside of the designated supervision area, with quality supervision from university faculty.

What do you like about this technology?
I like that I can supervise students who choose not to student-teach within close proximity to the university. Specifically, [at one time] I thought it was awesome that I was in Texas, my student teacher was in North Dakota, and this was all for the Sport Pedagogy program at University of Northern Colorado!

I like that the student teachers in remote placements are able to receive the same level of accountability, feedback, and supervision as student teachers whose placement schools are within driving distance. I like how much time is saved by not having to drive back and forth multiple times to these placement schools throughout the semester.

Additionally, with the Bluetooth earpiece, I like that I can hear everything the student teacher says, which is not something I am afforded as a supervisor in face-to-face settings. Similarly, I like that I can communicate with the student teacher via the earpiece (when necessary) without disrupting the flow of the lesson.

(continued)

Remote Supervision, Supervisor Perspective *(continued)*

How might the technology be improved (or what don't you like about it)?
- The earpiece is a bit large for some students.
- It would be helpful if we could provide students iPads with data plans so we didn't have to go through the placement school's Internet. In the same way, a data plan would allow us to observe outdoor lessons and other teaching spaces that do not have strong Internet connections.

What suggestions do you have for teachers or coaches in using the technology?
Take a chance on using technology to enhance your teaching and coaching. It will be messy at first, and there will be kinks to work out, but there are so many benefits to incorporating technology into your programs. For teacher educators, it's a great way to model tech for teacher candidates. For those who student-teach in remote locations, student teachers may not receive the same level of support or quality of feedback from someone else who is hired by the university to supervise, as that person may not have content expertise or understand or uphold the expectations set forth by the program or the university for student teachers.

Do you provide your students with any assignment directions related to the technology?
We did not provide written instructions for students, as they received hands-on training with the proper use of the technology before student teaching.

Go to the web resource to read about the experience from the perspective of the cooperating teacher and the student teacher.

Before using SVC with an intern, the supervisor must ensure that the intern knows how to set up and use the technology and determine whether SVC is feasible at the placement site. In order to determine feasibility of using SVC at a given site, consider the following questions for the intern and supervisor:

- Do both parties have all of the necessary equipment (figure 8.8)?
- Is the intern capable of managing the technology?
- Does the instruction location have Wi-Fi or cell service for smartphone data usage (if intern plans to use a smartphone and has an unlimited data plan)?
- Has the placement site's administration approved SVC for observations?

Some of the greatest potential concerns with SVC relate to the security, privacy, and safety of video-recording minors. However, if executed as we indicate here, the call involves no saved video recording because it uses a live video feed. Thus it is like a face-to-face observation that happens to take place through digital means. Still, it is compulsory to use SVC software that is encrypted. **Encryption** involves converting data into computer code in order to prevent unauthorized access, and it is used by Skype, FaceTime, and Google Hangouts. For example, Skype-to-Skype calls use the same 256-bit Advanced Encryption Standard (AES; also known as *Rijndael*) used by the U.S. government to protect sensitive data (Microsoft, 2018). Of course, the supervisor could video-record the SVC session via screen casting, but there is no reason to do so. Ultimately, it is paramount to gain permission for SVC from the placement site's administration, any cooperating teachers or coaches, and, if the administration feels it is necessary, parents and guardians of the students involved. As with traditional live observations, it must be stressed that no video will be recorded and saved and therefore that the live SVC will be comparable to an in-person visit.

Overall, on-site supervision may be more comprehensive than a remote observation using digital video technology. However, remote supervision using SVC offers several advantages when multiple on-site observations are not possible. In summary, "virtual observation enables highly qualified supervisors with direct connections to the university to provide meaningful observations and valuable feedback to [interns], while time and money otherwise spent on travel is significantly decreased or altogether eliminated" (Krause et al., 2018, p. 34).

Conclusion

Online instruction comes with many advantages and challenges. When designing and delivering online, hybrid, or flipped instruction courses, practitioners should apply best practices. Online course delivery can be enhanced through the use of screen recording videos. Online coaching also comes with unique challenges and opportunities for both sport coaches and health and wellness coaches. Using the equipment and recommendations described in this chapter can increase your chances for succeeding with online instruction and coaching as well as remote supervision via synchronous videoconferencing.

Key Terms

asynchronous online course—Student-centered approach in which learning content is delivered online, typically via email and a learning management system (LMS), and therefore unbound by constraints of time or place. Although assignments may require student interactions, students typically work through learning modules at their own pace and are not required to meet face-to-face (F2F) or to be online at any specific time (except possibly for a proctored final exam). Throughout the course, the instructor interacts with students and facilitates student exchanges via email and LMS functions (e.g., discussion boards, assignment feedback).

blended learning—Approach to teaching and learning in which at least some of the content and opportunities for interaction are delivered online as well as F2F. Students are often afforded some control over time, place, path, or pace. Blended learning practices are included in hybrid courses.

courseware—Term that combines *course* and *software* to refer to specifically built software for scoping and sequencing instructional content in order to deliver an entire educational course.

digital learning—Any type of learning that is accompanied by technology, or the effective use of instructional technologies to support teaching and learning. Digital learning can occur in online, F2F, and blended settings.

discussion board—Online forum that enables students to interact with classmates and the instructor through written commentary or by posting content (e.g., files, web links, videos), often in response to a question or discussion prompt posed by the instructor regarding the module's lesson content. Discussion boards are intended to facilitate discussion similar to that found in a well-implemented F2F classroom.

distance education course—Course in which the majority of classes are not held F2F and the majority of content is delivered at a distance; also referred to as a *distance learning course*. Historically, this approach took the form of correspondence courses conducted by means of the postal service, but today it typically refers to online instruction.

Distance education courses or entire programs can be delivered either fully online or in a hybrid fashion.

educational technology—All-encompassing term referring both to digital learning tools and to theoretical foundations for supporting teaching and learning through the use of technological processes and resources, which can be done in F2F, blended, and online settings.

encryption—Conversion of data into computer code in order to prevent unauthorized access.

face-to-face (F2F) course—"Brick-and-mortar" course for which all class meetings are held in person (i.e., on campus). A F2F course may use digital learning technologies or could be web facilitated—for example, using a learning management system or a website (e.g., to post the syllabus, assignments, and ancillary course materials).

flipped instruction—Pedagogical strategy that inverts the traditional classroom-based learning model so that a learning concept is first introduced to students online, outside of the classroom (often in the form of an instructional video), and F2F class time is reserved for what would traditionally be homework (i.e., application and problem-solving activities facilitated by the instructor in order to enable deeper understanding); also referred to as *flipped learning*. This type of web-facilitated course serves as one example of blended learning.

health coaching—Coaching that helps individuals with acute or chronic health conditions or health risks to modify their behavior in order to better manage their wellness, improve their health outcomes, and lower their health care costs.

hybrid course—Course in which some content is delivered online, thus reducing the number of F2F class meetings.

learning management system (LMS)—Web-based software that aids management of the learning process by helping the instructor administer the course, deliver learning content, document and track student progress, and facilitate online interactions between classmates and the instructor; also referred to as *course management system (CMS)*.

learning module—Sequenced collection of subject-related materials presented in a logical order to guide students through learning content and assessments. Learning modules can be designed to support a theme, group of concepts, or set of course goals or objectives. An online course is often divided into learning modules, which may center on one or more chapters of the course textbook or course objectives. This approach is often implemented by using organized folders and subfolders in a learning management system. Instructors can insert content including text, files, web links, videos, discussion boards, assignments, and exams. For example, an 8-week online course might be divided into eight 1-week learning modules, whereas a 16-week course might be divided into eight 2-week modules.

massive open online course (MOOC)—Course that is geared to serve a very large or even unlimited enrollment (100 or more students), offers open access (i.e., is free to anyone), is administered via the Internet, and is typically self-paced and auto-graded (e.g., in the form of multiple-choice exams).

online coaching—Person-to-person coaching for sport, fitness, health, or wellness that is delivered online (e.g., via videoconference, email, website, or LMS), may include telephone calls or text messaging, and in this text is distinguished from virtual self-coaching facilitated by artificial intelligent software.

online course—Course that is delivered completely or almost completely online—including all content, student–teacher interactions, and assessments—either synchronously or asynchronously. In some cases, additional student–teacher interactions may occur by telephone; typically, no F2F meetings are involved, with the possible exception of a proctored final exam.

An online degree program includes multiple online courses.

online learning—Form of distance education in which teaching and learning occur online, either synchronously or asynchronously; sometimes referred to as *virtual learning*, *cyber learning*, or *e-learning*.

screen recording video—Digital video recording of what is displayed on a user's computer or mobile device screen, with concurrent voice-over narration; also referred to as a *screencast*, which may also include the simultaneous transmission of the screen recording to others.

state virtual school—School that provides statewide online learning services for both students and teachers (e.g., supplemental online courses, professional development, educational programming) that are created, facilitated, and/or funded by the state.

synchronous online course—Course in which no F2F class meetings occur in a brick-and-mortar building but students do attend scheduled classes online with each other and the instructor all at the same time remotely through videoconferencing with chat or text features. Thus, students can ask questions and get an immediate response from the instructor through either instant messaging or audio; the instructor may set up multiple discussion or chat groups during an online lesson, much like small group work in a traditional classroom.

synchronous videoconferencing (SVC)—involves live two-way communication in which both audio and video are transmitted online allowing participants to interact with each other in real time remotely, typically using an app like Skype, FaceTime, or Google Hangouts.

virtual school—Educational institution that teaches students exclusively or mostly online through either synchronous or asynchronous courses.

web-facilitated course—Course that meets F2F but is augmented by the use of Internet-based technology (e.g., posting the syllabus online, using an LMS for students to submit assignments). A web-facilitated course is not a hybrid course because it does not reduce the number of F2F class meetings.

wellness coaching—Coaching that guides and motivates generally healthy individuals who wish to maintain or improve their overall health (e.g., through smoking cessation, good nutrition, weight management, physical activity).

Review Questions

1. Summarize the similarities and differences between online, synchronous, asynchronous, hybrid, blended, and web-facilitated courses.

2. Discuss potential advantages and disadvantages of online learning and instruction.

3. What equipment and software are commonly needed for online learning and instruction?

4. Identify some teaching recommendations for, and common components of, online courses.

5. What are some recommendations for online physical education in particular?

6. What is flipped instruction, and how might you use this technique in your teaching or coaching?

7. Identify the necessary equipment and summarize some tips for successful remote supervision using digital video technology (i.e., synchronous videoconferencing).

Discussion Questions

1. Considering online, hybrid, and face-to-face course formats, which do you prefer and why? Does your answer change depending on the course content? Please explain.

2. Would you feel comfortable teaching or coaching online? Why or why not?

3. Please describe one of your past online education experiences as a student (this could relate to any online training you have experienced if you have not taken an online course). Was it a good or bad experience? How so?

4. What do you think are the most important components or ingredients of an effective online course?

5. Identify one online teaching tool discussed in this chapter that you would like to integrate into your teaching. Please describe it, elaborate on how you would use it, and give examples.

6. How would you structure online physical education, health education, or coaching?

7. Would you like to be supervised remotely via synchronous videoconferencing? Why, or why not? What would be your major concerns (if any)?

PART IV

Technology
for Assessment

9

Wearable Technology for Assessment

Chapter Objectives

When you have completed this chapter, you will be able to do the following:

1. Define wearable technology and describe multiple wearable devices used for objective assessment in physical education, coaching, and personal health settings.
2. Effectively use heart rate monitors, pedometers, accelerometers, and GPS units in practical teaching and coaching environments.
3. Use objective data obtained from wearable technology to make valid evaluative decisions about students, athletes, and programs.
4. Describe pedagogical recommendations related to using common wearable technologies for assessment, as well as limitations and concerns about validity.

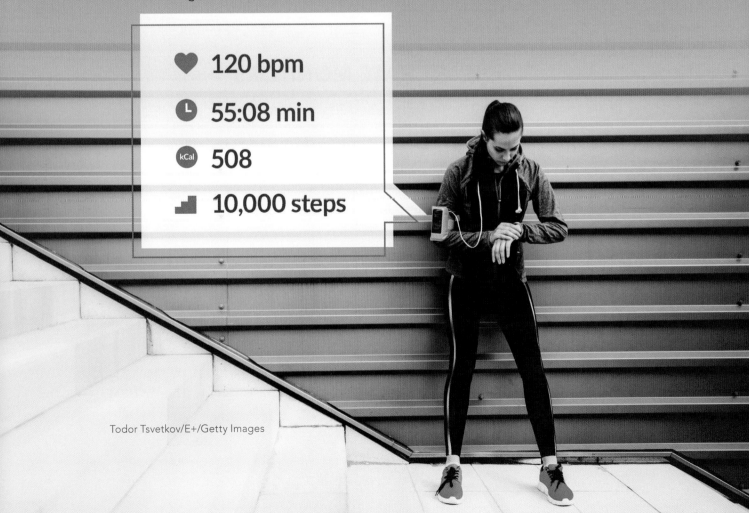

- ♥ 120 bpm
- 🕐 55:08 min
- kCal 508
- 📊 10,000 steps

Todor Tsvetkov/E+/Getty Images

Wearable technology includes various smart electronic devices (sometimes referred to as *wearables, wearable devices,* or *wearable activity trackers*) that can be worn on the body (e.g., smartwatch), integrated into shoes or clothing, or implanted subdermally. This technology uses smart electronics (i.e., micro-controllers), software, sensors, and connectivity features (e.g., Bluetooth, hardwire) to collect and share data, primarily to a website or connected mobile device app. According to an annual worldwide survey conducted by the American College of Sports Medicine (Thompson, 2019), wearable technology has been the number one fitness trend from 2016 to 2020 (the only exception was a drop to number three for 2018). Thus, since 2016, there has been no more popular type of technology for fitness professionals.

Prevalent forms of wearable technology for health and fitness include smartwatches, pedometers, accelerometers, heart rate monitors (HRMs), and global positioning system (GPS) tracking devices. These devices frequently track data such as heart rate, step count, energy expenditure, movement or activity time, speed or distance traveled, acceleration or intensity rate, pacing, sleep pattern, altitude change, and route. Practitioners can use these types of objective data to help with assessment and evaluation, and using these tools fits with a strong fitness education curricular model (Corbin & Le Masurier, 2014). However, when choosing wearable technology, we must consider not only the desired data but also the device's features, accuracy, cost, battery life, ease of use, and compatibility with any other devices you might use (Holden & Baghurst, 2018).

This chapter discusses common wearable technology options used for collecting student or athlete data and sharing it with a teacher or coach to facilitate assessment in physical education, health promotion and education, or sport settings. Wearable technology used for personal lifetime health and fitness is discussed in detail in chapter 6. This chapter focuses on heart rate monitors, pedometers, accelerometers, GPS units, and other examples of wearable technology used in coaching and health care. Though many wearable devices include a combination of these technologies, this chapter distinguishes several types. However, be sure to read the important warning in the sidebar titled Words of Caution for All Wearable Technology.

HEART RATE MONITORS

A **heart rate monitor (HRM)** measures and displays the user's heart rate (HR) in real time or records it for later analysis, or both. Due to strong correlation, HR can be used as both a guide for exercise intensity and a quantifiable way to assess individualized effort. Companies that make HRMs include Apple, Fitbit, Garmin, Heart Zones, Mio, Misfit, Polar, Scosche, Suunto, and TomTom.

There are two main types of HRMs: electrical and optical. An **electrical heart rate monitor** (also known as a **chest-strap heart rate monitor**) consists of a plastic-encased transmitter that is worn around the chest against the skin and held in place by a removable elastic chest belt. The chest-strap transmitter picks up electrical signals from the heart and sends them wirelessly to the wristwatch or other device. **Optical heart rate monitors** are most often worn either on the wrist (integrated into the underside of a watch) or on the forearm (integrated into an armband). They often collect HR data via an optical sensor through the process of **photoplethysmography (PPG)**, which uses light to measure blood flow.

Most HRMs continuously display the user's heart rate in beats per minute, which provides a measure of exercise intensity. This information constitutes biofeedback about an autonomic bodily function—in other words, a function that the body does not consciously control—thus enabling the user to control it by adjusting exercise intensity. Thus an HRM provides feedback that helps guide the user during a workout.

WORDS OF CAUTION FOR ALL WEARABLE TECHNOLOGY

A recent case study found that digital technology could enhance students' learning in physical education under certain conditions: (1) both teacher and learners are prepared to use it, (2) the specific physical education context and setting are appropriate for the technology's use, and (3) the technology clearly helps meet the lesson's learning objectives (Burne et al., 2018). Always make sure that these three conditions are met when you integrate any technology into your teaching or coaching practice, particularly with wearable technologies because of their recent mass popularity.

In addition, take care not to rely on wearable technology too much. A device may be inaccurate or need to be calibrated, or it may run out of battery power during a workout or competition. In addition, an athlete or student may develop a dependency on the wearable or the data it provides. One should be able to run, swim, cycle, or perform in any given sport by "feel"—that is, by self-perceived physical exertion and pace—while using the data provided by wearable technology not as a dictator but merely as an occasional guide. As Higdon (2007) has noted for runners:

> The heart-rate monitor is a great training tool, but some runners become so dependent on it that they forget what it means to run by feel. Others compute their maximum heart rates too high, so every "monitored" run is faster than it's supposed to be. Our point: Don't let your heart-rate monitor control your running. (para. 13)

(And *our* point: Don't let wearable technology control every workout or lesson!)

Before purchasing wearables to be used for assessment, consider the following questions (Alejo, 2018):

1. If applicable, are my colleagues and co-coaches on board with this purchase in order to facilitate a consistent, cohesive philosophy?
2. How much time can I commit to learning how to use the wearable, integrate it into my program, and collect and analyze data?
3. Does the anticipated data address specific objectives for learning or performance?
4. Is there a less expensive, more efficient way to collect the same data without using wearable technology?
5. Will I be able to understand and interpret the collected data?
6. Do other areas of my program need more attention before I integrate wearable technology for assessment?
7. Will I be able to ensure appropriate use of the technology to produce data that are valid and reliable?

Finally, know your setting, as well as local laws about sharing learners' biometric and activity tracking data with others. Some data may fall under regulations addressing informed or parental consent, the Health Insurance Portability and Accountability Act of 1996 (HIPAA), the Family Educational Rights and Privacy Act of 1974 (FERPA), or, for professional athletes, a collective bargaining agreement or specific contract exemptions (for more on legal aspects, see chapter 15).

What Type of HRM Is Most Accurate?

The gold standard for noninvasive measurement of HR is generally considered to be electrocardiography (ECG or EKG). However, because it involves placing 12 wired electrodes on the skin, it is impractical for measuring HR during nonlaboratory exercise. Of the remaining options, in general optical HRMs are more convenient and less cumbersome, but electrical (chest-strap) HRMs tend to be more accurate. For example, one study found that a chest-strap HRM was 99 percent accurate, whereas four wrist-worn HRMs ranged from 83 percent to 91 percent accuracy (Wang et al., 2017). Other studies have found accuracy rates of 94 to 97 percent across six wrist-based optical HRMs (Stahl et al., 2016) and 94 percent for an earbud optical HRM (Bunn et al., 2019). However, in late 2018 Polar released its Vantage Series optical HRMs, which may be more accurate due to the addition of a second light-emitting diode (LED), but its accuracy needs to be tested by means of unbiased empirical research. For now, while slight variations may exist across brands and models, electrical (chest-strap) HRMs are generally recognized as more accurate than optical HRMs.

Moreover, research indicates that optical wrist-worn HRMs are most effective at rest and decline in accuracy as exercise intensity increases (Claes et al., 2017; Terbizan et al., 2002; Wang et al., 2017). Of course, accuracy can also be affected by whether the HRM is worn correctly (Claes et al., 2017). In addition, research suggests HRMs tend to measure HR more accurately than they estimate energy expenditure (Lloyd et al., 2014; Wallen et al., 2016).

Electrical (chest-strap) heart rate monitor.

Figure 9.1 lists some common features of HRMs, as well as many features of activity-tracking devices.

Why Use HRMs?

In order for students or athletes to reach their fitness goals, they must learn to train at the right intensity or exertion level—that is, how hard or lightly one is working out. One of the easiest and most accurate ways to assess workout intensity is to continuously measure HR by means of an HRM. No two people are exactly alike in terms of physical conditioning, and the invaluable information provided by an HRM enables an individualized approach to exercise. Specifically, it gives each user an opportunity to learn to exercise safely according to his or her own level of conditioning and fitness.

In health education, students should learn about HR, target HR zones (THRZs), rating of perceived exertion, and self-monitoring of appropriate exercise intensities in conjunction with fitness principles in accordance with national standards for health education (Joint Committee on National Health Education Standards, 2007). Similarly, physical education teachers can use HRMs to help with assessment related to the National Standards for K-12 Physical Education—specifically, Standards 2 and 3, which address (respectively) applying knowledge of movement and performance, and achieving and maintaining a health-enhancing level

Figure 9.1   Common features of HRMs and activity trackers.

- Common HR data provided *during* a workout:
  - Current HR (displayed in beats per minute), average and peak HR, lowest HR, THRZs (e.g., endurance, aerobic, anaerobic variations) with warning alarms (if above or below desired zone), time in target heart rate zone
  - Recovery HR mode—to track how long it takes HR to return to normal resting rate
- HR data provided *after* a workout: all of the above plus RHR, percent of time in THRZ, and minutes above and below THRZ
- Stopwatch features—workout time, laps, interval and countdown timers, alarms, clock, date, data recall, lap memory size
- Estimated calorie counter (potentially helpful for pursuing weight-loss goals)
- Sleep monitoring—for tracking light, deep, or REM sleep and awake time
- Integrated GPS or foot pod (attached to shoe) to track speed, distance, cadence, and pace
- Embedded altimeter to track elevation changes
- Integrated pedometer or accelerometer to track daily steps, activity time, and estimated energy expenditure
- Options for display text size or nighttime display illumination
- Water resistance (varying depths) with swimming lap counter and stroke recognition
- Virtual training partner or coach to provide feedback derived from artificial intelligence
- Pairing with an app or website (e.g., Strava, Garmin Connect, MapMyRide, Polar Flow, Runkeeper) to permit additional workout data storage, analysis, maps, sharing (via social media or within the platform), or comparisons with others' workouts
- "Tethering," which wirelessly connects smartwatch HRM to smartphone to control phone functions such as texting, music, push notifications, fitness apps, and social media
- Coded transmitter to encrypt transmissions from HRM chest-strap sensor to wristwatch receiver, thus preventing other people's HRM signals from being sent to your watch (extremely important during group exercise). Note: most new chest-strap HRMs are coded.
- Battery replacement capability
- HRM chest-strap compatibility with exercise equipment so that a watch is unnecessary and HR is displayed on the equipment dashboard (e.g., Precor treadmills and Polar chest-strap HRM)
- Wireless tracking of multiple users' HRMs at once for an entire class or team (e.g., Polar GoFit, Polar Team Pro, Polar Club, Heart Zones, Ekho Team System)

Note: BPM = beats per minute, GPS = global positioning system, HR = heart rate, HRM = heart rate monitor, RHR = resting HR, REM = rapid eye movement, and THRZ = target heart rate zone.

of physical fitness (Society of Health and Physical Educators, 2014). Figure 9.2 provides examples of HRM uses in sport and physical training settings.

HRMs also come with drawbacks. For instance, depending on the model, one unit can cost anywhere from $25 to more than $500. Moreover, using them can eat up class time since it requires you to manage handing them out, collecting them, troubleshooting them (e.g., HR not appearing on the display), and replacing worn-out batteries or broken straps (which cost money). In addition, HRMs differ in the ease of battery replacement. Most units allow the user to replace the watch batteries, but some require the chest-strap batteries to be replaced by the manufacturer—if the consumer replaces them, then the water-resistance warranty is typically voided. All of these issues are amplified by large class sizes. But don't fret. This chapter discusses several ideas for overcoming these issues, and we firmly believe that the benefits of HRMs greatly outweigh the potential negatives.

Target Heart Rate

The first step in using HRMs with students or athletes is to determine individual training zones (i.e., target heart rate zones). A **target heart rate zone (THRZ)** indicates the exercise intensity that is needed in order to maximize cardiorespiratory benefits. This

Figure 9.2 Examples of HRM uses in sport and physical training.

- In physical education, HRMs can be used to objectively assess effort and guide students' individualized exercise intensities during class so that exercise is performed in their prescribed THRZ.
- In high-intensity intermittent sports (e.g., basketball), HRMs can help monitor exercise intensity, assess player fatigue and recovery levels, and quantify internal training load.
- HRMs can help find an athlete's HRmax in order to prescribe individualized training intensities.
- HRMs can help guide a specific workout's goal intensity by helping the user stay in the prescribed THRZ.
- On prescribed easy or recovery days, HRMs can help track workout intensity to ensure it is not too high so that the body is able to recover from previous hard workouts.
- For intensity-specific workouts (e.g., tempo or threshold workouts), HRMs can help users maintain proper intensity or effort levels, which is particularly helpful on undulating terrain where pace consistency is difficult.
- For high-intensity interval workouts, HRMs can help ensure that the desired intensity is achieved and can help individualize HR recovery for the appropriate amount of time between repeats (e.g., starting the next repeat when HR drops back to 120 BPM).
- HRMs allow you to analyze results of workouts, assessments, and competitions.
- HRMs allow you to track RHR and HR during known training paces. A HR that is unusually high or low may signify a problem (e.g., dehydration, heat or cold stress, sickness, lack of recovery, overtraining).

Note: BPM = beats per minute, GPS = global positioning system, HR = heart rate, HRM = heart rate monitor, HRmax = maximum HR, RHR = resting heart rate, and THRZ = target heart rate zone.

level of exercise (i.e., load) conditions the heart, lungs, and muscles without being overly strenuous. Intensity can be monitored during a workout by measuring heart rate (HR). The key to establishing personalized HR training numbers is to know one's resting HR (RHR), maximum HR (HRmax), HR reserve (HRR), and recommended exercise intensity levels.

Resting heart rate (RHR) is the number of heart beats in one minute at complete, uninterrupted rest. RHR typically ranges from 60 to 100 beats per minute (BPM) for individuals 10 years or older (including adults and seniors), and from 70 to 115 BPM for children ages 5 to 9 years (U.S. National Library of Medicine, 2019). Normally, a lower RHR signifies superior cardiorespiratory fitness, and well-trained athletes may have a RHR as low as 40 BPM.

RHR can be measured in several ways. The most accurate non-clinical method involves wearing a chest-strap HRM overnight, while sleeping, in order to determine average RHR. A less accurate best alternative is the pulse palpation technique—that is, while laying down flat on your back (i.e., supine position), feeling the pulse and counting the beats for 60 seconds. You can also count the number of beats in 15 seconds and multiply that number by four. The pulse can be checked at the carotid artery by placing the index and middle fingers on the neck to the side of the windpipe; another option is to check the radial pulse, which can be measured by placing the same two fingers between the bone and tendon on the thumb side of the wrist. When using the palpation technique, RHR is measured most accurately first thing in morning, before lifting one's head off the pillow. It can also be estimated in class or practice by asking students or athletes to lie down and rest for several minutes and then estimate RHR through the pulse palpation technique before engaging in physical activity.

Physical education teachers or coaches can consider tracking students' or athletes' RHR at least once every two weeks; some advanced athletes may journal their RHR every morning. Individuals who are starting an exercise plan may see their RHR decrease as their fitness improves. If, on the other hand, RHR is checked each morning and one day yields an abnormally high number, the cause *might* be one of the following:

- The individual needs more rest and did not recover from a previous hard workout.
- The individual's body has begun fighting an oncoming illness.
- The individual just woke up from a dream, which made the heart beat faster.

This information is particularly important for sport coaches, especially on days when a hard workout is planned. Expectations for the workout may have to be adjusted, and the workout plan may need to be changed. However, consistently delaying exercise because the individual incorrectly believes RHR is too high day-after-day should not be used as a repetitious excuse for never exercising—a physician may need to be consulted in this case.

The heart beats automatically, but heart rate can be affected by several factors. Table 9.1 offers a list of example factors that can affect HR either at rest or during exercise.

Maximum Heart Rate (HRmax)

HR training zones can be established by means of **maximum heart rate (HRmax)**, which is the highest number of times the heart can contract in one minute at maximal effort. HRmax typically decreases with age. It can be estimated in BPM by using one of the age-based formulas listed in table 9.2.

Though fast and relatively easy to use, these somewhat antiquated methods of predicting HRmax can be fairly inaccurate. For example, the Fox et al. (1971) formula can be 12 to 15 BPM too high or too low (Bayles & Swank, 2018). This imprecision can pose a major problem when prescribing exercise intensity based on age-predicted HRmax.

Table 9.1 Selected Factors That Affect Heart Rate

Age	RHR and HRmax tend to decrease with age.
Body position	HR is lowest in the supine position and higher when standing.
Body size and gender	HR is higher in individuals with proportionately smaller hearts (common in females), and vice versa.
Cardiac creep	HR slowly increases during a long workout even when the same pace is maintained due to several physiological factors (e.g., temperature regulation, hydration status, fatigue).
Fitness level	Lower HR typically signifies increased fitness level and more efficient heart function.
Hydration status	Dehydration can strain the heart and increase HR.
Intensity and pace	HR rises with increased intensity, pace, and training load.
Medical conditions	HR is affected by various conditions, such as cardiovascular disease, high cholesterol, and diabetes.
Medications	HR is increased by stimulants (e.g., nicotine, caffeine) and decreased by depressants (e.g., alcohol).
Mood	HR can be increased by situations that excite emotions (e.g., fight-or-flight response).
Other environmental factors	HR can be increased by training in high wind, at high elevation, or on changing terrain (e.g., hills, sand, mud).
Recovery levels	Fatigue may increase HR.
Smoking	Smoking acutely increases HR and chronically increases RHR.
Sport specificity	Training effects, differences in perceived exertion across activities and other factors may make it hard for athletes who are well trained in one sport (e.g., distance running) to elevate their HR as high in another sport (e.g., cycling).
Temperature	HR can be affected (typically elevated) by abnormally high or low temperature or humidity.
Type of physical activity	Some types of activities (e.g., sprinting) naturally elicit a higher HR than do others (e.g., billiards), and vice versa.
Water-based activity	Because water supports about 90 percent of body weight, HR tends to be 10 to 13 BPM lower for suspended water exercise than for the same effort on land.

BPM = beats per minute, RHR = resting heart rate, and HRmax = maximum heart rate.

Adapted from Benson (1998), Burke (1998), Kirkpatrick and Birnbaum (1997), and Laskowski (2018).

Lab-Based and Field-Based Tests for HRmax

Beyond estimations, HRmax can be measured via lab-based or field-based tests. Because these techniques entail elevated risks associated with maximal exercise testing—for example, chest pain, fainting, heart attack, and even death—they are more appropriate for advanced sport coaching, but *not* for health or physical education. However, HRmax tests can produce results that are more valid, which can assist in prescribing more accurate individualized recommendations for target HR.

An HRmax test should be performed only after obtaining a physician-signed medical clearance (i.e., sport physical), a completed and signed medical screening questionnaire (e.g., Physical Activity Readiness Questionnaire, or PAR-Q), and an informed consent and waiver. Moreover, the latter two should also be signed by a parent or legal guardian if

Table 9.2 Formulas for Age-Predicted Maximum Heart Rate

Formula creator	Target population	Formula	Example
Fox et al. (1971)	Healthy individuals of all ages	220 − age = APHRmax	*17-year-old:* 220 − 17 = 203 BPM
Tanaka et al. (2001)	Healthy adults	208 − (0.7 × age) = APHRmax	*36-year-old:* 208 − (0.7 × 36) = 208 − 25 = 183 BPM
Åstrand (1952)	Healthy individuals of age 4 to 33 years	216.6 − (0.84 × age) = APHRmax	*10-year-old:* 216.6 − (0.84 × 10) = 216.6 − 8.4 = 208 BPM

Note. APHRmax = age-predicted maximum heart rate. BPM = beats per minute. Across all formulas, age is calculated in years. Calculations presented here have been rounded to the nearest whole number.

the participant is under the age of 18 years. Again, HRmax tests are *not* recommended for general health and physical education settings and are more appropriate for advanced performance coaching environments. In addition, a maximal exercise test should only be administered by a certified exercise professional (e.g., clinical exercise physiologist) and only be conducted if the following conditions are met: (1) The test is performed under the supervision of a qualified health care provider who is able to recognize abnormal responses to maximal exercise as well as signs and symptoms of ischemic heart disease, (2) a written emergency plan exists and is rehearsed regularly, and (3) an automated external defibrillator (AED) is present (Bayles & Swank, 2018).

Common lab-based maximal exercise tests that elicit HRmax include treadmill protocols for active and sedentary males and females (e.g., Bruce protocol, Balke protocol) and for highly trained individuals (e.g., modified Åstrand protocol), as well as cycle ergometer protocols (e.g., Åstrand cycle ergometer protocol, Fox protocol, Storer-Davis protocol). Typically, cycle ergometer tests are used only if an injury precludes a safe treadmill test or if the person being tested is a trained cyclist or simply prefers cycling. For more information about testing protocols, see Bayles and Swank (2018).

Field-based tests for HRmax are typically sport specific. The athlete wears a chest-strap HRM and follows a maximal exercise protocol in the sport's usual environment while HR is tracked; the maximal (highest) HR reading is recorded. For example, figure 9.3 provides Benson's (1998) and Daniels' (2014) protocols for runners. Field-based tests also exist for swimming and cycling. As with lab-tests for HRmax, field-based tests should be used only with clearance from a physician and informed consent from the participant. Moreover, such tests should be administered only by trained medical exercise professionals who are specifically certified to administer maximal exercise tests—and only when the aforementioned conditions are met.

Target Heart Rate Zones

Earlier, we noted a formula that uses the number 220 minus age to estimate age-predicted HRmax (Fox et al., 1971), which in turn can be used to estimate HR training zone recommendations. This formula, however, does not account for individuals who differ considerably from the average. In contrast, the **Karvonen formula** (Karvonen & Vuorimaa, 1988) uses RHR to factor in an individual's current fitness level, thus resulting in a more individualized prescription for target heart rate zone.

Figure 9.3   Sample protocols for field-based testing of HRmax (running).

BENSON'S 3,200-METER RUN HRMAX FIELD TEST

- *Who.* Experienced runners with a good idea of their 3,200-meter (2-mile) race-time fitness level. (The protocol may need to be adjusted for faster runners if the 15-second increments increase the pace too quickly.)
- *Where.* 400-meter running track (8 laps)
- *Equipment.* Chest-strap HRM with stopwatch lap-split function
- *When to check HR.* At the end of each of the first 6 laps and then every 100 meters during the final 2 laps

Protocol	Example
1. Estimate current 3,200-meter race time.	• 12:00
2. Calculate 400-meter race pace (RP) for 3,200 meters.	• 1:30 pace per 400 meters × 8 laps = 12:00
3. Perform easy warm-up.	• Jogging, dynamic exercises (e.g., skipping, leg swings), striders
4. *Test start.* Jog lap 1 at RP + 1 minute.	• 1:30 + 1:00 = 2:30
5. Jog lap 2 at RP + 45 seconds.	• 1:30 + 0:45 = 2:15
6. Jog lap 3 at RP + 30 seconds.	• 1:30 + 0:30 = 2:00
7. Jog lap 4 at RP + 15 seconds.	• 1:30 + 0:15 = 1:45
8. Run laps 5 and 6 at RP.	• 1:30 (RP)
9. Run laps 7 and 8 as hard and fast as possible.	• Glance at HR reading on HRM every 100 meters and note the highest reading.
10. Perform a proper cool-down.	• Easy running and static stretching

DANIELS' 2-MINUTE HILL RUNNING HRMAX FIELD TEST

- *Who.* Designed for intermediate to advanced runners
- *Where.* Hill long enough to be run upward for at least 2 minutes continuously
- *Equipment.* Chest-strap HRM with stopwatch function
- *When to check HR.* At the end of each hill repeat
- *No hills.* Use the protocol given here but with 800-meter repeats at hard effort; perform the same HR comparisons between repeats.

Protocol

1. Find a suitable hill (see above).
2. Perform an easy warm-up, including easy running and dynamic warm-up exercises.
3. *Test start.* Run up the hill at 75 percent of full effort (i.e., moderately hard) for 2 minutes, then check HR. Walk or jog easily back down the hill.
4. Run up the hill at 100 percent of full effort for 2 minutes, then check HR. Walk or jog easily back down.
5. Run up the hill again at 100 percent for 2 minutes, then check HR. If this HR reading is *not* higher, you can assume that you have elicited HRmax (i.e., highest HR seen or recorded across the test).
6. Repeat hill runs at 100 percent until you do not see an increase in HR over the preceding repeat. Walk or jog easily back down after each repeat. HRmax will be the highest HR seen or recorded across all repeats.
7. Perform a cool-down (i.e., easy running and static stretching).

Notes: HR = heart rate, HRM = heart rate monitor, HRmax = maximum heart rate, and RP = race pace. One lap = 400 meters.

Adapted from R. Benson, Running, in *Precision Heart Rate Training*, edited by E.R. Burke (Champaign, IL: Human Kinetics, 1998), 65-90; and J. Daniels, *Daniels' Running Formula*, 3rd ed. (Champaign, IL: Human Kinetics, 2014).

Here is the Karvonen formula:

$$\text{Target heart rate} = [(\text{HRmax} - \text{resting heart rate})] \times (\text{prescribed \% intensity}) + \text{resting heart rate}$$

Notes: HRmax = maximum heart rate, and RHR = resting heart rate. HRmax is more accurate if an HRmax test is performed; otherwise, use the following formula: 220 − age in years = HRmax. The process of determining RHR is described earlier in this chapter.

Adapted from Karvonen and Vuorimaa (1988).

Heart rate reserve (HRR) consists of the difference between HRmax and RHR (HRmax − RHR = HRR) and is often used when prescribing exercise intensity levels (i.e., THRZs). As shown in table 9.3, recommendations for aerobic exercise put forth by the American College of Sports Medicine (Bayles & Swank, 2018) indicate that HR should be raised at least to a moderate intensity of 40 percent to 59 percent of HRR and that a reasonable upper intensity level for most exercisers would involve vigorous effort in the range of 60 percent to 89 percent of HRR. In lay terms, moderate-intensity exercise produces *noticeable* increases in breathing and heart rates, whereas vigorous intensity yields "substantial" increases in both. In order to produce health benefits, aerobic exercise should be regular, purposeful, continuous, and inherently rhythmic; should incorporate all major muscle groups; and should last at least 10 minutes per session (Bayles & Swank, 2018). A balanced exercise program should also include resistance, flexibility, and neuromotor (i.e., agility, balance, coordination) training.

Moreover, in order to minimize the risk of injury, an exercise program should follow the principle of progression. In other words, it should involve gradual progression of exercise intensity, duration, frequency, and accumulated volume, both from session to

Table 9.3 Aerobic Exercise Guidelines

Physical Activity Guidelines for Americans (U.S. Department of Health and Human Services):

- For children and adolescents (ages 6-17 years), at least 60 min MVPA per day, including VPA on at least 3 days per wk
- For adults, spread throughout the wk, at least 150-300 min per wk of MPA **or** 75-150 min per wk of VPA, **or** equivalent combination of MVPA

Aerobic Exercise Frequency and Duration Guidelines (American College of Sports Medicine):

30-60 min per day of MPA on at least 5 days per wk **or** 20-60 min per day of VPA on at least 3 days per wk **or** equivalent combination of MVPA on at least 3 to 5 days per wk

Intensity	% HRR	10-point scale of perceived exertion	General classification	Talk test	Sample activities
Moderate	40-59	4	Somewhat easy	Can talk but not sing	Power yoga Brisk walking Water aerobics
		5			
		6	Somewhat hard		
Vigorous	60-89	7	Hard	Can't say more than a few words	Lap swimming Cycling ≥10 mph (≥16 kph) Running
		8			
		9			
Maximal	90-100	10	Extremely hard	Can't talk	Sprinting

Resistance, flexibility, and neuromotor training are also required for a balanced exercise program. Key: kph = kilometers per hour, min = minutes, MPA = moderate PA, mph = miles per hour, MVPA = moderate to vigorous PA, PA = physical activity, VPA = vigorous physical activity, and wk = week.

Adapted from Bayles and Swank (2018) and U.S. Department of Health and Human Services (2018).

session and from week to week. A good rule of thumb is to increase weekly volume by no more than 10 percent from one week to the next and to avoid increasing intensity and overall volume at the same time (Daniels, 2014). Figure 9.4 provides an example using the Karvonen formula to prescribe THRZ for moderate- or vigorous-intensity workouts.

Performance-oriented sport coaches may consider using more specific HRmax training zone intensities. Here is an example for running (Daniels, 2014):

1. Easy running: 65 percent to 79 percent HRmax
2. Marathon-pace running: 80 percent to 89 percent HRmax
3. Threshold or tempo running: 88 percent to 92 percent HRmax
4. 10K zone running: 92.5 percent to 97 percent HRmax
5. Interval running: 97.5 percent to 100 percent HRmax
6. Repetition running: 100 percent HRmax

Thus aerobic-based performance sport requires narrower, more targeted training zones with periodic all-out efforts greater than 90 percent of HRmax, but that level of intensity is not appropriate for general physical education and rudimentary health benefits.

Figure 9.4 Karvonen formula example.

Characteristics: 15-year-old female with RHR of 65 BPM (no HRmax test performed)

1. Step 1:   220   −   15   =   205
                               (age in years)   (APHRmax)

2. Step 2:   205   −   65   =   140
                  (APHRmax)   (RHR)   (HRR)

3. Step 3:

140 (HRR)	×	0.40 (intensity)	+	65 (HRR)	=	121 (lower moderate THRZ)
140 (HRR)	×	0.59 (intensity)	+	65 (RHR)	=	148 (higher moderate THRZ)
140 (HRR)	×	0.60 (intensity)	+	65 (RHR)	=	149 (lower vigorous THRZ)
140 (HRR)	×	0.89 (intensity)	+	65 (RHR)	=	190 (higher vigorous THRZ)

4. Step 4:

Estimated moderate intensity THRZ is 121 to 148 BPM.
Estimated vigorous intensity THRZ is 149 to 190 BPM.

Notes: APHRmax = age-predicted maximum heart rate, BPM = beats per minute, HRR = heart rate reserve, RHR = resting heart rate, THRZ = target heart rate zone (i.e., training heart rate range). If appropriate, you can replace the first step with an HRmax test score for more accuracy, or, depending on your target population, you can use a different formula for age-predicted HRmax (see table 9.2). A moderate THRZ is recommended for unconditioned (i.e., less fit) individuals.

Using HRMs in Physical Education

In the past, it was nearly impossible to assess effort objectively and accurately for all students in a physical education class at the same time. Today, HRMs make it possible to do so, thereby facilitating potential success for every student. Specifically, HRMs help learners and practitioners align moderate- to vigorous-intensity exercise with the physical activity guidelines listed in table 9.3.

Some physical educators use collected HRM data to determine a portion of a student's grade based on time spent in the THRZ. For example, a teacher might award 30 points during a lesson—one point for each minute spent in the student's prescribed THRZ. This form of differentiated instruction allows for individualized exercise speed or pace; that is, students who are fitter must exercise at a higher rate in order to achieve their prescribed minimum THRZ intensity, whereas students who are less fit can succeed by attaining their THRZ at a slower pace. On the track, for instance, a fitter student might be required to run at a 7-minute mile pace, whereas a less fit student might need only to run or walk at a 12-minute mile pace, in order for them both to achieve their minimum THRZ intensity level.

HRM systems designed to handle a whole group, class, or team allow teachers and coaches the ability to wirelessly track each learner's HR in real time during exercise. Examples include Polar GoFit, Polar Team Pro, Polar Club, Heart Zones, and the Ekho Team System. These types of systems not only permit accessible oversight during exercise, but also enables expedited or automatic recording of the whole-group HR data for during or after the workout for either on-the-spot and later analysis.

In physical education, HRMs may be more appropriate at the secondary and college levels, particularly if using chest-strap HRMs or incorporating collected HR data as part of formal assessment. At the elementary level, wrist- or armband-mounted optical HRMs would be more appropriate for ease of use, and HR readings should be used only to give students informal feedback about appropriate exercise intensity levels—not for formal assessment. If you work with learners who are of middle school age or older, consider using figure 9.4 as one way for students to calculate their own THRZ while factoring in their estimated current fitness level by means of RHR.

Alternatively, many physical educators who teach a large number of students preset each HRM with the same estimated age-predicted THRZ. This level might fall into the following ranges based on 60 percent to 90 percent of APHRmax using the Åstrand (1952) formula:

- Lower elementary (approximately ages 5-7 years): 126 to 189 BPM
- Upper elementary (8-10 years): 125 to 187 BPM
- Middle school (11-13 years): 123 to 185 BPM
- High school (14-18 years): 121 to 181 BPM

This less-individualized technique is not recommended for performance sport coaching or when students of various ages (e.g., K-12) are using the same HRMs, but it can be used in settings where multiple students of similar age share the same HRM. Of course, a pre-set THRZ may not be appropriate for students who have a medical contraindication or an HRmax that differs considerably from the average. For more pedagogical considerations and suggestions, see figure 9.5.

When selecting an HRM, consider the following factors:

- Features and uses listed in figures 9.1 and 9.2
- Type of HRM—electrical chest-strap (more accurate) or optical wrist- or armband-mounted (easier to use and less invasive)
- Desired user feedback while exercising—for instance, exact BPM data or merely color-coded HR intensity indicator (e.g., blue = easy effort, yellow = moderate, red = hard)

Smartwatch with integrated optical heart rate monitor.

Guido Mieth/DigitalVision/Getty Images

- Need for integrated, concurrent, wireless tracking of all learners' HRs via practitioner's mobile device
- Ease of using integrated HRM software and hardware for data collection, storage, and dissemination

PEDOMETERS

Pedometers are portable, electronic, motion-detecting devices that count each step taken by the user. Simple waist-worn pedometers typically use a spring-suspended lever arm that moves up and down in response to vertical movements (and often makes a clicking sound), thus opening and closing an electronic circuit that counts steps. Normally, pedometers are worn on the waistband or shoe or integrated into a wrist-worn watch or smartphone app.

For lifetime health and wellness, pedometers are often used to estimate physical activity levels through daily step counts. In physical education, they can be used to objectively assess lessons (e.g., the amount of physical activity involved in a specific lesson) and students (e.g., the physical effort expended by a student)—both through estimated step counts—with the goal of students being moderately to vigorously active for at least half of class time during each lesson (Fröberg & Raustorp, 2019). Although movement intensity is not captured, pedometers still provide an objective measure of physical activity through step counts. Moreover, they are relatively unobtrusive and inexpensive (e.g., about $5 to

Figure 9.5   Tips for using HRMs in physical education and coaching.

- Read the owner's manual and search the web for step-by-step instructions or instructional videos relevant to the exact HRM model you are using. Consider also posting HRM instructions in the locker room and providing learners with an instructional video prior to their first use in the flipped instruction approach (see chapter 8).
- When using a chest-strap HRM:
    - For each use, put water or HRM gel on the back of the chest-strap electrodes before securing them to the chest.
    - A chest-strap HRM is typically worn just below the chest muscles (pectoralis major), well below the nipple line. For females, this area is typically just below the bottom of a sport bra or integrated into a bra specifically designed to integrate with an HRM. As a result, chest-strap HRMs must be put on by users in the privacy of a locker room or bathroom.
    - If the elastic band is not tight enough, then you may not find a signal when you initiate an HR signal search via the wristwatch receiver button; similarly, if the chest-strap slides down during activity, the signal may be lost. To avoid these pitfalls, make sure that the strap fits snugly against the chest and does not move during activity, while also ensuring that it does not restrict breathing. If the signal is lost, try sliding the chest-strap slightly up, down, or to the left or right; also check whether the transmitter's batteries are dead. The chest-strap can also be worn backward with the electrodes upright but across the back; this approach may be particularly helpful for individuals who are overweight or obese as the HRM may fit more snugly in place against the skin on their back compared to their front.
- For optical HRMs, make sure that the optical sensor (i.e., LED light) is tight against the skin and does not move with physical activity. It must be in constant contact with the skin in order to work properly. Wrist-mounted optical HRMs should be worn at least a finger's width up the arm from the wrist bone (i.e., the styloid process of the ulna).
- When using a set of HRMs that are shared across many classes or users throughout the day:
    - Number each HRM and assign each learner a number for the HRM that they will use each time. This approach allows for easy distribution and collection of HRMs and provides a quick way to take attendance (absentees are indicated by any HRM not collected). You can also track any problems with a specific numbered HRM (e.g., dead battery) and figure out who wasn't caring for it properly or accidently took it to the next class.
    - Acquire a class HRM organizer. For chest-strap HRMs, consider an HRM-specific carrying case organizer such as the Polar HRM classroom management system, which can be hung from a hook and cleanly numbers and separates the watches and chest-strap transmitters. For optical HRMs, consider a plastic case similar to a fishing tackle box with slots that can be easily numbered to accommodate the numbered HRMs.
    - For groups using chest-strap HRMs, ensure that the HRM transmitters are coded (i.e., encrypted – see figure 9.1) and that each leaner initiates the HR signal search on the receiver watch at least three feet (one meter) away from anyone else who is wearing a chest-strap transmitter so that HR signals do not get crossed. This will assist with avoiding a student's HRM transmitted signal being received by another classmate's HRM receiver watch.

(continued)

Figure 9.5 *(continued)*

- For reasons of sanitation, some practitioners require that each learner obtain their own appropriately sized HRM elastic strap that adheres to the plastic HRM electrode transmitter, which can get sweaty. Learners should be permitted to secure the plastic chest-strap under the shirt in a private area (e.g., locker room), which of course means that they must be able to retrieve the HRM before changing. After use, they can wipe the plastic transmitter clean with mild soap and water, dry them, and return them to the HRM organizer.

- Depending on how old your learners are, consider what you want the HRMs to display, whether either through a wristwatch-style HRM or projected on the wall if you are using a whole-group wireless HR tracking system. For instance, you might ask learners to monitor the total number of minutes spent in their THRZ (many HRMs have the capability to beep if the user is outside of the prescribed zone), current HR, total exercise time, lap time, time of day, average HR, or a combination of these options.

- If you factor the number of minutes spent in the THRZ into your grading, be prepared to see students jumping or running in place at the end of class in an attempt to get the last few seconds or minutes in their THRZ. Consider permitting students to come during breaks (e.g., recess, lunch, study hall) or before or after school to make up minutes missed or to earn bonus points. At the same time, consider user motivation—teachers and coaches should not act as a "heart rate police!" Don't single out or embarrass a student in front of the class for not being in their THRZ.

- Consider referring to HR-targeted lesson ideas from online resources or the following texts: Kirkpatrick and Birnbaum (1997), Polar (2010), and Swaim (2012).

- If you don't have enough HRMs for every student, consider dividing the class into groups and alternating which group uses the HRMs each session. Also, see chapter 16 for grant ideas to enable you to purchase more units.

- At the end of class, depending on the HRMs used, you may be able to have data (e.g., minutes spent in THRZ) downloaded via a whole-group wireless HR tracking system (e.g., Polar GoFit), downloaded via a hardwired multi-HRM docking station, or tracked individually by asking each learner to display their data for you to record manually. Learners can also keep an HR journal or portfolio (online or on paper) and record the data themselves, though you will need to conduct regular spot checks for accountability, particularly for older students who may lie about their readings. These journals can also include qualitative self-assessment and reflections on HR and workout data.

- If you use time spent in THRZ for assessment and a student is trying to cheat by wearing an HRM for another student or purposefully trying to cross HR signals, consider resetting the time spent in zone to zero on the watch for all parties involved immediately upon discovering the problem. If such behavior becomes a repeated problem, consult the student code of conduct for procedures related to academic dishonesty.

Notes: APHRmax = age-predicted maximum heart rate, BPM = beats per minute, HR = heart rate, HRM = heart rate monitor, THRZ = target heart rate zone.

$30) as compared with other wearables (e.g., HRMs, GPS units). Here are some examples of companies that make pedometers: 3DTriSport, Accusplit, Fitbit, Garmin, Omron, PedUSA, and Yamax.

Simple pedometers are used to track steps and estimate distance traveled in miles or kilometers, and increased daily step counts have been linked positively to lower prevalence of metabolic syndrome and several individual cardiovascular risk factors (Sisson et al., 2010). Pedometer data (e.g., step count, steps per minute, estimated distance, energy expenditure, activity time) are often integrated within other wearable devices. In addition, more advanced pedometers may track heart rate, sleep duration, activity recognition (e.g., walking, standing, sitting), and pulse oximetry (blood oxygen saturation); they may also feature mobile device connectivity, as well as activity alarms for long sedentary durations (i.e., a beep may occur after sitting for an extended time). They do not, however, account for the extra energy required for traversing hills or stairs, cannot track arm movements if worn on the waist, and cannot track the activities of swimming or cycling (McCarthy & Grey, 2015).

A properly positioned waist-worn pedometer.

TECHNOLOGY TIPS FROM THE FIELD

IHT Spirit System Heart Rate Monitors

Colleen Quinn-Maxwell
High School (Grades 9-12) Health and Physical Education Teacher and Sponsor of the Students Against Melanoma Club

What technology do you use regarding wearable technology?
IHT Spirit System Heart Rate Monitors.

What equipment and software are needed?
We have 32 HRM watches, a charging station, and cubby storage for housing the monitors, which are each numbered for class use. Also, we have a desktop computer with the IHT Spirit software installed (including stored participant data) with an Internet connection. We also have a class magnet board for directions to students regarding each class's use, including what teacher is using them. Finally, we also have cleaning wipes and replacement materials.

How do you use this technology?
- Students come to class and check our board of which assigned group or teacher is using the HRMs that day (we only have 32 HRMs, and some periods have 50 to 60 students).
- Each student is numbered in our IHT Spirit system so they can have individualized zones for performance based on their own resting heart rate (or a default is provided for teen use).

(continued)

IHT Spirit System Heart Rate Monitors *(continued)*

- Students get their monitor from our cubby system which is numbered and then they scan it in on the HRM reader. This also is a form of taking attendance for students. Once the monitor is put on their wrist, it will start reading their HR and performance in class. Blue zone is the lowest zone (light to moderate intensity), with yellow in the middle (moderate to vigorous intensity) and red being the highest zone (vigorous intensity).
- Students have been providing us with feedback for the last two months, and we have been tweaking things as new users, but now we are ready to start providing percentage challenges for the class period.
- Each activity for the day is already put into the IHT Spirit System prior to class, and a percentage goal for each zone depending on the activity (i.e., less active activities like badminton may expect more time in blue or yellow, while more active activities like handball require more time in yellow and red).
- Students now have challenges for percentages of time spent in the yellow zone and reaching the red zone. They should be out of the blue zone by the end of their three-minute warm-up, which varies each class.
- Each individual monitor shows the HR display, with the current HR beats per minute number and illuminated color that the student and teacher can view during the activity.
- At the conclusion of class, students individually scan back in on the HRM reader, view their data, receive teacher feedback, wipe down their monitor with an antibacterial wipe, and return the HRM to the numbered cubby.
- You can see the student sign-in time and sign-out time as well as data regarding HR zone and HR across the lesson. This is all archived for the students.
- At the conclusion of each school day, HRMs are placed on the charging system.

What lessons or activities do you use most often with the HRMs?
We have utilized them during all of our PE activities, trying to demonstrate the increase in heart rate (HR) during vigorous activities and the decrease in HR during light activities. All students rotate wearing the monitors, and we have a running database of their own HR and performance data for teachers to view and students to evaluate after class. We just began using the HRMs after receiving a district grant about five months ago.

Do you also use the HRMs for health education or coaching?
We have not used them for health education, but skills are taught in health about HR and exercise and the zones in which they will be working in during PE class.

What is your main objective for using HRMs?
We use HRMs to have authentic assessment of student performance in our PE classes. Our goal is to utilize this as an authentic and personalized assessment tool for our department when evaluating each student and their performance in our classes.

What do you like about the HRMs?
- We really like the increased accountability with students. We now have data to support student performance, and the ability to adapt to each student's individual needs is great.
- We love that the monitors have provided visual feedback for both the teacher and the student regarding in-class performance when they not only display an HR number but also illuminate either blue, yellow, or red, demonstrating what heart rate zone each student is performing in. We have noticed students having more drive and accountability for their own performance in class and pride in their performance when achieving the class goal. They are working collectively to meet each class goal as well, not just individually, and holding each other accountable with supportive words and encouragement to do more and try harder.

How might the technology be improved (or what don't you like about it)?
We have been mastering the technique of administering the monitors at the beginning of class and having students return them with the scanning and cleaning procedures. Our time has been cut down on this to almost normal changing time, but as we adjust our procedures, we hope to have students move right into warm-up and use the sign-in process with the monitor scan as our attendance as well—instead of losing the time to then have students sit and listen to instructions and take attendance.

What suggestions do you have for using this technology?
Start off slow with gradual implementation of the monitors to your expectations. There will be a learning curve for both you and the students for the following: (1) where to position the HRM on the wrist to acquire accurate HR data, (2) charging procedures, (3) setting up the computer station most effectively to coordinate procedures for students scanning the HRM during pickup and return, (4) careful positioning and removal of the HRM without ripping the strap, (5) implementing appropriate goals for HR zones, and (6) inputting data collectively with grading.

Courtesy of Collen Quinn-Maxwell.

Pedometer Accuracy

Pedometer models vary in their precision, and pedometer accuracy is affected by many factors—for instance, wearing a pedometer incorrectly (figure 9.6). Also, because stride length differs across individuals, some pedometers can be calibrated in order to provide more accurate distance estimates if software is not integrated to do so automatically (figure 9.7). Some pedometers also offer various settings to account for different modes of locomotion, such as walking, running, and shuffling; even so, the activity level of nonrhythmic and multidirectional stepping activities (e.g., cleaning, vacuuming, gardening) tend to be significantly underestimated in pedometer step counts (Toth et al., 2018). Other reasons for pedometer inaccuracy include incorrect positioning, extremely slow or inconsistent pace, and erroneous counting of steps in response to vibrations (e.g., within a moving vehicle) or up-and-down movements (e.g., standing and then sitting, ascending or descending a steep slope or set of stairs, engaging in certain sports such as tennis). In addition, the accuracy of some lower-end models may be reduced by improper positioning angles due to excessive midsection fat; this is not an issue for tri-axis pedometers, which work both horizontally and vertically (McCarthy & Grey, 2015).

Figure 9.6   Tips for wearing a waist-mounted pedometer.

- Read the directions for the specific pedometer you have, but most waist-mounted pedometers should be clipped firmly to the waistband or belt within several inches of the body's midline (i.e., belly button).
- Many models also offer a security strap which is only meant to catch the pedometer if it accidentally becomes unclipped.
- Do attach the pedometer directly to the waist-band of your shorts or pants, and the security strap clip (if included) to a pocket.
- Do *not* attach the pedometer to a pocket, top of a t-shirt, loose belt loop, or hang it from the security strap.

Ken Hively/Los Angeles Times via Getty Images   Jennifer Krause

Figure 9.7   Calculating stride length and wearing a waist-mounted pedometer.

Prior to adjusting the settings of the pedometer, measure your normal walking stride length.

1. At a usual walking pace, walk 10 steps as seen below:

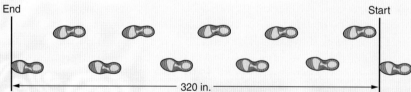

2. Measure from "Start" to "End" in inches as indicated.
3. Calculate the walking stride length through dividing the total distance by 10.
4. Example: Total distance = 320 inches. 320 / 10 = 32 inches
5. Walking stride length = 32 inches (or 2 feet and 8 inches)

Note: This stride length is specific to a "normal" walking pace. However, this procedure could also be replicated for faster-paced walking or running stride length.

Recommended Steps per Day

Daily step counts are often used as a way to motivate and estimate overall aerobic physical activity. Daily step count recommendations (figure 9.8) should fit with overall aerobic physical activity guidelines (table 9.3). Increases in physical activity can be facilitated by the constant user feedback pedometers or wearable step counters provide coupled with behavioral approaches such as goal setting and virtual or F2F coaching (U.S. Department of Health and Human Services, 2018). Overall, adults tend to average about 5,000 steps per day, 80 percent of which are categorized as light intensity (U.S. Department of Health and Human Services, 2018). Thus, practitioners must help individuals meet recommended daily step counts by facilitating appropriate programming.

Many sources (e.g., Tudor-Locke et al., 2008; U.S. Department of Health and Human Services, 2018) that address moderate to vigorous physical activity (MVPA) for adults recommend either setting a goal of 10,000 steps per day or increasing the number of weekly

Figure 9.8   Daily step count recommendations for healthy individuals.

Children (Ages 6 to 17 Years)

Recommended 60 minutes per day of physical activity = about 9,000 to 12,000 steps

Adults

- Target exercise volume = at least 7,000 steps per day, with a goal of 10,000 steps per day
- Most adults can meet aerobic exercise guidelines (table 9.3) by taking about 5,400 to 7,900 steps per day

Adult Step Count Estimates

- Moderate intensity exercise = about 100 steps per minute
- 1 mile (1.6 km) of walking = about 2,000 steps
- Walking at moderate intensity for 30 minutes = about 3,000 to 4,000 steps

Adult Activity Categories Based on Daily Step Count

- <5,000 steps per day = sedentary
- 5,000 to 7,499 steps per day = low active
- 7,500 to 9,999 steps per day = somewhat active
- 10,000 to 12,499 steps per day = active
- ≥12,500 steps per day = highly active

Additional Considerations

- Because of limitations in pedometer accuracy, consider steps per minute in combination with recommendations for frequency and duration (table 9.3) in order to attain aerobic exercise recommendations.
- Personalize daily step count goals after establishing baseline values (figure 9.9) and determining realistic and attainable health goals.
- Weight management typically requires taking more than the recommended minimum daily step count.
- A balanced exercise program should also include resistance, flexibility, and neuromotor training.

Adapted from Bayles and Swank (2018); and Tudor-Locke et al. (2008).

Figure 9.9 Sample procedures for setting a daily step count goal.

Plan exercise sessions and set step goals in an effort toward meeting exercise guidelines (table 9.3):

1. Set a goal for exercise time (e.g., certain number of minutes of brisk walking each day).

2. To establish a baseline, determine typical step counts by using a step counter to track the number of steps taken on several ordinary days with no purposeful exercise sessions. The majority of these steps would come during light-intensity activity.

3. Use a step counter to measure the number of steps taken while walking briskly for 10 minutes.

4. Use the result of step 3 (i.e., steps per minute during brisk walking) to calculate how many steps are needed in order to reach the exercise time goal set in step 1.

5. Determine a daily step goal by adding the baseline daily step count (from step 2) and the number of steps required to meet the goal for exercise time (step 4).

Example

1. 20 minutes
2. 5,200 steps per day (average daily baseline)
3. 1,100 steps for 10 minutes of brisk walking
4. 1,100 × 2 = 2,200 steps for 20 minutes of brisk walking
5. 5,200 baseline steps + 2,200 steps for 20 minutes of brisk walking = 7,400 (daily step goal)

Notes: An individualized progressive increase in daily steps (e.g., 10 percent per day) can be performed until an overall step goal is achieved (e.g., 10,000 daily steps). For example, an individual who starts at 6,000 daily steps can add 600 daily steps the following week.

Adapted from U.S. Department of Health and Human Services (2018).

steps taken by a certain percentage (e.g., 10 percent) from one week to the next until recommended exercise guidelines are met (table 9.3). For instance, brisk walking can contribute to daily moderate-intensity physical activity. Figure 9.9 elaborates on how to establish appropriate individualized step count goals. These procedures might be followed by health and physical educators who focus on lifetime health in order to help either child or adult students create individualized plans to incrementally achieve the recommended daily step counts listed in figure 9.8.

Pedometers in Physical Education

Appropriate instruction in physical education devotes at least 50 percent of class time to engaging students in MVPA (Society of Health and Physical Educators, 2015). To assess this benchmark, practitioners can use pedometers to track student step counts during class. For instance, Scruggs (2013) posits that 80 steps per minute would be an appropriate target to evaluate the 50 percent MVPA guideline for students in fifth

Accuracy of Commercial Pedometers

Many consumer-grade pedometers significantly undercount steps at walking speeds slower than 0.9 meters per second (about 2 miles per hour), which is particularly problematic for healthy older adults who walk at these speeds (Martin et al., 2012). One study tested the accuracy of six commercial pedometers—three wrist-worn (Fitbit Charge, Garmin vívofit 2, and Withings Pulse Ox) and three hip-worn (Fitbit Zip, Omron HJ-322U, Yamax Digi-Walker SW-200) for use while walking, running, and performing activities of daily living (Toth et al., 2018). Results indicated that, excluding the Withings Pulse Ox (which performed the worst), the pedometers captured 87 percent to 93 percent of hand-counted steps, which led the researchers to conclude that the majority of commercial pedometers may be accurate enough to inform positive behavior change (Toth et al., 2018). Some pedometers provide research-grade accuracy. One example is the ankle-mounted StepWatch, which has been found to have an error range of about only 4 percent to 5 percent; however, the costs of this device and the required additional software and accessories totals some $2,000, thus limiting the chances of using it in nonclinical settings (Aguiar et al., 2018).

Another study examined the accuracy of commercial waist-mounted pedometers in physical education among fifth-grade students and found that the devices significantly underreported step counts for skipping, galloping, and sliding as compared with walking and hopping (Smith & Schroeder, 2010). Tracking was least accurate for skipping and most accurate for walking. The researchers surmised that these differences may have resulted from unequal forces generated in the lead leg and the trail leg (which may not be strong enough to register a step) during skipping, galloping, and sliding. These results were supported by similar findings in a more recent study of waist-mounted pedometers used by fifth- and sixth-grade students (Smith et al., 2019). Thus, physical educators must be aware of the potential for movement-specific limitations.

through twelfth grades. According to this step count equivalence, physical education students should aim to attain at least the following numbers of steps, depending on total class time:

- 60-minute class × 80 steps = 4,800 steps during class
- 45-minute class × 80 steps = 3,600 steps
- 30-minute class × 80 steps = 2,400 steps

Remember that effective use of this guideline depends on the accuracy of the pedometer. Moreover, although these in-class step counts contribute toward the total number of daily steps recommended for children, more steps outside of class must be performed to entirely meet that recommendation (figure 9.8).

Sample numbered pedometer organizer system that can be hung on a cart or wall.

Reprinted by permission from Gopher Sport. www.gophersport.com/assessment/pedometers/classplus-fitstep-plus-packs

How Many Daily Steps Do Children and Adults Really Take?

Several studies have investigated average daily step counts for children and adults. One study that included 11,669 Canadian children of ages 5 to 19 years found that boys took an average of 12,259 daily steps, whereas girls averaged 10,906; for both sexes, weekday step counts were generally higher than weekend counts, counts declined with age, and seasonal variations were evident (e.g., fewer daily steps were taken during winter) (Craig et al., 2010). Another study tracked activity by 1,136 U.S. adults who wore a pedometer for two days and found that they took an average of 5,117 steps per day; the study also found that higher steps per day were positively associated with being male and single, being relatively younger and more educated, and having a lower body mass index (Bassett et al., 2010).

Practitioners can also use data from in-class step counts to objectively measure overall physical activity during a lesson, determine the effectiveness of specific activities for promoting physical activity during lessons, and make adjustments if benchmarks are not consistently met. They can also use step count data to estimate individual student effort; in fact, pedometer use has been found to motivate physical activity through self-monitoring and goal setting (Fröberg & Raustorp, 2019).

Integrating pedometers into practice requires effective management—namely, distributing units for use and collecting them afterward, as well as replacing batteries when necessary. Figure 9.10 lists pedometer considerations specific to physical education, and figure 9.11 lists suggested procedures for integrating pedometers into physical education. Many of these ideas also transfer well to health education settings. For a full review of pedometer use in physical education, see Fröberg and Raustorp (2019); for common pitfalls of using pedometers at the elementary level, see McCaughtry et al. (2008).

ACCELEROMETERS

Whereas pedometers count steps taken over time, accelerometers track both steps taken and intensity of movement. An **accelerometer** is an axis-based, motion-sensing, electromechanical device that reports intensity of movement by calculating acceleration forces in relation to gravity and converts the results into counts. Basic accelerometers (uniaxial units) are sensitive only to movement in the vertical plane (up and down), whereas more advanced models (biaxial or triaxial units) can also track anteroposterior (forward and backward) and lateral (side-to-side) movement. Depending on the model, an accelerometer may be attached to a shoe, connected to the body by means of a strap, sewn into an athlete's uniform, or simply clipped to the waist (this last type of unit is sometimes referred to as an activity tracker or combination accelerometer/pedometer). They are also commonly embedded within smartwatches and smartphones; for example, your smartphone probably uses an accelerometer to recognize whether you are holding it horizontally (in landscape view) or vertically (in portrait view) in order to automatically adjust when taking a digital picture.

Figure 9.10   Recommendations for integrating pedometers into physical education.

- Use pedometers to aid assessment of individual students' physical activity levels in relation to Standard 3 of the National Standards for K-12 Physical Education: Achieve and maintain a health-enhancing level of physical activity (Society of Health and Physical Educators, 2014).

- Use as motivation to increase both in-class and overall daily physical activity levels.

- Remember that pedometers tend to be more accurate for walking, running, and hopping and can significantly underestimate step counts for skipping, galloping, and sliding movements.

- Consider validating accuracy by one of the following means: (1) walking 100 meters with the pedometer, counting the number of steps taken, and comparing your count with the pedometer reading; and (2) performing a "shake test" by shaking the pedometer vertically 30 times and comparing the displayed step count with the actual number of shakes.

- If using a set of pedometers that are shared across many classes or students:

  - Number each pedometer and assign each student in each class a number for the pedometer they will use each time. This approach allows for easy distribution and collection, as well as a quick way to take attendance (absentees are indicated by any pedometer not collected). You can also track any problems with a specific numbered pedometer (e.g., change a dead battery, track down who wasn't caring for the unit properly, quickly determine who accidently took it to the next class).

  - Acquire a class pedometer organizer. Consider using either a plastic case similar to a fishing tackle box with slots that can be numbered to match pedometer numbering or, for example, a mobile storage cart with the attachable pocketed QuickID System from Gopher Sport.

  - If you don't have enough pedometers to give one to every student, consider dividing the class into groups and alternating which group uses the pedometers each day. To help you become able to purchase more units, see the ideas for grant writing and fundraising covered in chapter 16.

- To help prevent constant fiddling with the units by elementary students wanting to inspect their current step count during instruction, consider conducting group step-count checks periodically (e.g., every 10 minutes).

- Remember that pedometers may not be safe or durable enough for certain activities (e.g., contact sports).

- For students with visual impairments, consider using a talking pedometer (see chapter 7).

- Watch for students who may simply hold the pedometer in their hand and shake it vigorously in an attempt to dishonestly increase their step count.

Adapted from Fröberg and Raustorp (2019); and Lund and Kirk (2010).

Figure 9.11 Sample steps for including pedometers in physical education.

1. Teach students what a pedometer is, what it measures, and how to use it. Consider also providing learners with an instructional video prior to their first use in the flipped instruction approach (see chapter 8). Starting at the middle school level or beyond, if students each have their own pedometer, consider having them measure stride length (see figure 9.7) and input personalized data (e.g., age, gender) to activate advanced features.

2. Teach students time-efficient procedures for checking out and returning the pedometer and make sure that they are wearing the units correctly (baggy clothing may hinder accuracy).

3. If sharing pedometers across classes, teach students to reset them to zero at the beginning of each class.

4. Teach aerobic exercise guidelines (table 9.3) and how daily step count recommendations (figure 9.8) facilitate a healthy lifestyle.

5. Students can track and establish an average step count baseline across several PE class periods of similar length. Then, with your facilitation, they can set realistic goals for step counts during future PE class periods. Remind students to focus only on their own step counts—not those of their classmates. If students are able to wear their pedometers all day, at home and at school, then overall daily step count goals can be established and tracked. Then, students can aim to increase their step count by 10 percent each week until daily step count recommendations are reached.

6. As you either start or continue a fitness-focused unit (e.g., run/walk program, fitness stations, jumping rope, orienteering), ask students to quickly log or journal their step counts and compare them with their established goals. You can also track and compare total or average step counts for the class as a whole in order to monitor lesson-specific physical activity levels. Doing so may help you plan future programming or advocate to administrators and parents about how many steps students are taking during physical education.

7. Give students specific ideas for participating in individual and family-oriented physical activities both at home and in the community in order to maintain or increase their daily step counts.

Adapted from Fröberg and Raustorp (2019); Lund and Kirk (2010).

Accelerometers used in fitness wearables often report activity counts, intensity, duration, time of day of physical activity, and estimated energy expenditure, thus helping practitioners to assess learners' MVPA levels. One prime use of accelerometers is to aid in objective assessment of movement intensity. Moderate-intensity exercise equates to at least 2,020 counts per minute (3 metabolic equivalents [METs]), whereas vigorous-intensity exercise equates to at least 5,999 counts per minute (6 METs) (Troiano et al., 2008). Figure 9.12 provides samples of the reports that can be generated through an accelerometer's software or mobile app. Practitioners can use such reports to track each learner's movement intensity and compare intensities across activities or workout sessions.

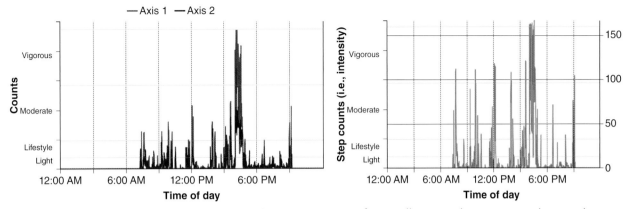

Figure 9.12   Sample ActiGraph GT1M accelerometer report for a college student wearing the accelerometer throughout the day and performing a $\dot{V}O_2$max test at about 4 p.m. The x-axis reflects time of day in both figures; the y-axis reflects counts (i.e., intensity) in the left example and step counts in the right example.

Seth Jenny

Regarding validity, as with pedometers, step counts and estimated energy expenditures derived from accelerometers tend to be more accurate for faster walking and for running (≤3 percent error), particularly on flat surfaces, and less accurate for slow walking (Abel et al., 2008). In addition, some evidence suggests that accelerometers placed on the ankle (specifically, the ActiGraph GT9X Link) is more accurate than hip- and waist-mounted units for predicted energy expenditure in both structured and simulated free or daily-living settings (Montoye et al., 2017). However, similar results may not be found for higher-intensity sporting activities or for activities that require significant arm movement. In fact, hip-worn accelerometers have been found to distinguish differences in physical activity associated with structured versus unstructured play in youth (Clevenger et al., 2018). In addition, a hip-worn, pedometer-style accelerometer (the New Lifestyles NL-1000), which includes an

Jennifer Krause

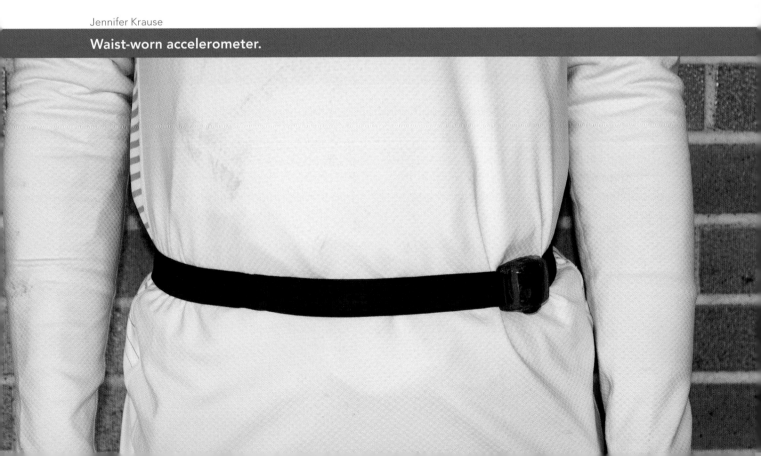

Waist-worn accelerometer.

MVPA timer, has been found to adequately measure MVPA across three school-related physical activity settings—specifically, classroom-based physical activity breaks, physical education lessons, and cross country running (McMinn et al., 2010).

GPS UNITS AND OTHER WEARABLE COACHING TECHNOLOGIES

Global positioning system (GPS) units, which typically take the form of wrist-worn digital watches or bike-mounted computers, integrate satellite triangulation technology to track exact changes in geographic location. Data provided by GPS units primarily include distance, speed, pace, and elevation. While GPS units are discussed in detail in chapter 6 relating to their use within lifelong health and fitness, we highlight their use as wearables for assessment in this chapter. Makers of wrist-worn GPS units include Apple, Coros, Fitbit, Garmin, Polar, Suunto, Timex, and TomTom. Makers of GPS cycling computers include Bryton, Garmin, Hammerhead, Pioneer, Polar, SRM, Stages, and Wahoo.

In addition to being used in physical education for activities such as geocaching (see chapter 6), GPS units are also commonly used by individuals to facilitate self-assessment in health and fitness and by sport coaches for tracking various assessment metrics. Beyond self-assessment, many athletes use data collected by wearable technologies such as GPS units to share their training experiences as they connect with coaches, fellow athletes, friends, or fans (see figure 9.13).

Wrist-worn GPS technology is commonly integrated into HRM watches, and it includes many other features listed in table 9.1 (e.g., altimeter, triaxial accelerometer, sleep monitor). GPS cycling computers often also assess speed, cadence, power, time, distance, HR, altitude, ascent and descent, and temperature. They may also offer other features, such as smartphone pairing, navigation, and saddle metrics with additional sensor integration. In addition, coaches can now use data analysis devices embedded into uniforms (e.g., in football, rugby) that include GPS and other technologies. If we discussed all wearable technologies used by coaches and athletes, this chapter would never end, but table 9.4 provides several examples.

INERTIAL MEASUREMENT UNITS (IMUs)

The **inertial measurement unit (IMU)** is a relatively new technology used to study kinesiology and assess the biomechanics of human movement, including accelerometry, for the purpose of exercise science and performance coaching. An IMU is a small electronic device that assesses and reports acceleration, angular velocity, and orientation through sensor fusion involving a combination of embedded accelerometers, gyroscopes, and magnetometers. Recent developments have integrated IMUs with GPS receivers so that data can be tracked even when GPS signals are lost (e.g., inside buildings or tunnels or in the midst of electronic interference). In regard to sport and physical activity, IMUs permit accurate assessment of global running metrics, such as vertical oscillation (i.e., amount of bounce), cadence (i.e., stride rate), and ground contact time. Additional calculations also enable measurement of body displacement and joint angles during movement. IMUs are increasingly being integrated into commercial fitness wearables. Of note, biomechanical data derived from IMUs are still less accurate than the results produced by a professional gait lab.

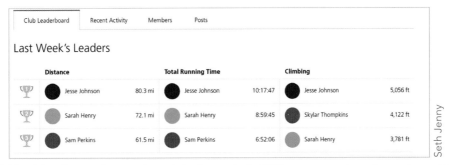

Figure 9.13   Members of a running club share their GPS smartwatch-collected weekly running distance, overall time, and elevation change online through Strava and post the image to Twitter.

Table 9.4   Selected Assessment Tools Using Wearable Technology

Product name	Description	Feature(s)	Resource
Catapult	Wearable technology integrated with Catapult AMS software, which addresses key data related to performance, health, and wellness	Specific real-time data provided depends on the specific Catapult product used	www.catapultsports.com
Garmin HRM-Run or HRM-Tri or Running Dynamics Pod	Chest-strap HRM that tracks running dynamics (i.e., factors impacting running economy) when paired with a compatible Garmin watch	Assessment of stride length, cadence, vertical oscillation (i.e., amount of bounce), vertical ratio (i.e., forward propulsion metric), and ground contact time (left and right foot)	www.garmin.com
Humon Hex muscle oxygen sensor	Wearable device worn on front of thigh (i.e., at the quads) that syncs with a smart device app	Measurement of muscle oxygen, thus enabling tracking of muscle exertion and lactate threshold in real time	https://humon.io
Polar Team Pro	Team tracking system featuring GPS, HRM, and inertial sensor	Real-time performance data, such as speed, intensity, distance, and HR measures	www.polar.com
STATSports Apex Pro Series	GPS, accelerometer, and Bluetooth technologies for indoor and outdoor athlete data tracking via wearable technology and mobile app	Connection to other sensors that allows tracking of distance, speed, HR, intensity, impacts, stress load, fatigue index, step balance, and metabolic metrics	https://statsports.com
WHOOP	Wrist wearable that synthesizes data into "strain" and "recovery" scores via its app	Collected data centered on HR, variability in HR, and sleep metrics	www.whoop.com
Wimu Pro	Hybrid wearable hub, for both indoor and outdoor team sports which collects data from external devices, wearables, and sensors and delivers processed data in real time on a single platform	More than 120 physiological, kinetic, and tactical processes monitored wirelessly in real time	www.realtracksystems.com
Zebra Motion-Works Sport	Wearable tracking software coupled with RFID technology	On-field tracking of player and ball movements in real time for athlete and coaching decisions, as well as immersive fan spectating	www.zebra.com

Notes: AMS = athlete management system, HRM = heart rate monitor, and RFID = radio-frequency identification. Product validity claims may need further investigation.

TECHNOLOGY TIPS FROM THE FIELD

Wearable Technology

Bradley Williams
- Riverbank, California
- 33-year-old male
- U.S. Air Force Veteran
- Professional Triathlete and Triathlon Coach
- Coaching website: www.kiscoaching.com
- Personal website: www.bw-tri.com
- Instagram and Twitter: @BW_TRI
- Facebook: www.facebook.com/bwtri
- Years of triathlon experience: 10 (4 as a professional)
- Standard: ranking as 25th-highest "70.3 Athlete in the World" according to the Ironman World Championship qualification point system; 70.3 World Championship Qualifier as a professional; four-time Ironman World Championship Qualifier as an amateur

In general, why do you use wearable technology?
To have in-depth knowledge and access to data during and after training.

Does your coach require you to use wearable technology?
Yes, a heart rate monitor and power meter—so that she can view the training data as we have a "remote" coaching relationship.

How does your coach access the wearable tech data?
www.trainingpeaks.com

How does your coach use the data collected from the wearable technology?
She uses the data to analyze if the workouts were executed as prescribed and if there are any signs of fatigue or noticeable decline in training performance.

What type of wearable technology do you use for running?
Garmin Forerunner 935. I use it for pacing, HR, time, etc. My main objective for using it is to track and analyze data during and post workout. I need TrainingPeaks online and the mobile app to analyze the data. I like TrainingPeaks as it is easy to use and provides multiple ways to analyze your data. However, the Garmin Forerunner 935 has a built-in wrist optical HRM, but it is inconsistent at best. It would be great to see optical HRM technology advance to where it is a reliable HR source.

What type of wearable technology do you use for swimming?
Garmin Forerunner 935. I use it during swims, with lap time and distance displayed. My main goal for using it is to keep track of distance and recovery/send-off times. I don't actually analyze the swim data; it just auto-uploads to TrainingPeaks and can be

analyzed in there if need be. I like that it is easy to use and accurate at keeping track of laps and distance. For other athletes and coaches, I don't actually suggest it to be used; rather, you should get used to using a proper pace clock and learning to work off of the clock. However, if you swim solo or lack the ability to use the pace clock, or do not have one, then the Garmin Forerunner 935 is a great resource. I personally lose track of laps, so it keeps me on track with distance per interval.

What type of wearable technology do you use for cycling?
Garmin Edge 520. I use it to keep track of time, distance, power, and HR. My main objective for using it is to execute workouts as prescribed and to be able to ride with power. In order to analyze the data, I use TrainingPeaks.com. I like that the Garmin Edge 520 is simple and easy to use! However, a longer battery life is the one thing that the Garmin Edge 520 loses over time and could be improved. My suggestion for other athletes using it is to not fill your screen with too much data. Keep it to what you need. I personally ride with 3sec Power, Lap Time, Lap Power, Lap HR, and Cadence for 99 percent of the time. I also have auto-lap set to 10K/6.2mi.

Garmin Vector 3 Power Pedals. I use it to collect power data and ride with power. My main goal using it is to hit goal power during workouts. I also use TrainingPeaks.com to analyze this data. I like the Garmin Vector 3 Power Pedals because they are easy to switch between multiple bikes. However, they can be unreliable at times (disconnecting the pedals from each other causing erroneous data). For other athletes, I suggest making sure you calibrate it before every ride and also reset install angles if switching between bikes.

What other type of wearable technology do you use for triathlon?
Halo Sport. I use the wearable neurostimulation device to prep the brain for workouts. Halo Sport is a brain stimulator that increases neuroplasticity. Mine could be improved by adding Bluetooth built into the device, which the latest model now has. For other athletes and coaches, I suggest reading the science to see if it is something you believe in.

Overall, what do you see as the benefits of wearable technology?
It can help you really dial in on your training. You are able to execute pacing better and, even more important for most people, you are able to go easy when you need to go easy. That way, when it is time to go hard, you are able to execute and deliver your best effort.

What are the greatest drawbacks to wearable technology?
Athletes can get caught up in the data and live and die by it. You still have to be able to listen to your body and not get so caught up in the data that it drives you crazy.

What do you do to try to minimize these drawbacks?
Always ensure that the athlete knows that the numbers are there for the training, but they won't always be reachable. Failure is okay, and it is not the end of the world. Never get so caught up in the data that you lose focus on the overall picture.

(continued)

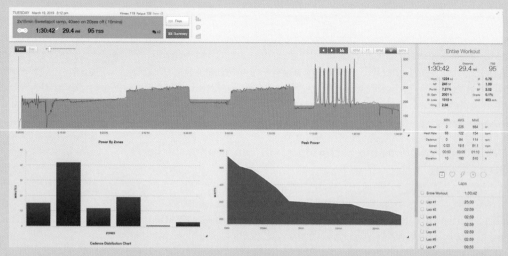

A TrainingPeaks screenshot from one of Brad Williams' indoor cycling workouts with the Garmin Edge 520 and Garmin Vector 3 Power Pedals. The top graph displays the structured workout with the power data overlaid in the form of the squiggly line. It is also possible to overlay additional data, such as cadence, heart rate, temperature, elevation, and speed. The lower left-hand bar graph, Power by Zones, signifies how much time Brad spent in each power zone. The lower right-hand graph, Peak Power, signifies the best power that Brad held for various durations during the ride. The far right-hand graph summarizes the workout, including such data as duration, distance, training stress score, work (in kilojoules), normalized power, grade, vertical ascent in meters, intensity factor, variability index, elevation gain and loss, and watts per kilogram (W/kg) of body weight. It also shows the minimum, maximum, and average for the following aspects: power, heart rate, cadence, speed, pace, elevation, and temperature.

Reprinted by permission from Brad Williams.

Professional triathlete Brad Williams wears the Garmin Edge 520 wristwatch and uses the Garmin Vector 3 Power Pedals, which provide objective data during and post-workout. When running, he uses the Garmin Forerunner 935 wrist-watch (with optical HR) which he primarily uses for pacing, HR, and running time. He also uses this same smartwatch for swimming workouts as he tracks distance, lap times, and recovery/send-off times during swim workouts.

Photo courtesy of Jay Prasuhn.

WEARABLE TECHNOLOGY FOR HEALTH EDUCATION

Wearable technology is not limited to sport and fitness but can also be found in the fields of personal health, health education, and health care. Some units provide objective assessment of health-related factors, whereas others focus on recovery or safety. Health-related wearables serve various purposes, such as helping to teach cardiopulmonary resuscitation (CPR), monitoring healthy behaviors beyond physical activity (e.g., sleep, nutrition), tracking data for health promotion and disease prevention, monitoring patients remotely, supporting adherence to medication instructions, helping with physical rehabilitation and recovery, improving safety, and reducing injury while improving ergonomics. Table 9.5 presents some examples of wearable technology related to health and safety; note that the validity of product claims may need further investigation because some of these technologies are very new.

Table 9.5   Examples of Wearable Technology Related to Health and Safety

Product name	Description	Feature(s)	Resource
Apple Watch Series 4	Wrist-worn unit with optical HR monitor that pairs with many health-related apps	Detection of hard falls; calls for emergency services if needed; ECG apps (approved by FDA and supported by AHA) to monitor for irregular heart rhythms and atrial fibrillation	www.apple.com/watch
Biostrap	Wrist-worn unit that monitors sleep and recovery markers aimed at improving health and performance	Mobile app pairing; tracking of sleep analytics (sleep stages), HR, HR variability, blood oxygen saturation, and respiratory rate	https://biostrap.com
Cercacor Ember	First-ever noninvasive hemoglobin tracking system for consumers; for use with smartphone and app	Tracking of up to 10 parameters, including hemoglobin, HR variability, and other blood markers; tracking body's response to training	www.cercacor.com
Dexcom G6 Continuous Glucose Monitoring (CGM) System	Replaceable glucose sensor and transmitter worn on skin; transmission of wireless signal to receiver or smart device (e.g., smartphone)	Wireless tracking of glucose levels on receiver or smart device with mobile app; help for managing diabetes with no finger sticks	www.dexcom.com
NormaTec Pulse 2.0 Full Body Recovery System	Compression massage sleeves for legs, hips, lower back, or arms	Useful for warming up or to facilitate recovery after a workout	www.normatecrecovery.com
OptiShokz Revvez	Sunglasses with embedded headphones that sit behind the ear and use bone conduction technology to deliver sound	Bluetooth sound delivered through the ear cartilage without silencing the outside world, thus enabling increased situational awareness and safety	https://optishokz.com
Practi-CRM	Wrist-worn band that provides feedback about CPR compression rate for manikin-based training	Warning diode that changes from green to red if compression rate is below 100 CPM or above 120 CPM	https://worldpoint.com

(continued)

Table 9.5 *(continued)*

Product name	Description	Feature(s)	Resource
Tracer360	Illuminated and reflective safety vest that provides 360-degree visibility for outdoor activities (e.g., cycling, road running)	Light weight (6.5 ounces, or 184 g), 40-hour battery life, rainproof, adjustable sizing	www.noxgear.com
WELT Smartbelt	Men's and women's traditional-looking belts with embedded accelerometer and sensor markers	Tracking of waist size, step counts, and sitting time via wireless mobile app	www.weltcorp.com
Upright Go 2 or Upright Necklace	Strapless (i.e., adhesive) or necklace posture corrector and training wearable that is placed on the upper back	Pairs with mobile app and provides feedback regarding sitting or standing up straight with a real-time vibration reminder when incorrect posture is detected	www.uprightpose.com

Notes: AHA = American Heart Association, CPM = compressions per minute, CPR = cardiopulmonary resuscitation, ECG = electrocardiogram, FDA = Food and Drug Administration, and HR = heart rate.

Conclusion

All kinds of wearable technology that assess physical activity are only tools. Individual motivation must be sustained by highlighting the "why" (i.e., appreciating how movement benefits daily life), the "way" (i.e., facilitating intrinsic motivation through the choosing of enjoyable physical activities), and the "do" (i.e., emphasizing learning more than achievement) (Segar, 2017). One accessible way to track exercise intensity is by using heart rate monitors. In general, pedometers are more accurate at counting steps than at estimating distance covered or calories burned, accelerometers are useful in tracking both steps taken and movement intensity, and GPS units primarily track speed and distance of movement. In addition, many wearable technologies integrate functions geared toward assessment related to coaching and health. Ultimately, the choice of whether to use a wearable device depends on the desired data, the validity of the data provided, price, and ease of use.

Key Terms

accelerometer—Axis-based electromechanical device that senses motion, reports intensity of movement by calculating acceleration forces in relation to gravity, and converts these digital signals into "counts" (three main types: uniaxial, biaxial, and triaxial).

electrical heart rate monitor (chest-strap heart rate monitor)—Two-part device that consists of a watch worn on the wrist and a transmitter that is worn against the skin around the chest, is held in place by a removable elastic chest belt, and picks up electrical signals from the heart and sends them wirelessly to the watch.

global positioning system (GPS) unit—Digital device (e.g., wristwatch, bike-mounted computer) that integrates satellite triangulation technology to track exact changes in geographic location, thus providing user data such as distance, speed, and pace.

heart rate monitor (HRM)—Device that displays the user's heart rate in order to guide exercise intensity (i.e., effort) or records heart rate data for later analysis or both (two types: electrical and optical).

heart rate reserve—Difference between resting heart rate and maximum heart rate.

inertial measurement unit (IMU)—Small electronic device now commonly integrated into GPS units that assesses and reports acceleration, angular velocity, and orientation through embedded accelerometers, gyroscopes, and magnetometers.

Karvonen formula—Formula that accounts for current fitness level via resting heart rate and assists in prescribing estimated target heart rate training zones (formula found in chapter 9).

maximum heart rate (HRmax)—Highest number of times the heart can contract in one minute at maximal effort.

optical heart rate monitor—Monitor that uses photoplethysmography to collect heart rate data via an optical sensor and is often worn on the wrist (i.e., on the underside of a watch) or forearm (i.e., in an armband).

pedometer—Portable electronic motion-detecting device that counts each step taken while wearing or carrying the device.

photoplethysmography (PPG)—Process of using light to measure blood flow —this technology is integrated into an optical heart rate monitor.

resting heart rate (RHR)—Number of heartbeats in one minute at complete, uninterrupted rest.

target heart rate zone (THRZ)—Intensity level or load at which exercise should be performed in order to produce cardiorespiratory benefits (i.e., conditioning the heart, lungs, and muscles) without being overly strenuous.

wearable technology—Smart electronic devices that can be worn on the body, integrated into shoes or clothing, or implanted subdermally that use smart electronics (i.e., micro-controllers), software, sensors, and connectivity features (e.g., Bluetooth, hardwire) to collect and share data, primarily to a website or connected mobile device app. (Sometimes referred to as wearables, wearable devices, or wearable activity trackers.)

Review Questions

1. Describe multiple ways to determine age-predicted, lab-based, and field-based maximum heart rate.

2. Based on aerobic exercise guidelines, what are the recommended heart rate training zones for moderate and vigorous intensity?

3. What are the recommended daily step counts for both children and adults?

4. What does an accelerometer measure?

5. List some wearable devices that include GPS technology and describe what each device measures.

6. Identify some health-related wearable devices and describe what they assess.

Discussion Questions

For each of the following questions, begin by describing your setting and the age of the participants.

1. What are your experiences with wearable technologies? Did they work? Were they accurate? What suggestions do you have for others who might use them?

2. What wearable technology would you use in your program? How and why would you use it? (If you are already using this technology, please describe how you use it.)

3. In great detail, describe how you would implement the use of heart rate monitors in your program?

4. What method would you use to determine maximum heart rate (HRmax), and how would you prescribe exercise intensity?

5. In great detail, describe how you would implement the use of pedometers or accelerometers in your program.

Other Forms of Technology for Assessment

10

Chapter Objectives

When you have completed this chapter, you will be able to do the following:

1. Identify a variety of technology tools for assessment.
2. Identify and describe types of quiz and survey technology.
3. Identify and describe types of video assessment.
4. Describe advantages of using technology for assessment.

Courtesy of Dannon Cox.

Assessment is arguably one of the most important yet most challenging aspects of teaching and coaching. When quality assessment is implemented, teaching and learning are enhanced. Assessment allows educators and coaches to measure students' achievement of standards and helps them make curricular and instructional decisions. Accountability, which has most commonly been assessed through the implementation of standardized testing in subjects such as math and language arts, is at the forefront of education. Although physical education, health education, and coaching have not yet reached this level of accountability in schools, national, state, and local standards feature assessment as one of the major goals teachers and coaches must accomplish. Table 10.1 displays assessment-related SHAPE America standards for physical educators, health educators, and coaches.

Table 10.1 Related Standards from SHAPE America

Profession	Standard(s)
Physical education	Select or create authentic, formal assessments that measure student attainment of short- and long-term objectives. (Society of Health and Physical Educators America, 2017, 5.a)
	Implement **formative assessments** that monitor student learning before and throughout the long-term plan, as well as **summative assessments** that evaluate student learning upon completion of the long-term plan. (Society of Health and Physical Educators America, 2017, 5.b, emphasis added)
	Implement a reflective cycle to guide decision making specific to candidate performance, student learning, and short- and long-term plan objectives. (Society of Health and Physical Educators America, 2017, 5.c)
Health education	Candidates collect and analyze needs-assessment data to plan relevant school health instruction and programs that meet the diverse needs of all learners and the community. (Society of Health and Physical Educators America, 2018, component 2.a)
	Candidates analyze and select assessment strategies, tools and technologies to determine their appropriateness for enhancing learning among all students. (Society of Health and Physical Educators America, 2018, component 4.b)
	Candidates implement a variety of formative and summative assessments that measure and monitor student progress, and that accommodate the diverse needs of all learners. (Society of Health and Physical Educators America, 2018, component 4.b)
	Candidates use assessment **data** to plan instruction, analyze student learning, reflect on implementation practices, provide meaningful **feedback** and adjust units and lessons so they meet the diverse learning needs of all students. (Society of Health and Physical Educators America, 2018, component 4.c, emphasis added)
Coaching	Implement appropriate strategies for evaluating athlete training, development and performance. (Society of Health and Physical Educators America, 2019, standard 34)
	Engage athletes in a process of continuous **self-assessment** and reflection to foster responsibility for their own learning and development. (Society of Health and Physical Educators America, 2019, standard 35, emphasis added)
	Adjust training and competition plans based on athlete needs and assessment practices. (Society of Health and Physical Educators America, 2019, standard 36)

Reprinted by permission, from J.M. Krause et al., "Let's Get Virtual: Observing Physical Education Field Experiences through Synchronous Video Conferencing," *Strategies* 31, no.1 (2018): 30-34.

Although there are many benefits to assessment, it can be challenging to implement when practitioners are faced with barriers, such as limited time for preparation, minimal class time, large class sizes, and lack of understanding of *how* and *what* to assess. Standards and resources are helping clarify the assessment process, but it is still seen as a challenge. Fortunately for today's professionals, there are many ways that technology has simplified and enhanced assessment opportunities.

Chapter 9 described various types of wearable technology for assessment, the use of which is common in physical education and coaching settings. This chapter will focus on other forms of technology for assessment, including fitness assessment software, web-based quizzes and surveys, and technology for **rubrics**, **video analysis**, and **data collection**.

HEALTH-RELATED FITNESS ASSESSMENT TECHNOLOGY

Chapter 9 described a variety of wearable technologies that can monitor aspects of fitness, such as heart rate, steps, and overall physical activity. There are, however, other aspects of fitness that cannot be measured with a wearable device. Fortunately, programs available to measure fitness sometimes include technology to enhance the tracking and reporting process.

One of the most commonly used fitness assessment programs is FitnessGram/ActivityGram (The Cooper Institute, 2014). It is the national test of the Presidential Youth Fitness Program, which helps educators teach fitness concepts, assess fitness, plan for improvement and maintenance of fitness levels, and empower students to be fit for life (National Fitness Foundation, 2019). The FitnessGram was first introduced in 1982 with an assessment in which students received a report card based on their performance in five areas of fitness: aerobic capacity, body composition, flexibility, muscular strength, and muscular endurance. The assessment is noncompetitive and is based on Healthy Fitness Zone standards organized by gender and age, which were established by The Cooper Institute to represent levels of fitness for good health. Classifications of fitness levels are the Healthy Fitness Zone, Needs Improvement Zone, and Needs Improvement—Health Risk Zone. Data from the FitnessGram allow for tracking of fitness levels over time; comparisons of fitness, academic achievement, and attendance; enhancement of physical education programs; creation of healthy school environments; and more. Although the FitnessGram assessments categories haven't changed much, the method of conducting, tracking, reporting, and sharing the tests and data has changed a lot since 1982. Almost every fitness test is integrated with technology, even in the most basic form. Table 10.2 displays FitnessGram tests that utilize technology.

Although technology such as a stopwatch or cadence CD seems simple, it helps make these tests more reliable, allowing consistency across all students. It also allows teachers the opportunity to better assist students while the technology does the counting. With regard to body composition assessment, the most basic form of technology would be a skinfold caliper; however, human error is of concern, because it takes consistency and skill to master this tool. There are several other technologies available to measure body composition, such as bioelectric impedance body composition analyzers. These scales, ranging from less than $100 to over $10,000 in price, work with sensors that send a small, safe electrical current through the body that measures the amount of resistance from body fat. Although it may be tempting to use one of these scales, be cautious with results, because these have been known to lack accuracy.

Tracking student data can also be completed with the FitnessGram software. Teachers simply import their class lists, create testing events, and enter student test results. Many different types of student reports can then be automatically generated, such as individual

Table 10.2 FitnessGram Tests That Use Technology

Test	Technology
Aerobic capacity: one-mile run	Stopwatch Scale to calculate $\dot{V}O_2max$
Aerobic capacity: PACER (progressive aerobic cardiovascular endurance run)	CD, audio cassette, or mp3 for music and timing
Aerobic capacity: walk test	Stopwatch Scale to calculate $\dot{V}O_2max$ Heart rate monitor
Body composition	Bioelectric impedance analyzer or skinfold caliper Scale
Muscular endurance: curl-up	CD, audio cassette, or mp3 for cadence
Muscular endurance: 90° push-up	CD, audio cassette, or mp3 for cadence
Muscular endurance: flexed arm hang	Stopwatch

and class score reports and student history reports (figure 10.1). Reports can be printed or emailed to students and parents in English or Spanish. Reports can also be generated for class -and school-level data.

In addition to fitness testing, FitnessGram also offers a three-day activity assessment for students to monitor and record daily physical activity patterns in 30-minute increments. They can generate a detailed report with active time and types of activity (figure 10.2). The ease of data input and reporting through the software, as opposed to keeping a written journal or log, makes this an attractive way to track activity.

QUIZ AND SURVEY TECHNOLOGY

Gathering and analyzing data on student knowledge of concepts, beliefs, and behaviors outside of the classroom can feel cumbersome and time consuming, particularly if it involves the use of paper and pencil. Simply checking for understanding with an entire class of students may not give the practitioner the information needed to truly gather levels of learning. Fortunately, there are several web-based assessment tools that can aid in collecting data from students for both formative and summative assessments.

When an instructor wants to gather student data, traditionally, a paper-and-pencil test or survey would be administered in class, collected by the teacher, and then graded by hand, one at a time, followed by entering results into a gradebook or spreadsheet. Additionally, if a teacher wanted to do a quick, formative check for understanding with a class, students might give a thumbs-up or thumbs-down signal, but they may feel pressured to answer a certain way after seeing how their peers respond. There are, however, several web-based software programs and applications that can aid in assessing learners' understanding to make this process more efficient and effective for everyone. Ideally, these are best used to gather different types of individual- and group-level student data, such as the following:

- "Get to know you" student information (name, interests, hobbies, favorite teams, etc.)
- Content interest surveys (information on what activities or topics students prefer to focus on for the year, semester, or unit)
- Sensitive content surveys (sensitive information, such as experiences with drug and alcohol use, that students may prefer to report anonymously)

FitnessGram Student Report

FITNESSGRAM®

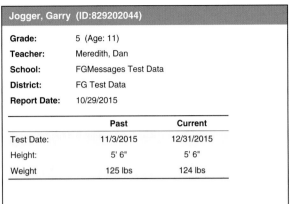

Jogger, Garry (ID:829202044)

Grade:	5 (Age: 11)
Teacher:	Meredith, Dan
School:	FGMessages Test Data
District:	FG Test Data
Report Date:	10/29/2015

	Past	Current
Test Date:	11/3/2015	12/31/2015
Height:	5' 6"	5' 6"
Weight	125 lbs	124 lbs

Aerobic Capacity

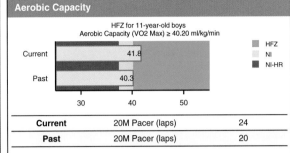

Current	20M Pacer (laps)	24
Past	20M Pacer (laps)	20

Congratulations! Your aerobic capacity is in the Healthy Fitness Zone and you are physically active most days. To maintain health and fitness, continue to participate in physical activities for at least 60 minutes each day. Keep your Body Mass Index (BMI) in the Healthy Fitness Zone.

Musculoskeletal Fitness

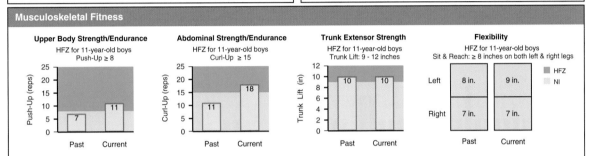

Your abdominal, trunk, and upper-body strength are all in the Healthy Fitness Zone. To maintain your fitness, be sure that your strength-training activities include exercises for all of these areas. Strength activities should be done at least 3 days per week.
In addition to aerobic and muscle-strengthening activities, it is important to perform stretching exercises to maintain or improve flexibility and some weight-bearing activity (e.g. running, hopping, jumping or dancing) to ensure good bone health at least 3 days per week.

Body Composition

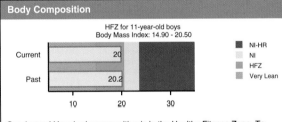

Good news! Your body composition is in the Healthy Fitness Zone. To maintain this healthy level of body composition, remember to:
-Be active for at least 60 minutes every day.
-Limit screen time to less than 2 hours a day.
-Make healthy food choices including fresh fruits and vegetables.
-Limit fried foods, foods with added sugars and sugary drinks.

Physical Activity

Reported Activity/Past 7 Days	Days	Goal
Aerobic activity for a total of 60 minutes or more	7	7
Muscle strengthening activity	3	3
Bone strengthening activity	2	3

To be healthy and fit, it is important to do some physical activity for a total of 60 minutes or more daily. Aerobic exercise is good for your heart and body composition. Muscular and bone-strengthening exercises are good for your muscles and joints.Congratulations! You are doing aerobic activity most or all days and muscular-strengthening exercises. Add some bone-strengthening exercises to improve your overall fitness.

HFZ: Healthy Fitness Zone; NI: Needs Improvement; NI-HR: Needs Improvement - Health Risk

FitnessGram.net

Figure 10.1 FitnessGram student report.

Reprinted by permission from The Cooper Institute, *FitnessGram Administration Manual*, 5th ed. (Champaign, IL: Human Kinetics, 2017).

ActivityGram Student Report

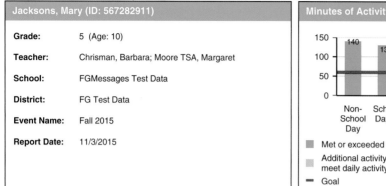

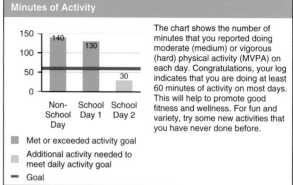

The chart shows the number of minutes that you reported doing moderate (medium) or vigorous (hard) physical activity (MVPA) on each day. Congratulations, your log indicates that you are doing at least 60 minutes of activity on most days. This will help to promote good fitness and wellness. For fun and variety, try some new activities that you have never done before.

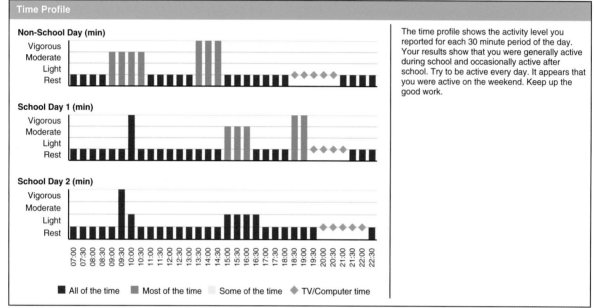

The time profile shows the activity level you reported for each 30 minute period of the day. Your results show that you were generally active during school and occasionally active after school. Try to be active every day. It appears that you were active on the weekend. Keep up the good work.

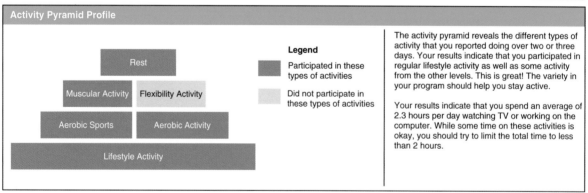

The activity pyramid reveals the different types of activity that you reported doing over two or three days. Your results indicate that you participated in regular lifestyle activity as well as some activity from the other levels. This is great! The variety in your program should help you stay active.

Your results indicate that you spend an average of 2.3 hours per day watching TV or working on the computer. While some time on these activities is okay, you should try to limit the total time to less than 2 hours.

ActivityGram provides information about your normal levels of physical activity. The ActivityGram report shows what types of activity you do and how often you do them. It includes the information that you previously entered for three days during one week.

Figure 10.2 ActivityGram student report.

Reprinted by permission from The Cooper Institute, *FitnessGram Administration Manual*, 5th ed. (Champaign, IL: Human Kinetics, 2017).

- Teacher assessment of knowledge or beliefs (multiple choice, true-false, short answer, rating scales, and essay questions; can be both formative and summative)
- Peer assessment (students assess each other's work, contributions, or efforts, particularly in group projects)
- Self-assessment (students assess their own work, effort, knowledge, beliefs)
- Teacher/coach evaluations (students answer questions about or rate the effectiveness of their instructor)
- Fitness assessments (students enter scores from fitness tests)
- Parent surveys (gather information from parents, such as interest in volunteering and rating their children in certain skills for a sport)

Depending on the purpose of the assessment, there are several technology-rich options for professionals to choose from that can enhance the administration and evaluation of quiz and survey assessments.

Learning Management System Assessments

As discussed in previous chapters, a learning management system (LMS) can provide educators with a way to manage their courses, particularly student data, with features such as assessments, assignments, surveys, and gradebooks. Educators can create assignments within the LMS and students can submit their assignments directly to the LMS course page, where the instructor can view and grade it according to the rubric created within the assignment. The grade is then entered by the instructor or generated with the rubric scores and automatically added to the gradebook. Additionally, an instructor can create a quiz or a survey within the LMS and students can complete it in class or anywhere with an Internet connection. Depending on the type of quiz or survey, it can be automatically graded if questions are closed-ended (e.g., multiple choice, true-false). Some common, helpful features of assessment within an LMS include:

- custom quiz and survey creation
- various question types (multiple choice, true-false, sequence/sort/order/rank, essay, short answer, etc.)
- custom rubric creation (point values, categories, criteria, etc.)
- time limits
- randomizing question order
- retake options
- various feedback options (text, audio, and video recording)
- gamification (badges, points, etc.)
- portfolios
- peer assessments
- time tracking
- association of standards with assessments
- anonymous surveys

Other Web-Based Survey and Quiz Programs

If you do not have access to an LMS or would like to just explore other options, there are many alternatives for easy, web-based survey and quiz programs that can easily be administered and evaluated. These are easily accessible and often affordable for teachers and coaches. Again, these offer opportunities to gather data from students without the use of paper and pencil, but they are found in stand-alone programs that are not typically integrated into an LMS or other grading system, although some can be connected.

Physical educators, health educators, and coaches can all take advantage of these web-based assessment tools for different purposes. For example, Krause, O'Neil, and Dauenhauer (2017) described how **classroom response systems** that poll students with a clicker can be worthwhile but are cumbersome in a physical education setting.

Using Plickers, a free classroom response app, may be a good alternative, and the only technology needed is the teacher's smartphone or tablet. The teacher provides students with individual printed Plickers cards (free online), each with unique visual codes and small letters, A, B, C, and D (figure 10.3). The teacher asks a question that requires a response of one of the four letters, and students select their answer by holding up their card with the correct letter on the top. The teacher holds up the smartphone or tablet and, using the app, scans all students' cards within seconds. Because each code is unique, the program collects each student's individual response and provides real-time results on individual and class levels.

Many physical education teachers have modified their Plickers cards to integrate them more easily into the PE setting by adding different types of answers to the card, such as thumbs-up or thumbs-down, emojis, numbers, levels of achievement, and more. Additionally, teachers have created magnetic versions of Plickers cards, often called Plagnets, that can be easily placed on a whiteboard or other magnetic surface in the gym space. There are many ideas on how to create your own Plagnets online, particularly on Twitter. One physical education teacher candidate shared the Plagnets she created for a class project that she later used in student teaching (see figure 10.4).

Plickers can be used in physical education, health education, and coaching. Physical educators can have students identify particular skill components they are feeling most successful or challenged with, such as the basketball free throw, where A = balance, B = eyes, C = elbow, and D = follow through. Health educators can quiz students on their knowledge of a particular topic, such as nutrition, by asking students to select the correct answer to the question: How many servings of vegetables do you need every day? Students would select their answer where A = 1-2, B = 3-5, C = 6-8, and D = 9-10. Coaches can also benefit from using Plickers with their athletes. If a coach wanted to focus on building teamwork, the team could be asked to assess how successful they were with collaboration and teamwork, where they would answer A = Very successful, B = Somewhat successful, C = Somewhat unsuccessful, and D = Unsuccessful.

Although using Plickers takes a little prep work to successfully implement (printing and assigning Plickers cards, entering questions into the app), the results can provide

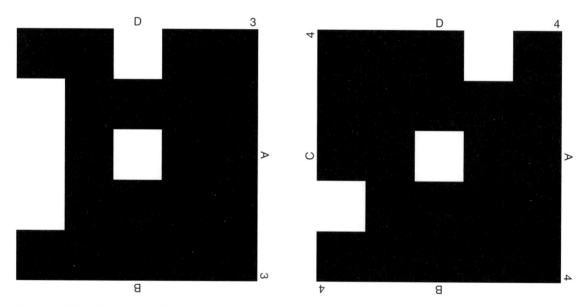

Figure 10.3 Plickers card.

practitioners with data that can help drive their instructional decisions. It is also a great assessment tool for programs without devices for all students. There are many other options available that assess individuals and classes, both for formative and summative assessment. Table 10.3 displays some of the most popular web-based quiz and survey assessment tools available today.

> Check out the web resource for resources on setting up and implementing web-based surveys and quizzes!

Administering Web-Based Quizzes and Surveys

Now that you have your quiz or survey created, you must find a way to administer it to your students. There are several things to consider before deciding how, when, and where to share it. First, what is the purpose of the assessment? Is it a test of knowledge to be graded? Are you looking for students to anonymously share personal beliefs about a particular topic that you'll summarize and share in the following class or practice session? Are you simply trying to check for understanding with the class or review for an upcoming exam? If you are using an LMS, students can access the quiz or survey from any device with an Internet connection; students simply log into the course in the LMS and complete the quiz online. If you are using other web-based programs, such as Survey Monkey or Google Forms, there are several ways for students and athletes to access them, such as the following:

Kendra Holtcamp PE
@kendrajPE

Made Plagnets today with large coin holders and ceramic magnets! Thank you, @PhysEdDepot for this great idea and @GarfieldPhysEd for the template! #PhysEd #plagnets #uncphysed #futurephysicaleducator @UNCSportPed

Figure 10.4 Twitter post of Plagnets created from large coin holders and ceramic magnets.

Reprinted by permission from Plagnets.

- Sending the URL link to each individual learner via email, text message, or other communication app (e.g., Remind)
- Posting the URL on a class or team website or social media page
- Displaying the URL on a screen, whiteboard, or paper for learners to then enter on their computers. Note that if the URL is long, it may be helpful to create a shortened version of the link using a website such as TinyURL.
- Create a QR code that leads directly to the URL for learners to scan with their tablet or smartphone. This could be displayed in class on a screen or paper or given to students on an exit ticket as they leave.

Although it is possible for students to complete the quiz during class time, the benefit of an online quiz is that it can be taken outside of class, so you can spend that time on other tasks. You may consider instituting some boundaries for your students, such as a specific window of time that they can access the quiz, time limits, and randomizing questions if you are concerned about cheating.

VIDEO FOR ASSESSMENT

One of the most valuable tools in physical education, health education, and coaching is video used for assessment. Traditional teaching often consists of subjective observations of performance and conclusions based on the instructor's perceptions and biases. For

Table 10.3 Web-Based Quiz and Survey Assessment Tools

Tool	Features	Price
EDpuzzle	• Create interactive online videos by embedding questions, notes, audio tracks or comments on a video, using existing videos or creating originals • Track what and when students view within the video and assesses student responses	Free (basic plan) or $8.50/month (pro teacher)
Edulastic	• Create standards-based assessments and get instant feedback from students through tech-enhanced exams • Sync to Google Classroom	Free (basic plan) or $100/year (premium)
Flipgrid	• Have students create short videos to respond to prompts; teachers, coaches, and peers can provide feedback	Free
FlipQuiz	• Create Jeopardy-style game show boards for test reviews in the classroom	Free (basic plan), $7/month or $70/year (pro)
Formative	• Create assessments that can be taken on any device using existing questions, upload and edit PDFs, give real-time feedback, track student growth, and integrate with other tools	Free (basic plan) or $12/month (premium)
Google Forms	• Create quizzes, questionnaires, and polls for individual assessments • Save data to Google Drive, download and export response data	Free
Kahoot	• Create quizzes and surveys in an engaging, game-based learning environment, including videos, pictures, and text • Have students respond to questions through their own devices, with the option to compete with one another	Free (basic plan), $1/month (plus), or $3/month (pro)
Plickers	• Create surveys and quizzes from a teacher device, scan students' answers with the app, and view results immediately	Free
Poll Everywhere	• Create polls and surveys online and display on the website or in a PowerPoint presentation • Have students respond via text message, Twitter, or through the website, with responses displayed in real time	Free (for groups of 40 or less)
Quizalize	• Create or use ready-made quizzes for whole-class formative assessment in a game-like format; students respond from any device • Integrate with Google Classroom	Free (basic plan, includes three classes and five activities) or $5.95/month (teacher premium)
Seesaw	• Students create digital portfolios of their work and can create videos of themselves doing the assignment or upload a file. Students can provide feedback to peers, and teachers can communicate with families.	Free (basic plan) or $120/year (plus)
Socrative	• Create activities (quizzes, exit tickets, quick questions) for students to complete on their own devices. Track student progress and keep in Google Drive or download. Space race feature allows students to compete in a game-based learning environment.	Free (basic plan, includes 50 students) or $59.99/year (pro for K-12 teachers)
Survey Monkey	• Create and deliver online polls. Use advanced features, such as skip logic, text analysis, summary reports, and data exports	Free (basic plan, includes 10 questions per survey) or $37-$99/month (paid)

Created from Quiz/Survey Assessment Tools.

example, if you were to observe a student perform an overhand throw, which is completed in just a few seconds, you may not be able to fully capture every critical element and therefore may not be able to accurately pinpoint where errors occurred to be corrected. The same idea goes for game events—a coach who is immersed in a basketball game may not be able to observe or remember every individual action and therefore may not be able to give the most accurate feedback or direction to the team. Video provides opportunities to observe students and athletes in action, with the ability to maximize analysis by providing more accurate, objective, and comprehensive feedback. Like they say, "The camera never lies."

There are many ways to incorporate video for assessment in physical education, health education, and coaching, such as **movement analysis**, **tactical analysis**, **project-based learning**, and assessment of one's own teaching. Video assessment can consist of different levels of use of video for analysis. Additionally, video can be used not only for instructor assessment and **peer assessment** but, perhaps even more importantly, student and athlete **self-assessment** as well. Each will be described with examples in the following sections. Note that this section will discuss video for assessment, whereas chapter 11 in this textbook will provide information regarding the video recording and editing process.

Basic Video Observation

One of the best ways to learn a new skill or tactic is to observe models perform it, both correctly and incorrectly. Physical education teachers can show video clips of motor skills, such as a cartwheel or tennis serve, on a large screen in the gymnasium to point out the critical elements to students. The benefit of displaying a video either in addition to or in place of a live demonstration is the ability to display the movement in slow motion, pause, and rewind to view again. Displaying good examples and poor examples of the skill performance is also helpful for students to learn what to do and not to do when performing the skill. Health education students can also benefit from analyzing existing video. For example, they may view a clip of a peer-pressure scenario and be asked to pinpoint refusal skills used by the actors in the video. This type of assessment is usually informal and instructional; however, embedding videos into a quiz tool, such as EDpuzzle or Kahoot, is possible. Coaches may also display video clips from professional competitions as an instructional tool to showcase and critique tactical actions performed by the athletes or teams.

Video Recording and Viewing

Recording and watching video can have many benefits for the instructor and learner, especially when viewed immediately. For example, a weightlifting club athlete may be working on perfecting the snatch lift. Her coach may try explaining to her that she needs to flatten her back; however, she *feels* like she has a flat back. The coach could then set up a video camera connected to a screen or a simple iPad on a tripod at an optimal angle. The athlete performs the lift again and then views her performance as many times as necessary to focus on her back positioning, with her coach providing feedback to help her understand the critical elements of this skill and where she needs to make modifications. This self-assessment, with the help of the coach, can help athletes make the improvements necessary to master their skills. Often, however, one-on-one instruction is not always possible, and video recording and playback can help students take control of their own learning. In addition to simple video recording and playback, there are alternatives that simplify this process. One example is the use of delayed video apps, such as BaM Video Delay ($7.99) or Video Delay Instant Replay (free), available in the App Store, or Replay It, available as an extension on Google Chrome. These applications record video and automatically delay the video display by a customized amount of time (e.g., 10 seconds

TECHNOLOGY TIPS FROM THE FIELD

Assessing Soccer Athletes with Technology

David Pinero
Youth Football Coach, Rebels Soccer Club, Chula Vista, CA
Private Soccer Coach, Youth-Adult
U.S. Soccer Federation F License Holder

What types of technology do you use for assessment of your soccer athletes?
There are a few video analysis apps that come to mind. Coach's Eye seems to be the most convenient one because it comes with an app. When we work on certain techniques, sometimes the technique is so quick that I can't catch something right away. Coach's Eye allows me to record it and later break it down with the athlete. We are visual and auditory learners, and it helps them see what they are doing wrong. For example, it helps the athletes to see themselves where they are hitting or not hitting the ball with their foot. Krossover is another one I use for the team, and they have added stuff where you can individualize it with techniques and tactics. I can break down every player by position group—the who, what, where, when, and why of the tactics I'm trying to teach. I can show a forward exactly where the weaknesses are and the best position they can be in to break down the line of defense to get a goal. There is also the PlayerTek vest that athletes can wear to track all of their

PlayerTek vest.
Courtesy Catapult Group International Ltd.

movements. It has a built-in accelerometer and connected GPS that connects to a tracking app and tracks things like distance covered during training and heat maps. I use it personally when I play for match day and use it for coaching some of my older clients. It is particularly great for players coming off injury to see progress as they recover. These are all really good investments to help visual learners.

What are some challenges that come with using this technology for coaching soccer?
Since I coach youth (U8), a big challenge is that it requires parental consent. This usually isn't a problem with my private clients, but it can be for the larger teams. With Coach's Eye, I don't like the price, and I have to record it on a certain angle on my phone to correct errors. Krossover hasn't developed full features yet, but they are working on it.

What suggestions do you have for other coaches with regard to using technology for assessment?
Video analysis is a good tool. The most success comes from the concept of visualization to see themselves. These apps and tools can help them improve.

PlayerTek vest app data.

Reprinted by permission from Catapult Group International Ltd.

to 2 minutes). This allows learners an opportunity to perform the skill and then view it on the screen immediately afterward without having to manipulate the recording device, which is especially helpful when teaching younger children or when you simply don't want anyone else to handle your device. Other features include multiple modes where you can set separate delays to see the action up to four times in a row. You can take it a step further by using a rubric to look for critical elements or other specific performance criteria for more objective assessment.

> Check out the web resource for more information on using technology for assessment.

Video Movement and Tactical Analysis

Although it is beneficial to simply observe performance on video, the introduction of applications and advanced software programs has greatly enhanced the ability and extent to which one can analyze movement and therefore determine how to improve performance. Video movement analysis apps provide users with the ability to not only record and view video but also to interact with the video to conduct an in-depth analysis with a variety of tools, such as rewind, fast-forward, pause, drawing tools (freestyle and angles), photo capture, StroMotion photos, audio recorded narration, sharing (emailing, downloading, posting), split screen comparisons, screen overlay comparisons, and more. Features vary depending on the program and version. There are many computer-based software and tablet- or smartphone-based applications available for movement analysis, ranging from simple and free to extensive and expensive. One of the most commonly used movement analysis programs is Hudl Technique (figure 10.5). This app, which is available for free, allows teachers and coaches the chance to record a student's performance and then analyze their technique. They can then share the analyzed video directly with the student. This free app, along with other low-cost programs, are often enough for K-12 teachers and coaches to get the desired analysis for an affordable price. They can also easily be used by students and athletes for peer-assessment tasks. For example, a physical education teacher could provide small groups with one tablet each with the Hudl Technique app installed. They could take turns capturing and analyzing video of one another performing a volleyball serve in a small-sided game. Students could rotate out of the game to watch their previously analyzed video and then become the next recorder. This allows the students to become more engaged in their peers' and their own learning, feedback, and performance. Collegiate and professional sports programs, on the other hand, may opt to use more advanced software, such as Dartfish, a computer-based software program that has all of the bells and whistles of the other apps but with many more options, including hosting videos on Dartfish TV, capturing live feeds, live video encoding, multivideo analysis, and more. Often, bigger athletic programs have individuals on staff to handle this analysis and relay the information to coaches for sharing with the athletes. The biggest difference is the price, with Dartfish cost-

Courtesy of Dannon Cox

Figure 10.5 Movement analysis with Hudl Technique.

ing up to $165 per month, whereas its simple app counterpart, Dartfish Express, is only $6.99. However, in order to take advantage of the features of the app, you must also join MyDartfish Mobile for $5.00 per month. In the end, even the simplest motion analysis software provides more options for analysis than simple video observation. Other popular movement analysis apps include Coach's Eye, iAnalyze, and Gamechanger.

> Check out the web resource for links to tutorials on using video analysis software and apps.

Although it is common to focus on individual athlete skill performance, the analysis of tactical movement in sport, such as offense, defense, possession, or transitions, is important for team dynamics and improvement of training and performance. Video tactical analysis programs, much like movement analysis programs, offer different features. One of the most common is the ability to tag specific tactical movements, events, or athletes in a contest. Dartfish software has the ability to create tags and note whenever that particular tag action takes place in the video. Later, the coach can select to view and even create a new clip of video of only the tagged portions of the video. This can be helpful if a coach wants to display a particular type of defense or showcase a specific player. Similar to Dartfish Express, Dartfish Note is a free app (with the $5.00 per month subscription) that allows coaches to customize buttons to define actions, view stats during the game, and share video collections with athletes and export statistics. Video tactical analysis apps are also useful for scouting, where video can be tagged for individual players, creating a highlight reel-like video. Athletes can also use this to create their own highlight reels to share. Other tactical analysis apps include Krossover (now with Hudl), Sportscode, and Performa Sports.

Video Feedback Improves Performance

Have you ever been told to correct your skill form when you were certain you were doing it the correct way all along? Often, athletes need to see themselves perform a skill to truly grasp feedback. Visual feedback is one of the most effective ways in which individuals learn motor skills (Magill, 2007), and video technology has been shown to be an effective tool for providing feedback and improving actual performance. Horseback riding skills of riders were improved simply by showing riders a video of themselves paired with feedback from the instructor (Kelley & Miltenberger, 2016). Video feedback has also been shown to improve sport performance through analysis of tactics when observing offensive and defensive play. For example, video analysis was used to determine the tactical responses of football teams with and without ball possession (Clemente et al., 2013). Physical education teachers and sport coaches could vastly improve the performance of their students and athletes through the use of video for assessment.

Video for Project-Based Learning

Video is also a great way to allow students to showcase their knowledge and skills and for teachers to assess them, with a proper rubric, through project-based learning (PBL). Teachers are called to try to assess students in authentic, real-world situations, which can be simulated through project-based learning activities. In addition, PBL offers students a chance to solve a real-world problem or question, provides them with choices for how to tackle it, includes a process of reflection and revision, and ends with a product that is applied in an authentic way. Video production offers students a way to produce something that is interesting and relevant to their own interests, as well as skills that will benefit them in the future. Video-based PBL can be accomplished in many settings; however, physical education and health education are particularly good subjects for implementation. For example, a health education class could be presented with the authentic problem of a teen vaping epidemic and a need to better inform them of the dangers of vaping. Students could then be tasked with creating video public service announcements that will be displayed on the monitor near the school's main office. With feedback and critiques from the teacher and peers, paired with guidance from a scoring rubric, teams of students can produce a video demonstrating essential knowledge of the dangers of vaping as well as other health education skills, such as resisting peer pressure.

Physical education is also a great subject area for project-based learning. Students could create a series of how-to videos on motor skills for elementary school students. Cox and Meaney (2018) described how physical education students created a show called *PE for Life*, in which they interviewed local community members who shared ways to live a healthy lifestyle, which led to incorporation of new activities in physical education. The key to using PBL with video is to ensure there is an authentic problem and allow students some choice in their approach to solving it.

CREATING AND UTILIZING RUBRICS WITH TECHNOLOGY

Although observing any type of performance on video is usually more valuable than simply observing with the naked eye, objectivity is still important. High-quality assessment almost always includes the use of a rubric to improve objectivity, increase reliability, and set expectations for mastery performance. No matter what type of analysis you are completing—whether it is students observing themselves on a delayed video app, students assessing their peers with a motion analysis app, or a teacher assessing health education students' public service announcement videos—a rubric should be used to guide the assessment and provide feedback. Creating rubrics can be challenging, but once they are produced, their usefulness far outweighs their trouble. Technology can aid in the creation of rubrics, making their integration into assessment more feasible. There are some websites and tools that have predesigned rubrics that can be used across multiple subjects, such as a class participation or behavior rubric. Others have some that can be customized or even made from scratch by selecting, modifying, or establishing criteria and scoring levels. These include checklists, rating scales, and holistic rubrics. Two of the most popular rubric websites are RubiStar and Quick Rubric. Rubrics can also be created and embedded into assessments within an LMS course, and results are automatically tallied and entered into the LMS class gradebook. These rubrics are premade or allow custom rubrics to be created, downloaded, and printed. There are also a few rubric apps available, including some specific to physical education, such as Easy Rubric and Easy Assessment. In the end, technology can aid in the development of rubrics, which are essential for good assessment practices.

DATA COLLECTION, MINING, AND REPORTING CONSIDERATIONS

There are several considerations that must be taken into account when using technology for assessment, particularly the collection of data, mining, and reporting results. Many of the web-based surveys, quizzes, and video analysis tools are easy to use and allow the instructor to collect valuable data. Some programs, such as Google Forms and Survey Monkey, are better at tracking student data than others. These and others offer ways to organize, export, and analyze the data collected either within the program itself (e.g., Survey Monkey) or export to other analysis programs (e.g., Microsoft Excel or Google Sheets). LMS-embedded assessment programs likely have the most seamless integration of data collection, data mining, data analyzing, and data reporting (e.g., gradebook) of all assessment technologies, because it is like a "one-stop shop."

LMS assessments can be limiting, however, depending on the program being used, which is one reason professionals sometimes seek out other options. One of the concerns with using other web-based assessments is data privacy. If you choose an option other than an official LMS—for example, using Google Forms to collect assessment data and export results to a Google Sheet—this system likely has no official connection to your school. This is problematic for several reasons. First, the school has no responsibility over the data, and if something goes wrong, you won't have their support. Second, there is always the risk of a data breach. Most sites, especially Google, offer password protection for your accounts and data, but there is always a risk when posting anything on the Internet. To protect yourself and your students, it is recommended that you not use full names or any other identifiers.

A third consideration is that some programs may not actually allow you to collect and save student data. It is suggested that you do your homework ahead of time. Can you create a class within the program? Can it save data to a spreadsheet and analyze it for you? Can you export your data? If data collection is not important to you for a particular formative assessment (e.g., a Jeopardy-style quiz game for review), then it is not a concern. However, you should be aware of the capabilities of the programs you choose and their ability to collect, store, and analyze data. Once you have collected your data, applying data mining techniques can help improve teaching and learning. Classifying student data into categories of achievement can help with learning who needs extra help and who needs extra challenges. Additionally, data mining can help with predicting achievement in the future.

One of the most useful benefits of assessment is being able to share the results with stakeholders. Some simple data analysis within a quiz or survey program, or the ability to create informative and interesting graphs to represent your data, is important for informing parents, administrators, students, and other individuals of the achievements and progress of your students. These can be presented in newsletters, posted on class websites or social media pages, shared verbally and visually at a PTA or faculty meeting, or emailed to just about anyone you deem appropriate.

Conclusion

This chapter described a variety of ways to use other technology for assessment. With the use of LMS assessment features, quiz and survey tools, and video analysis programs, there is a plethora of options for the enhancement and feasibility of assessment in physical education, health education, and coaching.

Key Terms

assessment—The process and tools educators use to gather data, measure, and document student behaviors, progression, and achievement.

classroom response systems—Interactive remote answering program where a teacher can collect responses from an audience.

data—Measurements or statistics used for analysis, decision making, or other information.

feedback—Process by which learners make sense of information about performance and use it to enhance their performance.

formative assessment—Methods that teachers and coaches use to conduct evaluations of student performance during a lesson or practice.

movement analysis—The practice of evaluating one's motor performance.

peer assessment—Assessment of students' work by other students of equal status.

project-based learning—Teaching method in which students apply knowledge and skills in response to an authentic and engaging question, problem, or challenge.

rubric—A scoring guide used to evaluate the quality of student performance.

self-assessment—Assessment of one's own performance.

summative assessment—Evaluation of student learning, performance, or achievement at the conclusion of an instructional unit.

tactical analysis—Analysis of performance of individual and team behaviors, such as movements and decisions within offense and defense.

video analysis—The practice of evaluating one's performance through viewing it on video.

Review Questions

1. What are the advantages of using web-based assessment tools?
2. List three web-based assessment tools that would be best to collect individual assessment data.
3. List three web-based assessment tools that could be used during class or practice to gather group data.
4. List three video analysis programs that could be used for skills or tactical analysis.
5. What is one challenge to consider when thinking about implementing assessment technology?

Discussion Questions

1. What are some benefits of using video for assessment?
2. Describe how you might incorporate video assessment into your teaching or coaching.
3. What are the benefits of using web-based assessment rather than traditional assessment?

Basic Digital Video Recording and Editing

Chapter Objectives

When you have completed this chapter, you will be able to do the following:

1. Explain common uses for digital video recording and editing by physical educators, health educators, and coaches.
2. Describe equipment options for recording digital video with a wireless microphone.
3. Demonstrate best practices for digital video recording and editing.
4. Create an edited digital video using a digital video editing software program.

Mieke Dalle/Photographer's Choice/Getty Images

You might ask yourself: Why do I need to learn about **digital video (DV)** recording and editing as a physical educator, health educator, or coach? There are many good reasons. Knowing how to effectively record and edit DV will assist with movement analysis (see chapter 10) and in providing visual feedback to your students or athletes so they may be able to improve motor performance. Also, video recording is particularly important for physical educators because they are encouraged to incorporate assessments using video analysis of students performing physical skills (Society of Health and Physical Educators America, 2016).

Moreover, as a health or physical educator with aspirations for National Board certification (National Board for Professional Teaching Standards, 2018), you will need basic DV recording and editing skills to submit the required teaching video samples for this process. Similarly, many health and physical education teacher preparation programs and state departments of education have adopted the Education Teacher Performance Assessment (edTPA), which requires preservice teachers to submit multiple DV samples of their teaching (Pearson Education, 2018). Often, successful completion of the edTPA requirements is compulsory for graduation or teacher certification. Figure 11.1 provides a nonexhaustive list of other reasons to learn rudimentary skills involved in recording and editing DV.

Thus, the purpose of this chapter is to provide a brief overview of simple recommendations for DV recording and editing. Practical tips regarding DV recording and editing are provided with specific attention being given to recording audio with a wireless microphone. First, let's briefly discuss the equipment and software needed.

Of note, before you purchase DV recording equipment or editing software, you should consider investigating whether your institution has an instructional technology center or library that signs out this type of equipment or provides access to computers with editing software installed. Commonly, teacher education programs will provide

Figure 11.1   Sample uses for digital video recording (and editing) for physical educators, health educators, and coaches.

- Formal assessment of preservice teachers for graduation or certification (e.g., edTPA)
- Process for health and physical education teacher National Board certification
- Promoting your athletes for recruiting purposes (i.e., athlete highlight videos)
- Culminating end-of-season highlight video (e.g., at end-of-season awards banquet)
- Remote student teacher or coaching internship supervision
- Communicating with program stakeholders (see chapter 3)
- Creating videos to motivate your students and athletes (see chapter 5)
- Simultaneous video challenges with other classes or teams (see chapter 5)
- Flipped instruction (i.e., flipped learning) (see chapter 8)
- Online synchronous and asynchronous instruction and coaching (see chapter 8)
- Student, athlete, teacher, and coach assessment, including peer and self-assessment (see chapter 10)
- Motion-analysis of physical skills (see chapter 10)
- Providing others professional development (see chapter 12)
- Program advocacy (see chapter 13)

this to their preservice teachers for field experiences and student teaching. In addition, practicing teachers and coaches may often be able to find this equipment through the school or community library. In order to acquire funding to purchase this equipment, practitioners will need to justify purchase requests with key monetary decision makers (e.g., principal, superintendent, athletic director, sport booster club, etc.). Some DV equipment and software makers provide educator discounts. More funding ideas are found in chapter 16 of this textbook. Moreover, legal aspects regarding video recording students and athletes is discussed in chapter 15, along with sample video and photo release forms.

DIGITAL VIDEO RECORDING EQUIPMENT

Recommended equipment for **DV recording** is (1) a DV camera device (e.g., DV camcorder, mobile device with a DV camera, etc.), (2) data storage (e.g., internal storage, memory card), (3) a tripod, and (4) a wireless microphone. Features and recommended pedagogical strategies for using each will now be discussed. Obviously, these types of technologies are always advancing, but these basic suggestions will provide you with a sufficient base of knowledge to make informed purchasing decisions.

Digital Video Camera Devices

In this text, a **DV camera** is defined as an electronic device that records live event motion picture information (including audio) to DV formats. Of note, many traditional point-and-shoot digital cameras and higher-end digital SLR (single-lens reflex) cameras also have DV capability (figure 11.2). However, these cameras are designed for capturing still images. Still pictures can also be captured via nearly all DV cameras. DV camera devices include traditional DV camcorders, action DV camcorders (e.g., GoPro HERO) and mobile devices with DV camcorders such as smartphones (e.g., iPhone, Samsung Galaxy) or tablets (e.g., iPad, Samsung Galaxy Tab, Amazon Kindle Fire). There are pros and cons to using each type of device, dependent on the situation.

Traditional DV Camcorders

A **DV camcorder** is a device that captures video and audio and records it via a hard drive or flash memory into media storage. Example DV formats include microDVD and mini-HD; common DV file formats are MP4, AVI, FLV (flash video), MOV (Apple QuickTime Movie), and WMV (Windows Media Video). Sample DV camcorder manufacturers include Canon, JVC, Olympus, Panasonic, Samsung, Sony, and Vivitar. See table 11.1 for a review of feature considerations when deciding on the best DV camcorder for your needs, as well as table 11.2 for a comparison of consumer versus professional DV camcorders. For most teaching and coaching situations, consumer DV camcorders are sufficient.

Figure 11.2   A digital SLR (single-lens reflex) camera with interchangeable lens and external microphone. Although these cameras are designed for capturing still images, newer models also capture DV.

Table 11.1 Traditional Digital Video Camcorder Feature Options

Feature	Function
Liquid crystal display (LCD) screen	Allows you to view video during and after recording; some include flip-out touchscreen capability (consider desired display size)
Viewfinder	Allows you to view and record the scene in bright light when an LCD screen may be difficult to see (particularly outdoors) or to conserve battery life (which an LCD may expend at a rapid rate)
Input ports	Options may include an external microphone port, flash memory card slot(s), or a LANC port (a hardwired remote system used when the DV camcorder is connected to a tripod—not compulsory)
Output ports	Options may include a headphone jack, or various ports to connect to an external hard drive, TV, or computer (e.g., FireWire, USB, HDMI)
Wi-Fi	Allows you to wirelessly transfer video and photos from the camcorder
Image stabilizer	Using a tripod is best; both optical and electronic stabilizers are effective
Resolution (pixel count)	Determines the image quality—a pixel is the smallest area of color in a DV picture; the higher the pixel count, the higher the resolution (i.e., playback image quality); minimum recommended is 1080p and is considered "full HD" (high-definition); 720p is a considerable step down and is considered "HD ready," or widescreen HD; "ultra HD" (i.e., UHD, 4K, or 8K) is the highest resolution quality; *Note:* pixel count is more important than whether the DV camcorder uses a CMOS or CCD image sensor
Change resolution option	Allows you to record lower-resolution video to conserve memory (i.e., data storage) – in other words, increase the number of DV recording minutes; and vice versa (i.e., record less minutes of DV, but at a higher resolution)
Zoom lens	Allows you to zoom video closer to an object (e.g., a 10x zoom lens will make the object appear 10 times closer); if you think you will zoom in a lot while shooting video, consider an optical zoom lens, which may provide DV that looks less pixelated compared to a digital zoom lens
Battery	Should include at least two hours of rechargeable battery capacity; some models offer a larger capacity battery or come with two batteries; if purchasing an extra battery, be sure you know the model number and consider an external battery charging unit so you can charge while using the camcorder
Remote control	Allows you to control camcorder from a distance (i.e., start recording, zoom, etc.)
Manual controls	Allows advanced users to manually adjust white balance, focus (helpful in low light), or exposure controls
Night mode / Night Vision	Allows you to record in low light or dark settings
Built-in projector	Projects playback on a screen or flat white wall; consider the lumen count (i.e., brightness level) and size of projection
Accessories	Accessories may include items such as carrying case, tripod, memory card, external charging unit, external microphone, external light, GPS for geotagging, compatibility with a standard tripod (screw-on base)

Note: Also, see the discussion later in this chapter titled DV camcorder data storage.

Some ideas adapted from Bourne (2009); and Consumer Reports (2018).

Table 11.2   Differences Between Consumer and Professional Digital Video Camcorders

Consumer	Professional
Cheaper (~$50-$300)	More expensive (~$1,500+)
Lightweight	Heavier
Smaller	Larger, bulkier
Handheld (can use a tripod)	Shoulder-mounted (assists with more steady shots)
Single lens	Allows for high-grade interchangeable lenses, filters, sun shields (permits macro and wide angle shots, deeper depth of field, more professional look, etc.)
One-button point-and-shoot record option	Manual controls (manual focus, white balance, aperture, speed and audio settings)
Lower video resolution output	Higher video resolution output (registers primary colors separately, resulting in crisper images)

Adapted from Steve's Digicams (2018).

However, professional DV camcorders may be needed for certain situations, such as:

1. when recording from far distances (e.g., football practice from an aerial view),
2. when high-level detail (i.e., increased image quality) is needed to replay frame-by-frame (i.e., slow motion) or when wanting to capture still frames from the DV,
3. when advanced audio is required (with a need for increased audio ports),
4. when filming in extreme high- or low-light situations, or
5. when high-level DV movement analysis (see chapter 10) is desired.

Action DV Camcorders

Action DV camcorders gained popularity through the GoPro brand. **Action DV camcorders**, also known as action-cams, are designed for capturing DV while immersed in an

A teacher recording a digital video while utilizing a tripod.

RoosterHD/E+/Getty Images

A kindergartener wears an action DV camcorder (e.g., GoPro Hero 4) attached with a chest strap during an elementary cross country race. See the video here: https://youtu.be/MEVzq9k8ibA

Seth Jenny

environment and participating in an activity. Most action DV camcorders are small and have an exterior or casing that is rugged, shock-resistant, and often waterproof at shallow depths. Sample action DV camcorder manufacturers include Garmin, GoPro, Panasonic, Polaroid, Sony, TomTom, Toshiba, and Vivitar. Of note, unless an external microphone is used, action DC camcorders are typically not recommended if audio capture is important (particularly if the camcorder resides within a protective waterproof case). Pros and cons of action DV camcorders are provided in table 11.3. Although this table can assist in determining whether an action DV camcorder is right for you, remember that each action DV camcorder offers diverse features.

Obviously, for movement practitioners, action DV camcorders are a unique tool for capturing video from the performer's perspective while participating in a physical activity or sport with little concern for damaging the camera. Often, these are used in outdoor adventure, water-based, or "extreme" sports (e.g., mountain biking, motocross, skiing, surfing, rock climbing, base jumping). There are many uses for action DV camcorders for sport coaches (e.g., viewing swim strokes from the underwater perspective). Preliminary research on the utilization of action DV camcorders to record and promote simulated learning experiences with preservice physical education teachers supported the device's portable nature and ability to capture the point-of-view perspective for later viewing and learning (Hyndman & Papatraianou, 2017). In addition, action DV camcorders are also beneficial for recording lessons for online physical education courses (Hyndman, 2017).

Mobile Device With DV Camera

Due to their prevalence and convenience, many people record DV with a mobile device. A **mobile device** can be defined as a portable handheld computing device with a rechargeable battery, often with a touchscreen display. Example mobile device categories include smartphones and tablets. A **smartphone** is a mobile phone with advanced computer features, such as a DV camera with microphone, touchscreen display, Internet capability, and the ability to run downloaded applications. Two popular kinds of smartphones are the iPhone and Samsung Galaxy. Up 35% from 2011, as of February 2018, 77% of all Americans owned a smartphone, including 94% of Americans ages 18 to 29 years old (Pew Research Center, 2018).

Similar to a smartphone, but not designed as a phone, **tablets** are thin and flat mobile computing devices with an operating system, typically with Internet accessibility, touchscreen display, and DV camera. Tablets are also capable of downloading and running computer applications, but usually are slightly larger than smartphones. For the purposes of this text, the iPad and iPod Touch, Samsung Galaxy Tab, and Amazon Kindle Fire are all examples of tablets. Over half (53%) of all Americans own a tablet computer (Pew Research Center, 2018).

Although many people record DV with mobile devices, there are several pros and cons to doing so (see table 11.4). Principally, audio capture without an external microphone can be extremely poor with mobile devices. Moreover, recording while holding the device vertically (i.e., portrait) rather than horizontally (i.e., landscape) will most likely pro-

Table 11.3 Pros and Cons of Action Digital Video Camcorders

Pros	Cons
As the name implies, permits action recording while immersed in performing an activity	Most do not include a zoom lens, so subject must be in close proximity
Rugged, shock-resistant, and often water-resistant (some require a casing)	The view is often a very wide angle and the subject may appear very far away on playback
Small and lightweight (most weigh between 2 and 8 ounces)	In most instances, does not suffice as a point-and-shoot camera due to the wide-angle field of view and lack of zoom capability (i.e., GoPro HERO is a special-purpose camera)
Hands-free recording with the use of accessories (e.g., chest strap; helmet cam; headband; wrist strap; clip attachment; handlebar, glass suction, or dashboard mount; selfie stick; tripod)	Most do not permit interchanging lenses
Variety of recording angles (based on mounting accessories)	Some do not have an LCD display (for playback and other touchscreen features); however, a monitor may be able to be used via a smartphone or tablet app with some models
Underwater or heavy rain recording capability (with waterproof models or cases)	Audio capture quality is typically lower, particularly if in a waterproof case; some models require an external microphone for any audio capture
Extreme wide-angle features	Battery can drain quickly, particularly if using the LCD display
Functions often include slow motion recording, burst mode (continuous still image capture effective for sports—i.e., 10 photos a second), and time lapse mode for intermittent still image or video capture (e.g., records a set amount of time every 30 seconds) while performing a long-duration activity (e.g., biking, hiking, running)	Mounting accessories can add to the overall cost (particularly name-brand accessories)
Many include image stabilization, ultra HD (4K or higher) recording option, and Wi-Fi capability for wireless data transfer	

Table 11.4 Pros and Cons of Recording Digital Video With a Mobile Device

Pros	Cons
Accessibility—it is likely you (and your students) have access to a smartphone or other mobile device within arm's reach at all times	Digital zoom in most mobile devices often results in pixelated playback compared to optical zoom lenses in traditional DV camcorders (tip: get as close as you can to your subject)
Familiarity—due to the pervasiveness of mobile devices, it is likely you (and your students) already have experience recording DV with a mobile device	Many mobile devices are not capable of recording in ultra HD (4K or higher) resolution
Easy and quick access to edit the video within the mobile device's applications without having to transfer the video file to a computer	Many mobile devices have limited data storage space and no memory card slots (tip: consider making space on your mobile device by storing data via the cloud [e.g., iCloud, Google Drive])
Easy sharing of the video files with others (e.g., social media, email, cloud file sharing)	Most mobile devices lack an adequate external light or night vision mode for recording in dark conditions
Easy access to movement analysis applications such as Hudl Technique or Coach's Eye (see chapter 10)	Most mobile devices have limited DV shooting options (i.e., limited manual controls)
Easy access to cast the video from the mobile device to a TV or monitor via Wi-Fi (e.g., Google Chromecast, Apple AirPlay)	Many tablets do not support an external microphone
Easy access to applications that permit augmented reality and other special effects while recording, such as Snapchat (see chapter 5)	

Swivl robotic DV motion tracking device with wireless microphone lanyard worn by the presenter.

Courtesty of Swivl

duce those infamous vertical "black bars" on either side of the video during playback on a widescreen display (i.e., TV, YouTube). Finally, zooming in on your subject usually degrades the clarity of the video on playback with mobile devices (i.e., pixelated look). However, probably the most important tip for attaining quality DV is to use a tripod. This type of equipment is discussed later in the chapter.

Robotic Digital Video Motion Tracking (With Wireless Microphone)

Several stand-alone DV recording devices and accessories now integrate robotic motion-tracking ability so a key subject (i.e., teacher, coach, athlete) can be automatically tracked with the camera via a remote control marker without the need for a videographer. For example, the Swivl (2018) is a 360-degree rotating (i.e., panning) and tilting robotic mount that connects to a smartphone or tablet (iOS or Android platforms) and via the Swivl app robotically tracks the movement of a wireless microphone lanyard worn by the presenter as DV and audio is captured. Designed to capture presentations and well-suited for recording lessons in a traditional classroom, new versions of the Swivl also provide the ability to integrate concurrent multiple wireless microphones and DV recording devices in order to capture small-group interactions as well.

In a sport setting, for instance, a Swivl may be effective for recording movements across a playing area of an athlete practicing alone. Trainers of dogs or horses might use a motion-tracking device like the Swivl to capture DV of the moving animal wearing the marker as the trainer provides commands to later share with clients (Patel, 2014). Distance education teachers might record face-to-face in-class lectures with DV motion-tracking devices with a wireless microphone to later post online for students to view (see chapter 8).

Some of the downsides to these types of devices is the range of the device (Swivl's range is approximately 30 feet) and that the device is not meant to be moved from its starting location once recording commences. Moreover, some robotic DV motion-tracking devices like the Swivl require an unobstructed line of sight from the device to the marker (e.g., wireless microphone lanyard), which is probably the biggest drawback to these particular devices. When line of sight is broken, the device does not know where the marker is and the DV camera may not be pointed at the presenter. This can be a major problem in gym or outdoor sports environments if people are constantly moving in front of the motion-tracking device. In a classroom, this can also occur temporarily if the presenter wearing the marker turns their back to the motion-tracking device. However, when line of sight is restored to the marker, the device then continues to track the marker again.

The SoloShot (2018), another DV motion-tracking device, was designed to track surfers from a far distance via an arm-worn remote control marker. A newer version of this device has a 600-foot range, 4K video with 65x optical zoom lens, does not require line of sight for the waterproof marker, and can be paired with an additional wireless microphone. Practitioners (or parents) might use the SoloShot to automatically record an individual wearing the arm-band during any outdoor activity. However, other DV recording suggestions will be discussed later in this chapter as certainly not all DV recording is automated.

DV Camcorder Data Storage

Data storage is one of the major DV camcorder equipment considerations. There are three primary DV camcorder **data storage** types: (1) internal storage (flash memory or hard drive), (2) removable memory card storage, or (3) a combination of internal and removable memory card storage. The biggest downside to DV camcorders with internal-only storage is that video must be deleted or transferred when capacity is reached. This is a bad situation if you are in the middle of recording something important. With DV camcorders that have removable memory card storage, you could simply swap memory cards without deleting any previously recorded video, then transfer video files from the removed memory card later.

Common DV camcorder memory card types include SD (secure digital), SDHC (SD high capacity), SDXC (secure digital eXtended capacity), and memory stick. Some devices (e.g., GoPro) require a "micro" version of these memory card types (e.g., microSD), which are smaller in size. In addition, an adapter may be used with micro memory cards in non-micro memory card devices (i.e., microSD-to-SD memory card adapter). When purchasing a memory card, be sure it is compatible with the DV camcorder. Typically, prior to your first recording, you should follow the camcorder's directions and format a new memory card within the camcorder, which deletes any pre-existing data on the memory card and prepares it for data storage on that device. Also, if you are borrowing a DV camcorder, consider purchasing your own corresponding memory card and remember to take it out of the camcorder prior to returning it. Always back up your video files on a hard drive, to another device, or to the cloud as soon as possible in case something happens to your memory card.

DV camcorder storage capacity (e.g., minutes of video) depends on the quality of video being recorded. The higher the resolution you record, the fewer minutes of recording time will be permitted until capacity is reached. 64GB and 512GB SDHC memory cards can hold up to about 7 hours and 116 hours, respectively, of HD video. Internal storage DV camcorders typically hold 30GB to 120GB, whereas some large capacity memory cards can hold up to 512GB or more. The larger the capacity, the more it costs. With most types of DV camcorders, the video files will need to be transferred to another device prior to editing the video.

Tripods

A **tripod** is a portable three-legged stand that, when attached to a DV camera, can elevate and provide stable video capture. For still photography, tripods are primarily used for long exposures (i.e., nighttime shots of traffic with blurred red taillights) or with long telephoto lenses (i.e., extreme close-up shots with big camera lenses). With any type of camera, built-in image stabilizers are often not enough to attain clear images and quality handheld DV footage.

Moreover, a tripod is required for effective panning. **Panning** is moving a camcorder along with a moving subject (i.e., tracking) or moving the camcorder across an entire scene (i.e., panorama). A tripod will allow you to smoothly track a moving object while recording video, such as recording a teacher walking around a classroom or gym, or tracking the ball movement during a sporting competition. In addition, almost all DV camcorders have a standard one-quarter-inch tripod mount (i.e., a hole with screw threading) on the underside that a plate on the tripod, which features the same standard size screw as the camera's mount, accepts. See figure 11.3 for advantages of using a tripod when recording video.

A **monopod**, also called a unipod, is a long single telescoping pole that can assist with stabilizing a DV camcorder. Although less steady and cannot stand alone like a tripod, monopods are commonly used in sport still photography when moving to various locations during game play and quick setup is necessary. In addition, mini tripods, also known as table or backpacker tripods, are typically less than 10 inches in height and can be used with lightweight and compact DV camcorders where they can rest on an elevated flat surface. Also, as discussed previously, action DV camcorders are commonly compatible with small and portable clamps, attachments, and other accessories that can help stabilize these camcorders across varying surfaces. Finally, special tripod mounts can be used for mobile devices (e.g., smartphones, tablets), which may be helpful for activities such as using video delay apps (see chapter 10). When purchasing these mobile device tripod accessories, be sure the mobile device can remain in its protective case while in use, because your screen is likely to be cracked if the tripod is accidentally knocked over while in use, particularly within a gym or playing field setting. Beyond a tripod, another crucial piece of often-neglected DV recording equipment is a wireless microphone.

Mieke Dalle/Photographer's Choice/Getty Images

A smartphone connected to a tripod mount, which is then screwed into the tripod. Similar mounts are made for all types of DV cameras, DV camcorders, and mobile devices.

Wireless Microphones

When recording in a large classroom, in a gym, or especially outside on an athletic field, it is necessary to use a wireless microphone in order to clearly record a speaker's voice. A **wireless microphone** system, also known as a radio microphone, allows you to collect audio from a person speaking via a microphone and wireless battery-powered transmitter to a receiver unit connected to a DV camcorder or mobile device. Unfortunately, this piece of equipment is not often used, because most people simply want to try to record DV with their smartphone. Then, when the DV is played back, it is often extremely hard to distinguish the speaker's dialogue.

One caveat to recording audio with a wireless microphone is that the audio capture is often limited to the person wearing the microphone. So, for example, if a teacher or coach wearing the wireless microphone poses questions to an entire class or team, you may hear the questions clearly on the recording, but the responses may be hard to hear. In addition, few things are more annoying than recording an entire lesson or coaching session wear-

Figure 11.3 Advantages of using a tripod when recording digital video.

- Stabilizes video recordings (i.e., reducing shakiness), particularly when zooming
- Ensures a level recording (many tripods come with a built-in level to assist with this)
- Allows recording of long classes or games without becoming tired from holding a camcorder
- Improves video sharpness (i.e., focusing), particularly in low light situations
- Allows you to pan more easily, smoothly, and fluidly while recording; following a moving object (i.e., panning) is compulsory in many physical activities and sports
- Allows you to increases creativity by modifying video angles (particularly with action DV camcorders)

Some text adapted from Goldstein (2009).

ing a wireless microphone and later realizing that no audio was ever recorded. Too often this happens to preservice teachers who try to borrow DV equipment 30 minutes prior to their teaching demonstration, without allowing time to familiarize themselves with it or determine if it is working properly. To avoid this, we recommend making a short test recording to make sure the wireless microphone audio is working. The individual operating the DV recording device can also listen to be sure the audio is being received via a connected earbud to the audio receiver, which is connected to the DV camcorder (this might be a cooperating teacher in a preservice teaching setting).

DIGITAL VIDEO RECORDING

As previously discussed, three common DV recording mistakes made by novices are (1) holding the mobile device vertically while recording, resulting in the aforementioned vertical "black bars" on either side of the video during playback, (2) poor audio capture because a wireless microphone is not used, making it difficult to hear the speaker's dialogue, and (3) shaky recording because a tripod was not used. Overcome these three common errors, and your DV recordings will be much enhanced. The tips in figures 11.4 and 11.5 will further assist you in improving the quality of your DV recordings.

After recording DV, if editing is not desired, most DV camcorders and mobile devices can be connected directly to a TV via HDMI cables (or composite video cables for older DV camcorder models) in order to play back the video. Additional HDMI adapters may be required for some mobile devices. Furthermore, screen mirroring apps on some mobile devices may permit viewing the video wirelessly, but additional streaming equipment (e.g., Apple TV, Google Chromecast, Roku) may be necessary if the TV is not Wi-Fi enabled.

Courtesy of Jaimie McMullen.

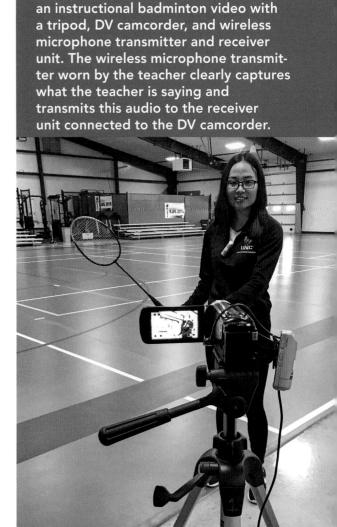

A physical education teacher creates an instructional badminton video with a tripod, DV camcorder, and wireless microphone transmitter and receiver unit. The wireless microphone transmitter worn by the teacher clearly captures what the teacher is saying and transmits this audio to the receiver unit connected to the DV camcorder.

Figure 11.4   Digital video recording tips.

- Test out all of the equipment the night before. Do *not* wait until 30 minutes before your lesson or coaching session and assume you will figure it out!
- Test the wireless microphone to make sure it is working—nothing is more frustrating than recording a whole session to later discover no audio was recorded.
- Bring extra batteries that are fully charged for your camcorder and wireless microphone transmitter and receiver.
- Bring a spare memory card—you don't want to run out of storage space while recording.
- If using a wireless microphone, the person recording may use an earbud connected to the wireless audio receiver to make sure the audio is being recorded.
- Try to avoid backlit recording conditions as much as possible (you want the light hitting the front of your subject, not coming from behind the subject).
- Fill the frame with your subject (also known as "framing").
- Get as close as you can to your subject (digital zoom often results in pixelated playback).
- Remember that using the LCD display will use more battery, as opposed to using the viewfinder (see table 11.1).
- Consider if a robotic DV motion-tracking device would work for your situation.
- If making an instructional video, consider making a script or storyboard with proposed content and preplanned filming angles for each scene, noting what will be said and by whom within each scene, and the final order and amount of time allotted for each scene in the final edited video.
- For sports skills, consider filming the entire skill (whole), as well as highlighting key aspects of the skill (part) from various video angles.

Note: Tips for creating a DV for online or flipped instruction are discussed in chapter 8.

DIGITAL VIDEO EDITING

Although the recording process is vitally important, effective editing is also essential to producing a quality DV. **DV editing** is the process of using computer software to manipulate and arrange video, digital images, text, and audio in order to structure and present a final DV product. Example professional DV editing computer software includes Adobe Premiere Pro, Final Cut Pro, and Vegas Pro. Some of these professional programs are also offered in a scaled-down, less complicated, and less expensive version, but some advanced editing features are not included (e.g., Adobe Premiere Elements, Final Cut Express, Vegas Movie Studio). Moreover, free DV software also exists (e.g., iMovie, Windows Movie Maker, Adobe Premiere Express via YouTube). Finally, DV editing mobile device apps, which are iOS or Android platform-specific, also allow users to edit video directly on the capturing device (e.g., FilmoraGo, Adobe Premiere Clip, iMovie, PowerDirector Video Editor App). Although it is recommended you read online reviews and research what features you specifically want, many find that the features offered in free or less expensive DV editing programs are adequate for creating a basic DV.

Figure 11.5 Digital video recording checklist.

Filming and Content

_____ Any filming with a mobile device is performed horizontally, with no "black bars" visible during playback.

_____ Video includes a clear and concise introduction (i.e., introduce speaker, video purpose) at the beginning and conclusion (i.e., review key points) at the end.

_____ Content is easily viewed (not cut off or too far away).

_____ Video provides a complete understanding of the content (i.e., the entire sport skill or content area is shown and explained at least once, not just a portion).

_____ Numerous video angles are used effectively to enhance understanding (when appropriate).

_____ Video scenes and verbal explanations are both used to enhance understanding (when appropriate), not just one or the other.

_____ Zooming within final edited video is not distracting.

_____ All presenters are dressed professionally (or in activity-specific attire).

Audio and Dialogue

_____ Audio capture sounds professional and wireless microphones are used (when appropriate).

_____ Any speaking within the video is clear and easy to hear.

_____ Content is well known by speaker(s), not read off script.

_____ Dialogue is professional, using correct grammar and pronunciation; and no inappropriate slang, gender-exclusive language (e.g., "you guys"), or repetitive distracting terms (e.g., "ah", "like", "you know").

Setting, Background, and Lighting

_____ Setting is appropriate for the content.

_____ Setting is free from distracting background sounds.

_____ Background is clear from visual distractions (i.e., no people shooting basketball behind someone speaking in a gym; no distracting pictures on wall behind the subject).

_____ Lighting is appropriate; and objects and people's faces can be seen clearly (i.e., not too dark with too much backlighting).

Note: This checklist is most appropriate after editing of the video occurs.

Adapted from Leight (2014).

Editing Equipment and File Retrieval

Table 11.5 provides a brief description of the equipment needed to edit DV. Please note that items marked with an asterisk (*) may not be necessary, depending on your needs and equipment. Moreover, if a memory card or Wi-Fi is not used to transfer the files to

Table 11.5   Digital Video Editing Equipment

Equipment	Purpose	Examples
Computer or mobile device	Using DV editing software and storing files	PC, Mac, smartphone, tablet
Audio/video cable, memory card, or Wi-Fi connection*	Transferring the video file, if not editing on the recording device	USB, FireWire, or memory card (or Wi-Fi connection for wireless file transfer or to edit online)
Editing software	Editing the DV	See examples provided in text
Video file(s)	Actual video file(s) to be edited	.mp4, .mov, .avi, .wmv, .mpeg, .mts
Still picture files*	Adding still images within DV	.jpg, .tif, .png, .gif, .tiff, .jpeg, .jfif
Audio files*	Adding additional music or audio to the DV (i.e., soundtrack)	.wav, .mp3, .aiff, .m4p, .wma, .ogg
Microphone*	Performing voice-over narration for the video	Built-in microphone or external microphone
Data storage capacity	Saving the finished DV	Internal device storage, USB flash drive, or memory card

Note: * = not required (dependent on specific circumstances).

be edited, most DV camcorders utilize a USB or FireWire cable in order to transfer the video files to a computer prior to editing (if not editing directly on the recording device).

Basic Editing Software and Common Editing Tools and Functions

Figure 11.6 shows a screenshot of typical editing software. First, most editing programs will offer some sort of menu, which provides functions for adding new media (video, audio, still images, text) as well as specific editing tools. A video playback area (i.e., **preview pane**) will allow you to view the edited version of the video. Finally, a **storyboard pane** (also called a **timeline**) will be included, which comprises the video or picture track, the audio track (sometimes only viewable if additional audio is added), and the text track (if you add text to overlay the video). Typically, a solid vertical line called the **scrub bar** overlays across all three tracks (video, audio, and text) on the timeline and assists the user in moving to precise video frames, which display within the video playback area. You can use the scrub bar to assist with locating exact areas within your video or audio tracks that you would like to manipulate (e.g., cut, trim, split, etc.). Figure 11.7 provides a description of the common basic editing tools and functions.

Editing Tips and Locating Tutorials

Because all DV editing software programs are slightly different, and new or updated versions continue to be released constantly, we suggest you view a video tutorial of the specific version of the editing software you intend to use. For example, you can visit Google or YouTube and search for the exact name and version of your editing software, along with terms like "tutorial" or "how to edit video" (for example, "Adobe Premiere Elements 2020 tutorial"). You can also search for how to perform specific editing tasks with search terms like "How do I add music in iMovie 2019?" Most computer software programs also include a "help" function within the menu, which will offer step-by-step directions of how to perform certain tasks within the program. Don't be afraid to use it. Figure 11.8 provides basic DV editing tips and considerations; figure 11.9 offers a checklist for DV editing.

1 Menu

2 Editing tools buttons

3 Video playback area (preview pane)

4 Storyboard pane (timeline)

5 Video/picture track

6 Audio track

7 Text track

8 Scrub bar

Figure 11.6   Digital video editing software screenshot: (1) Used to add new media and to access editing tools. (2) Shortcuts for editing functions. (3) Used to view the edited version of video. (4) Comprised of (5) video/picture track, (6) audio track, and (7) text track. (8) Solid vertical line that overlays across all tracks on the timeline and corresponds to the storyboard pane display; assists in precise video frame editing.

Figure 11.7   Common digital video terminology, editing tools, and functions.

USEFUL DV EDITING TERMINOLOGY

- *Video or audio clip:* An unedited episode of a video or audio segment
- *Aspect ratio:* The width-to-height ratio of the video display (standard definition video is 4:3, whereas high-definition video is 16:9)
- *Compressing a video:* The process of saving a video while reducing the amount of data within the video file, thus reducing the video file size and permitting quicker file transfer
- *Frame rate:* Rate at which video is captured each second (minimum frame rate should be 24 frames per second [fps]; other common frame rates are 29.97, 30, and 60 fps)
- *Resolution (pixel count):* 640 × 480 (SD),1280 × 720 (HD), 1920 × 1080 (HD) (see table 11.1)

VIDEO EDITING TOOLS

- *Templates and themes:* Software within DV editing programs that automatically combine video clips into a final video product, display the video with added animations or music, or incorporate various automated transitions between video clips
- *Import videos or still pictures:* Adding videos or still images to edit within the DV editing software program
- *Trim:* Removing the beginning or end of a video clip

(continued)

Figure 11.7 *(continued)*

- *Split:* Cutting a video clip into at least two sections, usually to move or delete portions
- *Splice:* Joining two video clips together
- *Fast motion or slow motion:* Speeding up or slowing down a video clip
- *Transitions:* Effect displayed between two video clips (fade, dissolve, wipe, etc.)
- *Visual effects (VFX):* Imagery created or manipulated beyond what was recorded (many software programs offer standard options like lighting effects, pixelization, cinematic overlays, animated effects, color replacement, etc.)

STILL IMAGE EDITING TOOLS

- *Panning and scrolling:* Horizontal (panning) or vertical (scrolling) movement across a still image, often combined with zooming in or out
- *Zooming:* Moving in or out across portions of the still image where attention is desired
- *Still image duration:* Time frame of how long the image displays in the video

AUDIO EDITING TOOLS

- *Import music or other audio:* Adding music or other audio track (e.g., narration) to the video
- *Trim/split/splice:* All of these terms apply as with video clips (music can be added or deleted from any point in the video)
- *Emphasize audio:* Accentuating the volume of the video audio, music, or narration within the final edited video
- *Fade in or out:* Audio levels of a clip can be manipulated for a fast, medium, or slow increase (in) or decrease (out) in volume at the beginning or end of a clip
- *Audio narration:* Adding spoken commentary to a video with an internal or external microphone; also called voice-over narration

TEXT EDITING TOOLS

- *Add text:* Titles, captions, or credits may be added to video clips (including size, color, font, background color, animations, etc.)
- *Text duration:* The length of time the text displays

Saving and Disseminating Digital Video Files

In order to be able to share your edited videos with others, there are a few key reminders regarding saving DV files. First, it is very important to know the difference between a DV editing software project file and a final movie file. A **project file** is the working file specific to the editing software you are using. You should save and back up a project file often so you don't lose your editing work. Of note, do *not* move or rename any original raw video or audio files that were imported into the editing software's project file and are being integrated into your edited video. If you do this, the DV editing software will not be able to locate these files for future editing within the project file.

Figure 11.8   Digital video editing tips.

VIDEO EDITING SUGGESTIONS

- If you are planning your scenes in the editing phase, it is too late. Be sure you have mapped out your ideas for your final edited video during the planning and filming phases.
- For instructional videos, determine the main concept to be covered and aim for a two- to five-minute finished product (for maintaining interest, it is better to make several short videos covering different concepts rather than one long video covering all concepts).
- Use slow motion or pausing to emphasize points (with text or audio narration) or for special effects.
- Depending on the resolution of the recorded video, slowing down the video too much may result in choppy playback.
- Avoid distracting or cheesy transitions between video clips.
- Don't always rely on the default length of time to display still images, which are often defaulted to display for seven seconds—view in "real time" and modify as needed.

TEXT EDITING SUGGESTIONS

- Consider including a title at the beginning of the video and credits at the end (cast, editor, director, producer, music credits, etc.).
- Text font and size should be relatively consistent throughout the video.
- Be sure the text appears at the appropriate time within the video.
- Be sure the text letters do not cover key components you want visible within the video.
- Be sure all text is correct (spelling, grammar, punctuation, etc.).
- Be sure the text color does not blend into the video background and is easy to read (i.e., don't display white text across a white sky).
- Be sure the text stays onscreen long enough to read and try to avoid too many words!

AUDIO EDITING SUGGESTIONS

- If adding a song to your video, consider using music that is royalty free (e.g., www. bensound.com) or has creative common licenses (e.g., http://freemusicarchive. org) to avoid copyright claims, particularly if uploading to YouTube or other video sharing platforms (see chapter 15).
- Be sure the video's soundtrack lyrics are appropriate for your setting (e.g., public school).
- At minimum, consider adding music to the beginning of the video to stimulate interest and set the tone, as well as using it as a transition to end the video during the credits.

Figure 11.9 Sample digital video editing checklist.

Text

_____ A title is included.

_____ Small amounts of text highlight key points and enhance video content understanding (e.g., critical elements of a sport skill, definitions of key terms).

_____ Credits are included (cast, editor, director, producer, music artists, and song titles).

_____ References are included (which support accuracy of content and provide viewer resources for where to learn more about the topic).

_____ All text is easy to read and contains no spelling, grammar, or punctuation errors.

Editing, Transitions, and Visual Effects

_____ Transitions between video clips are included. (_Note:_ Videos submitted for edTPA may require one complete unedited video.)

_____ Edited scene transitions and special effects are not distracting.

_____ Panning and zooming are used effectively with any still images.

_____ Repetition of the same scene is used effectively, when appropriate (e.g., showing a sport skill multiple times from differing angles).

_____ Slow motion is used effectively and does not display choppily.

_____ Visual effects are not distracting and complement the video pleasantly.

Audio and Music

_____ Music is used effectively in the video (e.g., during title, credits) and is consistent with the video's tone.

_____ Audio voice-overs added during the editing process are loud and clear enough to understand.

Final File

_____ Final edited video is no longer than five minutes.

_____ Final video is saved as an .mp4 file (do not share the editing program's project file).

Adapted from Leight (2014).

TECHNOLOGY TIPS FROM THE FIELD

Digital Video Recording, Editing, and Sharing

Seth Jenny
Cross country and track and field coach, grades 2-6
Grove City Athletics Club (http://grovecityac.org)
Grove City, Pennsylvania, USA

What types of technology do you use regarding digital video recording, editing, and sharing?
As a coach, I typically record digital video with my iPhone or GoPro, edit with a laptop and Windows Movie Maker, utilize free music for the videos from http://freemusicarchive.org, and share video with others via my YouTube channel (just search "Seth Jenny" in YouTube). After it is on YouTube, I post the web link to the club's Facebook page and Twitter account, as well as email it to parents through our online registration system (http://getmeregistered.com).

How do you use it?
My wife (another club coach as well) and I try to take video and still images of both the boys' and girls' teams at competitions with our iPhones. I also use pictures other parents text me or post to social media. We try to get footage of everyone, from the fastest to slowest. I then create simple videos put to music highlighting each kid.

My two boys in the club also love to take turns wearing the GoPro with chest strap during some races—it affords very unique camera angles. When they were younger I ran a few road races pushing a jogging stroller with the GoPro attached to the handle bars.

All parents or guardians sign off on video and picture sharing of their children when they register for the club.

Capturing audio for these videos is not too important so I don't need to use a wireless microphone.

What is your main objective for using this technology?
I want my young athletes to love running and physical activity for a lifetime. Many of them really enjoy watching themselves in the videos. I might also discuss with them racing strategy or running technique evident in the videos as well, but that is not the main goal of these videos. The main goal of the videos is to generate excitement for the club and try to recruit more kids to join as they see their peers having fun in the videos posted on social media—this strategy has worked!

What do you like about this technology?
Both the video editing program I use as well as the music I include within the videos are free downloads.

How might the technology be improved (or what don't you like about it)?
It can be very time consuming to download all the footage on my laptop, edit the video, upload the video to YouTube, and then share via social media. Moreover, if you have slow Internet, it can take a long time to upload the final video to YouTube.

What suggestions do you have in using the technology?
Don't try to use a professional editing software program if you are new to editing video. Most free or inexpensive editing programs are sufficient for basic video editing.

A **movie file**, then, is your finalized edited video; the rendered file. The **rendered** file is the final file that synthesizes everything you did while editing the project. Depending on the editing software used, to render the file (i.e., save the final movie file), you might select "Save Movie" or "Publish Movie." You often have options regarding the quality of the final movie file when saving. If file size is not a concern, then best quality should be selected, which will create a higher quality video, but larger file size. If you plan to upload this video to YouTube, Vimeo, or other web-based platform, you might consider selecting a compressed file version, which is a lower quality but smaller file size that will take less time to upload. The most common compressed type of video file is .mp4. Note that once you save a movie file, you cannot change this rendered file. If you would like to make any further edits to the video (e.g., you notice a misspelling in the text), you will need to do this in the DV editing project file, and then re-save (i.e., render) a new final movie file.

Lastly, because many email programs have file size attachment limitations and video files tend to be quite large, emailing them to others often proves difficult. Options might include compressing the file to a zip file prior to emailing, sharing files using online data storage (e.g., Google Drive, Dropbox, iCloud, Office 365), posting on social media (e.g., Instagram, Facebook, Twitter), or sharing links after you have uploaded the video to a video-sharing website (e.g., YouTube, Vimeo, TeacherTube, Twitch). Although YouTube is the most popular, creating a YouTube channel is beyond the scope of this book. However, simply search "Creating a YouTube Channel Tutorial" within YouTube for step-by-step directions. Be sure to select a recently posted video for the most up-to-date directions. See Technology Tips From the Field for a practitioner's perspective of recording, editing, and disseminating DV.

Conclusion

This chapter provided practical tips and suggestions regarding attaining DV equipment as well as a basic overview of simple DV recording and editing. Special attention was paid to capturing audio with a wireless microphone and using a tripod. Knowing how to effectively record and edit DV will not only assist with learner assessment, but the incorporation of self-created quality videos can also help enhance classroom management, augment instruction, deliver professional development, and advocate for your program. Will you take your program to the next level through the integration of DV?

Key Terms

action DV camcorders—Also known as action-cams (e.g., GoPro HERO); DV camcorders designed for capturing DV while immersed in an environment or participating in an activity.

data storage—Collective methods in which digital information is retained; for DV camcorders or DV cameras, this may be internal storage (e.g., flash memory or hard drive), removable memory card storage, or a combination of both.

DV (digital video)—Electronic version of motion pictures in which encoded data digital images are displayed in rapid succession with accompanying audio (if included).

DV recording—Video recorded in a digital format and saved via the data storage technique specific to the recording device (e.g., internal storage, memory card).

DV camcorder—A digital device that captures video and audio and records it via a hard drive or flash memory into media storage.

DV camera—An electronic device (e.g., DV camcorders, action DV camcorders, mobile devices with DV camcorders) that records live event motion picture information (including audio) to DV data storage formats; types include DV camcorders and mobile devices with DV camcorders.

DV editing—The process of using computer software to manipulate and arrange video, digital images or text, and audio in order to structure and present a final DV product.

mobile device—A portable handheld computing device with a rechargeable battery, often with a touchscreen display, such as smartphones and tablets.

monopod—Also called a unipod; consists of a long single telescoping pole that can assist with stabilizing a DV camera (similar to a tripod, but must be held constantly).

movie file—The finalized edited DV file (i.e., the rendered file) that is rendered typically by selecting "Save Movie" or "Publish Movie," depending on the DV editing software.

panning—Moving a camcorder along with a moving subject (i.e., tracking) or moving the camcorder across an entire scene (i.e., panorama), often through the use of a tripod or monopod.

preview pane—A video playback area within DV editing software that permits the user to view the edited version of the video prior to rendering the final movie file.

project file—The DV working file specific to the editing software being used; use this file to make changes to the DV project prior to saving (i.e., rendering) the final movie file.

rendering—Synthesizing and saving everything that was done while editing the DV project within the DV project file and converting it to the final movie file.

scrub bar—A solid vertical line within most DV editing software programs that overlays all three editing tracks (video, audio, and text) on the editing timeline (i.e., storyboard pane) and assists the user in finding exact video frames and audio sounds so that precise editing may occur (cut, trim, split, add transition, fade audio in and out, etc.).

smartphone—A mobile phone with advanced computer features, such as a DV camera with microphone, touchscreen display, Internet capability, and the ability to run downloaded applications (e.g., iPhone, Samsung Galaxy).

storyboard pane (i.e., timeline)—Comprised of the digital video track, the audio track, and the text track all layered and sequenced within the DV editing software program.

tablet—Thin and flat mobile computing device with an operating system, typically with Internet accessibility, LCD touchscreen display, and DV camera, that is capable of downloading and running computer applications (e.g., iPad and iPod Touch, Samsung Galaxy Tab, Amazon Kindle Fire).

timeline—See "storyboard pane."

tripod—A portable three-legged stand that, when attached to a DV camera, can elevate and provide stable video capture; for still photography, tripods are primarily used for long exposures or with long telephoto lenses.

wireless microphone—Also known as a radio microphone; allows you to collect audio from a person speaking via a microphone and wireless battery-powered transmitter to a receiver unit connected to a DV camcorder or mobile device.

Review Questions

1. What are some scenarios in which a physical educator, health educator, or coach might utilize digital video recording and editing skills?

2. What equipment or software is necessary to record digital video?

3. What features might be important to consider when selecting a digital video camcorder to purchase? (Consider what you would use it for.)

4. What are the pros and cons to recording with a mobile device?
5. What are the major considerations for recording quality digital video?
6. What equipment and software is necessary to edit digital video?
7. Name some common digital video editing tools and functions.
8. What are important things to remember when saving and sharing digital video files?

Discussion Questions

1. Do you think this book chapter is unnecessary? In other words, do physical educators, health educators, and coaches need to know how to record and edit digital video? Why or why not?

2. Describe how you might use digital video recording equipment. What digital video recording equipment would you need and what features of each would be important to accomplish this?

3. Because most people record digital video with their smartphone, are digital video camcorders or other digital video recording devices necessary for physical educators, health educators, or coaches? Why or why not?

PART V

Technology for Professional Development and Advocacy

12

Technology for Professional Development

Chapter Objectives

When you have completed this chapter, you will be able to do the following:

1. Identify a variety of high-quality online professional development opportunities.
2. Describe the types of formal and informal online professional development.
3. Determine which types of online professional development are appropriate for different needs.
4. Identify ways to manage a digital footprint.

Professionals in the physical education, health education, and coaching fields receive a great deal of knowledge and skills in their initial degree programs. Although this information is comprehensive and designed to ready individuals for teaching and coaching, the learning doesn't stop there. Great instructors spend their careers growing and learning new techniques and skills to stay abreast of the latest and greatest information through engagement in lifelong **professional development**.

There are many reasons why instructors might engage in professional development. The 2017 National Standards for Initial Physical Education Teacher Education state that "physical education candidates demonstrate behaviors essential to becoming effective professionals," and that they will "engage in continued professional growth and collaboration in schools and/or professional organizations" (Society of Health and Physical Educators America, 2017, p. 6). This is just the start to the expectation that teachers engage in professional development. Certified physical and health education teachers often need to earn continuing education credit every few years to maintain teaching licensure. For example, a certified teacher in the state of Virginia must earn 180 professional development points every five years. These points can be accumulated through a variety of subject-related activities, such as earning college credit, attending professional conferences, development of curriculum, publication of articles or books, and mentorship of other teachers (Virginia Department of Education, 2017). School districts often provide teachers with in-house workshops that can help them earn their professional development credits; however, many are not subject-specific and physical and health educators may prefer to pursue more relevant opportunities outside of the school walls. Teachers and coaches may also engage in professional development to increase qualifications or compensation. For example, a coach may complete additional first aid or other safety certifications to become more qualified for a specific coaching position, or a teacher may pursue a graduate degree to move up the pay scale. Most importantly, professional development offers teachers and coaches the opportunity to keep up to date in their field.

INFORMAL PROFESSIONAL DEVELOPMENT

Professionals who seek to connect with like-minded colleagues, gain new ideas, and have questions answered in a quick and less formal atmosphere can do so online through various web-based resources and networks, such as social media, websites, podcasts, forums, and e-newsletters.

Social Media

Social media consists of interactive virtual networks of individuals who can communicate, share media, and blog with one another **synchronously** and **asynchronously** through an online platform. Although social media is often used for personal networking among friends and family, it has evolved in a professional sense, and individuals may also use it to network with colleagues and seek new information and ideas.

There are several different types of social media. The following are most useful for professional development: social networks (e.g., Facebook, LinkedIn, Twitter, Voxer, Google+), media sharing (e.g., Instagram, Snapchat, YouTube, Vimeo), and bookmarking and content gathering (e.g., Pinterest). Physical educators, health educators, and coaches can engage with social media by networking with other professionals within their area of interest. There are several ways to accomplish this, ranging from simply following other professionals in the field to keep abreast of what they are sharing, to actively participating in dialogue about a particular topic. For example, educators and coaches using Twitter can search for a particular topic, such as volleyball, to view what others have posted about that topic. Users can also share ideas or post questions and include a key phrase, or hashtag (#) (e.g., #physed), as well as tag other individuals or organizations (e.g., @SHAPE_America) to attract other professionals, which usually leads to quick and multiple responses. Figure 12.1 displays a question posed from a health teacher looking for goal-setting activities.

Professionals can also participate in a Twitter chat, where a group of Twitter users meet at a predetermined time to discuss a topic using a particular hashtag. Questions will be posted by the chat leader and participants then respond using the hashtag. Twitter chats are quick (usually about one hour) and sometimes difficult to follow due to the number and speed of the responses. Similarly, a Twitter slow chat has the same concept, but only one question is posed and individuals can respond over the course of an entire day. Some examples of Twitter chats for teachers are #slowchatpe, #pechat, #espechat, and #healthedchat. Although there is a vast amount of information available through social media, be cautious—anyone can post just about anything, and you must be able to evaluate the quality of the idea and the source.

Joey Feith
@JoeyFeith

Here's how the new FMS Skill Posters and FMS Key Cards look like when printed/laminated. My G1 student we're using them today in #physed! Learn more here: thephysicaleducator.com/2018/09/12/the... #pegeeks

2:25 PM · Sep 12, 2018 · Twitter for iPhone

Sharing new ideas through social media.

Reprinted by permission from Joey Feith.

Another type of social media that allows for more in-depth discussion is Voxer, a free application that allows users to speak to one another in real time. This walkie-talkie-style social media app allows for multiple simultaneous users and specialized groups can be formed to focus on specific discussion topics. Given that physical and health educators can often feel isolated in their organizations, Voxer gives them an opportunity to connect with like-minded professionals (Vasily, 2016).

Although much professional development is still offered in traditional, face-to-face formats, such as in-person workshops, conferences, and trainings, advances in technology have provided opportunities for professional development to happen virtually anywhere, anytime. There has been a growing need for online professional development for teachers and coaches due to time constraints and frustration with lack of choice or autonomy (Elliott, 2017; Rodesiler, 2017). Online professional development comes in many formats and can range from informal seeking of information through a website search or chat with a distant colleague to formal completion of online degree programs. This chapter will showcase many of the online professional development opportunities available for physical educators, health educators, and coaches.

Websites, Forums, and E-Newsletters

There are several organizations and individuals who have created web-based resources for professionals to learn and grow. Physical educators, health educators, and coaches

Rebekah Sweat
@coachsweatPE

Does anyone have any ideas for a fun activity for a goal setting unit? This is for my health classroom. Thank you! #healthed #physed

3:55 PM · Sep 10, 2018 · Twitter Web Client

1 Like

Jeff Bartlett @bartletthealth · Sep 10, 2018
Replying to @coachsweatPE
My colleague @LaRocqueHealth & I have students take on the role of a wellness coach to develop a SMART Goal Game Plan for a "client" based on a personal wellness assessment #healthed

3

Reprinted by permission from Rebekah Sweat.

Figure 12.1   Health teacher uses hashtags (#physed and #healthed) to seek new ideas for an upcoming unit.

WHAT DOES THE RESEARCH SAY?

Social Media Use Among Teachers as Effective Professional Development

Online professional development, particularly social media, has been shown to be an effective means to growing as a teaching professional. Teachers are able to connect with one another and generate and share ideas through social media (Greenhow & Lewin, 2016). Goodyear, Casey, and Kirk (2014) found that physical education teachers' use of Facebook and Twitter supported their pedagogical innovation and shared practices through a community of practice. In order for it to be effective, however, professionals must first learn and be comfortable with the technology to increase satisfaction and gain benefits (Elliott, 2017; Tella, 2011). Therefore, engaging with online platforms you are already familiar with may enhance your professional development experience.

can benefit from websites that contain relevant information, standards, teaching and assessment ideas, job postings, and more. A great example is SHAPE America's website, which includes information on professional development opportunities, standards and guidelines, grants, events and conferences, and other resources and publications. Additionally, mySHAPE America is an interactive online community where professionals can connect with one another through social media sharing features, the SHAPE America blog, a member forum, and a member voices section with personal stories. Within the members-only forum, individuals can share and access documents, and special interest groups focus on particular topics, such as adapted physical education or physical activity programs. Other websites provide similar content as SHAPE America's, with other specific resources. PE Central, for example, includes content such as lesson planning and assessment ideas, best practices, and videos.

Podcasts

Many professionals seek out new information through listening to prerecorded audio files surrounding specific topics of interest. These audio files, or **podcasts**, are a great way to informally learn about current events, gather new ideas, or get to know professionals in the field. Many podcasts in the education and coaching worlds can be accessed directly from professional websites and listened to online or downloaded for offline listening. Table 12.1 includes a list of sources and podcasts related to physical education, health education, and coaching.

Check out the web resource for more information and activities on informal professional development.

FORMAL PROFESSIONAL DEVELOPMENT

Teachers and coaches who are seeking more formal avenues to grow as a professional may consider participating in online seminars, conferences, courses, or degree programs. These options may lead to earning credit, certification, or other forms of documented training that could enhance qualifications, compensation, or position within an educational or sport organization.

Table 12.1 Suggested Podcasts for Physical Educators, Health Educators, and Coaches

Focus	Sources	Podcast topics
Physical education	• Physedagogy • Online Physical Education Network	• Student-centered PE • Cooperative learning • Administrative support
Health education	• SHAPE America Podcast • CDC Healthy Schools Podcast	• Health education teacher leadership • Healthy eating and academic achievement
Coaching	• Sports Coach Radio • Winning Youth Coaching	• Effective team motivation • Your coaching purpose versus your coaching goals

Adapted from U.S. Department of Education Office of Educational Technology (2014).

Webinars

A **webinar** is an interactive, web-based seminar delivered synchronously through video conferencing software. The presenter and attendees can interact through two-way audio and video, instant messaging, polls or surveys, desktop sharing, and file sharing. Participants at the very least need a computer with Internet access and speakers, but would benefit from a microphone, headphones, and a webcam for full interactivity. Webinars can also be viewed from smartphones and tablets, depending on the software used by the presenter. Webinars are usually focused on a specific topic and are often short and concise. They may be recorded and available for viewing asynchronously after the session has ended; however, interactivity is no longer an option.

Benefits of webinars include the ability to attend from anywhere with an Internet connection, opportunities to directly interact and connect with the presenter and other attendees, and engagement in a focused session directly related to a topic of interest. On the other hand, a webinar, while relatively convenient, is scheduled for a specific date and time that may not fit the schedules of all those who wish to participate. These individuals may need to settle for accessing the archived webinar. Additionally, though many webinars are free of charge, some may require a fee to participate, depending on the source. The SHAPE America Online Institute, for example, offers a variety of webinars for physical education, health education, and coaching professionals. These include free and paid webinars where participants can earn contact hours and continuing education credits.

Online Conferences

A professional development conference typically consists of a collection of sessions, workshops, and speeches related to a particular topic area and is traditionally held over the course of a several days at a single location. Attendees travel to the conference and can select sessions of interest and network with colleagues throughout the planned events on-site. Although these conferences are beneficial, barriers such as time and cost often limit professionals' attendance, particularly for teachers and coaches. A worthwhile alternative to attending a traditional conference is an online conference. These conferences, similar to traditional conferences, host a series of web-based sessions, or webinars, on particular topics related to the conference theme.

Accessing an online conference usually requires online registration, a potential fee, and working sessions into your schedule. There is usually a set date and time for each session, and you will need access to your computer or device to view and participate synchronously. It is important to note the time zone of the conference and adjust your schedule to match as needed. Many conferences will also archive their sessions and allow you to view them on demand. Similarly to one-time webinars, participating in live online conference sessions allows for interaction with the presenter and other attendees. Online conferences typically have much lower registration fees compared to on-site conferences and some are even offered at no charge. Physical educators, for example, can register for free for the annual Connected PE Online Physical Education Conference. In 2018, this conference was held for seven days and had 21 sessions to choose from, with 500 available "seats" per session. Presenters included professionals who were experts in their session area, which included topics such as elementary fitness, feedback, motivation, assessment tools and strategies, flipped learning, and other technology. Similarly, health and physical educators also have the opportunity to attend the free #PhysEdSummit virtual conference yearly, which consists of 50-minute webcasts on best practices, teaching strategies, and resources. For those unable to attend live, all sessions were accessible on the PHYSEDagogy YouTube channel and website.

Single-Subject Certificate Courses

For professionals looking to gain additional credentials, single-subject certificate courses are a good option. A classic example is a first aid and CPR course, which is typically required of physical education teachers and coaches. These courses have traditionally been offered in classroom formats through organizations such as the American Red Cross or American Heart Association. They are now, however, offered in blended (online course plus hands-on sessions) and fully online formats, which adds convenience for attendees to complete on their own schedules. Completion of these courses will lead to a certificate or card. Coaches particularly benefit from completing coaching-specific certificate courses, as these are often required by youth sport programs, and many of these are offered online. Some examples of online coaching courses and certificates include general coaching courses, such as those offered through the Positive Coaching Alliance (~$30/course), sport-specific courses, such as the USA Track and Field's Coaching Track and Field basic course (~$85), or other safety courses, such as the National Alliance for Youth Sports' Concussion Training course (free).

Online College or University Programs and Courses

For individuals willing to invest more time and money into their professional development, many colleges and universities offer everything from single, one- to three-credit courses to entire degree programs in an online or hybrid format. Most of these courses, certificates, and degree programs are offered directly by the college or university, and students will need to pay for any required tuition, fees, and course materials. Courses may vary in terms of delivery mode (e.g., synchronous or asynchronous, assignment types, interaction level), but they are often hosted in a learning management system (e.g., Blackboard, Canvas, Desire2Learn, etc.) that helps with organization and delivery of the course. Some courses or programs may also be offered in a hybrid format, in which some of the course takes place online and other parts on campus. The University of Northern Colorado (UNC), for example offers a fully online master of arts in sports coaching degree program to enhance coaching knowledge and expertise and advance existing coaching practices. UNC also offers an online-hybrid program, the master of arts in teaching physical education and physical activity leadership, which meets online during fall and spring semesters, with one on-campus portion in the summer. Both of these programs, as well as other programs around the globe, are designed to meet the needs of working professionals through high-quality, online offerings.

IDENTIFYING APPROPRIATE AND HIGH-QUALITY ONLINE PROFESSIONAL DEVELOPMENT

Before engaging in online professional development, it is important to first think about why you are seeking it out in the first place. Do you simply have a question that can quickly be answered by another colleague in your field? Are you seeking new coaching strategies to implement in the coming season? Are you looking to earn credits for renewal or to earn more money? Are you looking to increase your professional network? These are important to ask yourself before deciding what professional development to select. Second, you must evaluate the quality of the online professional development to ensure you are getting accurate, up-to-date information, as well as to determine if it will satisfy your needs appropriately. The fact that the Internet is open to everyone and full of what seems like endless information can be both beneficial but also deceiving. There are plenty of reputable websites, webinars, and programs available to gain new information, but it is important to research and recognize the quality and credentials of each to ensure high-quality professional development experiences. When evaluating an online professional development, there are several characteristics that should be present. The quality checklist in figure 12.2 contains some important qualities to consider.

Additionally, college credit can also be earned by completing courses through other entities. PE Central, for example, has a professional development link that leads to informational articles, blogs, forums, and workshops. They offer both self-paced short online courses as well as traditional graduate online courses (offered through their partner, Adams State University) for professionals to improve teaching and earn continuing education credits, professional development hours, or graduate credit. For example, the

Figure 12.2 Online professional development quality checklist.

- [ ] Active participation by attendees
- [ ] High engagement and relevance to the subject
- [ ] Appropriately paced
- [ ] Led by skilled and knowledgeable facilitators
- [ ] Aligned with program goals
- [ ] Provides opportunities to make connections with other professionals
- [ ] Promotes reflection through online tools
- [ ] Includes results that can be immediately put into practice

Adapted from U.S. Department of Education Office of Educational Technology (2014).

Introduction to Teaching Personal and Social Responsibility short course costs $99.00, can be completed anytime, and will result in earning 10 PD hours and 1 CEU credit (for an extra charge). Another example is the Physical Education for Children With Autism course, which costs $499 plus the textbook, lasts for 12 weeks with set dates, and has an option for three graduate credits (additional $165).

Finally, there is a growing trend of Massive Open Online Courses (MOOCs), usually offered through universities in conjunction with other organizations, which are free online courses structured similarly to traditional online university courses, complete with lectures, quizzes, and discussions. MOOCs related to physical education, health education, and coaching are limited, but there is potential for growth in this area in the future. Two examples of MOOCs in this area are the Outstanding Physical Education Lessons and Youth Football Coaching: Developing Creative Players courses offered through the University of Birmingham in conjunction with FutureLearn.

BUILDING AND MAINTAINING YOUR PROFESSIONAL PRESENCE WITH TECHNOLOGY

Professional development is more than seeking new information to enhance your practice. It also involves the evolution of yourself as a professional. Given the multitude of opportunities for educators and coaches to participate and interact with others online, your online identity, or professional presence, is important to consider. There are several considerations to take into account about how you present yourself and suggestions on how to boost your professional presence online through e-portfolios, professional websites, and social media.

E-Portfolios, Professional Websites, and Social Media

A portfolio usually consists of a collection of artifacts that represent one's work and accomplishments. Portfolios for teachers and coaches may consist of lesson or practice plans, assessments, teaching or coaching videos, certifications, and other items that exemplify their work and are often used by beginning or transitioning professionals when seeking new positions. Traditionally, portfolios were kept in binders or folders and were only shown to a limited number of individuals; however, with modern technology, online or e-portfolios can be created to showcase work to a broader audience. Many teacher and coach preparation programs are turning to e-portfolios to gather and assess student achievements with regard to standards and accreditation, and students can then use the e-portfolios by sharing them with potential employers. For example, physical education and sport coaching major students at the University of Northern Colorado create a professional online portfolio website (figure 12.3) that includes a resume, teaching philosophy, professional development activities, and reflections and artifacts related to each of the National Standards for Initial Physical Education Teacher Education (Society of Health and Physical Educators America, 2017) or National Standards for Sport Coaches (Society of Health and Physical Educators America, 2005). In-service professionals who are not seeking new positions can build or transform their e-portfolios into personal websites that continue to showcase their work as a teacher or coach and can share that website with their community to allow parents, students, and other organization personnel to get to know them better. Although e-portfolios are created to showcase achievements, teachers and coaches can create other types of websites to build an online professional presence, such as a website created to host physical and health education or coaching information to be shared with students, athletes, and parents. These websites can include informa-

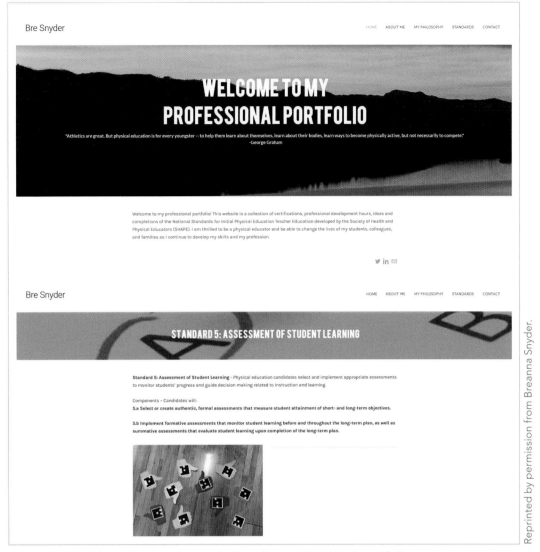

Figure 12.3 Physical education major's online professional portfolio.

tion about the instructor, as well as announcements, assignments, schedules, and more.

E-portfolios and professional websites have become increasingly easier to create. In the past, users needed to learn coding and purchase expensive software; however, advances in technology now allow anyone to create a website for little to no cost. Additionally, website design features are becoming more user friendly and intuitive, so it is simple to create one. Many schools and sport organizations have predetermined website platforms for teachers and coaches, which are connected to the organization's main website for easy navigation. If your organization does not have the capability for a website, however, professionals can use free or low-cost platforms, such as Google Sites, Weebly, and Wix.

As discussed earlier in this chapter, social media provides quick and easy access to networks of individuals and information. Because social networking is free to use and largely ubiquitous, many people use it for both personal and professional purposes. It is important to consider building your professional presence in this setting, but limiting per-

TECHNOLOGY TIPS FROM THE FIELD

Pursuing an Online Master's Degree in Sport Coaching

Dan Ogden, M.A.
Physical education teacher and football and track and field coach
Kalispell Middle School, Kalispell, Montana

Why did you pursue an online master's degree in sports coaching?
Sports were always a part of my life, and I wanted to be a professional in it. I love teaching, but I also really want to be a head coach. In order to do that, you need to have strong credentials and be competitive. I also wanted to move up on the teacher pay scale. As I always say, either you're getting better or you're getting worse. There's no such thing as staying the same, and I wanted to get better.

What are the highlights of an online degree program?
Convenience! The benefit of the online program is that I didn't have to leave the comfort of home and didn't have to travel for class. It was also somewhat self-paced, and I could work on it on my own schedule, which is great for a busy teacher/coach. I also enjoyed communication among classmates through discussion boards and sharing ideas with peers and professors.

What are the challenges associated with completing an online degree program?
At first it was awkward not having face to face contact . . . where you are interacting through a screen and it is hard to pick up on body language and being personal with people. Eventually, however, I grew to enjoy it, especially since I was in a cohort. It was a good thing to be a part of and get to know each other, even through the online format.

What suggestions do you have for other professionals considering an online degree program?
Study hard so you can play easy. Do your work early; be persistent. Know there's a time commitment. Rely on work ethic. Set aside time out of each week to get things done.

Mr. Ogden's introduction video for a course in his online master's degree program.
Courtesy of Dan Ogden.

sonal posts may be important. Every post, comment, share, follow, and hashtag should be intentional and should further the image you seek to portray of yourself as a professional.

Protecting Your Digital Footprint

Think about all of the activities you have engaged in through the web, including email correspondence, web searches, social media interactions (e.g., posts, connections, likes, followings, messages, shares, retweets), music and videos downloaded, photos uploaded, games played, app use, and more. Throughout all of your activity, you have created a digital identity, or **digital footprint**, which is the trail of personal information about yourself available online. This includes both active (voluntary online activity, such as uploading photos or commenting on a post) and passive (collected data, such as cookies or browsing history) content (Madden, Fox, Smith, & Vitak, 2007). Given the nature of trust that teachers and coaches are placed into within their positions, they must be able to manage their digital footprints to establish and maintain the respect of all stakeholders (e.g., students, parents, community members). The International Society for Technology in Education's Standards for Educators state that educators should "responsibly participate in the digital world," and particularly, "model and promote management of . . . digital identity" (ISTE, 2018). Although this chapter focuses on using online resources in a professional sense, it is important to understand that all of your online activity contributes to your digital footprint, and you should always be aware of the potential to contribute to this ever-important reputation you are creating for yourself. When thinking about managing your digital footprint, consider the tips offered in figure 12.4. Your digital footprint may be as important as your resume someday, and managing it is a critical skill for protecting your professional reputation (Hengstler, 2011).

Separate personal and professional profiles

Keep software up to date

Use strong passwords

Think before you post

Monitor yourself online

Maintain professional boundaries

Understand and update privacy settings

Be strategic about what you share

Figure 12.4 Tips to manage your digital footprint.

Check out the web resource to complete the Protecting Your Digital Footprint activity.

Conclusion

This chapter discusses the use of technology for professional development for physical educators, health educators, and coaches. There are many informal and formal online resources for professionals that provide opportunities for networking, knowledge generation, and overall growth. Teachers and coaches must be able to identify the purpose for the professional development and then evaluate its quality, all while keeping a professional digital footprint.

Key Terms

asynchronous—Not occurring at the same time.

digital footprint—Trail of personal information about yourself available online.

forum—A place, meeting, or medium where ideas are exchanged on a specific topic.

professional development—Specialized training to help educators improve knowledge, skill, and effectiveness.

podcast—Digital audio program (discussion or music) that can be downloaded from the Internet.

social media—Interactive virtual networks of individuals who can communicate, share media, and blog with one another synchronously and asynchronously through an online platform.

synchronous—Occurring at the same time.

webinar—An interactive, web-based seminar delivered synchronously through video conferencing software.

Review Questions

1. What are the advantages of online professional development?
2. List three types of informal and three types of formal online professional development.
3. Describe a type of online professional development that could be used for continuing education credit.
4. List three social media platforms where you could gain professional development.
5. How can you protect your digital footprint?

Discussion Questions

1. What type of online professional development is best for you at this point in your career?
2. How have you used social media in the past, and how could you incorporate social media into your professional development?
3. How could you build your professional presence online?

13

Technology for Advocacy

Chapter Objectives

When you have completed this chapter, you will be able to do the following:

1. Identify a variety of high-quality online advocacy resources and tools.
2. Identify a variety of ways to advocate for physical education, health education, and coaching using technology.
3. Determine which types of digital advocacy tools are appropriate for different needs.
4. Identify benefits and limitations of using technology to advocate for your needs.

Maskot/Getty Images

It is no secret that health and physical education and athletics have long been negatively stereotyped. The misconceptions of the value and content of physical and health education, as well as athletics, have led to reduced financial, political, and administrative support, as well as student and athlete participation. Many educators and coaches find themselves constantly standing up for their programs to prove their worth. With growing public awareness of the rise in obesity, decline in physical activity, and importance of health and physical fitness, a focus on the importance of physical education, health education, and athletics is warranted. Although professionals do their best to implement quality programs, they must rely on others to support their programs in order for them to be successful. To that end, there has been a surge in advocacy efforts to combat negative stereotypes and increase support for physical and health education. The challenge is finding a way to quickly and efficiently reach as many individuals as possible. The need for advocacy for these programs has reached an all-time high; thankfully, so has the capability of technology to help. This chapter will provide brief information on advocacy issues in physical education, health education, and coaching, followed by an overview of the following technology tools to aid in advocacy efforts:

- Online resources
- Email
- Virtual newsletters and infographics
- Teacher and coach websites
- Social media
- Digital video

ADVOCACY ISSUES IN PHYSICAL EDUCATION, HEALTH EDUCATION, AND COACHING

Advocacy, or communicating to persuade or influence others or bring about change, is a practice that all physical educators, health educators, and coaches should be able to accomplish. "Advocacy has the potential to shape or change policy in a way that can impact the health of thousands, if not millions, of people" (Galer-Unti, Tappe, & Lachenmayr, 2004, p. 287). Although many would consider their issues to be local to their school or program, some advocacy efforts lead to widespread support and change. Because of the importance of advocacy and the change it can effect, physical educators, health educators, and coaches are all expected to advocate in one way or another, as stated in their respective standards. See table 13.1 for standards related to advocacy.

Each profession has its own set of issues that could benefit from some level of advocacy, such as funding, administrative and leadership support, parental support, student and athlete buy-in, and political support.

There are several strategies often used to advocate for a cause. Prior to modern digital technology, individuals would have to hold on-site meetings, mail flyers, and make phone calls to connect with **stakeholders**, or individuals or groups who have an interest in decisions or activities of an organization, which might include students, parents, administrators, other teachers, policy makers, community members, and more. Now there are a variety of technology resources and tools available to enhance advocacy efforts, which are presented in the following sections.

Table 13.1   Advocacy Standards from SHAPE America

Profession	Standards
Physical education	Describe strategies, including the use of technology, for the promotion and advocacy of physical education and expanded physical activity opportunities. (Society of Health and Physical Educators America, 2017, 6.a)
Health education	Candidates advocate for health education as an essential component of the school community that supports the diverse needs of all learners and contributes to the school's mission. (Society of Health and Physical Educators America, 2018a, 5.f)
Coaching	Acquire and utilize interpersonal and communication skills . . . Sport coaches work to develop their oral and written communication skills to concisely and clearly communicate information, elicit community support, and advocate for the program. (Society of Health and Physical Educators America, 2019, standard 9) Provide accurate information about drugs and supplements to athletes and advocate for drug-free sport participation. (Society of Health and Physical Educators America, 2019, standard 20)

TECHNOLOGY TOOLS FOR ADVOCACY

It is important to understand what issue you are trying to advocate for and who your audience should be before deciding on what technology to use to aid in your efforts. Using a variety of technology tools can help you gather more information and connect with more stakeholders. Some groups may feel more comfortable with email, whereas others may use other modes, such as social media or blogs. Using a wide variety of technology resources to gather information and spread advocacy messages will ensure higher levels of engagement from the stakeholders you wish to reach. The following sections provide information about technology that can help enhance your advocacy efforts, with examples specific to physical education, health education, and coaching.

WHAT DOES THE RESEARCH SAY?

Advocacy Works

History shows that advocating for change works. "The greatest advancements in improving public health in the 20th century are the result of change in policy or regulation" (Thackeray & Hunter, 2010, p. 576). Advocacy efforts have led to changes in policy or regulations, resulting in—for example—the reduction of risky behaviors, such as tobacco use, motor vehicle crashes, and tooth decay (CDC, 1999a; 1999b). Advocates for women led to the passing of Title IX in 1972, which prohibits sex discrimination in any educational program or activity receiving any type of federal aid, giving girls and women an equal opportunity to participate in sports. Since then, girls' participation in high school athletics has increased more than 1000%. There is, however, a need for more advocacy—girls still get 1.2 million fewer participation opportunities than boys (Women's Sports Foundation, 2019). The Women's Sports Foundation hosts relevant information, position statements, research, and even an interactive messenger game (available on Facebook Messenger or Kik) that helps users navigate through the rights that Title IX protects in athletics.

Online Advocacy Resources

When it comes to learning ways to advocate for your profession, you can look to the Internet for resources. These resources may include position statements from professional organizations, research reports, policy guides, success stories, and links to other sources of information or events. SHAPE America's Advocacy Toolkit, for example, can be used by physical and health educators to inform themselves and other stakeholders of the importance of their subject areas. For example, if a school permits interscholastic sports and marching band as substitutes for physical education, the physical education teacher could advocate for policy change using the well-written and research-based position statement, *Physical Education Is Essential for All Students: No Substitutions, Waivers or Exemptions for Physical Education* (Society of Health and Physical Educators America, 2018b). The Toolkit also includes webinars, blogs, a legislative action center, and other guidance documents. Physical and health educators can visit other organization's resources online, such as Support Real Teachers and Society for Public Health Education, which contain general advocacy tips, videos, and other documents to help support these programs. Coaches can visit the National Alliance for Youth Sports, National Council of Youth Sports, and Positive Coaching Alliance websites for coaching-related events, information, and other resources. The National Council of Youth Sports website, for example, contains a Call to Action section, which provides information on the latest issues facing youth sports. Table 13.2 contains a list of reputable online sources to gather useful information for advocacy.

Email and Listservs

Electronic mail, better known as **email**, are messages sent between people using electronic devices. Although email seems like a simple tool, it may be one of the most logical ways to reach stakeholders, because most Americans have an email account for work or personal use and users check email regularly. If you already have access to the email addresses for a particular population, it would be relatively easy to send messages, links, or attachments to them via email. For example, to communicate with parents regarding their children's successes in physical education, it is simple to produce and attach a newsletter to a group email. There are times, however, when you wish to reach a bigger audience but do not have access to their email addresses. In this case, it may be beneficial to send your message through a **listserv**, which is an application that distributes messages to subscribers on an electronic mailing list. Professional teachers and coaches who

Table 13.2   Online Resources for Advocacy

Advocacy area	Resource
Physical education and health education	SHAPE America Adapted Physical Education National Standards Support Real Teachers PE Central Society for Public Health Education PE Links 4 U
Coaching	SHAPE America National Alliance for Youth Sports National Council of Youth Sports Positive Coaching Alliance NCAA

are members of professional organizations may subscribe to a listserv, which will send relevant messages to everyone who subscribes. You don't need to set up your own listserv to take advantage of them—you can ask organizations with many members to share your messages through their own listserv. For example, a school may have parents on their listserv and a professional organization will have teachers or coaches on theirs. Sending your message through these organizations, with permission, can reach a large audience.

Virtual Newsletters and Infographics

It was not long ago that teachers would send handwritten or typed notes or newsletters home with their students. Often serving as a friendly communication with parents and guardians about happenings in the school, newsletters were a great way to combine your news into one report that your audience can easily consume. Although informative, however, they were often lost in the shuffle of other papers sent home and could be wordy and unappealing. In the fast-paced world in which we live, many individuals prefer to receive information electronically; or if in print, prefer something eye-catching and easy to grasp at a glance. Virtual or electronic newsletters are just the ticket due to their low cost, attractive designs, ease of creation, and variety of options. Teachers and coaches can design simple yet effective virtual newsletters to inform parents of what their children are learning, share upcoming activities and events, and to advocate (e.g., brag about their program or ask for fundraising). If you want to take your virtual newsletter up a notch, incorporate **infographics**. Infographics are visual images that represent information or data at a glance, also referred to as *data visualization*. Figure 13.1 displays sample content ideas for your virtual newsletter.

Teacher and Coach Websites

Teachers and coaches can host a great deal of information on their professional website. Aside from announcements, upcoming events, lesson plans and practice schedules, learning tools, and more, the website can also serve in an advocacy capacity in several ways. First, a well-designed website can showcase a quality program to students, parents, administrators, and other stakeholders. By hosting valuable, educational information about your program, the website communicates to viewers the value of your profession. On the other hand, a disorganized, poorly designed website communicates just the opposite. Therefore, if you are going to host a website, be sure it is well executed. There are many simple website templates available to use if your organization does not have one for you. Weebly, Wix, and Google Sites all have a fairly intuitive, user-friendly interface that even the least experienced web designer can manage.

Not only can you share your program's highlights through your website, but you can include specific information, such as messages, research, statistics, photos, videos, and links to other websites. This content can be included as a way to advocate through education. For example, a coach may include statistics and facts on the dangers of anabolic steroid use on his team's website. This will bring parents' attention to the issue and inform athletes of the risks associated with it. Though indirect, it demonstrates the coach's stance on steroid use and advocates for the health of athletes.

Social Media

Using social media is one of the easiest ways to connect with stakeholders. All it takes is 280 characters (on Twitter), a few hashtags, and a tag or a handle, and you've sent your message to all of your followers and the followers of those you've tagged. There are several different social media options, including Twitter, Facebook, Instagram, Snapchat, Linke-

Virtual Newsletter Content

- Awards/achievements of you, your program/classes, your students
- Changes to the program
- Thanking stakeholders for their support
- Video highlighting successes or events that have occurred
- Tips to help students/athletes be successful
- Sample stories that have recently occurred within your program
- Sample stories that have recently occurred outside of your program, but are related
- Survey or poll to learn about stakeholder opinions or ideas
- Inspiring or humorous quotes
- Data/statistics from recent assessments/competitions
- Recommendations from related organizations related to your subject/sport (e.g., physical activity guidelines or water consumption recommendations)
- Highlight a student/athlete
- Photos of your program/students/athletes in action
- Call-to-action

There are several free or low-cost design software programs to choose from to create dynamic virtual newsletters, most of which have a free version, with the option for premium features or subscriptions for a fee:
- Canvas
- Easel.ly
- Piktochart
- Smore
- Vennage
- Visme

When creating your newsletter, there are some tips to consider to increase the attractiveness of your virtual newsletter:
- Create it for your target audience
- Leave plenty of (white) space
- Use a multi-column layout
- Minimize text
- Use graphics/visuals, but not too many
- Make it colorful, but keep them complementary
- Keep it simple and to the point

Once your virtual newsletter is created, you must find the best ways to share it with stakeholders. Depending on your audience, your newsletter can be sent via email, posted to a school/program or teacher/coach website, and shared via social media; and while it is a "virtual" newsletter, there is no rule that says it can't be delivered the old fashioned way – printed and sent home with students in a folder. While this is costly and cumbersome, it will provide an opportunity to reach stakeholders who do not have access to the internet or do not have email or social media accounts.

Figure 13.1 Content ideas for virtual newsletters.
Based on PHEA.

dIn, and more, as discussed in previous chapters. You can easily promote your program, profession, or team by sharing photos, videos, or ideas that showcase your students. You can also gain a lot of information to support your cause by connecting to professionals and organizations who might share relevant and timely information through social media. In order to reach as many stakeholders as possible, there are a few tips to follow:

- Ensure you have a professional social media presence
- Invite stakeholders to follow your social media handle through email, linking it on your website, or even just announcing it at the next meeting
- Connect with or follow stakeholders of interest
- Include photos or videos for more attention
- Tag stakeholders or stakeholder groups so you know they see your message
- Include relevant hashtags (#) that are related to the issue

Recently, an elementary physical education teacher in Colorado hosted her first Parents Love PE week, where parents were invited to attend and participate in their children's physical education class. She promoted her program and the event through Twitter with the hashtag #ParentsLovePE. She took pictures throughout the week and posted them on Twitter. As a bonus, she created labels with the hashtag and a creative message that were attached to water bottles she handed out to participating parents (figure 13.2). This was all in an effort to involve parents and promote her program.

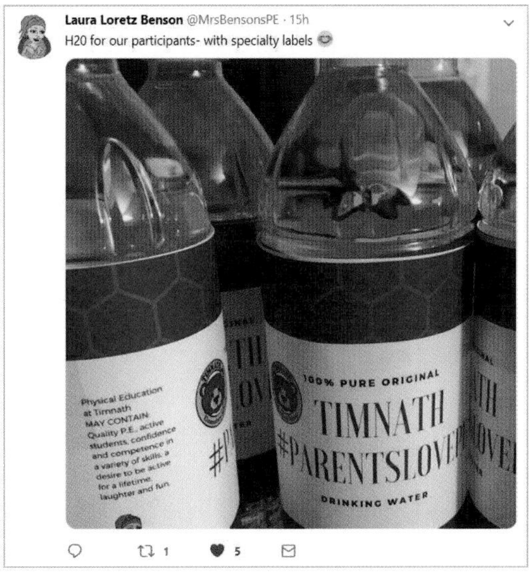

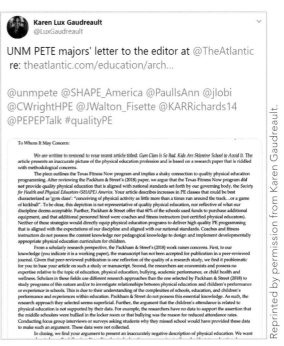

Figure 13.2 #ParentsLovePE water bottles.

Another example of using social media is to defend and advocate for physical education as a profession and a worthy subject in schools. In 2019, *The Atlantic* published an article in its education section titled "Gym Class Is So Bad, Kids Are Skipping School to Avoid It." This article caught the attention of many professionals and organizations, including SHAPE America, who shared an educated response to the article in defense of physical education via social media. A physical education teacher education coordinator at the University of New Mexico also shared a letter criticizing *The Atlantic*'s article via Twitter. She was able to strategically tag *The Atlantic* and SHAPE America to ensure that they and anyone else following them would see her tweet (figure 13.3).

Digital Video

Video is a powerful tool used to reach a broad range of audiences, and video capture, editing, production, and publishing have become relatively feasible tasks for anyone with a video camera or smartphone. There are many approaches to using digital video to advocate for your class. The video could be simply educational in nature. For example, a health educator could share a video on the newest dietary guidelines with students and parents in an effort to improve nutrition and curb unhealthy eating habits and obesity trends. Another example may be a physical education teacher who wants to convince her school district to increase physical education minutes to meet the recommendations set forth by SHAPE America. She could create a video to share with stakeholders on the importance and benefits of physical education. Although there are many pre-existing videos available to help advocate for the array of issues facing physical education, health education, and coaching professionals, it can be beneficial

To Whom It May Concern:

We are writing to respond to your recent article titled: *Gym Class Is So Bad, Kids Are Skipping School to Avoid It*. The article presents an inaccurate picture of the physical education profession and is based on a research paper that is riddled with methodological concerns.

The piece outlines the Texas Fitness Now program and implies a shaky connection to quality physical education programming. After reviewing the Packham & Street's (2018) paper, we argue that the Texas Fitness Now program ***did not*** provide quality physical education that is aligned with national standards set forth by our governing body, the *Society for Health and Physical Educators (SHAPE) America*. Your article describes increases in PE classes that could be best characterized as 'gym class': "conceiving of physical activity as little more than a times run around the track…or a game of kickball". To be clear, this depiction is not representative of quality physical education, nor reflective of what our discipline deems acceptable. Further, Packham & Street offer that 60% of the schools used funds to purchase additional equipment, and that additional personnel hired were coaches and fitness instructors (not certified physical educators). Neither of these strategies would directly equip physical education programs to deliver high quality PE programming that is aligned with the expectations of our discipline and aligned with our national standards. Coaches and fitness instructors do not possess the content knowledge nor pedagogical knowledge to design and implement developmentally appropriate physical education curriculum for children.

From a scholarly research perspective, the Packham & Street's (2018) work raises concerns. First, to our knowledge (you indicate it is a working paper), the manuscript has not been accepted for publication in a peer-reviewed journal. Given that peer-reviewed publication is one reflection of the quality of a research study, we find it problematic for you to base your article on such a study or manuscript. Second, the researchers are economists and possess no expertise relative to the topic of education, physical education, bullying, academic performance, or child health and wellness. Scholars in these fields use different research approaches than the one selected by Packham & Street (2018) to study programs of this nature and/or to investigate relationships between physical education and children's performance or experience in schools. This is due to their understanding of the complexities of schools, education, and children's performance and experiences within education. Packham & Street do not possess this essential knowledge. As such, the research approach they selected seems superficial. Further, the argument that the children's attendance is related to physical education is not supported by their data. For example, the researchers have no data to support the assertion that the middle schoolers were bullied in the locker room or that bullying was the reason for reduced attendance rates. Conducting focus group interviews or surveys asking students why they missed school would have provided these data to make such an argument. These data were not collected.

In closing, we find your argument to present an inaccurately negative description of physical education. We want

Figure 13.3 Advocating for physical education through Twitter.

Using Technology to Advocate for Physical Education

Jaimie McMullen, PhD
Associate Professor of Physical Education and Physical Activity Leadership, SHAPE Colorado President
University of Northern Colorado, School of Sport and Exercise Science

Why do you think it is important to advocate for physical education?
As a teacher educator, it is important to lead by example. I want students to see me advocating. I tell them that they need to advocate for their profession—so I feel the need to not only talk the talk, but also walk the walk. From a PE perspective, there is so much misinformation on who we are, what we do, and we need to continue to fight the good fight and let the world know that this is not their father's gym class.

What types of technology have you used to advocate for physical education?
I started as an undergraduate student at the University of Hawaii through the development of multimedia presentations, like videos on the purpose of PE. Then as a high school teacher in Iowa, my students used wearable technology that produced reports that were later shared with parents and community members. When I was teaching K-12 I would regularly reach out to the media to advocate for our program—they would publish articles about our program in the newspaper and sometimes our students would appear on the news. As I have progressed into higher education, I have tried to promote my physical education teacher education students through social media, like Twitter. This helps to highlight their accomplishments and celebrate them. Last week, for example, one of our graduates was doing something in the field that we try to teach our current students. It shows our current students that it is being done in the real world, and it was great to celebrate the good things our graduates are doing. Sharing this on Twitter was great for it.

What suggestions do you have for physical education teachers who wish to use technology to advocate for their programs?
People have to start somewhere. I teach a graduate level course on policy, advocacy, and leadership, where students create an infographic to promote physical activity to a specific stakeholder group. They also create a multimedia presentation on CSPAP. Change to Comprehensive School Physical Activity Programs that they could disseminate on their school's website. They also join Twitter. Some are active and others are anti-social media. I try to get them to understand that they should not join social media just to "like" each other's pictures, but rather to promote the things they are doing. Others can look to them for support, and parents at the school can follow to see what they are doing. If you share what you are doing in your program, it provides legitimacy to your program—another way to be accountable for providing quality PE and serve as an advocacy tool. Tech can help you share what you are doing with parents, administrators, policymakers, and others. Finally, technology is also helpful with data collection and dissemination. There is so much data located online—use the Internet as a tech tool. It is important to know where to find the data and know what data will help them.

How else have you involved your physical education teacher education students in your advocacy efforts related to technology?

If you look on social media, all of our state representatives have Twitter handles. I recently tweeted about a local legislative bill in Colorado and tagged the sponsoring representatives. They liked and retweeted it. There was an entire Twitter thread that started, and people shared their concerns about what the bill would do and concerns with quality. I then shared this thread with my preservice teachers so we could discuss the same concerns—and I used this as a learning opportunity. I also encouraged them to retweet about the bill so they can start to understand the impact of advocacy on their futures as professionals.

Jaimie McMullen
@DrJMcM

Super proud of my @UNCSportPed students who spent the day with me and @hillarymfranks at the Colorado State Capitol advocating for quality #health and #physed - they represented @UNC_Colorado very proudly! The future of the #physed profession is bright! @SHAPE_Colorado

Physical education major students lobbying for physical education shared via social media.
Reprinted by permission from Jamie McMullen.

to create your own, tailored to your specific issue and audience. Figure 13.4 displays a sample public service announcement project, with steps to plan content for an advocacy video on a topic of your choice. Once the plan and content are in place, you must then capture, edit, and publish your video.

Video Capture and Editing

Once well-planned and organized, video can be as elaborate or as simple as possible. If you are intending to capture live-action video, ideally, one would use a high-quality digital video camera mounted on a tripod. Additionally, using a wireless microphone is ideal to ensure audio is clear. If these tools are unavailable, using a smartphone to capture video is the most convenient option. If your video is not a live-action style, you may consider completing a screen capture of a visual presentation. For example, you could use Prezi to explain your idea through creative text and graphics. Using screen recording software, such as Camtasia, you can record your screen, then add video effects, transitions, audio, and more.

Once you have captured video, it will likely need some editing. Editing can include combining or cutting video clips and adding additional audio (e.g., voice-over, music), text layover, photographs, other external video content, and more. There are several video editing software programs available, such as iMovie, Windows Movie Maker, and Adobe Premiere, in addition to editing programs built into video capture programs, like Camtasia. If you are using your smartphone or tablet, there are several apps that provide user-friendly video editing capabilities, such as the iMovie app, available on IOS devices. Additionally, separate audio editing may be required; Audacity is one well-known program for doing so. If you are going to include music, sounds, or other images and are concerned about copyright issues, Jamendo, FreeSound, and Creative Commons contain

Figure 13.4 Advocating for physical education PSA video project.

As you know, physical education is among the most essential subjects in school, yet it continues to be marginalized. We need your help to educate the public on the importance of PE. You have been tasked to create a public service announcement (PSA) video to be shared with the world to save our profession. The health and well-being of our children are at stake! Use this template to plan your advocacy project.

CREATING AN OUTLINE

1. *Topic:* Determine the major focus for your video. What are the most important things to consider when advocating for PE? What does PE need in order to become as valued as it should be (a general overview of the importance of PE, focus on maximizing time allotted in schools, making it a graduation requirement, making it a requirement in your state, prioritizing it for ESSA funding, etc.)? _____

2. *Content:* Gather and organize facts, statistics, statements, and opinions that you collect on your issue (must be from reliable sources):

3.

Content type	Information
Facts, statistics, legislation	1. Sources used: 2. Sources used: 3. Sources used: 4. Sources used:
Opinions (be persuasive)	
Quotes from experts or well-known individuals	1. Sources used: 2. Sources used:

4. *Catchphrase:* Reinforce the main idea through a short and memorable catchphrase: _____

5. *Taking action:* Tell viewers what to do to help solve your issue (e.g., post on social media, complete a challenge, spread the word, etc.): _____

VIDEO PRODUCTION KEY REQUIREMENTS

- 1 to 3 minutes in length
- Use only footage and other materials you created yourself for this project or are licensed as free to use; do not use copyrighted music or materials
- Use any video program you would like to and are most comfortable with
- Involve your whole team in the video production!

content that can be used with some restrictions. See chapter 11 for more information on video capture and editing.

Video Publishing and Sharing

Where, when, and how you choose to publish your video will depend on your intended audience. If your goal is to simply convince the PTA to fundraise for new PE equipment, then a short video shown at the PTA meeting may be all that is needed. If you want to reach a larger audience, however, you'll need to share your video electronically. This can be done by attaching the video file (e.g., MP4) to an email message or directly posting the video to your website or social media page. Alternatively, you can publish your video on a video sharing website, such as YouTube or Vimeo, then share the link to the video with others easily through the same mechanisms.

Technology for Data Collection, Mining, and Reporting

An argument is always more persuasive when there is data to back one's position. Technology has made it quicker and easier to collect, analyze, and report data than ever before. The types of data you decide to use depends on the focus of your advocacy. For example, physical education teachers who wish to show the quality of their programs in terms of the amount of physical activity their students get (or don't get, due to barriers) can gather data with the use of technology. Students can wear heart rate monitors, accelerometers, or pedometers to gather minutes of moderate to vigorous physical activity, number of steps taken, or distance covered during physical education class. Advanced systems, such as the Interactive Health Technologies Spirit System, include heart rate monitors that record and store data that can then be shared with parents via email or printed and sent home with students. Whole-class data can be calculated and then shared with administration. Fitness-Gram also has a data collection and analysis mechanism with interactive reports on students' fitness levels in relation to the Healthy Fitness Zone.

In addition to mining your own students' data to advocate for your program, you can turn to online resources for additional support. For example, a high school health teacher who wants to advocate for stricter health education requirements in her school may use data from the Youth Risk Behavior Survey (concerning alcohol and tobacco use, dietary behaviors, and physical activity among youth) found on the Centers for Disease Control and Prevention website to convince her administration of the necessity. Many organizations already have visually appealing reports that can be shared; however, the YRBS data is available for download for those interested in running their own data reports. It is important to present the data you acquire—either from your own students or from pre-existing data found elsewhere—in a way that is simple yet effective. The mode in which it is presented (newsletter, email, etc.) will vary based on your audience; however, the presentation of the data is what is most vital. The use of visuals, such as graphs, charts, or other infographic-style features will help stakeholders better grasp the data than presenting them with a table full of numbers. Keep data simple and to the point with the most pertinent information conveyed. Remember, you can't argue with the numbers.

ADVANTAGES AND LIMITATIONS OF USING TECHNOLOGY FOR ADVOCACY

There are several advantages and limitations to using technology for advocacy. With the variety of options to advocate with technology, there are more opportunities to reach a greater audience. That said, you may have to actually use multiple technology tools to ensure you reach as many stakeholders as possible. It is a common assumption that people in modern society have Internet access with email and social media accounts. In fact, there is a **digital divide**, or a gap between demographics and regions who can readily use and access technology and those who cannot. Though younger generations tend to be more tech savvy and active users, you may have more difficulty reaching older generations who may not be familiar or comfortable with using modern technology. The same goes for individuals who simply do not have access to the Internet, either because of low socioeconomic status, lack of equipment, or location. Therefore, you cannot completely rely on technology for your advocacy efforts. It is necessary to continue traditional, face-to-face practices. You can, however, at least prepare for those meetings with resources you've found online.

Conclusion

This chapter discussed the use of technology for advocacy for physical educators, health educators, and coaches. There are many online resources and technology tools that provide opportunities for professionals to promote and gain support for their programs. Teachers and coaches must be able to identify the purpose of the advocacy and select the appropriate tool to engage stakeholders, all while considering the advantages and limitations of the technology.

Key Terms

advocacy—The practice of supporting, defending, or recommending on behalf of an idea or cause.

digital divide—The gap between demographics and regions who can readily use and access technology and those who cannot.

email—Short for electronic mail; sending and receiving messages electronically via computer.

listserv—An application that distributes messages to subscribers on an electronic mailing list.

Infographics—Visual images that represent information or data at a glance, also referred to as *data visualization*.

stakeholder—Individuals or groups who have an interest in decisions or activities of an organization.

Review Questions

1. What are the advantages of using technology for advocacy?
2. List three types of technology that can be used to advocate for physical education, health education, or coaching.
3. Describe how one could use video to advocate for their program.
4. How could you use technology to advocate for policy change related to your profession?

Discussion Questions

1. What is a common issue you might face as a professional, and how would you incorporate technology to help you advocate for this issue?
2. How have you used social media in the past, and how could you incorporate social media into your advocacy efforts?
3. How could you include advocacy in a professional website?

14

Technology Resources

Web Resource (online only).

Throughout the textbook, a variety of online resources are mentioned. In the field of technology, resources will always be changing. The resources listed in this chapter will be reviewed and updated as needed on a yearly basis. Chapter 14 will provide you with several tables of resources that vary in their intended audience. While these resources do not serve as an all-inclusive list, they do provide you with a variety of options to get you started on your journey to incorporate more technology in your program to enhance your teaching and learning. In this chapter, you will find links to websites, social media accounts, and technology-based professional organizations that you can use to further your education, to connect with groups and ask questions, and to identify people who are modeling what it looks like to advocate for their program using technology. This chapter also serves as a guide for you to do further research online. This chapter is not meant to be all-inclusive, but it is a starting point for you to jump-start your professional development online.

Refer to the instructions at the front of the book for how to access the web resource and chapter 14.

PART VI

Legal and Financial
Aspects of Technology

15

Legal Aspects of Technology Use

Chapter Objectives

When you have completed this chapter, you will be able to do the following:

1. Understand laws surrounding the use of the Internet with children under the age of 13.
2. Understand legal and fair ways to use content found on the Internet.
3. Understand how to protect student privacy while using technology.
4. Understand how to protect yourself and your students when using digital communication.

Innovations in technology have the capability to enhance student learning in a variety of ways, as discussed in previous chapters. Before taking advantage of these resources, however, practitioners should first be aware of the legal aspects of using technology in educational settings. Many new and seasoned practitioners are uninformed or misinformed about these issues (Schimmel & Militello, 2007). It can seem daunting to understand all of the legal aspects related to using technology in educational settings; however, you are responsible for making informed decisions in your daily practices. This chapter serves as a guide to help you better understand how to use technology within the law. This chapter focuses on four areas of interest:

1. Student use of the Internet
2. Copyright law
3. Student privacy
4. Digital communication

STUDENT USE OF THE INTERNET

Students frequently use the Internet as a resource to enhance learning. Information is readily available to supplement class projects, find videos, or communicate with friends and practitioners via email. Along with this abundance of educational resources, students also have access to explicit or mature content that is inappropriate to be used at school. Specifically in PK-12 settings, there are many safeguards in place to ensure students are using Internet resources safely. Before allowing students to use the Internet under your supervision, you should become aware of your school or district policies on acceptable use and the federal laws that limit content available to students.

Acceptable Use Policies

Schools or districts have commonly adopted **acceptable use policies (AUPs)** for Internet use. An AUP typically outlines how the Internet should be accessed and used by students and educational staff. Typically, an AUP contains the following information:

- Mission or goal statements of the district or institution
- Disclaimer statements
- Parental consent forms
- **Internet etiquette** statements (also known as netiquette)
- Consequences for inappropriate behaviors
- Network security statements (Flowers & Rakes, 2000)

Check out the web resource for more information on AUPs.

More often than not, practitioners complete training or sign agreements consenting to follow the school or district AUP. Some

Desktop computers are typically found in school technology centers.

Reprinted from Poder Learning Center. Daniel X. O'Neil. This photo is under the license of Creative Commons 2.0.

schools may also require students or guardians to sign consent forms agreeing to respect and follow the AUP. Before giving your students an assignment that requires the use of the Internet during class time, take some time to remind students about your schools' AUP, as well as consequences for inappropriate actions. If your students are accessing resources during class time or practice, be sure to monitor their use, because some content can get through school filters. Monitoring student use, especially if students use devices from home, will better ensure that students are following the school's AUP.

Children's Internet Protection Act

The **Children's Internet Protection Act (CIPA)** was created in 2000 in an effort to protect students under the age of 18 from "obscene or harmful content over the Internet." (Federal Communications Commission, 2015, p. 1). This law requires schools to provide safe Internet use policies if they wish to obtain federal money through the **E-rate program,** which helps schools purchase affordable broadband service. Schools that are CIPA compliant must ensure that minors do not have access to inappropriate content, are following safe practices when sending email and other types of electronic communication, do not participate in any unlawful uses of technology (such as hacking or downloading copyrighted materials), do not give out **personal identifying information (PII)** without permission, and are generally not exposed to harmful content (Federal Communications Commission, 2015). Along with knowing and understanding your schools' AUP, you should also be aware of any other Internet safety policies, and should seek school policies to follow when allowing students to use the Internet in class.

Children's Online Privacy Protection Act

The **Children's Online Privacy Protection Act (COPPA)** is a law that went into effect in 2000 to protect the privacy of children under 13. The goal of COPPA, which is enforced by the **Federal Trade Commission (FTC)**, is to protect the privacy of children by allowing parents to control what personal information about their children may be collected by **operators** of websites or online services, including apps, that are either directed to children or that knowingly collect personally identifiable information (PII) from children (Handler, 2015). COPPA requires the operators of websites directed toward children to include a clearly written privacy notice on their home page and anywhere on their site where user data are

A student editing a video at school using age-appropriate school programs.

Reprinted from Ivan Walsh. This photo is under the license of Creative Commons 2.0.

collected. The privacy policy must state who is collecting and maintaining the information, provide information about how to contact them, explain how the child's personal information will be used, and state whether information will be made available to third parties (COPPA, 2007). COPPA also requires operators to obtain **consent** from the child's guardian before collecting or using personal information from children. If you are using an app in a classroom that requires guardian consent, then you may *not* legally act in lieu of the child's guardian. Request consent from all guardians before using the app in your classroom. Some schools and school districts maintain lists of approved educational apps and websites. If you seek to use websites or apps with students under the age of 13, you should first check with your district to see if

Many students in a computer lab using school approved educational platforms.

you have access to an approved list. If this type of resource does not exist in the district, seek approval from your administrator before using the desired resource.

UNDERSTANDING COPYRIGHT LAWS

Various technologies now allow you to create and obtain lesson plans, presentations, and other supplemental learning resources. At the same time, you must be aware of your legal rights when using or sharing copyrighted materials. Mixed messages about "sharing" and "stealing" copyrighted works have left some educators confused and fearful (Hobbs et al., 2009). Although laws surrounding the use of copyrighted materials are quite complex, you have a duty to begin to understand them and teach them to your students.

What Is Copyright Law?

According to the U.S. Copyright Office, **copyright** law protects the rights of original authors' work and limits the ways in which the original works can be "perceived, reproduced, or otherwise communicated, either directly or with the aid of a machine or device" (U.S. Copyright Office, 2016, p. 8). Copyright law has generous terms for educators, with many exemptions for works that are being used for educational purposes under **fair use**. What this means is that you must be aware of the way you are using copyrighted materials and use them within the limits of the law. Realize again that there are some exceptions to copyright law that favor educators who are using the materials for **noncommercial** purposes to enhance student learning.

What Kind of Works Can Be Copyrighted?

Copyrighted works extend beyond books, movies, and songs. Any works that are original to an author, and are expressed in a **fixed** way (not just an idea), are subject to copyright laws. Section 102 of the copyright law provides a list of all works that can be copyrighted (U.S. Copyright Office, 2016, p. 8):

1. literary works;
2. musical works, including any accompanying words;

3. dramatic works, including any accompanying music;

4. pantomimes and choreographic works;

5. pictorial, graphic, and sculptural works;

6. motion pictures and other audiovisual works;

7. sound recordings; and

8. architectural works

As soon as someone has created something original and fixed, it is automatically protected by copyright without the need to apply for a special license or permit. The creator has exclusive rights to the original work for their whole lifetime, plus 70 years (U.S. Copyright Office, 2016). Some works cannot be protected by copyright. Copyright does not offer protection to a fact, "idea, procedure, process, system, method of operation, concept, principle, or discovery" (U.S. Copyright Office, 2016, p. 8). In some cases, people apply for **patents** to protect their work when they cannot be protected under copyright.

Legally Gathering Educational Resources From the Internet

As stated, one does not need to apply for special provisions for original and concrete works to be protected by copyright. The moment you create something new and tangible, such as a poem, a choreographed dance, or a video to share with students, the item is automatically protected. Navigating the Internet and acquiring resources to share with students without infringing on copyright laws can seem confusing. Fortunately, many resources can be used within the confines of a classroom for educational purposes. Consider the following suggestions to increase the likelihood that you are using content appropriately and abiding by copyright laws:

• Become familiar with the fair use doctrine and the four factors used to allow unauthorized use of copyrighted materials

• Use the Creative Commons and search for content that has limited copyright protections

Fair Use Doctrine

The fair use doctrine, found in Section 107 of the copyright law, is particularly of interest to practitioners who use copyrighted materials for educational purposes. Fair use allows unauthorized replication of copyrighted work without payment or permission for the following purposes (U.S. Copyright Office, 2016):

• Criticism

• Comment

• News reporting

• Teaching (including multiple copies for classroom use)

• Scholarship

• Research

Fair use, however, does not imply that everything used in an educational setting is free of penalty from copyright law. To determine if the use of a copyrighted material is fair, one must consider the four factors that are used to determine fair use decisions in court: the purpose of the use, the nature of the copyrighted work, the amount or substantiality of the portion used, and the effect of the use on the potential market (U.S. Copyright Office, 2016). See table 15.1 for a more detailed description of the four factors.

The fair use doctrine is still not explicitly clear, as you may have noticed. Basically, it is best to use copyrighted works in a transformative or new way, use small amounts of the work, and

Table 15.1 Four Factors of Fair Use

Factor	Description
The purpose of the use	This factor focuses on whether the work is **transformative** in some way, or if someone is making something new from the original work. For instance, a teacher may not simply photocopy half of a textbook to provide her students. However, if the teacher copies a portion of the book and then critiques it or uses it for a function different from its original purpose, then it is possible that the use of the work is fair use.
The nature of the copyrighted work	This factor focuses on two areas: whether the work is factual or fictional, and whether the work is published or unpublished. There are more protections for fictional works, so factual works can be shared more openly. Work that is unpublished is more protected because the original copyright holder stands to face a loss if the work is shared before it is published.
The amount or substantiality of the portion of work used	This factor relates to the amount of the work that is used. There is no concrete rule about how much work can be copied. As a general rule, the smaller the amount, the more likely it will be considered fair use. An exception would be if the "heart" of the work is copied (Russell, 2012), and this would most likely not be fair use.
The effect of use on the potential market	This factor relates to whether the work takes away sales or competes in any way with the original copyright holder. If the work is used in an environment where it is taking away possible sales (i.e., filming a performance at the theater), or is repeatedly shared without seeking approval from the copyright holder, then it does not qualify for fair use.

have a clear rationale for why the work is important. Many institutions offer helpful checklists that practitioners may use to help determine if they are within the fair use guidelines. Figure 15.1 highlights a fair use checklist obtained from Columbia University. This document was created to aid faculty and staff in higher education to make decisions about fair use of materials, but it can also be used by any practitioner attempting to use copyrighted resources.

Creative Commons

An alternative option to find materials without infringing on copyright is to use resources that have relinquished some or all of their copyright privileges. An increasingly popular way to look for these photos, videos, music, and other resources online is by using materials from the Creative Commons (CC). Often, works found on the CC only require an **attribution** be given to the author. By accessing the CC website, students and practitioners can find resources that have some of the rights removed without worrying about infringing on copyright. Works here can be repurposed or shared, as long as proper attributions are made. Through the CC, you can search for pictures that you want to modify or use "as is," for example, on brochures for commercial purposes. Figure 15.2 is a visual representation of the levels of copyright restrictions offered in the CC. Individuals who create materials that they would like to share can apply for a license through the CC and set the rules for which the item can be used. The fewer infringements you put on your new copyright through the CC, the more openly shared your work can be.

By following fair use guidelines and using the Creative Commons as a resource to gather supplemental class materials, you are less likely to be infringing on copyright, and you are modeling good ethics in class. This is not only important for you to know and model, but it is also important for you to teach your students so they do not violate copyright laws.

Figure 15.1   Fair Use Checklist.

Name:_____

Institution: _____

Project:_____

Date:_____

Prepared by: _____

PURPOSE

Favoring Fair Use

- ☐ Teaching (including multiple copies for classroom use)
- ☐ Research Scholarship
- ☐ Nonprofit educational institution
- ☐ Criticism
- ☐ Comment
- ☐ News reporting
- ☐ Transformative or productive use (changes the word for new utility)
- ☐ Restricted access (to students or other appropriate group)
- ☐ Parody

Opposing Fair Use

- ☐ Commercial activity
- ☐ Profiting from the use
- ☐ Entertainment
- ☐ Bad-faith behavior
- ☐ Denying credit to original author

NATURE

Favoring Fair Use

- ☐ Published work
- ☐ Factual or nonfiction based
- ☐ Important to favored educational objectives

Opposing Fair Use

- ☐ Unpublished work
- ☐ Highly creative work (art, music, novels, films, plays)
- ☐ Fiction

AMOUNT

Favoring Fair Use

- ☐ Small quantity
- ☐ Portion used is not central or significant to entire work
- ☐ Amount is appropriate for favored educational purpose

Opposing Fair Use

- ☐ Large portion or whole work used
- ☐ Portion used is central to or "heart of work"

(continued)

Figure 15.1 *(continued)*

EFFECT

Favoring Fair Use

☐ User owns lawfully purchased or acquired copy of original work

☐ One or few copies made

☐ No significant effect on the market or potential market for copyrighted work

☐ No similar product marketed by the copyright holder

☐ Lack of license mechanism

Opposing Fair Use

☐ Could replace sale of copyrighted work

☐ Significantly impairs market or potential market for copyrighted work of derivative

☐ Reasonably available licensing mechanism for use of the copyrighted work

☐ Affordable permission available for using work

☐ Numerous copies made

☐ You made it accessible on the Web or in other public forum

☐ Repeated or long-term use

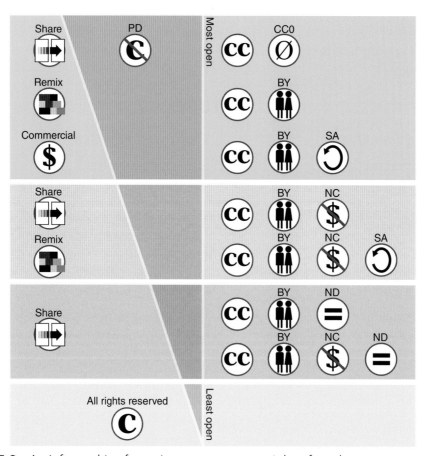

Figure 15.2 An infographic of creative commons copyrights, from least to most restrictive.

Use of Copyright in Distance Education

The **Technology, Education, and Copyright Harmonization (TEACH) Act** of 2002 specifically addresses the unique needs of teachers in **distance education** (Copyright Clearance Center, 2011) so that they are able to provide their students with the same resources that they provide students during face-to-face instruction. The TEACH Act specifies what content teachers may upload to an online platform for students to access. As a practitioner, you may upload resources for your students if they meet the criteria found in figure 15.3.

Uploading Student-Created Materials to the Internet

As stated, any new content created in a concrete way is automatically protected by copyright, without the need to apply for a license. This copyright law also applies to works your students or athletes create. According to **Family Educational Rights and Privacy Act (FERPA)**, you may not publicly post student work to the Internet without consent from the student or guardian. (You will learn about FERPA in more detail later in this chapter). After you have received permission to upload student work, you must give proper credit to the student. Consider what personal identifier you will use when posting the work, and discuss the identifier with the student's guardian. For instance, a guardian may wish that you not identify their child's work by name, but rather by their student number.

In addition to requesting permission to post student work, you should also be aware if the materials you are posting violate copyright in any way. Recall that fair use stipulates that you can use some copyrighted materials without permission for educational purposes. Once you post student work on the Internet, it may no longer be covered by fair use. For instance, if a student choreographed and performed a dance to a popular song, posting the entire video may infringe on the copyright of the song owner. Consult with your school or district's technology specialist before posting any materials that you suspect violate copyright protections. Again, this student work is acceptable for use in your private classroom, but may not be suitable to share on the public Internet.

Using Audio and Video Resources

Many practitioners use video or audio resources to complement their instruction. It is becoming more and more common for educators to stream music in class or watch videos to supplement lessons or analyze athlete performance. Section 110 of the copyright law deals specifically with the use of audio and video technology in nonprofit and educational settings (U.S. Copyright Office, 2016). Often, it is not an infringement of copyright law for educators to use legally purchased audio and visual resources in their classroom or other typical place of instruction. However, there are some instances where using these resources, even for educational purposes, is not considered acceptable and legal. The following guidelines should be used to determine whether you can acceptably use audio and visual materials in your institution:

- The activity must be a teaching activity and not recreation or entertainment.
- The activity must be put on by a nonprofit educational institution.
- The activity must take place in a classroom or other area used as a classroom for instruction.
- Videos or movies must have been lawfully made. (U.S. Copyright Office, 2016)

Note that there are exceptions to this law when using audio and video streaming services, which will be discussed later in this section.

Figure 15.3 TEACH Act checklist.

☐ My institution is a nonprofit accredited educational institution or a government agency.

☐ It has a policy on the use of copyrighted materials.

☐ It provides accurate information to faculty, students, and staff about copyright.

☐ Its systems will not interfere with technological controls within the materials I want to use.

☐ The materials I want to use are specifically for students in my class.

☐ Only those students will have access to the materials.

☐ The materials will be provided at my direction during the relevant lesson.

☐ The materials are directly related and of material assistance to my teaching content.

☐ My class is part of the regular offerings of my institution.

☐ I will include a notice that the materials are protected by copyright.

☐ I will use technology that reasonably limits the students' ability to retain or further distribute the materials.

☐ I will make the materials available to the students only for a period of time that is relevant to the context of the class session.

☐ I will store the materials on a secure server and transmit them only as permitted by this law.

☐ I will not make copies other than the one I need to make the transmission.

☐ The materials are of the proper type and amount the law authorizes:
- Entire performances of nondramatic literary and musical works
- Reasonable and limited parts of a dramatic literary, musical, or audiovisual work
- Displays of other works, such as images, in amounts similar to typical displays in face-to-face teaching

☐ The materials are not among those the law specifically excludes from its coverage:
- Materials specifically marketed for classroom use for digital distance education
- Copies I know or should know are illegal
- Textbooks, course packs, electronic reserves, and similar materials typically purchased individually by the students for independent review outside the classroom or class session

☐ If I am using an analog original, I checked before digitizing it to be sure:
- I copied only the amount that I am authorized to transmit
- There is no digital copy of the work available except with technological protections that prevent my using it for the class in the way the statute authorizes

Reprinted by permission from Georgia Harper.

Legal Use of Audio Resources

Music acquired legally, such as CDs or MP3s purchased by the practitioner or students or found in a school library, may be used in an **educational setting**. Educational settings are places such as classrooms, school gymnasiums, or school fitness centers. According to section 110 of the copyright act, music may be played for educational purposes (U.S. Copyright Office, 2016). Playing music in a dance class to help illustrate principles of tempo or rhythm absolutely falls under educational purposes. Listening to music in the school weight room would also be permissible, as long as the music was legally purchased. Instances that would fall outside of acceptable use would be broadcasting full songs at sporting events or school fundraisers. These would be considered **public performances** of music, and may require a permit. Playing music at public school events is common practice, but the legal implications are often overlooked. According to fair use, portions of songs may be used at these public events, but not a substantial part of the works (U.S. Copyright Office, 2016). Again, you should seek advice from your school administrator or district office if you wish to use audio resources outside of your typical classroom. Policies vary by school district, so be aware of your district policies before playing music at a public event. Subscription music streaming services do not follow the same rules as personal CDs or MP3s.

Recently, **music streaming services** have gained popularity. These services offer individuals a way to play full-length songs without requiring them to download and permanently store the files on their listening device. Previously, practitioners needed to purchase CDs or audio files, such as MP3s, for use in their classes. Music streaming services, such as Pandora, Spotify, and Apple Music, provide music to the user at little to no charge. Some of these services allow you to request specific songs, whereas others play a variety of songs within a specific genre requested by the user.

As mentioned previously, some music streaming services are offered free to the user, with optional upgrades for paid subscriptions. These services are very enticing for educators who may have limited funds. Some examples of free services include Pandora, Deezer, and Spotify. However, all three of the aforementioned streaming services have terms and services that restrict users from playing the music in educational settings, even in the background or for educational purposes. Spotify, for instance, has a statement in its terms and conditions related directly to use in schools, stating: "Spotify is for personal entertainment only and not for commercial use. This means it can't be played in public places such as bars, restaurants, stores, schools, etc." (Spotify, 2018). If you wish to use music streaming services in your classroom, you should research the levels of subscription they offer and be diligent of the terms and conditions. Representatives of these companies are available to help, too. For instance, after calling and speaking with a representative, we learned that Pandora offers a fee-based service called "mood music," which is marketed toward commercial businesses.

This fee-based service from Pandora allows businesses and schools to play the music in the background. Pandora Mood Music is a fee-based service, but serves as a viable option for practitioners who wish to legally play background music in their classroom (Pandora representative, 2018). Once again, you are cautioned to find out your district policy on streaming music in your classroom. Because these policies vary from institution to institution, speaking with your administrator or district office is recommended.

Reprinted from Streaming Music - Music Service - Smartphone by Blue Coat Photos. This photo is under the license of Creative Commons 2.0.

Legal Use of Video Resources

Similar to audio resources, videos acquired legally, such as DVDs purchased by the practitioner or videos from the school library, may be used in an educational setting. Using such videos in the classroom or in a coaching setting is allowed, as long as the videos are for educational purposes. For instance, playing a legally acquired documentary in class to help illustrate the controversy of body mass index (BMI) testing is permitted, but recording the Super Bowl and playing it back to analyze with your school football team is not. Copyright law permits video resources to be used in a classroom setting, not for public viewing. For instance, hosting a public movie night on the high school football field would require you to pay for a license to screen the movie, which can be very expensive. Paying in advance for a license will save you from facing a lawsuit later.

Because purchasing DVDs can become quite costly, it is becoming increasingly more common for educators to use free **video hosting services**, such as YouTube or Vimeo. Streaming these movies in your classroom is typically acceptable, depending on your district policy. A caveat is that you must ensure that the works you are using have appropriate copyrights. For instance, clips of full-length videos are commonly found on YouTube, and they are generally free of copyright violation. But in other instances, entire movies are illegally uploaded to YouTube before they can be flagged for removal. Online media websites, such as YouTube, claim that they attempt to monitor uploads to ensure the content is not in a violation of copyright, but they cannot catch all violations. In addition to not knowing if videos are uploaded legally, some online video websites require viewers to watch commercials. Some of these commercials may contain mature content or advertisements not appropriate in a PK-12 teaching environment. Many schools and school districts have blocked sites like YouTube districtwide because of explicit content. Be aware of your district policies on the use of YouTube, and seek out alternate sites such as Vimeo, TeacherTube, or GoNoodle to supplement your teaching.

Subscription video streaming service providers such as Netflix, Hulu, or Amazon Prime Video are also increasing in popularity in educational institutions, and can be easily accessed from home, work, or mobile devices. Although there are provisions in the copyright law about the use of video for educational purposes, those provisions do not supersede the terms of use of video streaming services (Ezor, 2013). Most streaming services make it clear in their terms and conditions that videos and television shows are for personal use only. Showing videos from personal streaming services in schools has been deemed illegal as well as unethical (Ezor, 2013). Educators who choose to use their personal accounts in their teaching institutions risk ramifications from the service provider, which may include having their personal accounts canceled. Be aware of your terms of use before playing a video from your personal video streaming service in class. However, Netflix realizes that some practitioners want access to educational videos without having to build up their personal DVD library, so they created a service called "Educational Screenings of Documentaries." Through this service, practitioners can screen specific documentaries for educational purposes. Films found in this Netflix program can be legally streamed in schools once a semester. It would not be surprising to see other video streaming services begin to follow the lead of Netflix to offer similar services.

CAPTURING AND SHARING STUDENT PHOTOS, VIDEOS, AND WORK

Many practitioners are turning to photo and video evidence to show student achievements. Videos can capture learning in all domains: psychomotor, cognitive, and affective. A video can easily be made of a student shooting a free throw in basketball, which the student can watch to self-assess or receive teacher feedback, and then a second video can be taken later in the year to record student growth. Students can record a dance video highlighting the use of movement concepts. Videos can capture students working together and highlight learning in the affective domain. After recording videos, you may wish to store them as evidence on your computer or share them with guardians. Some educators use web-based services that allow them to send pictures directly to parents throughout the day, engaging parents in student learning. Student photos and videos that are taken by the teacher are technically considered student records, and are therefore protected by the Family Educational Rights and Privacy Act (FERPA) (U.S. Department of Education, n.d.). FERPA was created by Congress to protect the privacy of students and parents. Student photos and videos can be taken and stored for use by the teacher without permission if they are for educational purposes, and if teachers take appropriate steps to keep the images secure. Extra precautions should be taken when capturing student photos and videos to be viewed by someone other than the teacher—for instance, to be posted on bulletin boards or displayed on the school website. Most schools distribute release forms to guardians requesting permission to take photos and videos of students for a variety of reasons. Guardians have the right to opt out of signing photo waivers, so you must keep note of who you cannot film or photograph.

Taking Videos for University Requirements or External Testing

Preservice health and physical education teachers should be aware of their university policy on video release forms when capturing student videos as part of their student teaching or for external accreditation services such as **edTPA**. During their student teaching semester, teacher candidates typically take videos to be viewed by their college professors or external scorers. Special caution should be taken to protect the rights of students in these instances. Typically, universities and other agencies require additional video release permission forms to be signed.

Posting Photos and Videos on Social Media

In addition to taking videos and photos for academic use, you may wish to post photos and videos of your students to highlight success in a competition, showcase exceptional work, or simply update parents on what their child is doing in physical education class. Some schools, individual teachers, and coaches create private social media accounts, using apps like Facebook or Instagram, that can only be accessed by parents or guardians (you will find more information about social media later in this chapter). These pages can be set up with multiple administrators to allow multiple practitioners to upload photos and videos to the private group. As noted previously, permission should be obtained from guardians before posting pictures of minors online. Guardians should have the ability to opt their student out of online posts, and practitioners should take precautions to not post pictures of students who do not have permission. In addition to social media platforms, some specific apps allow you to share photos and videos directly with parents. Apps such as Homeroom allow you to create private groups that can only be accessed by members you invite. Be aware that posting student grades on these sites is still a violation of FERPA, so take caution when deciding what artifacts to post on social media platforms.

Storing Student Data

It is typical for practitioners to store student data digitally, and practitioners are using technology to report more data than ever, from attendance to grades to fitness scores. According to FERPA, practitioners must ensure student privacy when storing any personally identifiable information (PII). It may seem overwhelming to ensure student safety online, especially because almost every digital interaction, whether simply searching for an image on Google or storing information online, is at risk of being monitored or compromised (Tudor, 2015).

Typically, school districts offer secure avenues for practitioners to upload required student information. These secure systems are beyond the scope of this textbook, but know that school administrators, district administrators, and state education representatives work diligently to provide secure student data systems. There are several additional steps that practitioners should follow to ensure student information is kept safe.

The first step to ensuring student safety is to protect your computer, tablet, USB drive, or any other device where you store student information. Adding a strong password to your computer, locking your office, and not leaving your school laptop in your car is the first step to keeping student data safe. This may seem straightforward and simplistic; however, there have been many reported cases of educators' personal laptops or tablets being stolen and thieves gaining access to countless years of private student information (Beaudin, 2017).

Next, be aware of how you are storing students' PII when using services other than school-based platforms. Most information that you record on a daily basis, such as attendance and grades, will be inputted directly on your school platform and stored securely in a system monitored by your district security team. However, if you are considering using educational apps or websites that collect student PII, you will need to take extra steps to increase student security.

1. Contact your school administrator to get approval to use the resource. Administrators are cautious about where PII is stored because of FERPA and student safety. Another concern administrators have is whether the terms and conditions of the app or website align with the district's safety policy. You or your administrator may need to request permission from the app's vendor to agree to the district's safety and privacy terms before you use it with students (Berdik, 2017).

2. Seek approval from guardians. Recall that COPPA requires guardians to grant permission before using apps that collect PII of students under the age of 13.

Finally, if you collect student data directly on your computer using programs like Microsoft Excel or Word, you should only keep it on your computer the year the student is in your class. At the end of the semester, delete any data connected to a student's PII that you no longer need. If deleting student data is not possible, or if you use this data to track progress over the years, consider saving student information to a USB that is password protected or locked in a secure location. If using a USB is not an option for you, consider saving student information by ID number instead of name. Students keep the same ID number every year, so you can keep record of student growth without linking the number to a student face or name.

DIGITAL COMMUNICATION

In this digital age, many people are turning to digital forms of communication, such as texting, emailing, and communicating through Facebook or Twitter. With 95% of teens having access to a smartphone, the use of digital communication is extremely common among all teens, regardless of gender, race, ethnicity, and socioeconomic background (Anderson & Jiang, 2018). With this rise in availability, you may ask yourself if it is acceptable for you to respond to a student email about an assignment or to send out a text reminder about the next day's tournament schedule. The answers to these questions traditionally come down to school ethics policies on communication. Some schools and school districts have policies banning all digital forms of communication with students, and others have guidelines that outline acceptable forms of digital communication (Todoric, 2011). Getting to know your district and school policies on digital communication is key, because there can be much variation between institutions. Figure 15.4 highlights district digital communication expectations from Community High School District 128 in Lake County, Illinois. This is a very well-written set of guidelines that will help guide you as you begin to navigate digital communication.

Figure 15.4   Digital communication expectations for teachers.

Community High School District 128 in Lake County, Illinois has adopted many common-sense guidelines that are worth highlighting here. The guidelines found on the school district website make reference to the TAP Test (communication should be *transparent, accessible,* and *professional*). This is a test developed by Mary Todoric (the *director of communications at Community High School District 128*), the district's technology director, and the superintendent's cabinet members, defining the acceptable criteria in which to communicate with students. Some key take-aways from the district expectations include the following:

- School employees should assume that everything sent to a student is public record.
- All communication with students should be professional.
- All communication should be made through school email accounts and district-approved tools, not personal accounts.
- The use of text messaging is not encouraged. School staff who wish to use text messaging to communicate in emergency situations (such as a coach sending a last-minute schedule change) must be communicated in advance with guardians.
- Online gaming with students is prohibited.
- Facebook fan pages can be used, but you must use district email to set up the account and may not post student names along with any images.
- Do not accept students as "friends" on any social media platforms.

Adapted from Todoric (2011).

Text Messaging

Some school districts have a policy against using personal phones to communicate with students. (Providing students with your office phone number is acceptable because it can be monitored by the district.) Text messaging is discouraged because communications over text message can often be informal and unprofessional. Students generally should not be communicating with their teachers via text messaging for educational purposes. Coaches, however, are more likely to use their cell phones to communicate with their athletes. Text messaging allows information to get to most students instantly, and coaches often have to update their athletes about changes in practice plans or emergencies. Schools and athletic teams often enforce phone policies that require parents or guardians to be copied on all text message communications. Guardians should be given a copy of the team text messaging policy prior to the start of the season. If students do not have access to cell phones, alternate methods of communication should also be offered.

Email

Students typically have access to instructors through email. Many school policies require you to use the school-provided

Youth texting on her cell phone.

Several examples of social media app icons.

Reprinted from Rosaura Ochoa. This material is under the license of Creative Commons 2.0.

email address (for instance, @school.edu) when communicating with students. Using the school email address means that your communication can be monitored, and more transparency is available to administrators. Emails should be professional and should be related to school or athletic team content. As with text messaging, email conversations should also copy the guardian.

Social Media

Social media may be used to promote classroom activities or team events. The use of social media should be strictly professional. You should not become personal "friends" or follow students on social media accounts, nor should they be able to "friend" or follow you. Be sure your personal social media accounts have adequate privacy filters. If you wish to set up social media pages for parents, students, or fans, seek approval from your administrator. As mentioned previously, some teachers and coaches create private social media pages or groups for their teams or their classes. These private social media pages should include all guardians and also administrators. Students should have the option to opt out of having their photos, videos, or class work displayed on social media.

WHAT DOES THE RESEARCH SAY?

Why Use Social Media, and How to Use It Correctly

Social media use has exploded in the last decade, with sites like Facebook having over 1.23 billion users (Protalinski, 2014), and Twitter having over 330 million users globally (Clement, 2019). Social media sites such as Facebook and Twitter are desirable places for educators to communicate with students because of the capacity to build learning communities, the ability for teachers to offer instant educational support, opportunities for peer-to-peer learning, and ongoing, public dialogue between students and practitioners (Carpenter & Krutka, 2014; Warnick et al., 2016). Experts suggest that educational employee policies should include the following statements:

- Schools should not prohibit employees from participating in online social networks.
- Schools should take action against employees who use social networks to post illegal material or material that directly affects their professional responsibilities.
- Schools should take action against employees who harass students.
- Schools should allow employees to post legal but controversial material.
- Employees must ensure privacy and that their role as an employee is not highlighted.
- Schools may forbid employees from directly contacting students to be "friends."
- Practitioners who use social networking for school work or athletic scheduling should ensure that opportunities are spread equally to students who are not on social networks.
- Practitioners who participate in political speech should do so in a way that disconnects themselves from the school identity.

Based on information from Warnick et al. (2016, pg. 792).

Conclusion

Health educators, physical educators, and coaches are all role models in the lives of youth. We all work together to model behaviors that are ethical and thoughtful. Being aware of the laws surrounding the use of technology will provide you with an ethical framework in which to make informed and safe decisions for your future students and their families. Continue to be educated on laws, regulations, and best practices in your community, so you keep your students safe and can be trusted to use the technology provided to you in an informed way.

Key Terms

acceptable use policy (AUP)—A policy adopted by a school or school district that outlines how the Internet should be accessed and used by students and staff.

attribution—The action of ascribing a work or remark to a particular author, artist, or person.

consent—To grant permission, or to agree.

Children's Internet Protection Act (CIPA)—A law requiring schools to provide safe Internet use policies if they wish to obtain federal money.

Children's Online Privacy Protection Act (COPPA)—A law requiring operators of websites or online services directed at children under 13 years of age to provide a detailed privacy policy and obtain consent from a guardian before supplying any personally identifiable information.

copyright—A form of protection grounded in the U.S. Constitution and granted by law for original works of authorship fixed in a concrete medium of expression. Copyright covers both published and unpublished works.

Creative Commons (CC)—A nonprofit organization that gives several tiers of less restrictive copyright licenses, known as Creative Commons licenses, to the public free of charge.

distance education—A form of learning in which the primary delivery mechanism is the Internet. These classes do not meet face-to-face, rather they meet completely or partially online.

educational setting—Any setting with the primary responsibility to provide early childhood education, elementary and secondary education, postsecondary education, or special education.

edTPA—A performance-based assessment used in teacher preparation programs that focuses on planning, instruction, and assessment. This subject-specific assessment system is online, and requires prospective teachers to submit a variety of videos to be assessed by highly trained educators.

E-rate program—A federal program that distributes money to schools to help cover phone services, Internet access, and Wi-Fi equipment and maintenance. All nonprofit schools with an endowment less than $50 million are eligible to receive E-rate funds.

fair use—Any copying of copyrighted material done for a limited and transformative purpose, such as to comment upon, criticize, or parody a copyrighted work. Such uses can be done without permission from the copyright owner.

Family Educational Rights and Privacy Act (FERPA)—A federal law that protects the privacy of student education records. The law applies to all schools that receive funds under an applicable program of the U.S. Department of Education.

Federal Trade Commission (FTC)—A federal agency that prevents fraudulent, deceptive, and unfair business practices.

fixed—A concrete or recorded medium of expression (not an idea or spoken word).

netiquette—A set of rules or etiquette that applies when communicating online.

music streaming services—Free or fee-based Internet-based subscription services that offer streaming of full-length music, without downloading songs.

noncommercial—Not intended to make profit.

operator—Any person who operates an online service or website who collects or maintains personal information from or about users.

patent—A government authority or license giving an exclusive right or title for a set amount to one owner, and thereby excluding others from making, using, or selling an invention.

personally identifying information (PII)—Information that can be used to distinguish or trace an individual's identity through linkages with other information. PII in education records includes both direct identifiers (such as a student's name, address, email address, phone number, or identification number) and indirect identifiers (such as a student's date of birth, employment information, religion, or medical information).

public performance—Performing or displaying a work at a place open to the public or at any place where a substantial number of persons outside of a normal circle of a family and its social acquaintances is gathered, including making a performance available online for the general public.

Technology, Education, and Copyright Harmonization (TEACH) Act—A law allowing educators to use copyrighted materials in educational settings that do not meet face-to-face if certain conditions are met.

transformative—Causing a substantial change in something or from the way it was intended to be used.

video hosting services—Internet-based services that allow users to upload their own videos and view videos posted by others.

video streaming services—Subscription Internet services that allow viewing of clips or full videos without downloading the videos to your device.

Review Questions

1. What is an acceptable use policy (AUP)? List three items that might be included in an AUP.
2. Compare and contrast the Children's Internet Protection Act (CIPA) and Children's Online Privacy Protection Act (COPPA).
3. Why might you teach students to use the Creative Commons (CC) for a class project? What copyright benefits does the CC offer your future students?
4. Describe the rights you have to use your personal music streaming subscription (such as Pandora or Spotify) in your future profession.
5. What are three strategies you could use to keep student data safe?

Discussion Questions

1. After reading this chapter, describe some steps you may need to take if you want to use music in your future program.
2. What do you think is the biggest legal barrier to using technology with students?
3. Think of a time you, or someone you know, may have infringed on copyright. What could you have done to prevent this from happening?
4. Look back at the section about text messaging. Will you give out your cell phone number in the future to send text messages to students and athletes? Why or why not?

16

Opportunities and Ideas for Acquiring Technology

Chapter Objectives

When you have completed this chapter, you will be able to do the following:

1. Understand how to use school and district resources to support technology use.
2. Use a variety of strategies to fundraise for your program.
3. Understand how to make smart technology purchases.

Monkey Business/fotolia.com

Throughout this textbook, you have learned a variety of ways to integrate technology in your program to enhance student learning. Although all of the suggestions in this book have an impact on learning, you may find yourself with limited technology resources and limited funds. It is not always realistic that your program will have the funds to acquire all of the tools you would like to implement. With limited funding, you will need to look for resources in your district, seek out routes to earn funding, and make wise technology purchases. Having a clear vision as to why you need the resources and how they will benefit your students will help drive your campaign.

This chapter focuses on the following areas of interest:

1. School- and community-based lending programs
2. School-based funding (school budget, PTA, booster clubs)
3. Fundraising and crowdfunding solutions
4. Grant writing (suggested grants and where to find more)
5. Smart technology purchases for your budget

SCHOOL AND COMMUNITY-BASED LENDING PROGRAMS

Practitioners are often faced with countless ideas for incorporating technology into their programs, making it overwhelming to decide which technology to choose. One solution is to look at the resources your school already has to offer. For instance, do you have portable projectors in a shared storage closet that you can check out and use in your teaching space? This is a perfect solution for projecting videos on the wall, providing students with instant feedback on their psychomotor skills, or showing another PE class from across the world to increase global awareness. Although the equipment may be bulky, your school likely has some older resources that you could borrow. If older projectors do not interest you, look into other types of technology initiatives you have at your school. Many schools now have one-to-one device initiatives, which enable all students access to a tablet or laptop. Some schools have "bring your own device" (BYOD) initiatives, which allow students to bring their smartphones, tablets, or laptops to school to use during the day (i-SAFE Ventures, 2016). If you are lucky enough to have class sets of devices to check out, you can add apps or programs to them as desired, according to your school policy. Throughout this book, there have been resources shared for both tablets and laptops that will enhance student learning.

If your school does not have tablets or laptops to borrow, another step would be to investigate if your district, community, or local university offers a lending library for physical education resources. In some districts, schools have the opportunity to check out shared equipment from a communal location. If you plan to use a technology resource for a limited period of time (i.e., a unit or a season), this would be an excellent option for you. See the sidebar for a few examples of curricular resources available across the country.

Speak with your administration or your district curriculum coordinator to find out if you have access to a resource like this in your area. If you do not have access to a lending library, reach out to colleagues at state or regional convention, and share resources amongst your programs. It would be beneficial to have an official document establishing some ground rules for borrowing equipment. Some sample questions on a borrowing contract include the following:

- What equipment is being borrowed, and in what quantity?
- How will the equipment be transported and where will it be stored?

CURRICULAR RESOURCES AVAILABLE ACROSS THE COUNTRY

PE EQUIPMENT LIBRARY

Location: Oakland, California

Description: The OUSD Physical Education Equipment Library (PEEL) has hundreds of items available for teachers to enhance their physical education programs.

Sample materials: General physical education equipment, DVDs, heart rate monitors, video cameras, stereos

Other: Practitioners must go in person to check out materials.

Website: www.ousd.org/Page/10320

GRANT WOOD AEA ADAPTED PHYSICAL EDUCATION

Location: Cedar Rapids, Iowa

Description: Differentiating instruction for diverse learners is easy when you have the right piece of equipment. Equipment available to check out in this collection supports general physical education, curriculum implementation, inclusive physical education placements, and specially designed adapted physical education classes. It can be used by all students for success.

Sample Materials: DVDs, orienteering equipment, portable sound sources, talking glow dice

Other: Prior approval is needed to check out some equipment.

Website: http://media2.aea10.k12.ia.us/display/017/wwk770?kw=*&fm=AP&ph=FIRST100&os=101&om=100&ot=215&oq=ZFMT&oq=AP&oq=

UNIFIED ARTS RESOURCE LIBRARY

Location: Albuquerque, New Mexico

Description: The Unified ARTS Resource Library is devoted to providing a wide variety of instructional materials to support Albuquerque Public Schools professionals.

Sample Materials: OT/PT-adapted PE materials, anatomy models, tape recorders, CDs, DVDs, audio textbooks

Other: There is an option to request other resources be added to the library.

Website: www.aps.edu/libraries/professional-libraries/unified-resources

- How do you properly use the equipment? How should students handle it?
- What established protocols will you use in your program with the equipment?
- Who will pay for any damages to the equipment?
- How long will the equipment be lent for? Who will bring it back?

Before committing time and efforts to obtain funding for your program, consider first looking for resources at your school, in your district, and amongst your colleagues throughout the state or region. Acquiring technology resources could be as easy as finding a district equipment library or asking a colleague to borrow a class set of pedometers. If you cannot find what you are looking for, you may need to consider investing in your own equipment.

SCHOOL-BASED FUNDING

If you are looking to make a big or small technology purchase, you have many options for finding funds. Every school or program has a different protocol to follow, but there are some typical sources of funding that you should look to first before looking into more complex solutions. Some typical sources for school-based funding come from:

- the school budget,
- a parent-teacher association (PTA), or
- a booster club

The School Budget

The first step to acquiring new technology is to look at your school's budget. State funding for public schools is typically allocated based on the number of students that are enrolled at the school. Often teachers have a set budget at the beginning of the year that they can use for supplies; however, it is not uncommon to have limited or no funds based on the school needs for the year. Although the intricacies of the school budget process are beyond the scope of this book, you do need to know that you, as a teacher, have the right to request funds from the school budget for your program. Coaches also typically have an annual budget, which is different from the budget for the health or physical educator. Your athletics director will help you determine your annual budget. If you are a practitioner that teaches and coaches, be sure you are using your funding for the appropriate purposes. Your teaching budget should not support your coaching, and vice versa.

An additional source of funding for health and physical education teachers is through the school's Title IV funds. When the **Every Student Succeeds Act (ESSA)** replaced **No Child Left Behind (NCLB)** Act in 2015, there were financial implications for schools beginning in the 2017-2018 school year. Now, as part of ESSA, physical and health education are part of a **well-rounded education**, thus opening up an avenue for additional funding. ESSA includes "a flexible block grant program under Title IV Part A, which is authorized at $1.6 billion in FY 2019" (Society of Health and Physical Educators America, 2018) (figure 16.1). Title IV Part A provides funding for activities in the three following areas:

1. Providing students with a well-rounded education

2. Supporting safe and healthy students (e.g., school mental health, drug and violence prevention, training on trauma-informed practices, health and physical education)

Title IV, Part A FY18 District Funding Estimates

Please fill out the information below in order to receive the estimated amount of funding that your school district will receive in July 2018 under Title IV, Part A of the Every Student Succeeds Act. This funding will be available to schools for the 2018-19 school year.

You will receive an email with the estimated amount of funding and links to SHAPE America resources to help you advocate for this funding to support health and physical education programs in your school district **within three (3) business days of your request.**

Name *

First   Last

Email *

Street Address *

Address Line 2

City *   State *

ZIP *

Official Name of School District *

Please only request the information from the district where you work. When filling out your district name, please do not use any abbreviations and double check to make sure it is spelled correctly to avoid any errors.

Submit

Figure 16.1 SHAPE America ESSA estimates request.

3. Supporting the effective use of technology (e.g., professional development, blended learning, and purchase of devices)

According to the SHAPE America ESSA fact sheet:

ESSA stipulates that each state will receive an allocation based on the Title I funding formula. Using the same Title I formula, the states will then allocate funds to school districts. Any school district that receives a formula allocation above $30,000 must conduct a needs assessment and then must expend 20% of its grant on safe and healthy school activities and 20% on activities to provide a well-rounded education. The remaining 60% of the allocation may be spent on all three priorities, including technology. However, there is a 15% cap on devices, equipment, software, and digital content. (Society of Health and Physical Educators America, 2018)

As previously mentioned, physical and health education teachers both qualify for funds allocated by Title IV as part of ESSA. This money, however, is not guaranteed. It is your role as a practitioner to create a plan and request funding from your program coordinator, administrator, or any other stakeholders responsible for allocating funds. SHAPE America proposes linking all of your requests to both the physical and health education national standards, as well as the International Society for Technology in Education (ISTE) standards (Society of Health and Physical Educators America, 2018) (table 16.1). The SHAPE America website (shapeamerica.org) provides a planning tool to help practitioners create a proposal to demonstrate their needs, as well as a template for writing a funding request letter. To reiterate, this funding is not guaranteed, but it is a great resource to begin looking for funding. If you do not get funding your first year, build your case and work to gain support from your school community again next year. Know that change sometimes takes time, and the extra time will help you build your case.

Parent-Teacher Association (PTA)

It is not always realistic to count on a school budget for obtaining funds. You may work at a school in a high-needs area where the budget is tight to help accommodate the

Table 16.1   ISTE Standards for Educators

Learner	Learn from and with others and explore promising practices that leverage technology.
Leader	Seek opportunities to support student empowerment, help shape and shared vision and advocate for student equity.
Citizen	Inspire students to contribute responsibly in the digital world and guide them to be curious, wise, empathetic, safe, and ethical.
Collaborator	Collaborate with others to improve practice, discover and share resources, and solve problems with others around the globe.
Designer	Design authentic, learner-driven activities and environments that recognize and accommodate learner variability.
Facilitator	Model creative expression, empower students to take ownership of their learning and create opportunities for students to innovate and solve problems.
Analyst	Use data to drive instruction and provide alternate ways for students to demonstrate competency and use assessment data to guide progress.

needs of your students. When weighing the basic needs of the students (such as food and safety) versus the needs of your program, you also may forego a portion of your annual budget to help in a higher area of need. If you are teaching at a school with limited to no budget, then you should consider approaching your parent-teacher association (PTA) to request assistance. The PTA is a group of family members who volunteer to advocate for the needs of students and align their projects with the strategic goals of the schools. The mission statement of the National PTA is "to make every child's potential a reality by engaging and empowering families and communities to advocate for all children" (National PTA, n.d.). The PTA can advocate on your behalf for ESSA funding, host fundraisers to support your program, or write grants through the National PTA website. Not all schools have PTAs, but most have some type of parent group working to ensure their students succeed. It is absolutely realistic to approach the PTA or parent group with requests for funds. The PTA might allocate a portion of the "Box Tops for Education" fundraiser to your program or perhaps raise money for technology resources that can be shared by a variety of teachers. Before approaching your PTA, it is best to speak with your administrator to find out the protocols at your school. You may be asked to sit in at a PTA meeting and pitch your needs or help run a fundraiser in conjunction with the group. Before approaching the PTA with requests, be sure to familiarize yourself with suggested steps for effective fundraising, shown in table 16.2.

Booster Clubs

A booster club is an organized group of parents that operate in the interests of athletes and the athletic program (Jensen & Overman, 2003). A primary purpose of booster clubs is to raise money for teams, especially when budget cuts prohibit teams from reaching their full potential. Booster clubs typically operate under a set of bylaws that are written by the athletic director, and they have specific rules to follow about financing athletic teams. Booster clubs sometimes have associated membership fees, hold fundraisers, or write grants to support teams. Each team typically has its own booster club. For instance, the gymnastics team would have a gymnastics booster club, and the wrestling team would have a wrestling booster club. When approaching a booster club for booster-generated funds, a coach should provide a written request. Booster clubs often have a mandatory

Table 16.2 Seven Steps to Effective Fundraising

Step	Description
1	Approach key stakeholders (principal, program coordinator, curriculum director, athletic director) to request approval to raise funds with the help of the PTA.
2	Write a clear and compelling needs statement with student learning outcomes included.
3	Set a monetary goal based on needs.
4	Construct a maintenance plan or have a plan to acquire additional funding if you are requesting items with batteries or consumable features.
5	Create a time line and a plan to manage incoming funds.
6	Follow through with your plan and be transparent with your stakeholders along the way. If the plan changes, request approval to proceed with amended plans.
7	Share the results with your supporters and donors. Use the equipment you requested and take plenty of pictures to post around the school and on any approved social media platforms. Send newsletters home to families, thanking them for supporting your cause. You never know when you'll need to request funds again, so any letters home should include lots of thanks to the PTA or parent group as well.

form that coaches should fill out when requesting funds. If your booster club does not have a form, then consider creating one. A simple Internet search of "booster club request form" will provide you with a variety of samples to choose from. A typical request form includes the following:

1. What is the purpose of the funds?
2. When are the funds needed?
3. How much money is requested? (Submit quotes from three vendors.)
4. How many students will benefit from the funds?
5. How will the activity benefit students who participate?
6. Will there be any matching funds from another source?
7. What efforts have been made to obtain money from other sources?
8. What activities have parents of student-athletes undertaken to support the project?

Before approaching the booster club, have a conversation with your athletic director about norms and protocols at your specific institution.

FUNDRAISING

If school-based funds are not readily available through the budget, the PTA, or a booster club, you can begin to think about holding your own fundraiser for the materials you need. Traditional **fundraising** efforts rely on students and their families to speak with people face-to-face and create connections between donors and those who will be benefitting from the funds. Donors typically have the option to pay in person, through secure websites, or via money apps such as Venmo or the Cash app. Money from this type of fundraiser typically comes directly from the school community, engaging parents, relatives, family friends, and community partners to help donate to the program. This type of fundraiser will be organized and run by you, the practitioner, and not an affiliated parent group. Although there seems to be endless possibilities for fundraising ideas, some typical practitioner-led fundraisers include the following:

- Community fun walks or runs with an entry fee or pledge system
- Product sales for profit (the "Y-Ties" fundraiser, candle fundraisers, book sales, coupon books, etc.)
- Restaurant fundraisers with a portion of the proceeds going to your program
- Weekend car washes

Before you select the fundraiser that you would like to implement, you must ask permission from your school stakeholders and determine the policies for raising money for individual programs. For instance, some practitioners are not allowed to keep all of the proceeds; they must split a portion among other programs at the school. Before organizing a fundraiser, refer to table 16.2 for a seven-step process to guide your planning.

Fundraisers can be quite time consuming, and can be tough to run on your own. Be sure you have clear goals to help you stay motivated along the way.

CROWDFUNDING

Sometimes, for a variety of reasons, teachers must look beyond traditional fundraisers. Some schools have policies that individual teachers cannot hold fundraisers for their individual programs, or fundraisers may be limited because the school is located in a low-income area. Whatever the case may be, you may need to look beyond your immediate community to support your cause. In this instance, you can seek support from alternate methods through **crowdfunding** websites. Crowdfunding is a way for practitioners to pitch their need for donations to a large range of Internet users (Reese & Miller, 2017). The reach for crowdfunding surpasses that of traditional fundraising, because projects can easily be shared beyond students' immediate family and community via social media. Although the list of crowdfunding websites is vast, table 16.3 provides a selection of websites frequently used by practitioners. Crowdfunding applications typically require a detailed budget, measurable student learning outcomes, and a convincing proposal that persuades potential backers that the cause is worthy of donation (Majumdar & Bose, 2018). Reese and Miller (2017) propose a four-phase process to obtaining crowdfunding:

- *Phase 1: Preplanning.* Before applying for funds, you must know your school or district policy for obtaining funds through a crowdfunding platform. You should do your homework and compare all of the platforms available before approaching administration. Be sure to research several of the crowdfunding resources from table 16.3. Different organizations have different requirements for obtaining funds, advertising on social

Table 16.3 Crowdfunding Platforms for Practitioners

Platform	Mission or vision statement	Goal or equipment requirements	Impact	Cost
Adopt-a-Classroom, Inc. (1998) www.adoptaclassroom.org	Advancing equity in education by powering today's classrooms to prepare tomorrow's graduates.	No goal requirements.	From 1998-2018, $35 million has been raised, and 177,712 classrooms have been adopted, benefitting 4.4 million students	They provide services for free by funding operating costs through vendor and corporate partnerships. Donors are welcome to donate an optional processing fee at checkout.
DonorsChoose (2010) www.donorschoose.org	We make it easy for anyone to help a classroom in need, moving us closer to a nation where students in every community have the tools and experiences they need for a great education.	No goal requirements. Projects must be fully-funded; no partial funding is accepted. Materials must be requested through one of the approved 20+ vendors.	Over $765 million raised for classroom project funding.	There are processing fees, fulfillment labor, and materials costs.
Fundly (2009) https://fundly.com	We empower people and organizations to support and nurture the causes and communities they care about.	No goal requirements.	Over $330 million raised	There is a platform fee of 4.9% and a 2.9% + $0.30 processing fees for credit cards.
GoFundMe (2010) www.gofundme.com	Free fundraising for the people and causes you care about.	Minimum goal is $1.00, maximum goal is $100 million. You can increase your goal amount any time.	Over $5 billion raised since 2010	There is no platform fee, but there are 2.9% + $0.30 processing fees for credit and debit cards.

media, structuring fees, and the like. For instance, through DonorsChoose, the applicant must choose resources from approved vendors; through Fundly, there are both platform fees and processing fees.

• *Phase 2: Project development.* After your project has been approved, you will begin formally planning the project. Determine what equipment you need based on the learning goals you wish to meet. You should consider how you will measure learning outcomes and have a clear plan about how to share the success of your project with donors. During this phase, you should also set time lines, determine your budget, and determine how you are going to sustain your project. Some crowdfunding platforms allow teachers to use money as it comes in, whereas others require you to wait until the fundraising campaign ends. Knowing this will help you create a solid time line.

• *Phase 3: Crowdfunding.* Start formally writing your proposal on your chosen platform. Table 16.4 provides you with some persuasive writing tips to help you write the best possible crowdfunding proposal. Each organization requires different formatting, so

Table 16.4 Crowdfunding Proposal Tips

Tip	Description
Be rational	Practitioners that are transparent about costs for the project, costs per item, and why they are reaching out to the community are more likely to be funded. Use facts and statistics to help donors see why you logically need the money (Majumdar & Bose, 2018).
Be authentic	Use pronouns and build trust with the donors. Tell your story and paint a picture of the students you will affect with your technology purchases. Do not fabricate uses—be truthful and authentic (Majumdar & Bose, 2018).
Share on social media and collect likes and comments.	Popular requests are more likely to be supported, and so are ones with community comments. Donors want to understand the status of the proposal, so be sure to respond to comments that donors post. Shares and comments also add to authenticity (Majumdar & Bose, 2018). The success of your crowdfunding campaign depends on you to be constantly promoting and interacting with donors.
Use images and videos	Providing compelling photo or video evidence of your needs and updating photos along the process increase the likelihood of being funded (Majumdar & Bose, 2018). Be authentic in the photos or videos you use, and ensure that the photos support the purpose of your project (Xu, 2018).
Timing, timing, timing!	Wait for an ideal time to launch your campaign. A campaign too close to the beginning of the year or after a big holiday break may hinder your success (Boitnott, 2017). Ask your administration what ideal times are for fundraisers at your institution, or ask parents and community members for input.
Enlist help	Reach out to your district grant writer or someone who has been successful at using crowdfunding in the past. Take advantage of experts who write persuasively and know the process well (Boitnott, 2017).
Be mindful	When constructing your budget, keep in mind that some crowdfunding sources operate in an "all or nothing" manner so that the integrity of the project is not compromised. If you select one of these platforms, consider splitting your project into two parts (Reese & Miller, 2017). Some crowdfunding platforms offer special funding events or have corporate partners who will match donations that meet their interests. Be mindful of your budget and special promotions so you can maximize your earnings.

read the expectations carefully. This proposal is what the public will see—even people who may not know you, your program, or your school. Although some applications can be completed in 30 minutes or so, take the time to draft and redraft your proposal to really provide an authentic and accurate story of why you need funding.

• *Phase 4: Concluding activities.* Depending on your crowdfunding platform, you will need to take different steps at the conclusion of your campaign. You may need to send thank-you letters, produce reports, upload pictures, or submit student work. Refer to chapter 15 if you are uploading student photos and student work so you do not infringe on copyright, and don't violate FERPA. Be sure you are transparent about how you are using your sources, and share funding successes with your administration and your school community. Remember, all of your current donors may choose to be *future* donors.

Crowdfunding requires lots of time, commitment, and promotion through social media. Successful campaigns are shared on various platforms beyond the immediate community. Take time to look at a variety of crowdfunding platforms and determine the best one to meet the needs of your program goals.

GRANTS

A final way to obtain funding for your program is through grant writing. Grant writing differs from fundraising because it requires you to submit a proposal up front, then wait to hear back from the grant committee either funding or denying your request. Depending on the type of grant you are writing, you may request a specific piece of technology or a specific dollar amount. You will put in a lot of work up front and at the end of the process, but you do not have to promote your grant like you would a fundraiser. The process of searching for a grant and writing a persuasive application can be challenging, but it is worth it in the end when your idea is funded. Another advantage to grant writing is that you are seeking resources beyond your immediate school community. You may teach in a community where funds are tight, and asking for money may seem inappropriate. Here are some practical tips that will help you prepare for writing your grant (Brett, 2016; Channing Bete Company, n.d.; Visovsky, 2015):

1. Prepare your materials.
   a. Know your needs and goals, including the budget request.
   b. Know the history and mission of your school or organization.
   c. Find a grant (identify several grants that meet your needs).
   d. Know the deadline for the proposal (allow plenty of time).
   e. Work with district grant writers or other experts at your institution.

2. Write the grant proposal.
   a. Provide a description of the project: be clear, concise, and specific. Avoid using acronyms and jargon whenever possible.
   b. Make a connection between the need for the funds and specific student outcomes.
   c. Adhere to the application guidelines. Do not include unnecessary information that will overwhelm the reviewer.
   d. Provide a detailed budget.

3. Before submission:
   a. Go through a checklist of the grant requirements.
   b. Proofread for spelling and grammar.
   c. Check paragraphs for length and readability.

4. After submission:
   a. Keep a copy of your application on your computer or print out a copy.
   b. Keep in touch with your funding source if you are awarded the grant (including any required follow-up information).
   c. Send a thank-you letter (whether you received the grant or not).

Grant writing can seem overwhelming, but the process is fairly straightforward. The more time and detail you put into your grant up front, the more likely you are to gain the funding you desire. Having a grant-writing team to review the proposal is extremely helpful, so enlist colleagues who have done this before. If you apply for a grant and do not get funding, then try again. Many grants have more than one cycle. You can ask for feedback from the grant committee, resubmit your application, or look for another grant that meets your needs.

The first place to look for a grant would be through your local school district. Sometimes there are opportunities to request funding from your district, so you are only competing for funds amongst a small group of practitioners in your district. Other local places to look would be your state SHAPE, AHPERD, or coaching association; local hospitals; and local health insurance providers (see tables 16.5 and 16.6 for more information on locating grants).

Search online for up-to-date grants from professional organizations.
Cnythzl/iStock/Getty Images

Table 16.5 Local and State Grants

Organization	Description
State SHAPE or AHPERD	Most state associations allocate some of their budget to grant opportunities for their members. After becoming a member of your state SHAPE or AHPERD, take a look at the grant opportunities. These opportunities vary from state to state. Some associations offer grants for travel to conferences, whereas others support requests for equipment. To find out more information about state associations, you can complete a web search, or go to www.shapeamerica.org and search "State Affiliate Websites" for a comprehensive list of all associations.
Local hospitals or health insurance providers	Local hospitals and health insurance providers often provide grants for initiatives that support health and wellness for community members. These resources typically support community funding opportunities that align with their missions of helping people live healthier lives.

Table 16.6 National Grants

Organization	Name of grant	Field	Description
Dick's Sporting Goods Foundation www.sportsmatter. org/getfunded.html	Sports Matter	Coaching	All youth sports teams are welcome to apply for funding through the Dick's Sporting Goods' Sponsorships and Donations program. Public and charter school teams also have the opportunity to submit a Sports Matter crowdfunding project through donorschoose. org, the largest crowdfunding supporter of students and schools.
Fuel Up to Play 60 www.fueluptoplay60. com/funding	Fuel Up to Play 60	Health and physical education	Schools may submit an application during more than one funding cycle per school year; however, total amount of money awarded may not exceed $4,000. Applicants must select one Healthy Eating Plan and one Physical Activity Plan. All applications must contain both Healthy Eating and Physical Activity Plans. Fuel Up to Play 60 monies and equipment, goods, and services are meant to fund and stimulate activities that lead to lasting change within the school environment.
Fund for Teachers https://fft.fund forteachers.org	Fund for Teachers	Health and physical education	Fund for Teachers (FFT) provides educators who possess a broad vision of what it means to teach and learn the resources needed to pursue self-designed professional learning experiences. FFT grants are used for an unlimited variety of projects, all designed to create enhanced learning environments for teachers, their students, and their school communities. This grant can be used for technology purchases that are aligned with learning goals.

Opportunities and Ideas for Acquiring Technology

Organization	Name of grant	Field	Description
The Connection https://internet.frontier.com/resources/grantsscholarships/social-media-in-the-classroom-grant	Social Media in the Classroom Grant	Health and physical education	There is so much opportunity for learning using social media. This grant can be used to bring in guest speakers to talk about social media or to purchase technology for the classroom!
The Nature's Bounty Foundation www.naturesbountyfoundation.com/Charity/Grants	Grant's Program	Health, physical education, and coaching	Requests made must support the areas of health and wellness.
Lockheed Martin www.lockheedmartin.com/en-us/who-we-are/communities/applying-for-contributions.html	STEM Education	Health, physical education, and coaching	Requests must align with one or more of Lockheed Martin's strategic focus areas—science, technology, engineering, and mathematics (STEM) education and military and veteran causes—or provide support to address the needs of the communities where our employees live and work.
SHAPE America www.shapeamerica.org/grants/SHAPE_America_Impact_Schools_Application.aspx	Impact Schools Grant Program	Health and physical education	The SHAPE America Impact Schools Grant Program identifies and provides funds and professional development opportunities to 10 eligible schools across the country. Funds raised for this program will be used to improve existing health and physical education programs and help teachers continue their studies and build expertise.
SHAPE America www.shapeamerica.org/grants/tommywilsonmemorialgrant.aspx	Tommy Wilson Memorial Grant	Health, physical education, and coaching	The grant supports recreational programs for individuals with disabilities. Grants are awarded for up to $1,500 total per year. Applicants may apply for $500 to $1,500. SHAPE America reserves the right to not award any funds in any given year.
Walmart Foundation http://giving.walmart.com/apply-for-grants	Community Grant Program	Health, physical education, and coaching	There are eight areas of funding for which an organization can apply. The ones most pertinent to technology purchases for health education, physical education, and coaching are listed here: *Quality of life:* Improving access to recreation, arts, or cultural experiences for low-income individuals and families in the United States *Education:* Providing after-school enrichment, tutoring, or vocational training for low-income individuals and families in the United States *Diversity and inclusion:* Fostering the building of relationships and understanding among diverse groups in the United States

SMART TECHNOLOGY PURCHASES FOR YOUR BUDGET

Throughout this chapter, you have read about tips to acquire funds for your program through various avenues. Regardless of the size of your budget, you must have a strategy and vision of what you want the technology to achieve. Purchasing equipment first and then tying it to student learning later is *not* the path to success. You should be able to clearly state how any new devices will be integrated in a meaningful way into your program. At every step of the process, you should be asking yourself, "What do I want my students to achieve?" (Walker, 2015). When making a purchase for your students, keep in mind your goals and take a look at some tips from experts that will help you make the best possible purchase (see table 16.7). Also, consider the following six key factors to making a wise technology purchase (Mears, 2006):

1. *The impulse buy.* Take your time deciding what to buy, and do not get distracted by things you see online or at conferences. Reckless spending sprees will get technology into the program quickly, but with poorly developed plans for use (Walker, 2015). Without adequate time to plan, you may end up with high-priced equipment that does not adequately serve your students. There may be similar products at lower prices, so do your work and take your time. Be aware of maintenance, contract renewals, or other consumable needs associated with your purchases as well. Money is often wasted or mismanaged because the technology is purchased without considering these specific features.

2. *Consider goals before technology.* Plan your purchases based on the needs of your students, rather than trying to make student learning fit the capabilities of the technology (Berger, 2017). For teachers, be sure you align your purchases with the state or national goals that inform your program. For coaches, ensure the equipment you purchase matches the goals you have for your athletes to improve their performance. Another consideration is ensuring the technology is developmentally appropriate. Perhaps your younger students would benefit most from pedometers, whereas your older ones would benefit from heart rate monitors (Society of Health and Physical Educators America et al., 2011). Think about the cognitive, physical, and emotional needs of your students before purchasing equipment.

3. *Assessment versus teaching versus teacher tasks.* Determine the purpose of the tool and consider equipment that serves multiple purposes. For instance, if you want equipment to give students instant feedback but also help you with assessment, look into resources such as the AssessLinkPE tool for skill analysis (AssessLink, n.d.). This tool allows you to film students in real time, show the video in slow motion, and also instantly score students on their biomechanics. If you can find a tool that enhances current practices and serves a variety of functions, then you are making a wise purchase.

4. *Purchase some materials now, more later.* Consider purchasing some equipment up front and the rest later. For instance, if you need 30 heart rate monitors and can only fund 15, then get a half-class set and have students share or rotate days. However, be cautious that you don't buy a portion of something that is unusable without the other part. For instance, if you purchase 20 dance pads for Dance Dance Revolution, but you can't afford the gaming system or the projector, then you just spent money on a project that might never be funded in the future, making the dance pads obsolete.

5. *Application limitations = money on a shelf.* Purchase a technology tool that has many uses, and won't be sitting on a shelf most of the year. Picking a cheaper version of a tool may seem appealing; however, the more expensive tool may have many applications. Mears (2006) calls this finding the "Swiss army knife" of technology.

6. *Cost = learning.* Do not purchase technology if you do not see a direct benefit to student learning outcomes. The latest and greatest technology resources might be appealing, but may have less of an impact than less expensive technology that appropriately meets the needs of your students.

Table 16.7   Tips for Purchasing Educational Technology

Tip	Description
Check your closets before you go shopping.	Do a thorough sweep of resources your program already has. Be sure to ask colleagues if they have any technology equipment that they do not currently use.
Compare apples to apples.	Compile a list of three to five vendors. Ask for the vendors to give you presentations to sell you on why their product is the best. Ask lots of questions.
Check references.	Ask the vendor for the names and contact information of other practitioners who have purchased the same equipment you're considering purchasing. Reach out to those programs and hear firsthand accounts of the technology in action.
Do a pilot test.	Ask your vendor if they are willing to let you pilot test the equipment before purchasing.
Research your vendor.	When purchasing from a vendor, find out how responsive they are to help with troubleshooting. Often, you are going to need assistance setting up or maintaining your purchase, so be sure you trust your vendor to support you.
Find creative savings.	Find out if you get discounts for purchasing in bulk or if there are any upcoming sales you should look out for. See if another program would be willing to collaborate with your purchase in order to cut costs.
Get a guarantee.	Your equipment purchase should work. Find out what is covered under the warranty or the money-back guarantee before proceeding.
Include your teaching or coaching team.	All key players in your program, including your teaching or coaching team and important stakeholders such as the athletics director, principal, and curriculum director, should understand your purchase, your goals, and how to use the equipment. The tools you purchase will stay with your program for many years to come.

Adapted from Slusser (2017).

So in the end, what should you purchase? This must be determined based on the needs of your program. One user on the PE Central Facebook page posted a question to its members asking what technology people would buy with $4,000. The majority of responses were heart rate monitors, smartboards, projectors, and iPads. What was missing from the post was: "Why?" Why make these purchases? How will this technology enhance student learning? Teaching with technology has many advantages if well planned, but also disadvantages if poorly planned. Instead of starting with the question "What would you buy?" consider starting with "Why are you interested in purchasing technology?" If you can't answer that question, then stop yourself from making an impulse buy.

Conclusion

Regardless of the size of your budget, you must have a strategy and vision of what you want the technology to achieve in your program. Having a goal will help you find or raise funds for your program and follow through with a plan to implement the technology in your program. With the content from this chapter, you should be more confident to find funding sources for your needs and understand the steps you should take to make informed technology purchases. Keep your student learning and performance at the forefront of your visions, and put in the work required to meet those goals. Share the work you do at local conferences and become a leader in utilizing technology in your district or state. There are many people who will turn to you as an expert in the field, so pass along all of your tech-savvy knowledge to your peers in your teaching and coaching circles.

Key Terms

crowdfunding—eliciting funding from a large group of people, or a crowd, using the Internet.

Every Student Succeeds Act (ESSA)—a law signed by President Obama in 2015 that provides a variety of provisions that will help schools better meet the needs of all students, and ultimately will help students achieve success. ESSA targets funding and resources for high-needs students and low -performing schools, transparency and assessment reports for communities, high academic standards in a variety of subject areas, and evidence-based intervention support.

fundraising—A persuasive activity that convinces donors to give money to a cause.

No Child Left Behind (NCLB)—A law signed by President Bush in 2002 that required schools to be accountable for measurable student outcomes. NCLB required states to create plans to boost the academic performance of all students, or risk losing Title I funding. NCLB lead to increased assessments for schools and students, and was ultimately replaced by ESSA in 2015.

well-rounded education—According to ESSA, a well-rounded education includes coursework in the arts, humanities, sciences, social sciences, English, and math. Coursework is provided that enables students to be critical and reflective thinkers.

Review Questions

1. List and describe three different ways you can obtain funding to support technology in your program.
2. What is the difference between fundraising and crowdfunding? List three advantages and disadvantages of each.
3. This chapter lists a variety of steps you should take before raising funds for your program. Which three do you believe are the most important, and why?
4. Look up a grant that you believe best fits your needs as a future practitioner (you can refer to tables 16.5 and 16.6 for ideas). Describe why you selected this grant, and list the steps you need to take to complete the application.

Discussion Questions

1. What type of fundraising sounds most realistic for you to lead in your future program? Why did you select this?
2. How would you convince a wary administration to use funds to purchase technology? What would be your top three arguments?
3. Describe a time that you were involved in fundraising. What were the pros and cons of this type of fundraising effort?
4. Navigate to your state professional organization home page and research what grants are available for you. How (if at all) could you use these grants to purchase technology?

REFERENCES

Chapter 1

Eberline, A., & Richards, K. (2013). Teaching with technology in physical education. *Strategies: A Journal for Physical and Sport Educators, 26*(6), 38-39.

International Society for Technology in Education. (2018). ISTE standards for educators. Retrieved from https://www.iste.org/standards/for-educators

Joint Committee on National Health Education Standards. (2007). *National health education standards: Achieving excellence* (2nd ed.). Washington, DC: American Cancer Society.

Krause, J.M. (2017). Physical education student teachers' technology integration self-efficacy. *The Physical Educator, 74,* 476-496.

Krause, J.M., Franks, H., & Lynch, B. (2017). Current technology trends and issues among health and physical education professionals. *The Physical Educator, 74*(1), 164-180.

Scrabis-Fletcher, K., Juniu, S., & Zullo, E. (2016). Preservice physical education teachers' technological pedagogical content knowledge. *The Physical Educator, 73*(4), 704-718.

Society of Health and Physical Educators. (2005). National standards for sport coaches. Retrieved from https://www.shapeamerica.org/standards/coaching

Society of Health and Physical Educators. (2014). *National standards and grade-level outcomes for K-12 physical education.* Champaign, IL: Human Kinetics.

Society of Health and Physical Educators. (2015). The essential components of physical education. Retrieved from https://www.shapeamerica.org//upload/TheEssentialComponentsOfPhysicalEducation.pdf

Society of Health and Physical America. (2017). National standards for initial physical education teacher education. Retrieved from http://www.shapeamerica.org/accreditation/upload/National-Standards-for-Initial-Physical-Education-Teacher-Education-2017.pdf

U.S. Department of Education, Office of Educational Technology. (2014). Online professional learning quality checklist. Retrieved from https://tech.ed.gov/wp-content/uploads/2014/11/Section-5-Online-Professional-Learning-Quality-Checklist-FINAL.pdf

U.S. Department of Education, Office of Educational Technology. (2017). Reimagining the role of technology in education: 2017 National Education Technology Plan update. Retrieved from https://tech.ed.gov/files/2017/01/NETP17.pdf

Chapter 2

Cox, D., Fan, X., Brooks, C., & Krause, J. (2018, October). *Top 10 learning management system components for health and physical educators.* Poster presented at the Society of Health and Physical Educators Colorado Convention, Aurora, CO.

Dietz, B., Hurn, J.E., Mays, T.A., & Woods, D. (2018). An introduction to learning analytics. In R.A. Reiser & J.V. Dempsey (Eds.), *Trends and issues in instructional design and technology* (pp.104-111). Boston, MA: Pearson.

Emmer, E.T., & Stough, L.M. (2001). Classroom management: A critical part of educational psychology, with implications for teacher education. *Educational Psychologist, 36*(2), 103-112.

Hughes, M. (2018). *A study on synthesizing PDM and MSs in K-12 environments* (Unpublished doctoral dissertation). Purdue University, West Lafayette, IN.

Jones, V. (1996). Classroom management. In J. Sikula (Ed.), *Handbook of research on teacher education* (2nd ed., pp. 503–521). New York, NY: Simon & Schuster.

Krause, J.M., Franks, H., & Lynch, B. (2017). Current technology trends and issues among health and physical education professionals. *The Physical Educator, 74*(1), 164-180.

Kyriakidis, G., & Papadakis, S. (2016, April). *Blended learning in K-12 education: A case study for teaching athletics in physical education.* Paper presented at the International Association for Blended Learning Conference, Kavala, Greece.

Landau, B.M. (2001, April). *Teaching classroom management: A stand-alone necessity for preparing new teachers.* Paper presented at the Annual Meeting of the American Educational Research Association, Seattle, WA.

Melnick, S.A., & Meister, D.G. (2008). A comparison of beginning and experienced teachers' concerns. *Educational Research Quarterly, 31*(3), 39-56.

U.S. Department of Education. (1974). *Family Educational Rights and Privacy Act.* Retrieved from https://www2.ed.gov/policy/gen/guid/fpco/ferpa/index.html?

Veenman, S. (1984). Perceived problems of beginning teachers. *Review of Educational Research, 54*(2), 143-178.

Chapter 3

Anastasiades, P.S. (2010a). K-12 educational videoconferencing applications in Greece and Cyprus. In A.C. Rayler (Ed.), *Videoconferencing: Technology, impact, and applications* (pp. 81-110). Hauppauge, NY: Nova Science.

Anastasiades, P.S. (2010b). Learning for K-12 students and teachers: Theory and practice: The conditions for an effective VC. In A.C. Rayler (Ed.), *Videoconferencing: Technology, impact, and applications* (pp. 179-198). Hauppauge, NY: Nova Science.

Anderson, M. (2015). How having smartphones (or not) shapes the way teens communicate [Web log post]. Retrieved from www.pewresearch.org/fact-tank/2015/08/20/how-having-smartphones-or-not-shapes-the-way-teens-communicate

Cranmer, G.A., & Sollitto, M. (2015). Sport support: Received social support as a predictor of athlete satisfaction. *Communication Research Reports, 32*(3), 253-264.

Filippone, M., & Survinski, M. (2016). The importance of etiquette in school email. *American Secondary Education; Bowling Green, 45*(1), 22–27. Retrieved from https://search.proquest.com/docview/1845747561/abstract/E60010EE785643C1PQ/1

Gorton, W. (2013, August 19). Head back to school with Drive: Student edition [Web log post]. Retrieved from https://drive.googleblog.com/2013/08/drivebts-teachers.html

Hartman, J.L., & McCambridge, J. (2011). Optimizing millennials' communication styles. *Business Communication Quarterly, 74*(1), 22-44.

Magid, L. (2017). Google now letting parents set up accounts for kids under 13 [Web log post]. Retrieved from https://www.mercurynews.com/2017/03/15/google-now-letting-parents-set-up-accounts-for-kids-under-13

Meishar-Tal, H., Kurt, G., & Pieterse, E. (2012). Facebook groups as LMS: A case study. *International Review of Research in Open and Distance Learning, 13*(4), 33-48.

Miller, M. (2008). *Cloud computing: Web-based applications that change the way you work and collaborate online.* Indianapolis, IN: QUE.

Moțățăianu, I.T. (2018). Technology-mediated communication in education. *Euromentor Journal, 9*(2), 48-54.

Näf, M. (2011). Doodle in the classroom: The benefits of online scheduling [Web log post]. Retrieved from https://elearnmag.acm.org/archive.cfm?aid=2003350

Pelton, L., & Pelton, T.W. (1996). *Building attitudes: How a technology course affects preservice teachers' attitudes about technology* (pp. 199–204). Presented at the Society for Information Technology & Teacher Education International Conference, Association for the Advancement of Computing in Education (AACE), Chesapeake, VA. Retrieved from https://www.learntechlib.org/primary/p/46765

Pew Research Center. (2018, February 5). Mobile fact sheet. Retrieved from www.pewinternet.org/fact-sheet/mobile/

Porterfield, K., & Carnes, M. (2014). *Why school communication matters: Strategies from PR professionals.* New York, NY: Rowman & Littlefield.

Price, R. (2017, May 6). Google Drive now hosts more than 2 trillion files [Web log post]. Retrieved from https://www.businessinsider.com/2-trillion-files-google-drive-exec-prabhakar-raghavan-2017-5

Rayler, A.C. (2013). *Videoconferencing: Technology, impact, and applications.* Hauppauge, NY: Nova Science.

Reich, J. (2015). Thinking about texting parents? Best practices for school-to-parent texting. Retrieved from http://blogs.edweek.org/edweek/edtechresearcher/2015/12/thinking_about_texting_parents_best_practices_for_school-to-parent_texting.html?cmp=SOC-SHR-FB

Rogers, E.M. (1995). *Diffusion of innovations* (4th ed.). New York, NY: Free Press.

Sadik, A. (2017). Students' acceptance of file sharing systems as a tool for sharing course materials: The case of Google Drive. *Education and Information Technologies, 22*(5), 2455-2470.

Smith, J. (n.d.). How does Remind comply with COPPA? Retrieved from https://help.remind.com/hc/en-us/articles/211758126-How-does-Remind-comply-with-COPPA

Society of Health and Physical Educators. (2009). Appropriate instructional practice guidelines, K-12: A side-by-side comparison. Retrieved from https://www.shapeamerica.org/upload/Appropriate-Instructional-Practice-Guidelines-K-12.pdf

Chapter 4

Association for Supervision and Curriculum Development (ASCD). (2014). *Whole school, whole community, whole child: A collaborative approach to learning and health.* Alexandria, VA: Author.

Bates, C.C., Huber, R., & McClure, E. (2016). Stay connected: Using technology to enhance professional learning communities. *Reading Teacher, 70*(1), 99-102.

Betcher, C., & Lee, M. (2009). *The interactive whiteboard revolution: Teaching with IWBs.* Victoria, Australia: ACER Press.

Boettner, E.T. (2011). Using bell ringers in the CTE classroom. *Techniques: Connecting Education & Careers, 86*(6), 8-9.

Clement, J. (2018, October). Number of apps available in leading app stores as of 3rd quarter 2018. *Statista.* Retrieved from https://www.statista.com/statistics/276623/number-of-apps-available-in-leading-app-stores/

Connolly, M. (2018). *Skill-based health education* (2nd ed.). Burlington, MA: Jones and Bartlett Learning.

D2L. (n.d.) Interpreting the quiz item analysis report. Retrieved from https://documentation.brightspace.com/EN/insights/-/instructor/d2l_insights_interpreting_quiz_item_analysis.htm

Decker, J. (2010). *Utilizing interactive whiteboards in the classroom* (Master's thesis). St. John Fisher College, Rochester, NY. Retrieved from https://fisherpub.sjfc.edu/mathcs_etd_masters/98/

Delacruz, S. (2014). Using Nearpod in elementary guided reading groups. *TechTrends: Linking Research & Practice to Improve Learning, 58*(5), 62-69.

Fryar, C.D., Chen, T., & Li, X. (2012). Prevalence of uncontrolled risk factors for cardiovascular disease: United States, 1999-2010. *NCHS Data Brief, 103*, 1-8.

Furdu, I., Tomozei, C., & Kose, U. (2017). Pros and cons gamification and gaming in the classroom. *Broad Research in Artificial Intelligence and Neuroscience. 8*(2), 56-61.

Gamification. (n.d.) In *Merriam-Webster*. Retrieved from https://www.merriam-webster.com/dictionary/gamification

Google. (2018a). G Suite for Education. Retrieved from http://services.google.com/fh/files/misc/google_edu_g_suite_for_education.pdf

Google. (2018b). G Suite Learning Center. Retrieved from https://gsuite.google.com/learning-center/products/#!/

Google. (2018c). Advanced search. Retrieved from https://www.google.com/advanced_search

Google. (2018d). Google Play. Retrieved from https://play.google.com/store?hl=en

Green, T., & Green, J. (2018). Flipgrid: Adding voice and video to online discussions. *TechTrends: Linking Research & Practice to Improve Learning, 62*(1), 128-130.

Hunt, N. (2005). Using Microsoft Office to generate individualized tasks for students. *Teaching Statistics, 27*(2), 45-48.

Institute for Teaching, Innovation and Learning (n.d.). 8 ways to use Poll Everywhere in your teaching. Retrieved from https://the12apps.files.wordpress.com/2015/11/8-ways-to-use-poll-ev-in-the-classroom.pdf

Ismail, M.A., & Mohammad J.M. (2017). Kahoot: A promising tool for formative assessment in medical education. *Education in Medicine Journal, 9*(2), 19–26.

Kowalski, K. (2016, March 3) When smartphones go to school. *Science News for Students*. Retrieved from https://www.sciencenewsforstudents.org/article/when-smartphones-go-school

Kuo, Y.C., Belland, B.R., & Kuo, Y.T. (2017). Learning through blogging: Students' perspectives in collaborative blog-enhanced learning communities. *Educational Technology & Society, 20*(2), 37–50.

Levy, L. (2014, November 19). 7 ways to deal with digital distractions in class. *Edudemic*. Retrieved from www.edudemic.com/7-ways-deal-digital-distractions/

March, T. (2000). The 3 R's of WebQuests: Let's keep them real, rich, and relevant. *Multimedia Schools Magazine, 7*(6). Retrieved from www.infotoday.com/MMSchools/nov00/march.htm

Marzano, R.J., & Haystead, M. (2009). *Final report on the evaluation of the Promethean technology*. Englewood, CO: Marzano Research Laboratory.

Martinelli, M. (2015, November 20). 20 ways I use my interactive flat panel to save time and my sanity. WeAreTeachers. Retrieved from https://www.weareteachers.com/20-ways-i-use-my-interactive-flat-panel-to-save-time-and-my-sanity/

McCrea, B. (2013, September 17). 6 ways teachers can use google hangouts. *The Journal*. Retrieved from https://thejournal.com/articles/2013/09/17/6-ways-teachers-can-use-google-hangouts.aspx?m=1

Microsoft. (2018a). Office 365 training center. Retrieved from https://support.office.com/en-us/office-training-center

Microsoft. (2018b). Shortcut keys in Office. Retrieved from https://support.office.com/en-us/article/shortcut-keys-in-office-e765366f-24fc-4054-870d-39b214f223fd

Microsoft. (2018c). Office accessibility center—Resources for people with disabilities. Retrieved from https://support.office.com/en-us/article/office-accessibility-center-resources-for-people-with-disabilities-ecab-0fcf-d143-4fe8-a2ff-6cd596bddc6d

Microsoft. (2018d). Create professional slide layouts with PowerPoint Designer. Retrieved from https://support.office.com/en-us/article/create-professional-slide-layouts-with-powerpoint-designer-53c77d7b-dc40-45c2-b684-81415eac0617

Miller, M. (n.d.) 12 ways to use Google Cardboard in your class. *Ditch That Textbook*. Retrieved from http://ditchthattextbook.com/2016/08/18/12-ways-to-use-google-cardboard-in-your-class/

Operating system. (n.d.). In *Merriam-Webster*. Retrieved from https://www.merriam -webster.com/dictionary/operating%20system

Persky, A., & McLaughlin, J.E. (2017). The flipped classroom—From theory to practice in health professional education. *American Journal of Pharmaceutical Education, 81*(6), 1-11.

Plump, C.M., & LaRosa, J. (2017). Using Kahoot! in the classroom to create engagement and active learning: A game-based technology solution for elearning novices. *Management Teaching Review, 2*(2), 151-158.

Ryan, M.D., & Reid, S.A. (2015). Impact of the flipped classroom on student performance and retention: A parallel controlled study in general chemistry. *Journal of Chemical Education, 93*(1), 13-23.

Seemiller, C. (2017). Curbing digital distractions in the classroom. *Contemporary Educational Technology, 8*(3), 214-231.

Selwyn, N., Henderson, M., & Chao, S.H. (2015). Exploring the role of digital data in contemporary schools and schooling—"200,000 lines in an Excel spreadsheet." *British Educational Research Journal, 41*(5), 767-781.

Smith, H.J., Higgins, S., Wall, K., & Miller, J. (2005). Interactive whiteboards: Boon or bandwagon? A critical review of the literature. *Journal of Computer Assisted Learning, 21*(2), 91–101.

Sommerville, J. (2017, August). Tips for making effective PowerPoint presentations. National Conference of State

Legislators. Retrieved from www.ncsl.org/legislators-staff/legislative-staff/legislative-staff-coordinating-committee/tips-for-making-effective-powerpoint-presentations.aspx

Strickland, J. (2005). Using webquests to teach content: Comparing instructional strategies. *Contemporary Issues in Technology and Teacher Education, 5*(2), 138-148.

Thomas, M., & Schmid, E. C. (2010). *Interactive whiteboards for education: Theory, research, and practice.* Hershey, PA: Information Science Reference.

Uncapher, M.R., Lin, L., Rosen, L.D., Kirkorian, H., Baron, N.S., Bailey, K., Wagner, A.D. (2017). Media multitasking and cognitive, psychological, neural, and learning differences. *Pediatrics, 140*(S2), S62-S66.

Walker, D.S., Lindner, J.R., Murphrey, T.P., & Dooley, K. (2016). Learning management system usage. *Quarterly Review of Distance Education, 17*(2), 41-50.

Wang, F.H. (2017). An exploration of online behaviour engagement and achievement in flipped classroom supported by learning management system. *Computers & Education, 114*, 79-91.

Wood, J. (n.d.). Taking charge of the web in your classroom. *Scholastic Teacher.* Retrieved from https://www.scholastic.com/teachers/articles/teaching-content/taking-charge-web-your-classroom/

YouTube. (2013). Steve Jobs iPhone 2007 presentation (HD). Retrieved from https://www.youtube.com/watch?v=vN4U5FqrOdQ

Chapter 5

Aguilar, V.S., Lamoth, C.J.C., Maurits, N.M., & Roerdink, J.B.T.M. (2018). Assessing dynamic postural control during exergaming in older adults: A probabilistic approach. *Gait and Posture, 60*, 235-240.

Althoff, T., White, R.W., & Horvitz, E. (2016). Influence of Pokémon Go on physical activity: Study and implications. *Journal of Medical Internet Research, 18*(12), 1-10.

Ameryoun, A., Sanaeinasab, H., Saffari, M., & Koenig, H.G. (2018). Impact of game-based health promotion programs on body mass index in overweight/obese children and adolescents: A systematic review and meta-analysis of randomized controlled trials. *Childhood Obesity, 14*(2), 67-80. doi:10.1089/chi.2017.0250

Armstrong, T., & Jenny, S.E. (2018). Increasing physical activity in schools 30 seconds at a time. *Strategies: A Journal for Physical and Sport Educators, 31*(1), 51-56. doi:10.1080/08924562.2018.1395670

Baltezarević, R. & Baltezarević, B. (2018). The impact of video games on the formation of eSports. *Facta Universitatis Series: Physical Education and Sport, 16*(1), 137-147. doi:10.22190/FUPES170614012B

Baranowski, T., Blumberg, F., Buday, R., DeSmet, A., Fiellin, L.E., Green, C.S., . . . Young, K. (2016). Games for health for children—Current status and needed research. *Games for Health Journal, 5*(1), 1-12. doi:10.1089/g4h.2015.0026

Baranowski, T., Thompson, D., Buday, R., Lu, A.S., & Baranowski, J. (2010). Design of video games for children's diet and physical activity behavior change. *International Journal of Computer Science in Sport, 9*, 3-17.

Brewer, L., Barney, D.C., Prusak, K.A., & Pennington, T. (2016). Effects of music on physical activity rates of junior high school physical education students. *Physical Educator, 73*, 689-703. doi:10.18666/TPE-2016-V73-I4-7024

Carey, C., Naugle, K.E., Aqeel, D., Ohlman, T., & Naugle, K.M. (2017). Active gaming as a form of exercise to induce hypoalgesia. *Games for Health Journal, 6*(4), 255-261. doi:10.1089/g4h.2017.0024

Cates, J.R., Fuemmeler, B.F., Diehl, S.J., Stockton, L.L., Porter, J., Ihekweazu, C., . . . Coyne-Beasley, T. (2018). Developing a serious videogame for preteens to motivate HPV vaccination decision making: Land of Secret Gardens. *Games for Health Journal, 7*(1), 51-66. doi:10.1089/g4h.2017.0002

Chen, S., Sun, H., Zhu, X., & Chen, A. (2014). Relationship between motivation and learning in physical education and after-school physical activity. *Research Quarterly for Exercise and Sport, 85*(4), 468-477.

Chu, C., Chen, F., Pontifex, M.B., Sun, Y., & Chang, Y. (2016). Health-related physical fitness, academic achievement, and neuroelectric measures in children and adolescents. *International Journal of Sport and Exercise Psychology, 17*(2), 1-16. doi:10.1080/1612197X.2016.1223420

Cortez, M.B. (2018, January 12). 3 ways college football programs innovate with VR. *EdTech.* Retrieved from https://edtechmagazine.com/higher/article/2018/01/3-ways-college-football-programs-innovate-vr

Cronin, C. (2018, January 9). How more than 2,500 virtual reality reps helped transform Case Keenum's game. *ESPN.* Retrieved from http://www.espn.com/blog/nflnation/post/_/id/265904/virtual-reality-played-a-role-in-transforming-case-keenums-game

Dayton, K. (2013, October 17). Technology in physical education at Wood Road Elementary (Ballston Spa) [YouTube video]. Retrieved from https://youtu.be/8aCfgVS4JsE

de Carvalho, I.F., Leme, G.L.M., & Scheicher, M.E. (2018). The influence of video game training with and without subpatelar bandage in mobility and gait speed on elderly female fallers. *Journal of Aging Research, 2018*, 1-6. doi:10.1155/2018/9415093

Donnelly, J.E., Hillman, C.H., Castelli, D., Etnier, J.L., Lee, S., Tomporowski, P., . . . Szabo-Reed, A.N. (2016). Physical activity, fitness, cognitive function, and academic achievement in children: A systematic review. *Medicine and Science in Sports and Exercise, 48*(6), 1197-1222. doi:10.1249/MSS.0000000000000901

Edmodo. (2017). Edmodo award badges. Retrieved from https://www.edmodo.com

Education Week Research Center. (2018). School leaders and technology: Results from a national survey.

Retrieved from https://www.edweek.org/media/school-leaders-and-technology-education-week-research.pdf

Entertainment Software Association. (2018, April). *2018 essential facts about the computer and video game industry.* Retrieved from http://www.theesa.com/wp-content/uploads/2018/05/EF2018_FINAL.pdf

Entertainment Software Association. (2019). *2019 essential facts about the computer and video game industry.* Retrieved from https://www.theesa.com/esa-research/2019-essential-facts-about-the-computer-and-video-game-industry

Finco, M.D., Reategui, E., Zaro, M.A., Sheehan, D.D., & Katz, L. (2015). Exergaming as an alternative for students unmotivated to participate in regular physical education classes. *International Journal of Game-Based Learning, 5*(3), 1-10. doi:10.4018/IJGBL.2015070101

Gabana, N.T., Van Raalte, J.L., Hutchinson, J.C., Brewer, B.W., & Pettitpas, A.J. (2015). The effects of music and a coxswain on attentional focus, perceived exertion, motivation, and performance during a 1,000 m ergometer rowing sprint. *Journal of Applied Sport Psychology, 27,* 288-300. doi:10.1080/10413200.2014.993775

Gao, Z., Podlog, L.W., & Harrison, L. (2012). College students' goal orientations, situational motivation, and effort/persistence in physical activity classes. *Journal of Teaching in Physical Education, 31,* 246-260.

Garn, A., Baker, B., Beasley, E., & Solmon, M. (2012). What are the benefits of a commercial exergaming platform for college students? Examining physical activity, enjoyment and future intentions. *Journal of Physical Activity and Health, 9*(2), 311-318. doi:10.7821/naer.2016.7.164

Gilchrist, S. (2018, August 13). Gaming system weds gym, academics for Pickerington middle-schoolers. *The Columbus Dispatch.* Retrieved from http://www.dispatch.com/news/20180813/gaming-system-weds-gym-academics-for-pickerington-middle-schoolers

Harms, J., & Ryan, S. (2012). Using music to enhance physical education. *Journal of Physical Education, Recreation & Dance, 83*(3), 11-56. doi:10.1080/07303084.2012.10598736

Herron, J. (2016). Augmented reality in medical education and training. *Journal of Electronic Resources in Medical Libraries, 13*(2), 51-55. doi:10.1080/15424065.2016.1175987

Hidi, S., & Renninger, K.A. (2006). The four-phase model of interest development. *Educational Psychologist, 41*(2), 111-127. doi:10.1207/s15326985ep4102_4

Hsiao, K. (2013). Using augmented reality for students [sic] health—Case of combining educational learning with standard fitness. *Multimedia Tools and Applications, 64*(20), 407-421. doi:10.1007/s11042-011-0985-9

Huang, Y., Churches, L., & Reilly, B. (2015). A case study on virtual reality American football training. Proceedings from the *2015 Virtual Reality International Conference.* Laval, France. Retrieved from https://dl.acm.org/citation.cfm?id=2806178

Jaakkolo, T., Liukkonen, J., Laakso, T., & Ommundsen, Y. (2008). The relationship between situational and contextual self-determined motivation and physical activity intensity as measured by heart rates during ninth grade students' physical education classes. *European Physical Education Review, 14*(1), 13-31. doi:10.1177/1356336X07085707

Jenny, S., & Armstrong, T. (2013). Distance running and the elementary-age child. *Journal of Physical Education, Recreation & Dance, 84*(3), 17-25. doi:10.1080/07303084.2013.763709

Jenny, S.E., Chung, J.J., Rademaker, S.M., & Schary, D.P. (2017). Learning a sport through video gaming: A mixed-methods experimental study. *Loading: The Journal of the Canadian Game Studies Organization, 10*(17), 1-20.

Jenny, S.E., Hushman, G.F., & Hushman, C.J. (2013). Preservice teachers' perceptions of motion-based video gaming in physical education. *International Journal of Technology in Teaching and Learning, 9*(1), 96-111.

Jenny, S.E., Keiper, M.C., Taylor, B.J., Williams, D.P., Gawrysiak, J., Manning, R.D., & Tutka, P.M. (2018). eSports venues: A new business opportunity. *Journal of Applied Sport Management, 10*(1), 34-49. doi:10.18666/JASM-2018-V10-I1-8469

Jenny, S.E., Manning, R.D., Keiper, M.C., & Olrich, T.W. (2017). Virtual(ly) athletes: Where eSports fit within the definition of "sport." *Quest, 69*(1), 1-18. doi:10.1080/00336297.2016.1144517

Jenny, S.E., Noble, K.M., Hamill, S.D., & Schary, D.P. (2017). Virtual and authentic tennis: Differences and similarities of three common tennis strokes performed by collegiate players. *FACTA UNIVERSITIS Series: Physical Education and Sport, 16*(3), 525-541. doi: 10.22190/FUPES181218048J

Jenny, S.E., & Schary, D. (2014). Exploring the effectiveness of learning American football through playing the video game "Madden NFL." *International Journal of Technology in Teaching and Learning, 10*(1), 72-87.

Jenny, S.E., & Schary, D.P. (2015). Motion-based video game and authentic wall/rock climbing: Motivations and perceptions of novice climbers. *International Journal of Technology in Teaching and Learning, 11*(1), 35-49.

Jenny, S.E., & Schary, D.P. (2016). Virtual and "real-life" wall/rock climbing: Motor movement comparisons and video gaming pedagogical perceptions. *Sports Technology, 8*(3-4), 100-111. doi:10.1080/19346182.2015.1118110

Jenny, S.E., Schary, D.P., Noble, K.M., & Hamill, S.D. (2017). The effectiveness of developing motor skills through motion-based video gaming: A review. *Simulation and Gaming: An International Journal of Theory, Practice and Research, 48*(6), 722-734. doi:10.1177/1046878117738552

Jenny, S.E., & Thompson, R.M. (2016). Pokémon Go: Encouraging recreation through augmented reality gaming. *International Journal of Technology in Teaching and Learning, 12*(2), 112-122.

Joint Committee on National Health Education Standards. (2007). *National Health Education Standards: Achieving excellence* (2nd ed.). Washington, DC: American Cancer Society.

Kakinami, L., O'Loughlin, E.K., Dugas, E.N., Sabiston, C.M., Paradis, G., & O'Loughlin, J. (2015). The association between exergaming and physical activity in young adults. *Journal of Physical Activity and Health, 12*, 789-793. doi:10.1123/jpah.2013-0447

Karageorghis, C.I., Hutchinson, J.C., Jones, L., Farmer, H.L., Ayhan, M.S., Wilson, R.C., & Bailey, S.G. (2013). Psychological, psychophysical, and ergogenic effects of music in swimming. *Psychology of Sport and Exercise, 14*, 560-568. doi:10.1016/j.psychsport.2013.01.009

Keiper, M.C., Manning, R.D., Jenny, S., Olrich, T., & Croft, C. (2017). No reason to LoL at LoL: The addition of esports to intercollegiate athletic departments. *Journal for the Study of Sports and Athletes in Education, 11*(2), 143-160. doi:10.1080/19357397.2017.1316001

Kostka, A. (2018, July 14). FanFest attendees compete in virtual reality Home Run Derby. *The Washington Times.* Retrieved from https://www.washingtontimes.com/news/2018/jul/14/fanfest-attendees-compete-virtual-reality-home-run

Larkin, T.L., & Belson, S.I. (2005). Blackboard technologies: A vehicle to promote student motivation and learning in physics. *Journal of STEM Education, 6*(1-2), 14-27.

Lee, K., Ahn, H., & Kwon, S. (2017). Music's effect on exercise participants by exercise session. *Journal of Applied Sport Psychology, 29*(2), 167-180. doi:10.1080/10413200.2016.1220991

Lipovaya, V., Lima, Y., Grillo, P., Barbosa, C.E., Souza, J.M., & Duarte, F. (2018). Coordination, communication, and competition in eSports: A comparative analysis of teams in two action games. Proceedings from the *16th European Conference on Computer-Supported Cooperative Work—Exploratory Papers. Reports of the European Society for Socially Embedded Technologies, 2*(1). Retrieved from https://dl.eusset.eu/bitstream/20.500.12015/3122/1/ecscw2018-exploratory-paper-11.pdf doi:10.18420/ecscw2018_11

Manlapaz, D.G., Sole, G., Jayakaran, P., & Chapple, C.M. (2017). A narrative synthesis of Nintendo Wii Fit gaming protocol in addressing balance among healthy older adults: What system works? *Games for Health Journal, 6*(2), 65-74. doi:10.1089/g4h.2016.0082

Martens, R. (2012). *Successful coaching* (4th ed.). Champaign, IL: Human Kinetics.

Mast, D., de Krom, J., & de Vries, S. (2015). Exploring the application of interactive video projection in physical education. Proceedings from the *Ninth International Conference on Tangible, Embedded, and Embodied Interaction.* Stanford, CA. Retrieved from https://dl.acm.org/citation.cfm?id=2687901

Mills, M. (2013, February 4). PBS survey finds teachers are embracing digital resources to propel student learning. *Public Broadcasting System.* Retrieved from http://www.pbs.org/about/blogs/news/pbs-survey-finds-teachers-are-embracing-digital-resources-to-propel-student-learning/

Moholdt, T., Weie, S., Chorianopoulos, K., Wang, A.I., & Hagen, K. (2017). Exergaming can be an innovative way of enjoyable high-intensity interval training. *BMJ Open Sport and Exercise Medicine, 3*(1), 1-7. doi:10.1136/bmjsem-2017-000258

Monedero, J., Lyons, E.J., & O'Gorman, D.J. (2015). Interactive video game cycling leads to higher energy expenditure and is more enjoyable than conventional exercise in adults. *PLoS ONE, 10*(3), 1-12. doi:10.1371/journal.pone.0118470

National Association of Collegiate Esports. (2019). NACE. Retrieved from https://nacesports.org

Nation-Grainger, S. (2017). "It's just PE" till "It felt like a computer game": Using technology to improve motivation in physical education. *Research Papers in Education, 32*(4), 463-480.

Ni, M.Y., Hui, R.W.H., Li, T.K., Tam, A.H.M., Choy, L.L.Y., Ma, K.K.W., . . . Leung, G.M. (2019). Augmented reality games as a new class of physical activity interventions? The impact of Pokémon Go use and gaming intensity on physical activity. *Games for Health Journal, 8*(1), 1-6. doi:10.1089/g4h.2017.0181

Ning, W.N., Pope, Z., & Gao, Z. (2015, February 23). Associations between adolescents' situational motivation and objectively-determined physical activity levels in physical education. *JTRM in Kinesiology.* Retrieved from https://files.eric.ed.gov/fulltext/EJ1060199.pdf

PE Central Videos. (2018). Interactive games online course introductions [YouTube video]. Retrieved from https://youtu.be/gbq9ge3WuZk

Pew Research Center. (2018). Teens, social media, and technology 2018. Retrieved from http://assets.pewresearch.org/wp-content/uploads/sites/14/2018/05/31102617/PI_2018.05.31_TeensTech_FINAL.pdf

Rau, P.P., Gao, Q., & Wu, L. (2008). Using mobile communication technology in high school education: Motivation, pressure, and learning performance. *Computers & Education, 50*(1), 1-22.

Rodríguez-Aflecht, G., Jaakkola, T., Pongsakdi, N., Hannula-Sormunen, M., Brezovszky, B., & Lehtinen, E. (2018). The development of situational interest during a digital mathematics game. *Journal of Computer Assisted Learning, 34*(3), 259-268.

Rosly, M.M., Halaki, M., Rosly, H.M., Cuesta, V., Hasnan, N., Davis, G.M., & Husain, R. (2017). Exergaming for individuals with spinal cord injury: A pilot study. *Games for Health Journal, 6*(5), 279-289. doi:10.1089/g4h.2017.0028

Roure, C., & Pasco, D. (2018). Exploring situational interest sources in the French physical education context. *European Physical Education Review, 24*(1), 3-20. doi:10.1177/1356336X16662289

Sheehan, D., & Katz, L. (2010). Using interactive fitness and exergames to develop physical literacy. *Physical and Health Education Journal, 76*(1), 12-19.

Simons, M., Chinapaw, M.J., Brug, J., Seidell, J., & de Vet, E. (2015). Associations between active video gaming and other energy-balance related behaviours in adolescents: A 24-hour recall diary study. *International Journal of Behavioral Nutrition and Physical Activity, 12*(32), 1-6. doi:10.1186/s12966-015-0192-6

Smith, C. (2016, November 15). 75 incredible Pokémon Go statistics. *DMR.* Retrieved from http://expanded ramblings.com/index.php/pokemon-go-statistics/

Society of Health and Physical Educators. (2005). *National standards for sport coaches* (2nd ed.). Reston, VA: Human Kinetics.

Sun, H., & Gao, Y. (2016). Impact of an active educational video game on children's motivation, science knowledge, and physical activity. *Journal of Sport and Health Science, 5*(2), 239-245. doi:10.1016/j.jshs.2014.12.004

Superdata. (2017). Esports courtside: Playmakers of 2017. Retrieved from https://www.superdataresearch.com/market-data/esports-market-report/

Support Real Teachers. (2018). Projector uses in physical education. Retrieved from https://www.supportreal teachers.org/projector-uses-in-physical-education.html

Sween, J., Wallington, S.F., Sheppard, V., Taylor, T., Llanos, A.A., & Adams-Campbell, L.L. (2014). The role of exergaming in improving physical activity: A review. *Journal of Physical Activity and Health, 11,* 864-870. doi:10.1123/jpah.2011-0425

Szabo-Reed, A.N., Willis, E.A., Lee, J., Hillman, C.H., Washburn, R.A., & Donnelly, J.E. (2017). Impact of three years of classroom physical activity bouts on time-on-task behavior. *Medicine and Science in Sports and Exercise, 49*(11), 2343-2350. doi:10.1249/MSS.0000000000001346

Taylor, L., Kerse, N., Klenk, J., Borotkanics, R., & Maddison, R. (2018). Exergames to improve the mobility of long-term care residents: A cluster randomized controlled trial. *Games for Health Journal, 7*(1), 37-42. doi:10.1089/g4h.2017.0084

The PE Geek Apps. (2017). Turn your school into a fitness game. Retrieved from http://monsuta.fitness/

Wang, R., DeMaria, S., Goldberg, A., & Katz, D. (2016). A systematic review of serious games in training health care professionals. *The Journal of the Society for Simulation in Healthcare, 11*(1), 41-51. doi:10.1097/SIH.0000000000000118

Warburton, D., Bredin, S.S., Horita, L.T., Zbogar, D., Scott, J.M., Esch, B.T., & Rhodes, R.E. (2007). The health benefits of interactive video game exercise. *Applied Physiology, Nutrition, and Metabolism, 34*(4), 655-663. doi:10.1139/H07-038

World Health Organization. (2018). Gaming disorder. Retrieved from http://www.who.int/features/qa/gaming-disorder/en/

Yodice, J. (2018, June 8). NMAA adds video gaming for upcoming school calendar. *Albuquerque Journal.* Retrieved from https://www.abqjournal.com/1182456/nmaa-adds-video-gaming-for-upcoming-school-calendar.html

Chapter 6

Althoff, T., White, R.W., & Horvitz, E. (2016). Influence of Pokémon Go on physical activity: Study and implications. *Journal of Medical Internet Research, 18*(12), e315.

Ameringen, M., Turna, J., Khalesi, Z., Pullia, K., & Patterson, B. (2017). There is an app for that! The current state of mobile applications (apps) for DSM-5 obsessive-compulsive disorder, posttraumatic stress disorder, anxiety, and mood disorders. *Depression and Anxiety, 34*(6), 526-539.

Angrisano, A., Petovello, M., & Pugliano, G. (2012). Benefits of combined GPS/GLONASS with low-cost MEMS IMUs for vehicular urban navigation. *Sensors (Basel), 12,* 5134-5158.

Aylett, C. (2017, January 26). The impact of technology on social interactions [Blog post]. Retrieved from www.linkedin.com/pulse/impact-technology-social-interactions-christine-aylett

Blaz. (2019, January 19). The best watches for hiking 2019 [Blog post]. Retrieved from https://besthiking.net/best-watches-for-hiking-2015

Brown, A. (2017, September 11). Younger men play video games, but so do a diverse group of other Americans [Blog post]. Retrieved from www.pewresearch.org/fact-tank/2017/09/11/younger-men-play-video-games-but-so-do-a-diverse-group-of-other-americans

Bruno, L.E. (2018). Embracing technology and pop culture trends in physical education: Ready, set, (Pokémon) go. *Journal of Physical Education, Recreation & Dance, 89*(4), 45-51.

Colder Carras, M., Van Rooij, A.J., Spruijt-Metz, D., Kvedar, J., Griffiths, M.D., Carabas, Y., & Labrique, A. (2018). Commercial video games as therapy: A new research agenda to unlock the potential of a global pastime. *Frontiers in Psychiatry, 8,* 300.

Conkle, J. (Ed.). (2019). *Physical education for lifelong fitness: The physical best teacher's guide* (4th ed.). Champaign, IL: Human Kinetics.

Eysenbach, G. (2001). What is e-health? *Journal of Medical Internet Research, 3*(2), e20.

Garattini, C., Wherton, J., & Prendergast, D. (2012). Linking the lonely: An exploration of a communication technology designed to support social interaction among older adults. *Universal Access in the Information Society, 11*(2), 211-222.

Griffiths, C., Harnack, L., & Pereira, M. (2018) Assessment of the accuracy of nutrient calculations of five popular nutrition tracking applications. *Public Health Nutrition, 21*(8), 1495-1502.

Hayes, T. (2014, November 29) What's inside a fitness tracker anyway? [Blog post]. www.digitaltrends.com/wearables/whats-inside-fitness-tracker-anyway

Hödl, C., & Pröbstl-Haider, U. (2017, July). Geocaching in Austrian national parks. *Eco.Mont (Journal on Protected Mountain Areas Research), 9*(2), 42-51.

Insel, T., & Wang, P. (2009). The STAR*D trial: Revealing the need for better treatments. *Psychiatric Services, 60*(11), 1466.

International Data Corporation. (2017, November 30). Worldwide wearables market grows 7.3% in Q3 2017 as smart wearables rise and basic wearables decline, says IDC [Press release]. Retrieved from www.idc.com/getdoc.jsp?containerId=prUS43260217

Iqbal, M. (2019, April 29). Pokémon GO revenue and usage statistics (2019) [Blog post]. Retrieved from www.businessofapps.com/data/pokemon-go-statistics

Iyadurai, L., Blackwell, S.E., Meiser-Stedman, R., Watson, P.C., Bonsall, M.B., Geddes, J.R., Holmes, E.A. (2018). Preventing intrusive memories after trauma via a brief intervention involving Tetris computer game play in the emergency department: A proof-of-concept randomized controlled trial. *Molecular Psychiatry, 23*(3), 674-682.

Joint Committee on National Health Education Standards. (2007). *National Health Education Standards, second edition: Achieving excellence*. Washington, DC: American Cancer Society.

Kim, J. (2017). Smartphone-mediated communication vs. face-to-face interaction: Two routes to social support and problematic use of smartphone. *Computers in Human Behavior, 67*, 282-291.

Kleiboer, A.M., Smit, J., Bosmans, J., Ruwaard, J., Andersson, G., Topooco, N., . . . Riper, H. (2016). European comparative effectiveness research on blended depression treatment versus treatment-as-usual (E-COMPARED): Study protocol of a randomized controlled non-inferiority trial in eight European countries. *Trials, 17*(1), 387.

Laczo, L. (2018, August 29) The Netflix of fitness aka streaming workout classes: Peloton, Tonal, and a lot more. . . . Retrieved from https://shapescale.com/blog/fitness/streaming-workout-classes/

Li, J., Theng, Y.L., & Foo, S. (2014). Game-based digital interventions for depression therapy: A systematic review and meta-analysis. *Cyberpsychology, Behavior, and Social Networking, 17*(8), 519-527.

McNeil, C.B., & Hembree-Kigin, T.L. (2010). *Parent-child interaction therapy*. New York, NY: Springer Science & Business Media.

Merry, S. N., Stasiak, K., Shepherd, M., Frampton, C., Fleming, T., & Lucassen, M. F. G. (2012). The effectiveness of SPARX, a computerised self help intervention for adolescents seeking help for depression: Randomised controlled non-inferiority trial. *BMJ : British Medical Journal, 344*(7857), 16-16.

Mojtabai, R., Olfson, M., Sampson, N.A, Jin, R., Druss, B., Wang, P.S., . . . Kessler, R.C. (2011). Barriers to mental health treatment: Results from the National Comorbidity Survey Replication. *Psychological Medicine,*

41(8), 1751-1761. Retrieved from http://doi.org/10.1017/S0033291710002291

Murphy, S.P. (2008). Using DRIs for dietary assessment. *Asia Pacific Journal of Clinical Nutrition, 17*, 299-301.

Pangrazi, R., Beighle, A., & Sidman, C.A. (2007). *Pedometer power: Using pedometers in school and community* (2nd ed.). Champaign, IL: Human Kinetics.

Patel, A., Schieble, T., Davidson, M., Tran, M.C.J., Schoenberg, C., Delphin, E., . . . Bennett, H. (2006). Distraction with a hand-held video game reduces pediatric preoperative anxiety. *Pediatric Anesthesia, 16*(10), 1019-1027.

Rieck, T (2018). 10,000 steps a day: Too low? Too high? Retrieved from https://www.mayoclinic.org/healthy-lifestyle/fitness/in-depth/10000-steps/art-20317391

Rouse, M. (2016). Augmented reality gaming (AR gaming). Retrieved from https://whatis.techtarget.com/definition/augmented-reality-gaming-AR-gaming

Russoniello, C.V. (2009) The effectiveness of casual video games in improving mood and decreasing stress. *Journal of Cyber Therapeutic Rehabilitation, 2*(1), 53-66.

Schlatter, B.E., & Hurd, A.R. (2005). Geocaching: 21st-century hide-and-seek. *Journal of Physical Education, Recreation & Dance, 76*(7), 28-32.

Shin, G., Jarrahi, M.H., Fei, Y., Karami, A., Gafinowitz, N., Byun, A., & Lu, X. (2019). Wearable activity trackers, accuracy, adoption, acceptance, and health impact: A systematic literature review. *Journal of Biomedical Informatics, 93*, 103-153.

Shepherd, M., Psych, D., Merry, S., Lambie, I., & Thompson, A. (2018). Indigenous adolescents' perception of an eMental health program (SPARX): Exploratory qualitative assessment. *Jmir Serious Games, 6*(3), e13. doi:10.2196/games.8752

Society of Health and Physical Educators. (2014). *National Standards and Grade-Level Outcomes for K-12 Physical Education*. Reston, VA: Author.

Society of Health and Physical Educators. (n.d.). National Standards for Sport Coaches. Retrieved from www.shapeamerica.org/standards/coaching

Steinheimer, L. (2017, March 19). Why your GPS-enabled smartwatch may show different data than your friend's. Retrieved from www.digitaltrends.com/outdoors/how-gps-watches-work

Team COROS. (2019, February 15). GPS accuracy—What's right and what's not. Retrieved from https://coros.com/article.php?id=8

Van Orden, K.A., Witte, T.K., Cukrowicz, K.C., Braithwaite, S.R., Selby, E.A., & Joiner, T.E., Jr. (2010). The interpersonal theory of suicide. *Psychological Review, 117*(2), 575. Retrieved from http://search.proquest.com.ezproxy.gvsu.edu/docview/503982094?accountid=39473

Waldinger, S. (2016, December 16). What to do about those difficult relationships at the holidays? [Blog post]. Retrieved from https://robertwaldinger.com/category/blog

World Health Organization. (2011). mHealth: New horizons for health through mobile technologies. Retrieved from www.who.int/goe/publications/goe_mhealth_web.pdf

World Health Organization. (2017). The World Health Organization definition of health. Retrieved from https://8fit.com/lifestyle/the-world-health-organization-definition-of-health

Zhang, F., & Kaufman, D. (2016). A review of intergenerational play for facilitating interactions and learning. *Gerontechnology, 14*(3), 127-138.

Chapter 7

AbleGamers. (2018). The AbleGamers charity. Retrieved from https://ablegamers.org

AbleNet. (2019). BIGmack. Retrieved from www.ablenetinc.com/bigmack

Adapted Physical Education National Standards. (2008). Certification. Retrieved from https://apens.org/certification.html

American College of Sports Medicine. (2019). ACSM/NCHPAD certified inclusive fitness trainer. Retrieved from www.acsm.org/get-stay-certified/get-certified/specialization/cift

Americans with Disabilities Act. (1990). Public Law 101-336. Retrieved from www.ada.gov

Americans with Disabilities Act Amendments Act. (2008). Public Law 110-325. Retrieved from www.ada.gov

Besombes, N. (2018). Execution and mindgame in fighting games: Two facets of videomotricity in esports. *Movement & Sport Sciences, 2*, 1-17. doi:10.1051/sm/2018008

Bofolli, N., Foley, J.T., Gasperetti, B., Yang, S.P., & Lieberman, L. (2011). Enjoyment levels of youth with visual impairments playing different exergames. *Insight: Research and Practice in Visual Impairment and Blindness, 4*(4), 171-179.

CapGame. (2018). CapGame facilitates access to video games for the disabled public. Retrieved from www.capgame.fr

Cunningham, G.B. (2015). *Diversity and inclusion in sport organizations* (3rd ed.). Scottsdale, AZ: Holcomb Hathaway.

Enabling Devices. (2019). [Home page.] Retrieved from https://enablingdevices.com

Eveleth, R. (2012, July 24). Should Oscar Pistorius's prosthetic legs disqualify him from the Olympics? *Scientific American*. Retrieved from www.scientificamerican.com/article/scientists-debate-oscar-pistorius-prosthetic-legs-disqualify-him-olympics

Exercise Connection. (2018). Autism exercise specialist certificate. Retrieved from www.autismexercisespecialist.com

Fanfarelli, J. R. (2018). Expertise in professional Overwatch play. *International Journal of Gaming and Computer-Mediated Simulations, 10*(1), 1-22. doi:10.4018/IJGCMS.2018010101

FlagHouse. (2019). FlagHouse: Resources for sport, recreation, special needs, and more since 1954! Retrieved from www.flaghouse.com

Game Accessibility Guidelines. (2019). [Home page]. Retrieved from http://gameaccessibilityguidelines.com

Gasperetti, B., Milford, M., Blanchard, D., Yang, S.P., Lieberman, L., & Foley, J.T. (2011). Dance Dance Revolution and EyeToy Kinetic modifications for youth with visual impairments. *Journal of Physical Education, Recreation and Dance, 81*(4), 15-17, 55. doi:10.1080/07303084.2010.10598459

HelpKidzLearn. (2017). [Home page]. Retrieved from www.helpkidzlearn.com

Hodge, S.R., Lieberman, L.J., & Marata, N.M. (2012). *Essentials of teaching adapted physical education: Diversity, culture, and inclusion.* Scottsdale, AZ: Holcomb Hathaway.

Hofmann, A. (2019, February 5). Accessible esports: Technically feasible, but lacking social visibility. *REHACARE Magazine.* Retrieved from www.rehacare.com/en/Topic_of_the_Month/Topics_of_the_Month_2019/May_2019:_Real_inclusion_through_virtual_possibilities

Hoyt Running Chairs. (2019). The blade. Retrieved from https://www.hoytrunningchairs.com

Individuals with Disabilities Education Improvement Act. (2004). Public Law 108-446. Retrieved from https://sites.ed.gov/idea

Innovative Products. (2019). Electronic POSS-I-BOWL 2000 ball release. Retrieved from www.bowlingramps.com

International Paralympic Committee. (2011, April 2). IPC policy on sport equipment. Retrieved from www.paralympic.org/sites/default/files/document/120203164107739_Sec_ii_Chapter_3.10_IPC_Sport_Equipment_Policy.pdf

Invictus Active. (2019). Invictus active trainer. Retrieved from https://www.invictusactive.com

Jenny, S.E., Hushman, G.F., & Hushman, C.J. (2013). Preservice teachers' perceptions of motion-based video gaming in physical education. *International Journal of Technology in Teaching and Learning, 9*(1), 96-111.

Jenny, S.E., & Schary, D.P. (2016). Virtual and "real-life" wall/rock climbing: Motor movement comparisons and video gaming pedagogical perceptions. *Sports Technology, 8*(3-4), 100-111. doi:10.1080/19346182.2015.1118110

Jenny, S.E., Schary, D.P., Noble, K.M., & Hamill, S.D. (2017, October 30). The effectiveness of developing motor skills through motion-based video gaming: A review. *Simulation and Gaming: An International Journal of Theory, Practice and Research*, 1-13. doi:10.1177/1046878117738552

Kloos, A.D., Fritz, N.E., Kostyk, S.K., Young, G.S., & Kegelmeyer, D.A. (2013). Video game play (Dance Dance Revolution) as a potential exercise therapy in Huntington's disease: A controlled clinical trial. *Clinical Rehabilitation, 27*(11), 972-982. doi:10.1177/0269215513487235

Laughlin, M.K., Murata, N.M., Gonnelli, M., & Larranaga, J. (2018). Assistive technology: What physical educators need to know. *Journal of Physical Education, Recreation and Dance, 89*(3), 38-45. doi:10.1080/07303084.2017.1417930

Lee, G. (2013). Effects of training using video games on the muscle strength, muscle tone, and activities of daily living of chronic stroke patients. *The Journal of Physical Therapy Science, 25*(5), 595-597. doi:10.1589/jpts.25.595

Lee, H., Huang, C., Ho, S., & Sung, W. (2017). The effect of a virtual reality game intervention on balance for patients with stroke: A randomized controlled trial. *Games for Health Journal, 6*(5), 303-311. doi:10.1089/g4h.2016.0109

Lepore, M., Gayle, G.W., & Stevens, S. (2007). *Adapted aquatics programming: A professional guide* (2nd ed.). Champaign, IL: Human Kinetics.

Lieberman, L. J., & Houston-Wilson, C. (2009). *Strategies for inclusion: A handbook for physical educators* (2nd ed.). Champaign, IL: Human Kinetics.

Lipovaya, V., Lima, Y., Grillo, P., Barbosa, C.E., Souza, J.M., & Duarte, F. (2018). Coordination, communication, and competition in esports: A comparative analysis of teams in two action games. Proceedings of the 16th European Conference on Computer-Supported Cooperative Work—Exploratory Papers: *Reports of the European Society for Socially Embedded Technologies.* doi:10.18420/ecscw2018_11

Lotan, M., Hadash, R., Amrani, S., Pinsker, A., & Weiss, P.L. (2018). Improving balance of individuals with intellectual and developmental disability through a virtual reality intervention. *Journal of Physiotherapy & Physical Rehabilitation, 3*, 76. doi: 10.4172/2573-0312-C1-002

Malinverni, L., Mora-Guiard, J., Padillo, V., Valero, L., Hervas, A., & Pares, N. (2017). An inclusive design approach for developing video games for children with autism spectrum disorder. *Computers in Human Behavior, 71*, 535-549. doi: 10.1016/j.chb.2016.01.018

Martin, M. (2017, June 2). How Killer Instinct player Wheels is overcoming disability to be a pro. *Yahoo Sports.* Retrieved from https://sports.yahoo.com/killer-instinct-player-wheels-overcoming-disability-pro-204002264.html

McNamara, S. (2018, August 8). Integrating AT into adapted physical education. *Center on Technology and Disability.* Retrieved from https://youtu.be/cCim6loyVrA

Microsoft. (2019). Xbox adaptive controller. Retrieved from www.xbox.com/en-US/xbox-one/accessories/controllers/xbox-adaptive-controller

Morelli, T., Foley, J., Columna, L., Lieberman, L., & Folmer, E. (2010, June 19). VI-tennis: A vibrotactile/audio exergame for players who are visually impaired. *Proceedings of the Fifth International Conference on the Foundations of Digital Games,* Monterey, CA. 147-154. doi:10.1145/1822348.1822368

Morelli, T., Foley, J., & Folmer, E. (2010, October 25). VI-bowling: A tactile spatial exergame for individuals with visual impairments. *Proceedings of the 12th International ACM SIGACCESS Conference on Computers and Accessibility,* Orlando, FL. 179-186. doi:10.1145/1878803.1878836

National Consortium for Physical Education for Individuals with Disabilities. (2020). *Adapted physical education national standards* (3rd ed.). Champaign, IL: Human Kinetics.

QIAT Leadership Team. (2012). Self-evaluation matrices for the quality indicators in assistive technology services. Retrieved from https://qiat.org/indicators.html

QuadStick. (2019). QuadStick: A game controller for quadriplegics. Retrieved from www.quadstick.com

RehabTool. (2004). What's assistive technology? Retrieved from http://rehabtool.com/at.html

Resonance House. (2019). Shadow's Edge. Retrieved from www.shadowsedge.com

Re-vibe Technologies. (2019). Re-vibe connect: Vibration reminder watch. Retrieved from https://revibetech.com

Rosly, M.M., Halaki, M., Rosly, H.M., Cuesta, V., Hasnan, N., Davis, G.M., & Husain, R. (2017). Exergaming for individuals with spinal cord injury: A pilot study. *Games for Health Journal, 6*(5), 279-289. doi: 10.1089/g4h.2017.0028

Scanlan, J.N. & Novak, T. (2015). Sensory approaches in mental health: A scoping review. *Australian Occupational Therapy Journal, 62*(5), 277-285. doi: 10.1111/1440-1630.12224

Snoezelen Multi-Sensory Environments. (2019). What is Snoezelen? Retrieved from www.snoezelen.info

Society of Health and Physical Educators. (2019a). [Home page]. Retrieved from www.shapeamerica.org/

Society of Health and Physical Educators. (2019b). Unified physical education. Retrieved from www.shapeamerica.org/ResourcesPublications/Unified_PE

Special Olympics. (2019). Special Olympics unified champion schools. Retrieved from www.specialolympics.org/our-work/unified-champion-schools

Susquehanna Esports. (2019). Susquehanna Soniqs. Retrieved from https://susquehannaesports.com

Switch In Time. (n.d.). Switch In Time: Accessible software. Retrieved from www.switchintime.com

Tar Heel Gameplay. (n.d.). Welcome. Retrieved from https://tarheelgameplay.org

3dRudder. (2019). Foot powered motion controller made for gaming. Retrieved from www.3drudder.com

United Sates Census Bureau. (2018, November). Americans with disabilities: 2014. Retrieved from www.census.gov

US Games. (2018). Exer-gaming. Retrieved from https://www.usgames.com/p-e-activities/exer-gaming

Wheelers' Paramill. (2019). The paramill-wheelchair treadmill. Retrieved from https://wheelersparamill.com

Wilcox, B.J., Wilkins, M.M., Basseches, B., Schwartz, J.B., Kerman, K., Trask, C., . . . Crisco, J.J. (2016). Joint-specific play controller for upper extremity therapy: Feasibility study in children with wrist impairment. *Physical Therapy, 96*(11), 1773-1781. doi: 10.2522/ptj.20150493

World Health Organization. (2011). World report on disability. Retrieved from www.who.int/disabilities/world_report/2011

World Health Organization. (2018, January 16). Disability and health. Retrieved from www.who.int/en/news-room/fact-sheets/detail/disability-and-health

Zabala, J.S. (2005). Ready, SETT, go! Getting started with the SETT framework. *Closing the Gap, 23*(6), 1-3. Retrieved from www.joyzabala.com

Chapter 8

Allen, I.E., & Seaman, J. (2015). Grade level: Tracking online education in the United States. Babson Survey Research Group. Retrieved from www.onlinelearningsurvey.com

American Council on Exercise. (2019). ACE. Retrieved from www.acefitness.org

Artistic Dressage. (2019). Artistic dressage. Retrieved from www.artisticdressage.com

Bus, K., Peyer, K.L., Bai, Y., Ellingson, L.D., & Welk, G.J. (2018). Comparison of in-person and online motivational interviewing–based health coaching. *Health Promotion Practice, 19*(4), 513-521. doi:10.1177/1524839917746634

Casanova, A. (2019). What exactly is a virtual race? Retrieved from www.active.com/running/articles/what-exactly-is-a-virtual-race

CoachUp. (2019). CoachUp. Retrieved from www.coachup.com

Corbin, C., & Le Masurier, G. (2014). *Fitness for life* (6th ed.). Champaign, IL: Human Kinetics.

Corbin, C., Le Masurier, G., & Lambdin, D. (2018). *Fitness for life: Middle school* (2nd ed.). Champaign, IL: Human Kinetics.

Daum, D.N., & Buschner, C. (2012). The status of high school online physical education in the United States. *Journal of Teaching in Physical Education, 31*, 86-100.

Daum, D.N., & Buschner, C. (2018). Research on teaching K-12 online physical education. In K. Kennedy & R.E. Ferdig (Eds.), *Handbook of research on K-12 online and blended learning* (2nd ed., pp. 321-334). Pittsburgh, PA: ETC Press. Retrieved from http://repository.cmu.edu/etcpress/82

Davies, C.A., Spence, J.C., Vandelanotte, C., Caperchione, C.M., & Mummery, W.C. (2012). Meta-analysis of Internet-delivered interventions to increase physical activity levels. *International Journal of Behavioral Nutrition and Physical* Activity, *9*(52), 1-13. doi:10.1186/1479-5868-9-52

Digital Learning Collaborative. (2018, September 5). Digital learning landscape brief: State virtual schools. Retrieved from www.digitallearningcollab.com/state-virtual-schools

Evergreen Education Group. (2017). Keeping pace with K-12 online learning 2016. Retrieved from www.evergreenedgroup.com/keeping-pace-reports

Everhart, K., & Dimon, C. (2013). The impact of course delivery format on wellness patterns of university students. *Education, 133*(3), 310-318.

Ginder, S.A., Kelly-Reid, J.E., & Mann, F.B. (2018). Enrollment and employees in postsecondary institutions, fall 2017; and financial statistics and academic libraries, fiscal year 2017: First look (preliminary data) (NCES 2019-2021). U.S. Department of Education. Washington, DC: National Center for Education Statistics. Retrieved from https://nces.ed.gov/pubs2019/2019021.pdf

Groundspeak. (2019). Geocaching [YouTube channel]. Retrieved from www.youtube.com/user/GoGeocaching

Healy, S., Block, M., & Judge, J. (2014). Certified adapted physical educators' perceptions of advantages and disadvantages of online teacher development. *Palaestra, 28*(4), 14-16.

Hew, K.F., & Lo, C.K. (2018). Flipped classroom improves student learning in health professions education: A meta-analysis. *BMC Medical Education, 18*(38), 1-12. doi:10.1186/s12909-018-1144-z

Huffman, M.H. (2016). Advancing the practice of health coaching: Differentiation from wellness coaching. *Workplace Health and Safety, 64*(9), 400-403. doi:10.1177/2165079916645351

International Association for K-12 Online Learning. (2019). iNACOL. Retrieved from www.inacol.org

Juniu, S., Hofer, M., & Harris, J. (2012, February). Physical education learning activity types. College of William and Mary, School of Education, Learning Activity Types Wiki. Retrieved from http://activitytypes.wm.edu/PhysicalEducationLearningATs-Feb2012.pdf

Kooiman, B.J., Sheehan, D.P., Wesolek, M., & Retegui, E. (2016). Exergaming for physical activity in online physical education. *International Journal of Distance Education Technologies, 14*(2), 1-16. doi:10.4018/IJDET.2016040101

Kooiman, B.J., Sheehan, D.P., Wesolek, M., & Retegui, E. (2017). Moving online physical education from oxymoron to efficacy. *Sport, Education and Society, 22*(2), 230-246. doi:10.1080/13573322.2015.1015978

Krause, J.M., Douglas, S., Lynch, B.M., & Kesselring, L. (2018). Let's get virtual: Observing physical education field experiences through synchronous video conferencing. *Strategies, 31*(1), 30-34. doi:10.1080/08924562.2017.1394241

Lammers, E., Bryant, G., Michel, L.S., & Seaman, J. (2017, June 12). Time for class: Lessons for the future of digital learning in higher education, 2017 update. Retrieved from http://tytonpartners.com/library/time-class-2017-2

Loyola University New Orleans. (2019). Self-assessment of online learning readiness. Retrieved from http://cnh.loyno.edu/lim/self-assessment-online-learning-readiness

Magda, A.J., & Aslanian, C.B. (2018). *Online college students 2018: Comprehensive data on demands and preferences.* Louisville, KY: Learning House. Retrieved from www.learninghouse.com/knowledge-center/research-reports/ocs2018

MarylandOnline. (2018). Specific review standards from the QM higher education rubric (6th ed.). Retrieved from www.qualitymatters.org/sites/default/files/PDFs/StandardsfromtheQMHigherEducationRubric.pdf

MarylandOnline. (2019a). Quality matters. Retrieved from www.qualitymatters.org

MarylandOnline. (2019b). Specific review standards from the QM K-12 rubric (5th ed.). Retrieved from www.qualitymatters.org/sites/default/files/PDFs/StandardsfromtheK-12RubricFifthEdition.pdf

Means, B., Toyama, Y., Murphy, R., Bakia, M., & Jones, K. (2010). *Evaluation of evidence-based practices in online learning: A meta-analysis and review of online learning studies.* Washington, DC: U.S. Department of Education.

Microsoft. (2018). Does Skype use encryption? *Skype Help.* Retrieved from https://support.skype.com/en/faq/FA31/Does-Skype-use-encryption?

Mohnsen, B. (2012). Implementing online physical education. *Journal of Physical Education, Recreation and Dance. 83*(2), 42-47. doi:10.1080/07303084.2012.10598727

National Society of Health Coaches. (2019). NSHC. Retrieved from www.nshcoa.com

O'Neil, K., & Krause, J. (2017, January 5). *PETE university supervisors' perceptions of use and feasibility of live remote supervision.* Presented at the National Association of Kinesiology in Higher Education National Conference. Orlando, FL.

Peloton. (2019). Peloton. Retrieved from www.onepeloton.com

Society of Health and Physical Educators. (2014). *National standards and grade-level outcomes for K-12 physical education.* Reston, VA: Author and Human Kinetics.

Society of Health and Physical Educators. (2016). *2016 shape of the nation: Status of physical education in the USA.* Reston, VA: Author.

Society of Health and Physical Educators. (2018). *Guidelines for K-12 online physical education.* Reston, VA: Author.

Ubell, R. (2017, February 6). Online cheating. *Inside Higher Ed.* Retrieved from www.insidehighered.com/digital-learning/views/2017/02/06/robert-ubell-online-cheating-and-what-colleges-can-do-about-it

U.S. Department of Education. (2018). List of 2017 digest tables. *Digest of Education Statistics.* Retrieved from https://nces.ed.gov/programs/digest/2017menu_tables.asp

U.S. Department of Health and Human Services. (2018). *Physical activity guidelines for Americans* (2nd ed.). Washington, DC: Author. Retrieved from https://health.gov/paguidelines/second-edition/pdf/Physical_Activity_Guidelines_2nd_edition.pdf

Venable, M. (2018). 2018 online trends in education report. Retrieved from www.bestcolleges.com/perspectives/annual-trends-in-online-education

Vida Health. (2019). Vida. Retrieved from www.vida.com

Wellcoaches. (2016). Wellcoaches school of coaching. Retrieved from https://wellcoachesschool.com

Zhang, Y., Liu, H., & Lin, C. (2018). Research on class size in K-12 online learning. In R.E. Ferdig & K. Kennedy (Eds.), *Handbook of research on K-12 online and blended learning* (2nd ed., pp. 273-283). Pittsburgh, PA: ETC Press. Retrieved from http://repository.cmu.edu/etcpress/82

Chapter 9

Abel, M.G., Hannon, J.C., Sell, K., Lillie, T., Conlin, G., & Anderson, D. (2008). Validation of the Kenz Lifecorder EX and ActiGraphGT1M accelerometers for walking and running in adults. *Applied Physiology, Nutrition & Metabolism, 33*(6), 1155-1164. doi: 10.1139/H08-103

Aguiar, E.J., Moore, C.C., Ducharme, S.W., & McCullough, A.K. (2018). Validation of step counters in the free-living context. *Medicine & Science in Sports & Exercise, 50*(10), 2180. doi: 10.1249/MSS.0000000000001662

Alejo, B. (2018, December 26). Before athlete tracking. Retrieved from https://twitter.com/Coach_Alejo/status/1078040483170078733

Åstrand, P. (1952). *Experimental studies of physical working capacity in relation to sex and age.* Copenhagen, Denmark: Musksgaard.

Bassett, D.R., Jr., Wyatt, H.R., Thompson, H., Peters, J.C., & Hill, J.O. (2010). Pedometer-measured physical activity and health behaviors in U.S. adults. *Medicine & Science in Sports & Exercise, 42*(10), 1819-1825. doi: 10.1249/MSS.0b013e3181dc2e54

Bayles, M.P., & Swank, A.M. (2018). *ACSM's exercise testing and prescription.* Philadelphia, PA: Wolters Kluwer.

Benson, R. (1998). Running. In E.R. Burke (Ed.), *Precision heart rate training: For maximum fitness and performance,* (pp. 65-90). Champaign, IL: Human Kinetics.

Bunn, J., Wells, E., Manor, J., & Webster, M. (2019). Evaluation of earbud and wristwatch heart rate monitors during aerobic and resistance training. *International Journal of Exercise Science, 12*(4), 374-384.

Burke, E.R. (1998). *Precision heart rate training: For maximum fitness and performance.* Champaign, IL: Human Kinetics.

Burne, G., Ovens, A., & Philpot, R. (2018). Teaching physical education with digital technologies: A self-study of practice. *Revista Brasileira de Educação Física Escolar, 4*(2), 93-108.

Claes, J., Buys, R., Avila, A., Finlay, D., Kennedy, A., Guldenring, D., . . . Cornelissen, V. (2017). Validity of heart rate measurements by the Garmin Forerunner 225 at different walking intensities. *Journal of Medical Engineering & Technology, 41*(6), 480–485. https://doi.org/10.1080/03091902.2017.1333166

Clevenger, K.A., Moore, R.W., Suton, D., Montoye, A.H.K., Trost, S.G., & Pfeiffer, K.A. (2018). Accelerometer responsiveness to change between structured and unstructured physical activity in children and adolescents. *Measurement in Physical Education and Exercise Science, 22*(3), 224-230. doi: 10.1080/1091367X.2017.1419956

Corbin, C.B., & Le Masurier, G.C. (2014). *Fitness for life* (6th ed.). Champaign, IL: Human Kinetics.

Craig, C.L., Cameron, C., Griffiths, J.M., & Tudor-Locke, C. (2010). Descriptive epidemiology of youth pedometer-determined physical activity: CANPLAY. *Medicine & Science in Sports & Exercise, 42*(9), 1639–1643. doi: 10.1249/MSS.0b013e3181d58a92

Daniels, J. (2014). *Daniels' running formula* (3rd ed.). Champaign, IL: Human Kinetics.

Fox, S.M., III, Naughton, J.P., & Haskell, W.L. (1971). Physical activity and the prevention of coronary heart disease. *Annals of Clinical Research, 3*, 404-432.

Fröberg, A., & Raustorp, A. (2019). Integrating the pedometer into physical education: Monitoring and evaluating physical activity, pedagogical implications, practical considerations, and recommendations. *The Physical Educator, 76*(1), 135-155. doi: 10.18666/TPE-2019-V76-I1-8608

Higdon, H. (2007, July 9). Make every run easier. *Runner's World*. Retrieved from https://www.runnersworld.com/training/a20797305/make-every-run-easier

Holden, S.L., & Baghurst, T.M. (2018). Considerations when choosing a fitness tracking device. *Strategies, 31*(3), 54-56. doi: 10.1080/08924562.2018.1445891

Joint Committee on National Health Education Standards. (2007). *National health education standards, second edition: Achieving excellence*. Washington, DC: American Cancer Society.

Karvonen, J., & Vuorimaa, T. (1988). Heart rate and exercise intensity during sports activities: Practical application. *Sports Medicine, 5*(5), 303-311. doi 10.2165/00007256-198805050-00002

Kirkpatrick, B., & Birnbaum, B.H. (1997). *Lessons from the heart: Individualizing physical education with heart rate monitors*. Champaign, IL: Human Kinetics.

Laskowski, E.R. (2018, August 29). What's a normal resting heart rate? Mayo Clinic. Retrieved from https://www.mayoclinic.org/healthy-lifestyle/fitness/expert-answers/heart-rate/faq-20057979

Lloyd, L.K., Crixell, S.H., & Price, L.R. (2014). Is the Polar F6 heart rate monitor less accurate during aerobic bench stepping because of arm movements? *Journal of Strength & Conditioning Research, 28*(7), 1952-1958.

Lund, J.L., & Kirk, M.F. (2010). *Performance-based assessment for middle and high school physical education* (2nd ed.). Champaign, IL: Human Kinetics.

Martin, J., Krc, K., Mitchell, E., Eng, J., & Noble, J. (2012). Pedometer accuracy in slow walking older adults. *International Journal of Therapy and Rehabilitation, 19*(7), 387-393.

McCarthy, M., & Grey, M. (2015). Motion sensor use for physical activity data: Methodological considerations. *Nursing Research, 64*(4), 320–327. doi: 10.1097/NNR.0000000000000098

McCaughtry, N., Oliver, K.L., Dillon, S.R., & Martin, J.J. (2008). Teachers' perspectives on the use of pedometers as instructional technology in physical education: A cautionary tale. *Journal of Teaching in Physical Education, 27*(1), 83-99. doi: 10.1123/jtpe.27.1.83

McMinn, D., Rowe, D.A., Stark, M., & Nicol, L. (2010). Validity of the New Lifestyles NL-1000 accelerometer for measuring time spent in moderate-to-vigorous physical activity in school settings. *Measurement in Physical Education and Exercise Science, 14*(2), 67-78. doi: 10.1080/10913671003715516

Montoye, A.H.K., Conger, S.A., Connolly, C.P., Imboden, M.T., Nelson, M.B., Bock, J M., & Kaminsky, L.A. (2017). Validation of accelerometer-based energy expenditure prediction models in structured and simulated free-living settings. *Measurement in Physical Education and Exercise Science, 21*(4), 223-234. doi: 10.1080/1091367X.2017.1337638

Polar. (2010). Lessons for life: Individualizing health and physical education with heart rate and activity monitoring. Retrieved from https://www.polar.com/sites/default/files/b2b/pe/lessons_for_life_e-version.pdf

Polar. (2018, September 13). Introducing the new Polar Vantage Series—The next-generation multisport watches. Retrieved from https://www.polar.com/blog/polar-vantage-series-next-generation-multisport-watches

Scruggs, P.W. (2013). Pedometer steps/min in physical education: Does the pedometer matter? *Journal of Science and Medicine in Sport, 16*(1), 36-39. doi: 10.1016/j.jsams.2012.05.011

Segar, M.L. (2017). Activity tracking + motivation science: Allies to keep people moving for a lifetime. *ACSM's Health & Fitness Journal, 21*(4), 8-17.

Sisson, S.B., Camhi, S.M., Church, T.S., Tudor-Locke, C., Johnson, W.D., & Katzmarzyk, P.T. (2010). Accelerometer-determined steps/day and metabolic syndrome. *American Journal of Preventative Medicine, 38*(6), 575–582. doi: 10.1016/j.amepre.2010.02.015

Smith, J.D., & Schroeder, C.A. (2010). Pedometer accuracy in elementary school children while walking, skipping, galloping, and sliding. *Measurement in Physical Education and Exercise Science, 14*(2), 92-103. doi: 10.1080/10913671003715540

Smith, J.D., Schroeder, C.A., & Smith, R.M. (2019). Pedometer accuracy and metabolic cost in elementary school children while walking, skipping, galloping, and sliding. *The Physical Educator, 76*(1), 1-23. doi: 10.18666/TPE-2019-V76-I1-8392

Society of Health and Physical Educators America. (2014). *National standards and grade-level outcomes for K-12 physical education.* Reston, VA: Author.

Society of Health and Physical Educators America. (2015). *The essential components of physical education.* Reston, VA: Author.

Stahl, S.E., An, H., Dinkel, D.M., Noble, J.M., & Lee, J. (2016). How accurate are the wrist-based heart rate monitors during walking and running activities? Are they accurate enough? *BMJ Open Sport & Exercise Medicine, 2*(1), 1-7. http://dx.doi.org/10.1136/bmjsem-2015-000106

Swaim, D.L. (2012). *Heart education: Strategies, lessons, science, and technology for cardiovascular fitness.* Champaign, IL: Human Kinetics.

Tanaka, H., Monahan, K.D., & Seals, D.R. (2001). Age-predicted maximal heart rate revisited. *Journal of the American College of Cardiology, 37*(1), 153–156.

Terbizan, D.J., Dolezal, B.A., & Albano, C. (2002). Validity of seven commercially available heart rate monitors. *Measurement in Physical Education and Exercise Science, 6*(4), 243–247.

Thompson, W.R. (2019). Worldwide survey of fitness trends for 2020. *ACSM's Health & Fitness Journal, 23*(6), 10–18. doi:10.1249/FIT.0000000000000526

Toth, L.P., Park, S., Pittman, W.L., Sarisaltik, D., Hibbing, P.R., Morton, A.L., . . . Bassett, D.R. (2018). Validity of activity tracker step counts during walking, running, and activities of daily living. *Translational Journal of the American College of Sports Medicine, 3*(7), 52-59. doi: 10.1249/TJX.0000000000000057

Troiano, R.P., Berrigan, D., Dodd, K.W., Mâsse, L.C., Tilert, T., & McDowell, M. (2008). Physical activity in the United States measured by accelerometer. *Medicine and Science in Sports and Exercise, 40*(1), 181-188. doi:10.1249/mss.0b013e31815a51b3

Tudor-Locke, C., Hatano, Y., Pangrazi, R.P., & Kang, M. (2008). Revisiting "how many steps are enough?" *Medicine and Science in Sports and Exercise, 40*(7 Suppl.), S537–S543. doi: 10.1249/MSS.0b013e31817c7133

U.S. Department of Health and Human Services. (2018). *Physical activity guidelines for Americans* (2nd ed.). Washington, DC: Author. Retrieved from https://health.gov/paguidelines/second-edition/pdf/Physical_Activity_Guidelines_2nd_edition.pdf

U.S. National Library of Medicine. (2019, March 7). Pulse. *Medline Plus.* Retrieved from https://medlineplus.gov/ency/article/003399.htm

Wallen, M.P., Gomersall, S.R., Keating, S.E., Wisløff, U., & Coombes, J.S. (2016). Accuracy of heart rate watches: Implications for weight management. *PLoS ONE, 11*(5), 1-11. doi:10.1371/journal.pone.0154420

Wang, R., Blackburn, G., Desai, M., Phelan, D., Gillinov, L., Houghtaling, P., & Gillinov, M. (2017). Accuracy of wrist-worn heart rate monitors. *JAMA Cardiology, 2*(1), 104-106. doi:10.1001/jamacardio.2016.3340

Chapter 10

Clemente, F.M., Couceiro, M.S., Martins, F.M.L., Mendes, R., & Figueiredo, A.J. (2013). Measuring tactical behavior using technological metrics: Case study of a football game. *International Journal of Sports Science & Coaching, 8*(4), 723-739.

Cooper Institute. (2014). *FitnessGram®/ActivityGram®.* Retrieved from www.cooperinstitute.org/fitnessgram

Cox, D.G. & Meaney, K.S. (2018). Lights, camera, project-based learning! *Strategies, 31*(1), 23-29.

Kelley, H., & Miltenberger, R.G. (2016). Using video feedback to improve horseback-riding skills. *Journal of Applied Behavior Analysis, 49*(1), 138-147.

Krause, J.M, O'Neil, K., & Dauenhauer, B. (2017). Plickers: A formative assessment tool for K-12 and PETE professionals. *Strategies, 30*(3), 30-36.

Magill, R.A. (2007). *Motor learning and control: Concepts and applications* (9th ed.). New York: McGraw Hill.

National Fitness Foundation. (2019). *Presidential youth fitness program.* Retrieved from https://pyfp.org

Society of Health and Physical Educators America. (2017). *National standards for initial physical education teacher education.* Retrieved from www.shapeamerica.org/accreditation/upload/National-Standards-for-Initial-Physical-Education-Teacher-Education-2017.pdf

Society of Health and Physical Educators America. (2018). *National standards for initial health education teacher education.* Retrieved from www.shapeamerica.org/uploads/pdfs/2018/accreditation/HETE-Standards_2018d.pdf

Society of Health and Physical Educators America. (2019). *National standards for sport coaches.* Retrieved from www.shapeamerica.org/standards/coaching

Chapter 11

Bourne, J. (2009, August 24). Equipment for video podcasting, part 1: Basic cameras. *Peachpit.* Retrieved from www.peachpit.com/articles/article.aspx?p=1383762

Consumer Reports. (2018). *Camcorder buying guide.* Retrieved from www.consumerreports.org/cro/camcorders/buying-guide

Goldstein, M. (2009). 7 reasons why you should use a tripod. *Photography Blog.* Retrieved from www.photographyblog.com/articles/7_reasons_why_you_should_use_a_tripod/

Hyndman, B.P. (2017). A simulation pedagogical approach to engaging generalist pre-service teachers in physical education online: The GoPro trial 1.0. *Australian Journal of Teacher Education, 42*(1). doi:10.14221/ajte.2017v42n1.6

Hyndman, B. & Papatraianou, L. (2017). The technological integration of a simulation pedagogical approach for physical education: The GoPro PE trial 1.0. *Learning Communities: International Journal of Learning in Social Contexts, Special Issue: 2017 30th ACHPER International Conference, 21,* 6-18. doi:10.18793/LCJ2017.21.02

Leight, J.M. (2014). *Technology for physical education teacher education: Student handbook of technology skills: Instructions and assessments* (2nd ed.). Author.

National Board for Professional Teaching Standards. (2018). *Elevating teaching, empowering teachers.* Retrieved from www.nbpts.org

Patel, A. (2014, December 26). 15 uses for the Swivl. *The Coolcat Teacher Blog.* Retrieved from www.coolcatteacher.com/15-uses-swivl/

Pearson Education. (2018). *edTPA.* Retrieved from www.edtpa.com

Pew Research Center. (2018). *Mobile fact sheet.* Retrieved from www.pewinternet.org/fact-sheet/mobile/

Society of Health and Physical Educators America. (2016). *Standards-based physical education student progress report: Introduction and guidance on usage.* Reston, VA: SHAPE America.

SoloShot. (2018). *SoloShot 3: Your robotic cameraman.* Retrieved from https://soloshot.com

Steve's Digicams. (2018). *Consumer vs professional video camcorder: 4 major differences.* Retrieved from www.steves-digicams.com/knowledge-center/how-tos/camcorder-operation/consumer-vs-professional-video-camcorder-4-major-differences.html#b

Swivl. (2018). *Swivl.* Retrieved from www.swivl.com

Chapter 12

Elliott, J.C. (2017). The evolution from traditional to online professional development: A review. *Journal of Digital Learning in Teacher Education, 33*(3), 114-125. https://doi.org/ 10.1080/21532974.2017.1305304

Goodyear, V.A., Casey, A., & Kirk, D. (2014). Tweet me, message me, like me: Using social media to facilitate pedagogical change within an emerging community of practice. *Sport, Education and Society, 19*(7), 927-943.

Greenhow, C., & Lewin, C. (2016). Social media and education: Reconceptualizing the boundaries of formal and informal learning. *Learning, Media and Technology, 41*(1), 6-30.

Hengstler, J. (2011). Managing your digital footprint: Ostriches v. eagles. In S. Hirtz & K. Kelly (Eds.), *Education for a Digital World 2.0* (pp. 89-139). Vancouver: Open School BC.

International Society for Technology in Education (ISTE). (2018). *ISTE standards for educators.* Retrieved from www.iste.org/standards/for-educators

Madden, M., Fox, S., Smith, A., & Vitak, J. (2007). *Digital footprints. PEW internet & American life project.*

Retrieved from www.pewinternet.org/files/old-media/Files/Reports/2007/PIP_Digital_Footprints.pdf

Rodesiler, L. (2017). For teachers, by teachers: An exploration of teacher-generated online professional development. *Journal of Digital Learning in Teacher Education, 33*(4), 138-147. https://doi.org/10.1080/21532974.2017.1347535

Society of Health and Physical Educators America. (2005). *National standards for sport coaches.* Retrieved from www.shapeamerica.org/standards/coaching/

Society of Health and Physical Educators America. (2017). *National standards for initial physical education teacher education.* Retrieved from www.shapeamerica.org/accreditation/upload/National-Standards-for-Initial-Physical-Education-Teacher-Education-2017.pdf

Tella, A. (2011). Reliability and factor analysis of a Blackboard Course Management System success: A scale development and validation in an educational context. *Journal of Information Technology Education, 10,* 55-80.

United States Department of Education Office of Educational Technology (USDOE). (2014). Online professional learning quality checklist. Retrieved from https://tech.ed.gov/wp-content/uploads/2014/11/Section-5-Online-Professional-Learning-Quality-Checklist-FINAL.pdf

Vasily, A. (2016). Using social media for #ProfessionalDevelopment. *Journal of Physical Education, Recreation, and Dance, 87*(6), 5.

Virginia Department of Education. (2017). *Virginia licensure renewal manual.* Retrieved from www.doe.virginia.gov/teaching/licensure/licensure_renewal_manual.pdf

Chapter 13

Centers for Disease Control and Prevention (CDC). (1999a). Achievements in public health, 1900-1999: Fluoridation of drinking water to prevent dental caries. *Morbidity and Mortality Weekly Report, 48*(41), 933-940.

Centers for Disease Control and Prevention (CDC). (1999b). Achievements in public health, 1900-1999 motor-vehicle safety. A 20th century public health achievement. *Morbidity and Mortality Weekly Report, 48*(18), 369-374.

Galer-Unti, R.A., Tappe, M.K., & Lachenmayr, S. (2004). Advocacy 101: Getting started in health education advocacy. *Health Promotion Practice, 5*(3), 280-288.

Society of Health and Physical Educators America. (2017). *National standards for initial physical education teacher education.* Retrieved from www.shapeamerica.org/accreditation/upload/National-Standards-for-Initial-Physical-Education-Teacher-Education-2017.pdf

Society of Health and Physical Educators America. (2018a). *National standards for initial health education teacher education.* Retrieved from www.shapeamerica.org/uploads/pdfs/2018/accreditation/HETE-Standards_2018d.pdf

Society of Health and Physical Educators America. (2018b). *Physical education is essential for all students: No substitutions, waivers or exemptions for physical education* [Position statement]. Reston, VA: Author.

Society of Health and Physical Educators America. (2019). *National standards for sport coaches.* Retrieved from www.shapeamerica.org/standards/coaching/

Thackeray, R., & Hunter, M. (2010). Empowering youth: Use of technology in advocacy to affect social change. *Journal of Computer-Mediated Communication, 15,* 575-591.

Women's Sports Foundation. (2019). *You have the right to play.* Retrieved from www.womenssportsfoundation. org/advocate/

Chapter 15

Anderson, M., & Jiang, J. (2018, May 31). Teens, social media & technology 2018. Retrieved August 31, 2018, from www.pewinternet.org/2018/05/31/teens-social-media-technology-2018/

Beaudin, K. (2017). The legal implications of storing student data: Preparing for and responding to data breaches. *New Directions for Institutional Research, 2016*(172), 37-48. https://doi.org/10.1002/ir.20202

Berdik, C. (2017, January 18). The best way to protect students' personal data. *Slate.* Retrieved from www. slate.com/articles/technology/future_tense/2017/01/ how_to_protect_students_personal_data.html

Carpenter, J.P., & Krutka, D.G. (2014). How and why educators use Twitter: A survey of the field. *Journal of Research on Technology in Education; Eugene, 46*(4), 414-434. Retrieved from http://search.proquest.com/ docview/1632517880/abstract/B1603196ED044BF3PQ/1

Children's Online Privacy Protection Act (COPPA). (2007). In *Encyclopedia of Small Business,* (3rd ed., vol. 1, pp. 183-185). Detroit, MI: Gale. Retrieved from http://go.galegroup.com.ezproxy.gvsu.edu/ps/i. do?p=GVRL&u=lom_gvalleysu&id=GALE|CX2687200 109&v=2.1&it=r&sid=GVRL&asid=34be6f14

Clement, J. (2019). Number of monthly active Twitter users in the United States from 1st quarter 2010 to 1st quarter 2019 (in millions). *Statista.* Retrieved from www.statista. com/statistics/274564/monthly-active-twitter-users-in-the-united-states/

Copyright Clearance Center. (2011). The TEACH Act. Retrieved from www.copyright.com/wp-content/ uploads/2015/04/CR-Teach-Act.pdf

Ezor, J.I. (2013). Streaming while teaching: The legality of using personal streaming video accounts for the classroom. *Albany Law Journal of Science & Technology, 23*(1), 221.

Federal Communications Commission. (2015). *Children's Internet Protection Act (CIPA).* Retrieved from http:// transition.fcc.gov/cgb/consumerfacts/cipa.pdf

Flowers, B.F., & Rakes, G.C. (2000). Analyses of acceptable use policies regarding the Internet in selected K-12 schools. *Journal of Research on Computing in Education, 32*(3), 351. Retrieved from http://search. proquest.com.ezproxy.gvsu.edu/docview/274754895?a ccountid=39473

Handler, C. (2015, February 4). School's out: COPPA's limiting reach in the classroom. *Mondaq Business Briefing.* Retrieved from http://link.gale-group.com/apps/doc/A400173591/GRGM?u=lom_ gvalleysu&sid=GRGM&xid=003e4a3a

Hobbs, R., Jaszi, P., & Aufderheide, P. (2009). How media literacy educators reclaimed copyright and fair use. *International Journal of Learning and Media, 1*(3), 33-48. doi:10.1162/ijlm_a_00026

National School Public Relations Association. (2010). *Setting expectations on e-communication.* Retrieved from www.nspra.org/trendtracker_april_2010

Pandora representative, personal communication, July 16, 2018.

Protalinski, E. (2014, January 29). *Facebook passes 1.23 billion monthly active users.* Retrieved from https:// thenextweb.com/facebook/2014/01/29/facebook-passes-1-23-billion-monthly-active-users-945-million-mobile-users-757-million-daily-users/

Russell, C. (2012). *Complete copyright.* Chicago, IL: American Library Association.

Schimmel, D., & Militello, M. (2007). Legal literacy for teachers: A neglected responsibility. *Harvard Educational Review, 77*(3), 257-284; 392-393. doi:10.17763/ haer.77.3.842n787555138746

Spotify. (2018). *Can I use Spotify at my business or school?* Retrieved from https://support.spotify.com/ us/using_spotify/the_basics/use-spotify-in-my-bar-restaurant-store-school-etc/

Todoric, M. (2011). Guidelines for acceptable electronic communication with students. *The Education Digest, 77*(3), 47-49. Retrieved from http://search.proquest. com.ezproxy.gvsu.edu/docview/1933090265?accoun tid=39473

Tudor, J. (2015). Legal implications of using digital technology in public schools: Effects on privacy. *The Journal of Law and Education, 44*(3), 287.

U.S. Copyright Office. (2016). *Copyright law of the United States and related laws contained in Title 17 of the United States Code.* Retrieved from www.copyright. gov/title17/

U.S. Department of Education. (n.d.). *FAQs on photos and videos under FERPA.* Retrieved from https:// studentprivacy.ed.gov/faq/faqs-photos-and-videos-under-ferpa

Warnick, B.R., Bitters, T.A., Falk, T.M., & Kim, S.H. (2016). Social media use and teacher ethics. *Educational Policy, 30*(5), 771-795. https://doi.org/10.1177/0895904814552895

Chapter 16

AssessLink. (n.d.). *AssessLinkPE: SD skill testing for physical education.* Retrieved November 30, 2018, from www.assesslinkpe.com

Berger, R. (2017). *Unbundling school technology purchases.* Retrieved November 10, 2018, from www.forbes.com/sites/rodberger/2017/10/16/unbundling-school-technology-purchases/

Boitnott, J. (2017). 10 tips to make your crowdfundig campaign successful. Retrieved November 10, 2018, from https://www.entrepreneur.com/article/303855

Brett, C. E. W. (2016). Need funding? tips on where to find and how to apply for grants. *Strategies, 29*(5), 52-55.

Channing Bete Company. (n.d.). *Tips for finding—and getting!—the funding you need.* Retrieved November 10, 2018, from http://preview.channing-bete.com/special-pdfs/fundingtips.pdf

i-SAFE Ventures. (2016). *i-SAFE direct—Smart schools, smart technology, smart choices.* Retrieved November 10, 2018, from www.isafeventures.com/2016/10/25/i-safe-direct-smart-schools-smart-technology-smart-choices-2/

Jensen, C., & Overman, S. (2003). *Administration and management of physical education and athletic programs* (4th ed.). Long Grove, IL: Waveland Press.

Majumdar, A., & Bose, I. (2018). My words for your pizza: An analysis of persuasive narratives in online crowdfunding. *Information & Management, 55*(6), 781-794. https://doi.org/10.1016/j.im.2018.03.007

Mears, B. (2006). Making wise technology purchases. *Journal of Physical Education, Recreation & Dance; Reston, 77*(8), 10-12. Retrieved from http://search.proquest.com/docview/215760516/abstract/136D6ED994814BD5PQ/1

National PTA. (n.d.). *Mission statement & values—About PTA.* Retrieved November 11, 2018, from www.pta.org/home/About-National-Parent-Teacher-Association/Mission-Values

Reese, J., & Miller, K. (2017). Crowdfunding for elementary science educators. *Science and children; Washington, 54*(6), 55-59. Retrieved from http://search.proquest.com/docview/1863560173/abstract/E6406A05563C46CEPQ/1

Slusser, J. (2017, October 6). *10 tips for smarter EdTech purchasing.* Retrieved November 10, 2018, from www.gettingsmart.com/2017/10/10-tips-smarter-edtech-purchasing/

Society of Health and Physical Educators America. (2018). *Title IV, part A of the Every Student Succeeds Act: Student support and academic enrichments grants.* Retrieved from www.shapeamerica.org/uploads/pdfs/2018/advocacy/Title-IV_A-Fact-Sheet-2018.pdf

Society of Health and Physical Educators America, Ayers, S., & Sariscsany, M.J. (2011). *Physical education for lifelong fitness: The physical best teachers guide* (3rd ed.). Champaign, IL: Human Kinetics.

SPARK. (n.d.). SPARK grant finder tool for physical education grants. Retrieved November 02, 2018, from https://sparkpe.org/grants/grantfunding-resources/

Visovsky C. (2015). Writing a Successful Grant: Tips and Tools. *Journal of the advanced practitioner in oncology, 6*(3), 279–280.

Walker, T. (2015, December 1). *Are school districts getting smarter about education technology?* Retrieved from http://neatoday.org/2015/12/01/school-districts-getting-smarter-education-technology/

Xu, Ting (2018). Learning from the crowd: The feedback value of crowdfunding. Retrieved November 18 from https://ssrn.com/abstract=2637699

INDEX

Note: The italicized f and t following page numbers refer to figures and tables, respectively.

A

ability switches 136, 147-148, 155
AbleGamers 154
AbleNet 140*t*
accelerometers 113*t*, 224-228, 234
acceptable use policies 31*t*, 33, 49, 308-309, 323
Access (Microsoft) 56
accessibility 138, 155
Accessibility Checker 58, 80
access limitations 31*t*, 32
accommodations 138, 155
accountability with on-demand coaching 121, 122
accountability with online courses 181
action DV camcorders 259-260, 261*t*, 274
ActivityGram 239-240, 242*f*
activity limitations 137, 155. *See also* students with disabilities
activity trackers. *See* wearable activity trackers; wearable technology
adapted physical activity 149, 155
adapted physical education
  defined 139, 155
  national standards 138*t*
  professional development 136-137
adaptive controllers 154
adaptive sports 139, 149, 155
Adaptive Tech Solutions 140*t*
addressing email messages 35
Adopt-a-Classroom 332*t*
advanced Google searches 65, 65*f*
advocacy
  data gathering for 301
  defined 12, 292, 302
  online tools 294-297
  sample technology applications 8*t*, 10*t*, 11*t*
  standards 293*t*
  technology's pros and cons 301-302
  using video 297-301, 300*f*
aerobic capacity tests 240*t*
aerobic exercise guidelines 211-212, 211*t*
Alerts (Google) 68, 68*f*
alternate text 58
altimeters 112, 113*t*, 133
Amazon 140*t*

American Printing House for the Blind 140*t*
Americans with Disabilities Act 138
amplifying sound devices 142
Anatomy Learning app 75*t*
ancillary materials, for online courses 171
Android apps 74
animations 60
Apple App Store 74, 124
Apple Watch 233*t*
apps
  adapted physical education 143, 151*t*
  attendance 21, 22*t*
  augmented reality 98, 99-100, 116-117
  behavior management 23, 24, 26-27
  coaching 11*t*, 19
  data management 27
  defined 80
  equipment management 25
  group management 22, 23*f*
  hydration tracking 126
  mental health 127-129
  messaging 36-37
  music 87
  nutrition tracking 124-126
  on-demand fitness 121
  polling 69
  quiz and survey 244-245, 246*t*
  reminder 42, 44, 46
  skills analysis 8*f*
  social media 281
  student data sharing 319
  tournament 21
  translation 30, 37, 65
  use in health education 73-74, 75*t*-77*t*
  video assessment 247-250
  videoconferencing 46, 102
  video editing 78, 266, 299
  video management 77-78
  workout 102
Artistic Dressage 186-187, 186*t*
AssessLinkPE tool 338
assessment
  creating and using rubrics 252
  data collection 252-253
  data management systems 27
  defined 12, 253
  for online courses 177-178, 177*t*
  health-related fitness 239-240

LMS tools 17, 18*f*, 78-79, 243, 245
online physical education 183*t*, 184-185
purposes 238
quiz and survey technology 240-245
sample technology applications 8*t*, 10*t*, 11*t*
SHAPE America standards 41
using accelerometers 226, 227*f*
using heart rate monitors 213, 218
video technology 245-251
AssetTiger 25
assistive technology. *See also* students with disabilities
  defined 136, 155-156
  for cognitive impairments 145-147
  for hearing impairments 142-145
  for physical disabilities 147-150
  for visual impairments 140-142
  sample apps 150-152, 151*t*
  suggested pedagogical approach 139
  types 136, 137*t*
  video games 152-155
asynchronous, defined 280, 290
asynchronous online courses 161, 174, 187, 195
asynchronous video 48-49
athlete management systems 19, 21-24, 28
Atlantic article on physical education 297
attendance apps 21, 22*t*
attributions 312, 323
audio equipment
  for digital video 264-265, 266*f*, 267*f*, 299
  for screen recording videos 171, 173
  for videoconferencing 47-48
audio resources, legal uses of 271*f*, 299-301, 315, 317
augmented reality
  defined 98, 105
  gamification and 99-100
  to promote physical activity 116-117
auto-grading 177*t*
award certificate templates 104
Awesome Eats 75*t*

B

badges, digital 104, 105
BAND app 45*t*
bandwidth 47, 49
barometers 112, 113*t*, 133
battery life indicators 113*t*
beep balls 141-142, 156
beep boxes 142
behavior management tools 23-24, 26-27
bell-ringers 64, 80
Benson's HRmax field test 210*f*
Best Summary technique 67
Beyond Sight 140*t*
bias 139, 156
BIGmack 145
bioelectric impedance analyzers 239
biometric headphones 114*t*
biometric identification 178
Biostrap 233*t*
blended learning 161-163, 195
blindness 140-142
BlockPosters.com 79
blogs 66-67, 80
Blood Pressure Evaluation app 75*t*
Bluetooth 20, 28, 87, 105
Bodimojo 75*t*
body composition tests 240*t*
Book Creator 72-73
booster clubs 330-331
Born Fitness 121
BouncyBalls.org 79
Bracket app 21
brain boosters 72
Brain Pop 75*t*
brainstorm polls 70*t*
budget management tools 25

C

calculation with spreadsheets 63
Calendly 43*t*
Calm app 128
Calm Counter 26
cameras
    digital video 257-263
    for online instruction 164, 171, 173-174
    motion-sensing 94*f*, 96*f*
    videoconferencing 48, 67*f*, 191*f*
CapGame 154
Carbon Footprint ACP 75*t*
Cardboard (Google) 65-66, 66*f*
cardiac creep 208*t*
Catapult 229*t*
CBT (cognitive behavioral therapy) 129, 133
Central Athlete 186*t*
Cercacor Ember 233*t*
certificate courses 284
certifications 123, 185, 280. *See also* professional development
cheating in online courses 177, 178
cheating with heart rate monitors 216

chest-strap heart rate monitors
    accuracy 204
    basic features 202, 205
    battery replacement 206
    resting heart rate measurement with 207
    use in field testing 209, 210*f*
    use in physical education 213, 215
Children's Internet Protection Act 309, 323
Children's Online Privacy Protection Act (COPPA) 34, 49, 309-310, 323
Choreographed YouTube plank challenge 101*f*
Chrome extensions 64
CK (content knowledge) 5, 6*t*
ClassDojo 24, 24*f*, 45*t*, 75*t*
ClassPass 121
classroom management 8*t*, 17. *See also* management
classroom response systems 8*t*, 243-245, 253
ClassroomScreen.com 79
clickable image polls 70*t*
clip art 60
closed captioning 144, 156
cloud-based file sharing 10*t*, 38-40, 49, 67-68
coaching
    advocacy in 292, 293*t*
    certifications 185
    classroom response systems in 243-245
    digital file sharing for 40
    management standards 16*t*
    online 121-122, 123, 160, 185-187, 188-189
    overview of technology's benefits 9-10
    podcasts 283*t*
    sample technology applications 11*t*, 19
    SHAPE America standards 127*t*, 131*t*, 238*t*
    using heart rate monitors 215-216
    video assessment in 247
coaching-enhancement programs 11*t*
Coach's Eye 248
CoachUp 186, 186*t*
coded transmitters 205*t*
cognitive behavioral therapy (CBT) 129, 133
cognitive impairments 145-147
cognitive worksheets 95*f*
collaborative tools 10*t*, 17, 40
colleges, online instruction 284-286, 288
collegiate esports 91
communication
    AT for students with disabilities 145
    defined 12, 49
    email overview 33-36

importance to sport participation 48
legal issues 320-322
LMS tools 17, 18*f*, 33
of student behavior data 24
overview of technology 30-33
scheduling and reminder tools 40-44, 43*t*, 45*t*
standard technologies 132
technology benefits and barriers 32-33
text messaging 36-37
via social media 37-38
video-based 44-49
communication apps 11*t*
Community High School District 128 320, 321*f*
competitive polls 70*t*
competitive video gaming 91
compressing video 269*f*, 274
conferences 283-284
Connected PE Online Physical Education Conference 284
Connection, The 337*t*
consent 34, 49, 310, 323
content knowledge (CK) 5, 6*t*
continuing education requirements 280
controllers, adaptive 154
COPPA. *See* Children's Online Privacy Protection Act (COPPA)
copyright
    legal uses of works 311-318, 312*t*, 313*f*-314*f*, 316*f*
    music 271*f*, 299-301, 317
    overview of protections 310-311, 323
course calendars 18*f*
course gradebooks 27
course management systems 16-19. *See also* learning management systems
courseware 161, 195
Crazy Children's Dentist Simulation 75*t*
Creative Commons 312, 314*f*, 323
crowdfunding 331-334, 333*t*, 340
CTS 186*t*
CXC Academy 186*t*
cycle ergometer tests 209
cycling, video game 90-91

D

daily step counts 220-222, 221*f*-222*f*, 224
Dance activities, technology tips 103
Dance Dance Revolution 94, 153
Daniels' HRmax field test 210*f*
Dartfish 250
data, defined 253
data collection 252-253, 301
data management systems 17, 27, 252-253
data storage 263, 274, 319-320
Deaflympics 139, 156

deafness 142-145
dehydration 208*t*
delayed video apps 247-249
Design Ideas function (Power-
     Point) 61, 62*f*, 80
Dexcom G6 233*t*
Dick's Sporting Goods Foundation
     336*t*
Dietary Guidelines for Americans
     123, 133
dietary reference intakes (DRIs)
     123, 133
digital badges 104, 105
digital beeping devices 141-142
digital divide 302
digital footprint 289, 290
digital learning 161, 195
digital message communicators
     145, 156
digital natives 4, 5, 12
digital sensory stimulation 145-
     146, 156
digital sound beacons 142, 156
digital video. *See also* video
     as advocacy tool 297-301, 300*f*
     distributing 270-274, 301
     editing tools and tips 266-268,
          269*f*-270*f*, 271*f*-272*f*, 273,
          299301
     overview 256, 274
     recording equipment 257-265
     recording tips 265, 266*f*, 273,
          299-301
disability, defining 137-138, 156.
     See also students with dis-
     abilities
discrimination 138, 156
discrimination index 79
discussion assignments, online
     174, 175*f*, 176*t*
discussion boards
     defined 195
     for online courses 161, 167,
          175*f*, 176*t*
     LMS tools 18*f*, 78
     sample assignment 169*f*
     sample prompt 168*f*
displays in health education 55
distance education 160, 195, 315,
     323. *See also* online instruc-
     tion
diversity 138, 156
document management tools 25,
     67-68. *See also* Google Drive
Don Bradman Cricket 88
DonorsChoose 332*t*
Doodle 42, 43*t*
downvote polls 70*t*
DRIs (dietary reference intakes)
     123, 133
D2L Brightspace 165, 166*f*
DV camcorders 257-260, 258*t*, 261*t*,
     263, 274
DV cameras 257-263, 274
DVDs, workout 121

DV editing 274
DV recording 257, 274. *See also*
     digital video

E
Easy Attendance 22*t*
Eat This Much app 75*t*
editing digital video 266-268, 269*f*-
     270*f*, 271*f*-272*f*, 273, 299-301
editing emails 35
Edpuzzle 73, 246*t*
edTPA 319, 323
education, technology's benefits
     4-6
educational settings 317, 323
educational technology 163, 195
Edulastic 246*t*
eHealth resources 126, 133
electrical heart rate monitors 202,
     204, 234. *See also* chest-
     strap heart rate monitors
electrocardiography 204
electronic mail. *See* email
elliptical machines 119*t*-120*t*
email
     as advocacy tool 294-295
     basic considerations 33-34
     defined 302
     etiquette 34-35
     file sharing via 35-36
     policies 321-322
     setup 34
     use in online instruction 165-
          167
emotional scale polls 70*t*
Enable Mart 140*t*
Enabling Devices 140*t*
encryption
     defined 49, 194, 195
     for synchronous videoconfer-
          encing 192, 194
     of activity tracker transmis-
          sions 205*t*
     of personal information 33
     of shared files 39
energy expenditure, with motion-
     based video games 93
Entertainment Software Rating
     Board 95*f*
e-portfolios 286-287, 287*f*
EquiFITT 186*t*
equipment
     digital video recording 257-265
     for online instruction 164, 171,
          172, 173
     for viewing webinars 283
     fundraising for 330*t*, 331-334,
          332*t*, 333*t*
     lending programs 326-328
     music 87-88, 89*f*
     obtaining grants for 334-335,
          336*t*-337*t*
     remote supervision 191*f*, 192,
          193-194
     school-based funding for 328-
          331

     smart purchases 338-339
     videoconferencing 47-48
     video editing 267-268, 268*t*
equipment management tools 25
E-rate program 309, 323
esport 91, 105, 153
etiquette 34-35, 308, 323
Every Student Succeeds Act 328-
     329, 340
exams 177-178, 177*t*. *See also*
     assessment
Excel (Microsoft) 56, 62-63
extrinsic motivation 84, 105

F
Facebook 282, 322
Facebook Messenger 30
face-to-face interactions 131, 160,
     187, 195
fade in or out 270*f*
fair use 310, 311-312, 312*t*, 313*f*-
     314*f*, 315, 323
Family Educational Rights and
     Privacy Act (FERPA)
     defined 28, 50, 323
     digital file sharing and 27, 40,
          315
     videos subject to 319
Federal Trade Commission 309,
     323
feedback, defined 253
feedback tools 69-73, 170, 251
FERPA. *See* Family Educational
     Rights and Privacy Act
     (FERPA)
file sharing
     cloud-based 10*t*, 38-40, 67-68
     options 25
     via email 35-36
file storage 25
First Aid app 75*t*
fitness. *See* physical health and
     fitness
fitness coaching, online 121-122,
     186-187
fitness equipment 117-121, 119*t*-
     120*t*. *See also* equipment
FitnessGram 239-240, 240*t*, 241*f*
fitness-on-demand services 121
504 plans 138, 156
fixed works 310, 323
FlagHouse 140*t*
Flipgrid 48-49, 77, 246*t*
flipped classrooms 74, 80
flipped instruction 179-181, 179*f*,
     196
flipped learning 18*f*
FlipQuiz 246*t*
focus, technologies for helping
     146-147
Fooducate 75*t*
footwear, smart 114*t*
Formative 246*t*
formative assessments 238*t*, 253
formulas, spreadsheet 62

forums 282, 290
frame rate 269*f*
Fuel Up to Play 60 336*t*
Fund for Teachers 336*t*
Fundly 332*t*
fundraising 330*t*, 331-334, 332*t*,
    333*t*, 340. *See also* technol-
    ogy funding

G

Game Accessibility Guidelines
    153-154
game-based learning 71
Gamer Sensei 186*t*
Games for Health Journal 96
gamification
    defined 80, 99, 105
    in health education 71
    LMS tools 18*f*
    with AR 99-100
gaming disorder 97, 105
Garmin Edge 520 231, 232
Garmin Forerunner 935 230-231,
    232
Garmin HRM 229*t*
Garmin Vector 3 Power Pedals
    231, 232
Garmin vívofit jr. 2 110-111
geocaching 114-116, 171
Giant Timer 19
Global Navigation Satellite System
    112
Global Positioning System
    defined 105, 133
    personal monitors 111-112,
        113*t*-114*t*, 228-232, 234
    use with augmented reality 98
Gmail 34
GoFundMe 332*t*
golf watches 114*t*
GoNoodle 72, 102
Google Alerts 68, 68*f*
Google applications in health edu-
    cation 63-68
Google Cardboard 65-66, 66*f*
Google Classroom 38, 64
Google Docs 64
Google Drive
    document sharing via 25,
        38-39, 64, 67-68
    for file management 10*t*, 67-68
    sample home page 38*f*
Google Duo 67
Google Family Link 34
Google Forms 43*t*, 64-65, 246*t*
Google Hangouts 67, 67*f*
Google Play 74
Google Scholar 68
Google Translate 30, 65
Gopher Sport 140*t*
GPS watches 111-112, 113*t*-114*t*,
    228-232
GradeBook Pro 27
gradebooks 27
grading for online courses 174,
    176*t*, 177*t*

grading rubrics. *See* rubrics
GrandPad tablet 132
Grant Wood AEA Adapted PE 327
grant writing 334-335, 336*t*-337*t*
group management tools 21-22,
    23*f*, 24, 24*f*
GroupMe 30
G Suite for Education 63-64
guest speakers 67
Gulp app 75*t*
Gym Closet 140*t*
gyroscopes 112, 113*t*, 133

H

Halo Sport 231
Hammersmith, Matthew 188-189
Hangouts Meet 38
hashtags 281, 297
headings, for students with dis-
    abilities 58
headphones, biometric 114*t*
health and wellness coaching 185
health coaching 185, 196
health education
    advocacy in 292, 293*t*
    certifications 280
    classroom response systems in
        243-245
    digital file sharing 39-40
    display tools 55
    Google applications in 63-68
    LMS tools 78-79
    management standards 16*t*
    Microsoft applications in 56-63
    overview of technology's ben-
        efits 8-9, 10, 11
    podcasts 283*t*
    sample technology applications
        10*t*
    SHAPE America assessment
        standards 238*t*
    smartphone apps 73-74, 75*t*-77*t*
    student involvement tools 69-73
    video assessment 247, 251
    video games in 94-96
    video integration 74-78
    wearable technology for 233,
        233*t*-234*t*
    websites 79-80
health promotion using video
    games 94-96
health-related fitness. *See* physical
    health and fitness
hearing impairments 142-145
heart rate, factors affecting 208*t*
heart rate monitors (HRMs)
    common features 205*t*
    defined 133, 202, 234
    GPS watches as 113*t*
    reasons for using 8*t*, 111, 204-
        206
    training with 203, 206-212
    use in physical education 213-
        214, 215-216, 217-219
heart rate reserve 211, 234
Heja app 44, 45*t*

HelpKidzLearn 155
high-tech assistive technology 137*t*
high-visibility devices 141
hip-worn accelerometers 227-228
HitCheck 75*t*
homemade videos 104
home workout services 121-122
HRM. *See* heart rate monitors
    (HRMs)
Hudl Technique 249-250
Humon Hex 229*t*
hybrid courses 163, 164, 178-179,
    184, 196
hydration trackers 126
hyperlinks 58-59

I

icebreaker polls 70*t*
iDoceo 22*t*
IEPs (individualized education
    plans) 138, 156
IHT Spirit System Heart Rate
    Monitors 217-219
image quality 48
images in PowerPoint 61
Immune System—Wiki Kids 75*t*
impairments 137, 156. *See also* stu-
    dents with disabilities
importing video 269*f*
impulse buying 338
iNACOL standards 165, 166*t*
inclusion 138, 156
Independent Living Aids 140*t*
individual behavior management
    tools 23, 26-27
individualized education plans
    (IEPs) 138, 156
individuals with disabilities. *See*
    students with disabilities
Individuals with Disabilities
    Education Improvement Act
    138, 139
inertial measurement units 228,
    235
infographics 295, 302
Innovative Products 140*t*
instruction, defined 12
instructor feedback, for online
    courses 170
interactive touchscreens 55, 80
interactive video game cycling
    90-91
interactive video projection 99,
    100*f*, 105
interactive whiteboards 11*t*, 55, 80
interest development 85-87, 86*t*
International Society for Technol-
    ogy in Education (ISTE) 12.
    See also ISTE standards
Internet connections
    accommodating lack of 181
    editing online documents with-
        out 64
    loss during quizzes 177
    percentage of U.S. homes with
        30

Internet etiquette 308, 323
Interval Timer Pro 19
intrinsic motivation 84, 105
introductions 167, 169*f*
Invictus Fitness 186*t*
iOS apps 74
iPads 193
ISTE standards 4-5, 4*t*, 5*t*, 7, 9, 329*t*

J

Jenny, Seth 273
Jitterbug phone 132
Johnson, Neve 46
Jones, Dayton 153
journal articles, searching for 68
journals, LMS tools 18*f*
Juggernaut 186*t*

K

Kahoot! 10*t*, 71, 246*t*
Karvonen formula 63, 209-211,
    212*f*, 235
Keep It Simple Coaching 186*t*
keyboard shortcuts 56, 57*t*, 62, 80
KIDZ BOP 90*f*
Kinderboard 141
Kinect Sports Rivals Rock Climb-
    ing 93
knowledge types 5, 6*f*, 6*t*
Krossover 248

L

language barriers
    for text messages 37
    technology pros and cons 32,
        33
    translation apps 30, 37, 65
Laughlin, Rachel 125
leaderboard polls 70*t*
learning management systems
    assessment tools 243, 245, 252
    communication features 17, 18*f*,
        33
    defined 50, 196
    document sharing via 25, 38
    gradebooks 27
    in health education 78-79
    overview 17-19, 18*f*, 28
    use in online instruction 161,
        174, 178
learning modules 161, 168, 196
legal issues
    avoiding copyright violations
        271*f*, 299-301, 311-318
    in digital communications 320-
        322
    mandates for students with dis-
        abilities 137-139
    overview of copyright protec-
        tions 310-311
    students' use of Internet 34,
        308-310
    use of students' images and
        data 318-320
lending programs 326-328
liability 184
lifetime fitness model 109, 109*f*

lifetime health technologies 108
lifetime sport technologies 122-123
listservs 294-295, 302
lists for students with disabilities
    58
live-streamed coaching 121
local and state grants 336*t*
Lockheed Martin 337*t*
loneliness 130-131
low-tech assistive technology 137*t*
Lynch, Brandy 193-194

M

Madden NFL 88
magnification devices 141
management
    attendance and behavior 21-24
    budgets, equipment, and docu-
        ments 25
    course- and sport-based tools
        16-19
    data and assessments 17, 27
    defined 12, 16, 28
    sample technology applications
        8*t*, 10*t*, 11*t*, 16*t*
    SHAPE America standards 16*t*
    time- and task-based tools
        19-21
maps, in GPS watches 113*t*
massive open online courses 161,
    196, 286
MaxiAids 140*t*
maximum heart rate 207-209, 209*t*,
    210*f*, 211, 212, 235
McMillan Running 186*t*
McMullen, Jaimie 298-299
Medgic—AI for Skin 75*t*
medications, heart rate effects 208*t*
meditation tools 114*t*
Meetup 132
memory cards 263
mental health 108, 126-130
message communicators 145
mHealth resources 126, 133
microphones
    for remote synchronous video
        191*f*
    for screen recording videos
        171, 173
    for videoconferencing 47-48
    with digital video 264-265,
        266*f*, 275
Microsoft Office 56-63
mid-tech assistive technology 137*t*
MindShift CBT 128
mobile devices
    as virtual reality viewers 65-66
    defined 274
    DV cameras in 260-262, 261*t*
    finding apps for 73-74
    ownership statistics 36, 85
    remote supervision with 193-
        194
    screen recording videos 171,
        172
    time management tools 19

tripods for 264
monopods 264, 275
Monsuta Fitness 98
motion-based video games. *See
    also* video games
    defined 105
    for students with disabilities
        152-155
    motivation with 90-94
    rehabilitation with 96-97
    teaching tips 95*f*-96*f*
    use in online physical educa-
        tion 185
motion-tracking devices 262-263
motivation
    defined 84, 105
    rewards and 104
    with augmented and virtual
        reality 98, 99-100
    with gamification 99-100
    with interactive video 99, 100*f*
    with music 87-88, 89*f*-90*f*
    with technology 85-87, 100-104
    with video games 88-97
motor skills, teaching with video
    games 92-93
movement analysis 247, 249-250,
    253
movie files 270, 275
MP3 players 87
Mullis, Adam 103
multiple-choice polls 70*t*
muscular endurance tests 240*t*
music
    management tools 19-20, 87-88,
        89*f*
    motivation with 87-88, 89*f*-90*f*
    royalty free 271*f*, 299-301
music streaming services 317, 323
My3 app 128
MyPlate 123
mySHAPE America 282

N

narration 270*f*
national grants 336*t*-337*t*
National Health Education Stan-
    dards PreK-12 8, 9*f*, 127*t*,
    131*t*
National Standards for Initial
    Health Education Teacher
    Education 8
National Standards for Initial
    Physical Education Teacher
    Education 7
National Standards for K-12 Physi-
    cal Education 6, 7, 7*f*
National Standards for Sport
    Coaches (NSSC) 9-10
Nature's Bounty Foundation 337*t*
near field communication 113*t*
Nearpod website 72
negative transfer 95*f*
Netflix 318
netiquette 308, 323
newsletters 295, 296*f*

Nights Out app 76*t*
No Child Left Behind Act 328, 340
noncommercial purposes 310, 323
NormaTec Pulse 2.0 233*t*
NSSC (National Standards for Sport Coaches) 9-10
nutrition trackers 75*t*, 123-126

O

OD_Bike_Safety 76*t*
Ogden, Dan 288
OneNote (Microsoft) 56
one-to-one device initiatives 326
one-way communications 36, 44
online coaching
    approaches 121-122, 185-187
    certification for 123
    defined 196
    growth of 160
    practitioner interview 188-189
    sample services 186*t*
online conferences 283-284
online courses 161-163, 196. *See also* online instruction
online document sharing 10*t*, 25, 38-40, 67-68
online instruction
    advantages and disadvantages 162*t*-163*t*
    assessment in 177-178
    assignments 174-177, 178-179
    coaching 121-122, 123, 160, 185-187
    common features 165-171
    course structures 161-163
    equipment and software 164
    flipped instruction in 179-181
    for physical education 181-185
    growth in popularity 160
    pedagogical tips 170
    professional development via 284-286
    remote supervision in 187-194
    screen recording videos 171-174
online learning 160, 196
online quiz and survey tools 243-245, 246*t*
online quiz tools 10*t*
operating systems 73-74, 80
operators (online) 309, 324
optical heart rate monitors 202, 204, 215, 235
OptiShokz Revvez 233*t*
OUSD Physical Education Equipment Library 327
Outlook (Microsoft) 56
overhand throw 7

P

Pacifica—Stress & Anxiety 76*t*
Pandora 317
panning 264, 270*f*, 275
Paralympics 139, 150, 156
paramobile devices 148, 156
parental consent 34
parent-teacher associations 329-330

participation restrictions 137, 156. *See also* students with disabilities
patents 311, 324
PDFcandy.com 79
PE Central 285
pedagogical content knowledge 5, 6*t*
pedagogical knowledge 5, 6*t*
pedometers
    accuracy 219-220, 223
    defined 133, 235
    reasons for using 110-111, 214-217
    suggested goals with 220-222, 221*f*-222*f*
    use in physical education 222-224
peer assessment 247, 253
peer interactions, online 176*t*
peer workshops 64
Peloton 121, 186*t*, 187
Period Tracker 76*t*
personal identifying information 309, 319-320, 324
personal interest 85, 86*t*, 105
personalizing text messages 37
personal trainers 123, 187
personal websites 286-289
photoplethysmography 202, 235
#PhysEdSummit conference 284
physical activity, integrating technology with 100-104
physical disabilities 147-150. *See also* students with disabilities
physical education
    advocacy in 8*t*, 292, 293*t*, 297-299, 300*f*
    assessment standards 41
    Atlantic article 297
    certifications 280
    classroom response systems in 243-245
    digital file sharing 39-40
    flipped instruction 179
    management standards 16*t*
    online courses 181-185, 183*t*
    overview of technology's benefits 6-8, 10, 11
    podcasts 283*t*
    sample technology applications 8*t*, 19
    SHAPE America assessment standards 238*t*
    using heart rate monitors 213-214, 215-216
    video assessment 247, 251
    with pop culture trends 117
physical health, defined 108
physical health and fitness
    activity trackers for 109-114
    assessment technology 239-240
    benefits 108-109
    fitness center equipment for 117-121

lifetime sport technologies 122-123
    nutrition and hydration trackers for 123-126
    online coaching 121-122, 186-187
    recreational activities for 114-117
Pinero, David 248-249
Pistorius, Oscar 150
pixel count 258*t*
Plagnets 244, 245*f*
PlayerTek vests 248, 249*f*
Plickers
    as assessment app 8*t*, 244-245, 246*t*
    as attendance app 21
podcasts 282, 283*t*, 290
Pokémon Go 98, 116-117
Polar Team Pro 229*t*
policies
    acceptable use 31, 33, 49
    communication 30, 320-322
    email etiquette 35
    privacy 309-310
    social media use 37-38
Poll Everywhere 69-70, 69*f*, 246*t*
polling tools 42, 69-70, 70*t*, 246*t*
pool entry devices 148
pop culture trends 117
portfolios 286-287, 287*f*
possessing technology knowledge 5
PowerPoint (Microsoft) 56, 59-62, 174
Practi-CRM 233*t*
Pregnancy Tracker 76*t*
prejudice 139, 156
presentation software 59-62
Presidential Youth Fitness Program 239
preview pane 268, 275
privacy
    importance to communications 33
    laws protecting 34, 49, 309-310
    of phone numbers 36
    of videoconferencing 194
    of web-based assessment 252
    protecting with classroom management systems 27
proctoring for online assessments 178
professional development
    choosing programs 285-286
    defined 12, 290
    establishing online presence 286-289, 295
    formal approaches 282-285
    informal approaches 280-282
    overview 280
    sample technology applications 8*t*, 10*t*, 11*t*
project-based learning 247, 251, 253
project files 270, 275

Project Lift 186*t*
prostheses 149-150, 156
PTSD Coach 128
public performances 317, 324
public service announcements 300*f*
Publisher (Microsoft) 56
pulse palpation technique 207
Purple Robot 128

Q
Q&A polls 70*t*
QR codes 20
Quality Matters 165, 166*t*
Quick Access Toolbar 56
Quick Response codes 20, 28
Quinn-Maxwell, Colleen 217-219
Quit That! app 128
Quizalize 246*t*
Quizizz 76*t*
Quiz Show Game (PowerPoint) 62
quizzes
    advantages and disadvantages of online 177*t*
    LMS tools 177-178, 243, 245
    remote administration 178, 245
    sample web-based tools 246*t*
    traditional 240
    using classroom response systems 243-245

R
racing, virtual 184
racing wheelchairs 149
RandomLists.com 79
ranking polls 70*t*
Real Time CPR Guide 76*t*
recording digital video 257-265, 266*f*, 273
Recovery Record 125
Recycle Coach 76*t*
references (vendor) 339*t*
rehabilitation using video games 96-97
relationships, healthy 130-131
release forms 319
remediation areas 181
Remind app 11*t*, 42-44, 45*t*, 46
reminder tools 42-44, 45*t*
remote coaching. *See* online coaching
remote supervision 190-194, 190*t*, 191*f*
rendered video files 270-274, 275
research findings
    coach-athlete communication 48
    daily step counts 224
    game-based learning 71
    on advocacy 293
    online instruction 164
    online physical education 182
    on motion-based video games 93
    on online professional development 282

on social media use 322
on technology use in health and physical education 10
on video feedback 251
pedometer accuracy 223
technology's impact on classroom management 17
video gaming for students with disabilities 152
resistance training sensors 114*t*
resolution (video) 258*t*, 263, 269*f*
resources for online courses 169-171
response times, email 35
responsive formatting 80
resting heart rate 207, 235
Revibe Connect watch 146-147
revisions histories 64
rewards 23, 104
ribbon (Microsoft Office) 56, 56*f*
Rise Above the Disorder 130
robotic motion tracking 262-263
roster apps 21, 22, 22*t*
rowing machines 120*t*
rubrics
    creation and basic functions 252
    defined 253
    for WebQuests 72
    in online instruction 165, 166*t*, 175*f*, 176*t*, 184
Runcoach 186*t*
runners, visually impaired 142
Ryan Leech Connection 186*t*

S
Safety for Kid apps 76*t*
scheduling tools 40-42, 43*t*
Scholar (Google) 68
school-based technology funding 328-331
Schoology 17
School Specialty 140*t*
Screencast-O-Matic 78, 171*f*
screening, mental health 128
screen readers 58
screen recording videos 171-174, 196, 299
scrolling 270*f*
scrub bar 268, 275
Section 504 138
security of student data 319-320
Seesaw app 44, 45*t*, 76*t*, 246*t*
self-assessment 238*t*, 247, 253
self-control in email messages 35
self-efficacy 117, 133
Semi-Pro Cycling 186*t*
Sensory Magic 146
sensory rooms 146, 156-157
sensory stimulation activities 145-146
SETT framework 139
SHAPE America
    advocacy resources 293*t*, 294, 329
    assessment standards 238*t*

coaching standards 127*t*, 131*t*
grant program 337*t*
high school student standards 112, 115*f*
management standards 16*t*
mental health standards 127*t*
nutrition standards 124*t*
online physical education stance 182
professional development resources 282
social health standards 131*t*
teacher education standards 41, 127*t*
technology use forums 10
SignUp app 43*t*
SignUp Genius 43*t*
single-subject certificate courses 284
situational interest 85, 86-87, 86*t*, 105
skill-based approach 54
sleep trackers 113*t*
Slide Master (PowerPoint) 61
slides, PowerPoint 59-62
SLR cameras 257, 257*f*
smart balls 99-100
smart footwear 114*t*
smartphones
    accelerometers in 224
    as virtual reality viewers 65-66
    defined 260, 275
    DV cameras in 260
    finding apps for 73-74
    ownership statistics 36, 85, 320
    time management tools 19
smart rings 114*t*
smartwatches 20, 205. *See also* wearable technology
smart wheelchairs 148
smoking 208*t*
Smoking Cost Calculator 76*t*
Snapchat 98
Snoezelen Multi-Sensory Environment 146
social health 108, 130-133
social media
    as advocacy tool 8*t*, 295-297
    as communication tool 37-38
    defined 290
    legal issues 319, 322
    LMS tools 18*f*
    professional development via 280-281
    professional presence on 287
    social health promotion via 132
Society of Health and Physical Educators. *See* SHAPE America
Socrative 246*t*
SoloShot 263
Solve the Outbreak app 76*t*
songs. *See* music
sound beacons 142, 156
spam 37, 50
SPARX 129

speakers, wireless 87, 89*f*
special education 138, 157. *See also* students with disabilities
special needs 136, 157. *See also* assistive technology; students with disabilities
Special Olympics 139, 157
Spinlife 140*t*
splicing video 269*f*
splitting video 269*f*
sport
   adaptive 139, 149, 155
   online coaching 186-187
   technologies for 122-123
Sportaid 140*t*
sport video games 88-90, 105
Spotify 317
spreadsheets
   defined 81
   for equipment and supplies management 25
   for sharing assessment data 27
   for test scoring 63
   Microsoft Excel 56, 62-63
Stack-Up 130
stairway to lifetime fitness model 109, 109*f*
stakeholders
   advocating with 292, 293, 295-297
   defined 292, 302
   sharing classroom results with 24, 253
Standard Drinks Calculator 77*t*
Standards for Educators (ISTE) 4, 4*t*, 5
Standards for Students (ISTE) 5, 5*t*, 7, 9
state virtual schools 160, 196
stationary bikes 120*t*
STATSports Apex Pro Series 229*t*
step counts 110-111, 220-224, 221*f*-222*f*. *See also* pedometers
StepWatch 223
stereotypes 139, 157, 292
stopwatches 19, 205*t*
storyboard pane 268, 275
streaming services 317, 318
Strength Ratio 186*t*
stress management tools 114*t*
stride length 219, 220*f*
student introductions 167, 169*f*
student involvement tools 69-73
student management systems 21-24
students with disabilities. *See also* assistive technology
   AT for cognitive impairments 145-147
   AT for hearing impairments 142-145
   AT for physical disabilities 147-150
   AT for visual impairments 140-142
   legal mandates 137-139
   Microsoft Office features for 58

physical education technology for 26-27
   sample apps 150-152, 151*t*
   types of ATs for 136, 137*t*
   video gaming for 152-155
student work, uploading 315, 319
subject lines 35
subscription video streaming services 318
summative assessments 238*t*, 253
Super Hero Toilet Time Bathtub app 77*t*
Survey Monkey 246*t*
surveys 18*f*, 240-243, 245, 246*t*
Susquehanna Soniqs 153
SwimSwam 186*t*
Switch in Time 155
Swivl 262
Sworkit 102, 103
Sworkit Kids 77*t*, 102
syllabi for online courses 167
synchronous, defined 280, 290
synchronous online courses 161, 170, 197
synchronous videoconferencing 187, 190-194, 197
synchronous video technologies 44-48, 50, 190-194, 190*t*, 197

T
tables for students with disabilities 58
tables of contents 58-59
tablets
   defined 260, 275
   DV cameras in 260
   finding apps for 73-74
tactical analysis 247, 250, 253
Tailwind Coaching 186*t*
Taliaferro, Andrea 26-27
talking devices 140-141
Talkspace 128
TAP test 321*f*
target heart rate zone 206-207, 209-212, 212*f*, 213, 216, 235
Tar Heel Gameplay 155
task management tools 20-21
TEACH Act 315, 316*f*, 324
TeacherKit 22*t*, 77*t*
team selection apps 21-22, 23*f*
Team Shake 22, 23*f*
TeamSnap 20
Teamstuff 19
Team Timer 19
technological, pedagogical, and content knowledge (TPACK) 5, 6*f*, 6*t*, 12
technology, defined 4, 12
Technology, Education, and Copyright Harmonization Act 315, 316*f*, 324
technology funding
   fundraising 330*t*, 331-334, 332*t*, 333*t*
   grants 334-335, 336*t*-337*t*
   lending programs 326-328
   school-based 328-331

technology in education
   for motivation 85-87, 100-104
   general benefits 4-10
   sample applications 8*t*, 10*t*, 11*t*
   smart purchases 338-339
technology knowledge 5
technology management 79-80. *See also* management
technology-mediated communication 30, 50
Technology Tips
   adapted physical education 143-144
   dance activities 103
   digital video 273
   in physical education for students with disabilities 26-27
   integrating technology into health and physical education 11
   lifetime fitness instruction 125
   online coaching 188-189
   online professional development 288
   on using technology for advocacy 298-299
   reminder tools 46
   remote supervision 193-194
   video assessment 248-249
   wearable technology 217-219, 230-232
teleconferencing 35, 50
telephone use in online teaching and coaching 165, 188
templates
   award certificates 104
   defined 81
   digital video 269*f*
   discussion board 175*f*
   Microsoft Word 57
   PowerPoint 61
tests, scoring 63
tethering 205*t*
text formatting 58, 60
text in videos 272*f*
text messaging 36-37, 321
therapeutic video games 129-130, 132-133
timelines 268
time management tools 19-20, 26
Time Timer 26
Title IV funds 328-329
Title IX 293
Todoric, Mary 321*f*
token economies 26
touchscreens 55, 80
TPACK (technological, pedagogical, and content knowledge) 5, 6*f*, 6*t*, 12
Tracer360 234*t*
trackers
   activity 109-114, 111*f*, 113*t*-114*t*, 115*f*
   for students with disabilities 146-147
   mental health 128
   nutrition and hydration 123-126

traditional elliptical machines 119*t*
traditional video games 88, 105
training
    adaptive sports 149
    HRM use 203, 206*f*
    personal 123, 186, 188-189
    resistance sensors 114*t*
    standards 10
    using GPS data 112-113
    virtual reality 98
TrainingPeaks 186*t*, 188, 189, 230, 232*f*
transformative works 312*t*, 324
transitions (video) 269*f*, 272*f*
translation apps 30, 37, 65
translation services 37
treadmills 119*t*, 209
treatment apps, mental health 128
trilateration 111, 133
trimming video 269*f*
tripods 262, 263-264, 265*f*, 275
troubleshooting 31*t*
tutorials, for video editing software 268
Twitter
    as advocacy tool 295, 297, 298-299
    professional development and 281, 282
    use policies 322

U

under-desk elliptical machines 120*t*
Unified ARTS Resource Library 327
United in Stride 142
universal design for instruction model 138, 138-139, 157
universities, online instruction 284-286, 288
updates, video game 95*f*
Upright Go 2 234*t*
upvote polls 70*t*

V

Vida Health 185, 186*t*
video. *See also* digital video
    as advocacy tool 297-301, 300*f*
    assessment with 245-251
    avoiding copyright violations 315, 318
    of students 318-319
    use in adapted physical education 143, 144-145
    use in health education 74-78
    use in online coaching 185, 186-187
    use in online instruction 161, 167, 168, 171-174, 180-181, 187-194
video analysis 239, 253
video calls 44-48, 50
video chat 102*f*
videoconferencing. *See also* online instruction

as professional development tool 283-284
    defined 50
    guest speakers via 67
    LMS tools 38
    overview of technologies 44-48
    use in online instruction 161, 165, 190-194, 190*t*
video-delay apps 11*t*
video editors 78, 266
video games
    competitions 91
    for students with disabilities 152-155
    health and wellness promotion 94-97
    mental health 129-130
    motion-based 90-94, 95*f*-96*f*, 96-97, 105
    sedentary 88-90
    social health 132-133
video hosting services 318, 324
video remote interpreting 144, 157
video streaming services 318, 324
virtual coaching. *See* online coaching
virtual newsletters 295, 296*f*
virtual races 184
virtual reality
    defined 105
    for students with disabilities 152
    mental health apps 129-130
    motivation with 98
    smartphones as viewers 65-66
virtual schools 160, 197
visual effects 269*f*
visual impairments 140-142
visual notification devices 142-144
voice-overs 171, 173, 174
Voice Typing 64
Voxer 281

W

Wait Timer Visual Timer Tool 26
Walmart Foundation 337*t*
Warner, Lisa 11
warranties 339*t*
watches, GPS 111-112, 113*t*-114*t*
Waugh, Robert 143-144
wearable activity trackers
    common features 205*t*
    defined 133
    major types 109-114, 111*f*, 114*t*
    sample assignment using 115*f*
wearable technology
    accelerometers 224-228
    defined 235
    for students with disabilities 146-147
    GPS devices 112, 113*t*, 228-232
    heart rate monitors 202-214
    overview 202
    pedometers 110-111, 214-224
    reporting group data 301

use in health education 233, 233*t*-234*t*
    use in online physical education 184
web-based document sharing 10*t*, 25, 38-40, 67-68
webcams 171, 172, 173-174, 191*f*
web-facilitated courses 163, 197
webinars 10*t*, 283, 290
WebQuest 72, 81
websites. *See also* online instruction
    crowdfunding 331-334, 332*t*
    for professionals 286-289, 295
    in health education 72, 79
    legal issues for students' use 308-310
    legal use of resources from 311-312, 313*f*-314*f*
    professional development 281-282
    uploading student works to 315
    video sharing 274
welcome messages 165-167
Wellcoaches 186*t*
wellness coaching 185, 197
wellness trackers 114*t*
well-rounded education 328, 340
Wellworks For You 186*t*
WELT Smartbelt 234*t*
wheelchairs 148-149
whiteboard apps 11*t*, 55, 80
whole-school model 54, 54*f*, 81
WHOOP wearable device 229*t*
WiFi Presentation Remote 77*t*
wikis 10*t*, 18*f*
Williams, Bradley 230-232
Wimu Pro 229*t*
wireless microphones 264-265, 266*f*, 275
wireless speakers 87, 89*f*
Without Limits 186*t*
Women's Sports Foundation 293
Word (Microsoft) 56, 57-59
workout DVDs 121
world cloud polls 70*t*

X

Xbox Adaptive Controller 154

Y

Youth Risk Behavior Survey 301
YouTube
    channels 274
    copyright issues 318
    in health education 77
    with dance activities 103

Z

Zebra MotionWorks Sport 229*t*
zooming 258*t*, 261*t*, 262, 266*f*, 270*f*

Seth E. Jenny, PhD, teaches within the department of public health at Slippery Rock University of Pennsylvania. He previously taught within the department of physical education, sport, and human performance at Winthrop University and the department of health, exercise, and sport sciences at the University of New Mexico. Dr. Jenny has over 20 years of health, physical education, and coaching experience across K-12 and higher education settings, where he has been an early proponent of integrating technology into teaching and coaching. He has worked as a U.S. Air Force exercise physiologist and has coached athletes across all ages and abilities, from elementary athletes to Olympic competitors. Dr. Jenny has created and taught face-to-face, online, and hybrid technology courses for undergraduate and graduate students studying health and physical educa-tion teacher education, coaching, and sport management.

Seth Jenny

He is a certified health education specialist (CHES), an American College of Sports Medicine exercise physiologist (ACSM-EP), and holds Level 2 (youth specialization) coaching certifi-cation from USA Track and Field. Dr. Jenny is an active scholar, providing more than 100 professional presentations and publishing over 40 peer-reviewed academic journal articles within his prime areas of research: esports, motion-based video gaming, and elementary-age distance running. In 2016, he was named the Research and Scholarship Faculty Member of the Year within the College of Education at Winthrop University. Dr. Jenny cofounded and is the acting president of the nonprofit Grove City Athletics Club (Grove City, Pennsylvania), where he is a volunteer coach for elementary cross country and track and field athletes. He spends his spare time with his family and training for marathons, with a personal best of 2:48:30 (6:25 mile pace for 26.2 miles).

Jennifer M. Krause, PhD, is an associate professor of physical education and physical activity leadership (PEPAL) in the School of Sport and Exercise Science at the University of Northern Colorado (UNC). She also serves as coordinator of the physical education K-12 teaching program at UNC and is a research faculty member of the University of Northern Colorado Active Schools Institute. Dr. Krause has over 15 years of experience teaching health and physical education in K-12 and teacher preparation settings and coaching youth sport. She currently teaches undergraduate- and graduate-level courses related to physical education and coaching technology, assessment, health education methods, and teacher and coach action research. She also mentors doc-toral students in the PEPAL program at UNC.

Courtesy of University of Northern Colorado

Dr. Krause's major line of research explores technologi-cal, pedagogical, and content knowledge preparation and self-efficacy among preservice physical education teachers, as well as the technology training and experiences among physical education teacher educators. Dr. Krause has published over

20 peer-reviewed research and professional articles and delivered over 80 research and professional presentations at international, national, and regional meetings. Dr. Krause received the 2017 University Physical Education Teacher of the Year Award from SHAPE Colorado. She currently serves on the editorial board for *Strategies: A Journal for Physical and Sport Educators* and is a member of the SHAPE Colorado board.

Tess Armstrong, PhD, is an assistant professor in the department of movement science at Grand Valley State University. Dr. Armstrong has published numerous articles related to youth physical activity, and she has given more than 20 research and professional presentations at local, state, national, and international conferences. She has nine years of experience teaching at the preK-5 level and in teacher preparation programs. Dr. Armstrong currently teaches classes related to assessment in physical education; teaching methods of fitness, of dance, and of elementary physical education; and physical education for classroom teachers. She is actively involved in supervising preservice teachers at the university level.

Courtesy of Grand Valley State University

Chapter 4 contributing author **Matthew Cummiskey, PhD**, is an associate professor at West Chester University, training future health and physical education teachers. He taught K-12 health and physical education for 5 years and has taught within higher education for 13 years. Dr. Cummiskey enjoys implementing technology in his classes to enhance motivation, involve students, promote learning, and showcase technology modalities students can implement. His technology-related scholarship includes two book chapters; two articles in *Journal of Physical Education, Recreation & Dance*; 14 articles in the journal of the Pennsylvania State Association for Health, Physical Education, Recreation and Dance (PSAHPERD); three SHAPE America national conference presentations; and four SHAPE America Eastern District technology presentations. Dr. Cummiskey currently teaches the course Assessment and Technology (HPE 347) at West Chester University.

Matthew Cummiskey

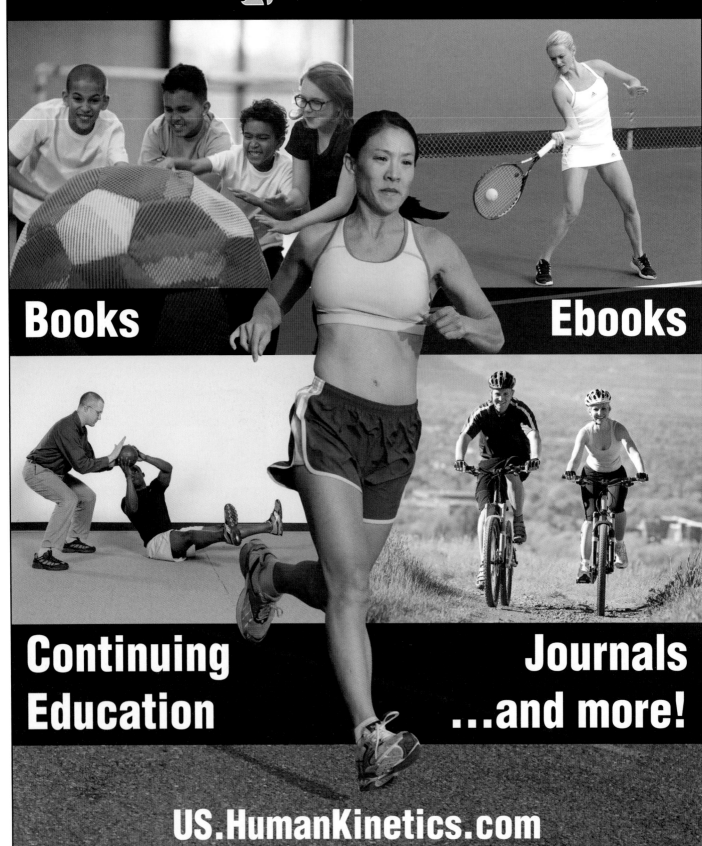